BRITAIN'S COMMUNISTS
THE UNTOLD STORY

CW01019432

I dedicate this book to my parents
who lived as communists should

BRITAIN'S
COMMUNISTS
THE UNTOLD STORY

BY **JOHN GREEN**
WITH CONTRIBUTIONS BY
ANDY CROFT AND GRAHAM STEVENSON

Britain's Communists: the untold story
by John Green with contributions by Andy Croft and Graham Stevenson

First published in Britain in 2014 by
Artery Publications
11 Dorset Road
London W5 4HU

Book design by Michal Boncza
Front cover based on a design by Galina Green, utilising a badge by Jeff Sawtell
Printed by Russell Press

ACIP catalogue record for this book is available from the British Library
ISBN 978-0-9558228-4-1

Other books by the author:

Stasi Hell or Workers' Paradise
Engels: A Revolutionary Life
Ken Sprague – People's Artist
Afon Ystwyth – the story of a river
Red Reporter – covert correspondent for East Germany
Wings over the Valley – a Bird Watcher's Wales Diary

Contents

ACKNOWLEDGEMENTS	9
INTRODUCTION	13
AN ALTERNTIVE NARRATIVE	21
WRITERS AND THE BATTLE OF IDEAS (ANDY CROFT)	35
INFLUENCE AMONG PROFESSIONAL WORKERS	63
FILM – 'THE MOST IMPORTANT OF THE ARTS'	93
TRADE UNIONS – THE MAIN FOCUS	117
THE DAILY WORKER AND THE MORNING STAR	145
INTERNATIONALISM – A CORNERSTONE OF PARTY POLICY	159
THE STRUGGLE AGAINST FASCISM	187
THE PARTY AND THE SECOND WORLD WAR	193
THE YOUNG COMMUNIST LEAGUE AND THE STUDENT MOVEMENT	215
THE PEACE MOVEMENT	229
THE WOMEN'S MOVEMENT	245
COMMUNISTS AND THE LABOUR PARTY – A FRAUGHT RELATIONSHIP	263
THE 'ENEMY WITHIN' (GRAHAM STEVENSON)	289
SUMMING UP	309
BIBLIOGRAPHY	321
FOOTNOTES	327
INDEX	337

'The validity of the socialist aim is to advance beyond the predatory phase of human development.'

ALBERT EINSTEIN

ACKNOWLEDGEMENTS

Much of the historical background for this book has been culled from the excellent volumes, History of the Communist Party of Great Britain, written by James Klugman (Vols. I and II), Noreen Branson (Vols. III and IV), John Callaghan (Vol. V) and Geoff Andrews (Vol. VI). I am deeply indebted to all these writers for their pioneering research which has meant that I was able to save valuable time by not having to reference every original source. Francis Beckett's book Enemy Within, and the various publications written or edited by Kevin Morgan also proved to be valuable resources. I would particularly like to thank Andy Croft, himself an acknowledged expert and author of books on the Communist Party and its impact on British culture, for writing the chapter, Writers and the Battle of Ideas, an earlier version of which was first published in Communisme 87 (Paris, 2006), and Graham Stevenson for his invaluable help in tracing biographies and for writing the chapter, The 'Enemy Within'. Bert Hogenkamp very kindly gave me permission to make extensive use of his pioneering research on film and the Left in Britain for the chapter, Film – 'The Most Important of the Arts'. And Ken Keable gave me permission to use information included in his fascinating book London Recruits: The Secret War Against Apartheid for the chapter, Internationalism and the Party. I am also very grateful to professor Nicholas Deakin for taking the time to read my draft manuscript and for offering perceptive and useful comments, and to Christine Lindey, who took time off from writing her own forthcoming book on the Artists International Association to read my chapter on the AIA and correct some glaring mistakes, as well as making some very useful suggestions. My thanks are also due to my long-time collaborator, Michal Boncza, for making a perceptive critique and giving very useful tips for research; and for his enormous patience during late rewrites and above all for once again dedicating his design skills to the project. I am grateful also to Tom Sibley and Roger Seifert for allowing me to use material included in their excellent biography of Bert Ramelson and for Tom Sibley's pertinent comments on the chapter, Trade Unions – the Main Focus, and to Mick Costello for reading the chapter on the Daily Worker and Morning Star and making very helpful comments, Thank you Galina for your cover design and keen eye for grammar and proofing as well as useful suggestions for text improvement. Dave Cope, John Foster, Peter Frost, Sally Groves, John Haylett, Nicola Seyd, Jo Stanley, Philippa Lloyd, Kevan Nelson and Nick Wright have all given me help and criticism in one way or another. and unnamed others have also allowed me to use their own personal reminiscences and provided additional information. I owe more than I can express to my mother and father for their kind, tolerant and understanding parenting and for encouraging me to make up my own mind on all matters. Bruni de la Motte has, as always, been my most valuable critic and has been an essential corrective to my impatience and dreadful tendency to cut corners.

Throughout the text I use the capitalised term 'Party' to refer only to the Communist Party of Great Britain or its successor The Communist Party of Britain, because it simplifies things and, among its members, sympathisers and even some of its enemies, the CPGB was invariably referred to succinctly as 'The Party'. For anyone wishing to fully grasp what it meant to belong to the Party in its heyday and what an ordinary member was expected to do, there is no better source than John Gorman's vivid and riveting description in his autobiography Knocking Down Ginger. For those who would like to read more biographies of communists, the best and most comprehensive source is Graham Stevenson's online Communist Biographies.[1]

I would also like to stress here that anyone described in the text as a 'communist' refers to those who have at some time in their lives been members of the CPGB or the YCL it in no way implies that they still are members of any communist organisation or that they still consider themselves to be communists. I have made every attempt to ensure that the facts and information included here are accurate and correct, but there will undoubtedly be the odd mistake or omission. I can only apologise in advance if any are found, and take full responsibility for them.

'Die Ideale sind ruiniert, rettet die Ruine!'
(The ideals are ruined, save the ruins!)

SLOGAN PAINTED ON THE SQUATTED 'TACHELES' ARTISTS'
CENTRE IN BERLIN, FOLLOWING THE DEMISE
OF THE GERMAN DEMOCRATIC REPUBLIC

'He saw history as a gigantic act of reparation,
rescuing the defeated from the "enormous condescension"
of posterity.'

RAPHAEL SAMUEL WRITING ABOUT E.P.THOMPSON[2]

Introduction

'Just as other nations have taken power into their own hands, so also the people of our country will take power in their own way, on the basis of their historical conditions and traditions.'

BRITISH ROAD TO SOCIALISM (1958)

Growing up in a communist household and over a lifetime getting to know many communists not only in the UK, but worldwide, I became increasingly aware of how my own experience gave me a diametrically different image of communists from the one purveyed in the media and found in the popular imagination. I long pondered on the idea of putting together a narrative, based on my own experience and perceptions, which would counter that 'official' imagery.

The trigger for actually doing so came while I was attending a lecture at Gresham College, in central London, given by professor Nicholas Deakin and titled: 'Middle-class Recruits to Communism in the 1930s'. In his opening remarks he said that, 'Until recently, these 1930s communists had been too easily dismissed as Stalin's useful idiots or as children of the bourgeoisie suffering from acute class guilt'. He offered a refreshing re-assessment of the lives of individual communists and, for me, demonstrated that a proper re-assessment was not only long overdue, but necessary.

The Provost of the College introduced the lecture by saying that he

BRITAIN'S COMMUNISTS: THE UNTOLD STORY

and, he assumed, probably most members of the audience of a certain age, undoubtedly knew a communist either in their own families or in their circle of friends. Whether valid or not, this indicated how ubiquitous communists were in society, certainly among that generation born during the first or second decade of the 20th century.

In his lecture, Deakin quoted Karl Miller, who said, 'One of the most dismal prejudices to be encountered in Anglo-America has been the worsening failure to imagine how decent people could choose to be communists in the 1930s'.[3] The issues raised in Deakin's lecture were the spark for what I attempt to explore in the following pages.

Since the demise of the communist-ruled countries of Eastern Europe there has been a renewed interest in the history of communism and the Communist Party of Great Britain. So much that has been written about communism in the past, from Koestler's Darkness at Noon, and The God that Failed, through Orwell's 1984 to Martin Amis's Koba the Dread and Courtois's The Black Book of Communism: Crimes, Terror, Repression,[4] has very much reduced the communist experience to the model and experience of the Soviet Union. This focus has marginalised and occluded the expe-riences of ordinary communists in western countries like Britain.

The mainstream portrayal of communists, if they were mentioned or discussed at all, was inevitably as agents of the Soviet Union, carrying out Stalin's orders, as subversives out to under-mine British democracy and impose a Soviet-style totalitarian system on the country. Because of this perception the Party has been the focus of British secret service surveillance and Special Branch raids throughout its history, as it and its members were deemed by the establishment to be a dire threat to the country's stability. How far is this perception accurate or representative?

Did you know that Sylvia Pankhurst of the renowned suffragette family, together with fellow suffragette, Ellen Wilkinson, were founding members of the Communist Party? That leading Labour politicians like Peter Mandelson and Dennis Healey were at one time members of it or of its youth wing, the Young Communist League (YCL)? Or that the composer Benjamin Britten, while not a member, was very close to the Party and collaborated with communist writers like Randall Swingler and with communist composer Alan Bush? That the writer of musicals Lionel Bart and the actor Alfie Bass were also members, or that the writer Hilary Mantel fleetingly belonged to the YCL? Even Tony Blair, before anyone knew who he was, wrote for the

Party's theoretical journal, Marxism Today. The Morning Star – the paper cooperatively owned by its readers, but widely perceived as 'the Communist Party's daily paper', was supported by such figures as future Labour leader Michael Foot and comedian Spike Milligan who both spoke at the paper's celebratory events in London's Festival Hall. Perhaps you would be surprised to hear that the Communist Party was even, for a time, represented in the House of Lords? Wogan Philipps, 2nd Baron Milford was, unsurprisingly, the only member of the Party ever to sit in the House of Lords, from 1962 onwards. In his maiden speech he called for its abolition! Looking abroad, did you know that Picasso was a member of the French Communist Party for most of his life or that the world famous Brazilian-born architect Oscar Niemeyer was also a life-long communist?

Those just mentioned may be simply exceptional individuals, but what about the tens of thousands of others who joined the Communist Party or were sympathisers over the decades? What was it about the ideas of communism that could attract such a diverse number of individuals in considerable numbers, not just ordinary working people, but intellectuals, artists and professionals?

So many people make significant and positive contributions to our society, but it is invariably only those who in their contributions represent the values of the ruling class who are accorded status and historical significance. The communist movement, from the start, set itself against entrenched privilege and wealth and has therefore been suppressed and marginalised by mainstream narratives that are largely dominated by that privileged class. Its members – overwhelmingly ordinary working people – have been stigmatised and dismissed from history.

Do most communists resemble those caricatured by stand-up comedian Alexei Sayle in his sketches about his 'Stalinist' family, taking their holidays in Albania? Or, as more sinisterly portrayed by Peter Sellars in the Boulting brothers' film I'm All Right Jack: the humourless shop steward, Fred Kite, a slimy and devious individual, hoodwinking the docile workers? Or, are they, in the main, woolly-headed idealists who simply let themselves be duped by Moscow?

A fashionable cliché that is heard so often from those dismissing communist ideas, is that if you weren't a communist in your twenties you were heartless but if you were still a communist in your forties, you were brainless. How far is that valid? If the idea of communism is so insidious, but at the same time asinine, are communists then manipulative and unscrupulous or just naïve idiots? If they are, surely they can be easily exposed? But then why has the ruling élite and the largely obsequious media spent so much time and effort denigrating communism and communists? What magical or hypnotic force does the idea possess that it could attract so many people – from the working class, middle class and intelligentsia?

In response to an advert I placed in the Morning Star, in 2013 asking communists or former communists what had motivated them to join the Party, the overwhelming number responded similarly, that they wished to see more equality and justice in society and a more peaceful world. It was as basic as that. How far such responses are typical I can't judge, but they do give an indication of what many communists were looking for by joining the organisation.

Interestingly, the poet Jackie Kay, in her autobiography Red Dust Road, also sketches a very different picture of a communist family – the one in which she grew up in working class Glasgow. Her stepfather, John Kay was the Party's Industrial Organiser for Scotland and her stepmother was also a Party activist. It was courageous of them to adopt a black child and bring her up in working class Glasgow at a time when racism was rife. No doubt, for her parents, the idea of adopting a black child was at the same time an expression of their internationalist outlook and also gave them the opportunity, together, of challenging society's endemic racism head-on.

The role of the Communist Party and of communists in Britain has been either completely ignored or written out of most official histories of the country since the party was founded in 1920. Even Left and sympathetic writers often, invariably unintentionally, ignore its role. To take just one example: Sarah Boston's book, Women Workers and the Trade Unions, for example, doesn't even include the Communist Party in her index, and writes about leading women communists like Jessie Eden (later McCulloch), one of the leaders of the Birmingham Lucas workers, without mentioning her political allegiance.

Many people would probably laugh out loud if it were suggested to them that communists and communism had probably had a tangible affect on their own lives. Would an ardent countryside rambler, for instance, know that it was a brave Manchester communist, Benny Rothman, who led the first mass trespass on Kinder Scout in the Pennines in 1932, which paved the way for the present-day right of access to the countryside which all of us now enjoy? He also remained a life-long campaigner on nature conservation issues.

How many would know that the inventor of the zoom lens and fibre optics was a founding member of the Communist Party? Harold Hopkins FRS, a leading British physicist and twice nominee for the Nobel Prize perfected the zoom lens for the BBC in 1954. But, perhaps even more importantly, he was responsible for the development of fibre optics, now an essential tool in medical diagnostic work, and rod-lens endoscopes for keyhole surgery. Those inventions are taken for granted today both in the cinema industry and in medicine. In addition to his enormous body of theoretical work, Hopkins's many other inventions are in daily use throughout the world. If you undergo keyhole surgery there will be a communist, if not under the bed, then lurking behind the operating team!

Communists in London led the illegal occupation of London's tube stations during the War so that citizens could find shelter and survive during Nazi bombing raids. They also led some of the first post-war squatting activities to protest at the lack of adequate housing after the War, adding impetus to the Labour government's mass council house building policy. These are just a few of the things connected with communists that have probably impacted in some way on our lives today.

Much of the ingrained traditional anti-communism finds its literary alibi in a few key sources. Two of the main ones, in the Anglo-Saxon world, being the works of Orwell and Koestler, mentioned above. These two writers wrote with the inevitable vitriol and bitterness of apostates, and their essential message is succinctly expressed in the title of Koestler's The God that Failed.

It is also conveniently overlooked by those who instrumentalise these books in order to frighten people off communist/socialist ideas and communists, that while Orwell used Stalin's Russia as his template for 1984, he made it abundantly clear that he was writing about the dangers of totalitarianism in general, not specifically about the Soviet Union, even though that was his model. In his The Road to Wigan Pier, Orwell wrote that socialism was urgently needed: either a 'socialist party' had to be formed in Britain or 'fascism is coming', he said.[5]

While the experiences and writings of such authors certainly cannot be decried as mere calumny or dismissed as irrelevant, they are the experiences of just two individuals. However, the prominence given them reveals the role they have been enlisted to play by the powers that be, to demonise the very idea of communism. Their publication and dissemination has been subsidised and avidly promoted by western governments; they are the perennial books included in school examination papers, they have been made into films and innumerable doctoral theses have been written about them. How valid, though, is such a traditional, dystopian picture as a portrayal of communism and communists?

The communist idea is also far from being an alien one, as sometimes portrayed by its detractors. It has had a long gestational history in Britain, too. There have been a whole number of individuals and groups throughout our history who have espoused communistic ideas. In the Middle Ages there was John Ball ('When Adam delved and Eve span, who was then the gentleman?') and Wat Tyler, who led the first poll tax rebellion, followed in the 17th century by Gerrard Winstanley and the 'communistic' Levellers, active during the English Revolution. In the 18th century Tom Paine stands out as a champion of Republicanism, egalitarianism and a classless society. The Chartist Movement during the 19th century inspired many socialist thinkers and had a seminal influence on the ideas of early British communists like William Morris, as well as on Karl Marx and Friedrich Engels, the founders of modern communism. Both Marx and Engels spent most of their adult lives in England and absorbed many of its political and historical traditions which influenced their thinking in no small way. No ideas emerge from a vacuum, they all have their precedents and precursors, and the ideology of communism is no different. Such ideas of social change, though, will always be tempered, once an attempt is made to implement them, by quotidian circumstances. Take those countries which have had communist-led governments: the practical reality has reflected more the specific national traditions than the ideals of the movement's theoreticians.

Even royalty has found Marxist ideas of interest. The future Empress of Germany, Princess Victoria Adelaide Mary Louise, the eldest daughter of Queen Victoria, was precociously intelligent and incredibly well-read. After reading about Karl Marx and perhaps even some of his own writing, she asked a close acquaintance and politician, the superbly named Sir Mountstuart Elphinstone Grant Duff to sound him out and report back to her.

In early 1879, Duff sent Marx an invitation for free drinks at the Devonshire Club. He reported back to the Princess the following day, noting that his impression of Marx was 'not at all unfavourable and I would gladly meet him again'. He also told her that he had suggested to Marx that if the rulers of Europe came to an understanding amongst themselves for a reduction of armaments which might greatly relieve the burden on the people, then what would become of the Revolution which he expected. Marx responded by saying that such an agreement was an impossibility. Duff concluded his report by telling the princess: 'They are too dreamy to be dangerous except just in so far as the situation with its mad expenditure on armaments is obviously and undoubtedly dangerous. If however within the next decade the rulers of Europe have not found means of dealing with this evil without any warning from attempted revolution I for one shall despair of the future of humanity at least on this continent.' I'm sure the princess's interest in Marx and his ideas was speedily diverted towards more genteel preoccupations.

An Alternative Narrative

'The most valuable attribute we all possess is life. It is given us only once and we should use it in such a way that we will have no torturing regret later over futile, wasted years, never know the shame of an unworthy, trivial past, and so live that, when dying, we can say: my whole life and all my energy has been dedicated to the most wonderful cause in the world – the struggle for human liberation.'

NIKOLAI OSTROVSKY

This book is an attempt to offer a different narrative and an assessment of the more positive role of communists and the Communist Party in British life throughout the 20th century, and to counter many of the clichés, the prejudice and the accepted shibboleths. It is also an attempt to offer an alternative historical and social narrative.

Communists exist in the popular imagination, if at all, as marginal conspiratorial groups fomenting violent revolution and, while the Soviet Union still existed, working as its agents. The James Bond thrillers helped perpetuate such images. In terms of who communists actually were or are, what they have done and how they have behaved, the majority will know very little if anything.

This book will deal almost entirely with the past – the period of the existence of the Communist Party of Great Britain, even though one of its successors, the Communist Party of Britain still exists and is active. However, anyone who is at all interested in recent history or politics would find it difficult to discover any account of the role communists have played in the life of the country, apart from in a few academic papers.

The daily newspaper most closely associated with the Communist Party, the Morning Star, is still being published daily and its pages cover national and international politics and general news, it carries theatre and book reviews and a weekly jazz column, it has regular feature contributions from Labour Party MPs, the Green Party, Welsh and Scottish nationalists and others from the broad Left. is, though, rarely, if ever, mentioned or quoted by the mainstream media and is studiously ignored by the BBC in its round-up of the country's daily papers. It is invisible – why?

What I am attempting to do here is to redress the balance, to demonstrate that communists do belong in the mainstream of British society, despite the Party's small size and its lack of electoral support. In each of the chapters, I examine a separate aspect of life in which communists have been particularly active and influential. Not everyone will wish to read every detail in every chapter, but hopefully readers will find in at least some of the chapters information that is of particular interest and which will help illuminate their own perceptions.

As professor James Hinton put it, 'The essence of the Communist Party as it developed in Britain was the focussing of socialist political life outside the "legitimate" arena of electoral politics, in the politics of the street, the housing estate and, above all, the factory.' That is what makes it very different to the main political parties.[6] It was the party you joined if you wanted to see radical social change, rather than mild reform.

In the eyes of the ruling forces in the West, communism and the Communist Party, throughout 20th century and into this one, were perceived as the demons to be fought unrelentingly if democratic societies were to survive; communism was the main enemy, threatening us all with tyranny. A compliant and largely subservient media reiterated those views ad nauseam. However, the fact that so many ordinary people, professionals, artists and intellectuals were attracted to communism over many years indicates that there could be a very different perception.

In Britain, the Communist Party, even though it never became a mass party as those in France and Italy did, was a significant player in the political life of the country. Its input, particularly in the trade union movement and the struggles for the rights of working people, was enormous. But also in a wide variety of other areas of public life the input of communists was often pioneering.

The Communist Party was the first political party to wage an early and unremitting struggle against colonialism and racism, several of its members facing persecution and enduring imprisonment for their devotion to these causes. It was also the only political party to offer forthright opposition to fascism right from the outset. On gender equality and on recognition of gay rights it was also in the vanguard. Communists played significant roles in influencing government education policy; they were successful in winning and organising artists for many progressive causes; they helped create a more focussed and politicised student body and they continually gave considerable support to the various peace movements as well as organising scientific professionals and academics in support of disarmament and the banning of nuclear weapons. The ongoing demand for sufficient decent social housing, opposition to slum landlordism and high rents were also campaigns in which communists played central roles. Communists were always prominent in the general left-wing movement in the country and invariably gave leadership in key struggles and campaigns. Their commitment, organising ability and political understanding were widely recognised as essential ingredients for the success of any popular struggle. They were, in the main, characterised by their self-sacrifice, devoting many hours of their leisure time to supporting Party policies and working in local and national organisations at all levels for no material reward or recognition.

The contribution made by communists to life in Britain has never been properly acknowledged, or has been credited to others, and today that contribution has been totally eclipsed or, if mentioned at all, then traduced. Communists have been invariably treated like the embarrassing relative no one wants at the family get-together because they are too loud and outspoken, liable to bring family skeletons out of the cupboard and refuse to comply with accepted decorum. Its members have been ridiculed, besmirched and dismissed and the false steps or mistakes made by the Party distorted out of all proportion. That is why I feel it is important to offer redress to the tens of thousands of those who gave unstintingly over a shorter or longer period to the ideas of justice, equal opportunity and peace through the Communist Party. Many worked unstintingly, campaigning for better facilities in their localities, fighting for the underpaid and giving support to the underdog, attending tedious branch committee meetings, marching on demonstrations and standing in the cold and rain on picket lines. They weren't people bent on social destruction, overthrowing democratic governments or intent on imposing a Soviet style regime, but were concerned more with trying to build a 'Jerusalem in our green and pleasant land'.

As one rare example of public respect afforded a communist, I would like to mention here the case of the renowned physicist and peace campaigner J.D. Bernal, a life-long communist who made no secret of his politics. At a concert to commemorate his 70th birthday, held at London's Queen Elizabeth Hall in 1972, among the great and the good who attended or sent friendly messages were Benjamin Britten, Asa Briggs, Sir Adrian Boult, Yehudi Menuhin, Lord Blackett, John Berger, Michael Ayrton, Sir Hugh Casson, Dame Barbara Hepworth, Sir Julian Huxley, Pastor Niemöller, Lord Ritchie-Calder, CP Snow and Sir Solly Zuckermann. Surely this in itself demonstrates that communists could be recognised and respected for their social contribution. But this recognition, if given at all, was invariably expressed in private and was certainly given little, if any, coverage in the media.

J.Hinton noted perceptively:

'Because Britain never had a mass communist party, unlike France or Italy, historians of the labour movement have inclined to minimise its significance...Out of all proportion to its formal membership, the Communist Party organised or influenced extra-parliamentary currents which did much to determine the force and direction of the over-all Labourist tide in Britain. History with the Communist Party left out is likely to miss important aspects of the dynamics of the British Labour movement'.[7]

This is particularly true of the period during the peak of Labour's power in the 1940s. Communist Party influence was then at its height, until the onset of the Cold War in 1947. It was also at this time that the Party adopted a more reformist policy, abandoning the Bolshevik template for taking power; and this new approach could have led to a rapprochement with Labour had Attlee's government responded favourably.

When one examines the early twentieth century historical context for the great upsurge in Communist Party membership and widespread interest in communism it becomes clear why it proved such an attractive proposition for many. The beginning of the twentieth century saw the most devastating world war, followed by the great economic crash in the twenties, together with mass unemployment, soon to be followed by the rise of fascism and the Second World War. Clearly, the capitalist system of profit-chasing was incapable of guaranteeing peace, prosperity or full employment. The Soviet example of long-term planning, the guarantee of full employment and a policy of peaceful coexistence looked like a promising and attractive alternative.

The aftermath of both the First and Second World Wars brought with it a radicalisation of society throughout Europe. The wars had given the men at the front and the women left behind to struggle for survival – often by joining the workforce for the first time – a new sense of dignity, of their social rights and aspirations. These changes inadvertently brought about a crumbling of the old order. There was also a serious questioning of the pre-war societies that were left behind and a de-termination by the rank and file who had taken part in those wars to make sure that a post-war society would be different.

The 1960s with the Civil Rights Movement in the US, the anti-Vietnam War movements in many countries of Europe, together with young people's growing sense of their own power, brought about a similar questioning and demand for radical change, but this time largely confined to students and young people.

More recently, despite the announcement of the 'End of History' in 1989, we have experienced the deepest worldwide economic recession since the twenties and, once again, the ideas of Marx and a discussion of socialist alternatives are assuming a renewed relevance.

Politically, much of the twentieth century has been coloured, on a global scale, by the conflict between the capitalist and the communist worlds, at least until the collapse of East European socialism in 1989. For many, particularly in the third world, communism represented an ideal goal for humanity: the creation of a society characterised by equality, solidarity, community and peaceful coexistence. For its enemies, however, it was a bogeyman, its adherents intent on setting up tyrannical systems of government and representing a dire threat to Western freedoms.

Certainly during the late 1920s through to the mid-1940s communism as an ideology reached a peak of attraction. In Western Europe and the United States hundreds of thousands were attracted to its ideas and to the Communist Party; intellectuals and artists in their thousands joined or strongly sympathised with communism. In the underdeveloped world, including the colonial countries, communism offered the perspective of liberation and independence from imperial domination and oppression. Its attraction became so potent that western governments everywhere introduced draconian measures to combat its ideas; films and literature were banned and individual members were placed under surveillance and persecuted; in the colonial countries the situation was worse – communist parties were banned and their followers hounded, imprisoned and even killed.

In the USA in 1947, in the wake of Truman's introduction of a loyalty oath and the activities of the House Committee on Un-American Activities (HUAC), the Communist Party was forced to register as an 'agent of a foreign power' and its members and sympathisers were hounded and harassed in one of the biggest political witch hunts to be carried out by any modern industrialised nation. In West Germany the Communist Party, which had been outlawed, its members persecuted and decimated by Hitler, was once again banned in 1956.

Communism, whether from a positive or negative standpoint impacted on, and affected the lives of, all of us who lived through this period. In the following pages I will examine the ways in which the Communist Party of Great Britain and its individual members had an impact on life in Britain. What sort of people were these communists, what did they wish to achieve and what did they actually accomplish?

A whole number of biographies and autobiographies have been written by and about individual communists and these are a rich source of information in terms of their protagonists' background, motivation and lives, but most are only known and possibly read by a handful of sympathisers or interested academics. I have made full use of a number of them for this book (see bibliography).

To begin to understand how people became communists, what motivated and inspired them, the logical place to begin is with the Bolshevik Revolution in Russia in 1917. For us today it is virtually impossible to imagine the impact the Russian Revolution had on people throughout the world. One cannot exaggerate the earth-shattering effect it had on world politics and social relations. The First World War was dragging to its end – the worst, senseless mass slaughter experienced in generations. Those who had gone through it were determined such wars should never happen again and many also wanted to make sense of their horrendous experiences by helping to build a new world free of want, poverty and injustice. For ordinary working people, the poor and oppressed, the Russian Revolution was an ardent inspiration and gave them a sense of historical fulfilment: working people had, for the first time in history, actually taken over the reins of power and abolished Tsarist tyranny. So why shouldn't this happen elsewhere?

Among the powerful, the rich and the whole capitalist class, on the other hand, the revolution sent shudders of horror down their spines; all of a sudden their wealth and privileged positions in society were called into question. Those seemingly unshakable class hierarchies were everywhere, and now more than ever, under threat.

The Soviet Union became the first 'workers' state', the first country governed, it seemed, by its own working people. It inspired not only manual workers and agricultural labourers, but scientists, artists, writers and musicians around the world. The list of these is substantive, from people like Pablo Picasso, Rabindranath Tagore, Arthur Miller, Diego Rivera, Paul Robeson, Harry Belafonte to Bernard Shaw, Sidney and Beatrice Webb, from Charlie Chaplin, John Reed, Albert Einstein to Frédéric and Iréne Joliot-Curie. All were thrilled about this attempt to remodel a class-ridden society, to do away with hierarchies of all sorts and to provide everyone with equal opportunities. The reasons why these hopes and aspirations were not fulfilled is a different story and not the subject of this book.

It is widely forgotten today that immediately following the successful Bolshevik revolution the West, in the form of British, French and US forces, together with the Italian special Corpo di Spedizione, as well as contingents from Romania, Greece, Poland, China and Serbia, all invaded the Soviet Union in support of the White Russians, in an attempt to strangle the new socialist state in its cradle. The Japanese also, concerned about their northern border, sent the largest military force from the east, numbering about 70,000 soldiers. So the young Soviet Union, still floundering in the chaos and ruins bequeathed it by the First World War, found itself immediately embroiled in a new fight for its very existence. This fact, too, won the young Soviet Union much sympathy and goodwill on the part of working people from around the world. It also led to the entrenchment of a siege mentality in the Soviet Union and to an increased militarisation and centralisation of power.

Within a short space of time the revolution led to the setting up of communist parties in many other countries of the world, including in Britain in 1920. As Marx and Engels had said, in their Communist

Manifesto, half a century earlier: 'A spectre is haunting Europe – the spectre of communism'. Once the armed interventions by the western powers in the Soviet Union had been repulsed and it was realised in the West that communism wasn't going to be stopped by armed might alone, the ruling classes of all countries went on the propaganda offensive: communism had to be vilified, damned and ridiculed if the spread of its infectious ideas was to be stemmed. That set the stage for the continuous stream of anti-communist rhetoric and distortion that followed, and it has never ceased. This is not to imply that communism itself and individual communists are beyond reproach or that there is nothing to criticise, condemn or repudiate in communist theory or practice – the Stalinist tyranny is only the most glaring example of such a case. However, no language and no flights of imagination were too wild not to be enlisted in attacking the ideas: communists believed in free love and undermined the bastions of marriage, they wanted everything to be owned by the state, children would be taken from their parents and become the property of the state; everyone would live in communes and be dragged down to the same level; there would be no freedom of choice; a one-party system, like that in the Soviet Union, would be imposed etc.

I remember my father telling me how a teacher in his secondary school demonstrated to the class what socialism would mean, by taking a pocket watch, dismantled it, and handing out the small cogs, springs and screws to the individual pupils. That, he said, was what socialist equality meant! A friend told me a similar story: her father, trying to dissuade her from becoming a communist, told her that the communists make you share toothbrushes.

It was, of course, Karl Marx and his close collaborator Friedrich Engels in the 19th century who were instrumental in creating the basis for the world communist movement. It is their ideas, known today generically as 'Marxism' which laid the basis for the philosophy and the goals of the world's communist parties.

While the Soviet Union and its Communist Party, certainly in its early days, played a dominant and guiding role for the world's communist parties, it is, nevertheless, a caricature to portray each and every national communist party as merely an agent of Soviet power. The idea of monolithic parties taking their orders from Moscow and stifling all and every opinion that deviated from the 'party line' while in part true – certainly during the pre-war years – does not reflect the complex reality of the communist movement. Particularly, in Britain, the Party followed very closely its own line, based on local circumstances, even if on occasion loyalties to the Soviet Union overrode these.

While there is no doubt that the Soviet Communist Party, particularly under Stalin, did try to impose its discipline on the world communist movement, this was not always successful or even effective in many cases. Certainly in the early years of the communist movement – at least until the outbreak of the Second World War – communists, as well as many on the non-communist Left, looked up to and admired the Soviet Union for what it had achieved and saw it as one of their chief obligations to defend and protect this 'first workers' state'. However this didn't necessarily mean accepting everything the Soviet Union did or what the Soviet Communist Party said – there were many within the Party who disagreed with various policies, but such disquiet was rarely expressed publicly. It was kept within 'the movement' in order to maintain an outward show of unity.

Despite the British Party's admiration of, and early allegiance to, the Soviet Union, it certainly didn't follow the Stalinist model of tight central control and discipline. Professor Kevin Morgan, in his substantial research on the Party during the war years found that, 'there was an underlying democratic ethos to much of the party's work at this time'.[8]

Most people who joined the communist parties, in whatever country, invariably did so because they wanted to change the systems in their own countries for the better and saw their responsibilities as first and foremost to their own nation and their own people. The picture of a party stifling discussion and debate is at variance with many members' experience.

Interestingly and significantly, a number of those members who left the Party after a time, for whatever reasons, often recalled enjoyable and exciting days discussing politics with no holds barred, in smoky pubs, small meeting rooms or in comrades' homes; they missed those stimulating and invigorating debates and, once outside, they felt as if they had abandoned their family. Almost anyone who has once been a member of the Communist Party is in some way indelibly stamped by the experience and, more often than not, in a positive way.

When the Marxist historian Eric Hobsbawm died in 2012, the media were replete with eulogies praising his historical insights, but expressing bemusement at his adherence to the communist cause to the end of his life, as if it were an eccentric tic. Why does there appear to be such a lack of understanding or empathy as to why so many of his generation joined in the first place and often remained loyal to the cause of their youth? Most writers on communism make little effort to understand the reasoning behind an adherence to communist ideas or the Communist Party. Such allegiance is invariably dismissed in a patronising fashion as a 'belief' or 'blind faith': Marxism is a religion and Das Kapital is its Bible.

Reams have been written and countless words uttered about the naivety, the delusions, stupidity and even culpability of those – communists and sympathisers – who gave their support to the Soviet Union over many years. Historians have delivered enough evidence to demonstrate that the Soviet Union (and, to a lesser or equal extent, its East European allies) under Stalin was a place of arbitrary and widespread criminality on the part of the state and the leaderships of the institutionalised communist parties. So, quod erat demonstrandum, anyone supporting the Soviet Union or communism must also have been criminal or culpably naïve in some way or other. However, this supposition is open to question. An apparently logical connectedness between the Soviet Union and individual communists active in other countries needs to be looked at in its historical context.

Certainly in those early years, at least until the death of Lenin, and despite some unsavoury incidents and isolated acts of criminality that are always by-products of war, the general attitudes of those who didn't feel immediately threatened by communism was one of tacit approval and support. A tyrannical Tsarist empire had been overthrown. And even up until the end of the Second World War support was still widespread abroad, despite Stalin's show trials in the thirties and his decimation of the old Bolshevik leadership. It was only with the repression of the Hungarian uprising in 1956 and the intervention in Czechoslovakia in 1968 that support for the Communist Party fell away sharply.

One of the big factors in explaining that continued widespread support for the Soviet Union both internally and externally – something not often discussed – has been the role played by the Jewish Diaspora. Anti-Semitism of the worst sort was endemic throughout Tsarist Russia and its empire. The new Soviet government under Lenin promised equality for all races and oppressed minorities within the old Tsarist Empire. For Jews this opened up the prospect of genuine freedom for the first time in history. Also, those tens of thousands of Jews who had earlier fled the pogroms and settled in the USA, Britain and other countries, identified readily with the young Soviet state and began to play significant roles in communist parties and the Left in their new countries of residence. Unsurprisingly, perhaps, the CPGB set up a Jewish Bureau in 1937 and it later published a newsletter, the Jewish Clarion (from 1947-64).

For Western capitalism, the young Soviet state represented a dire threat to the system of profit-making and every means was taken to isolate and exterminate it. The West's bellicosity towards the Soviet Union continued right up until 1941, when a belated rapprochement came about in the face of the seemingly unstoppable German military onslaught. A formal alliance was then forged between the Soviet Union, the main western European powers and the USA to wage a joint war against the Nazis. However, in 1945 at the closing stage of Second World War, already before the guns had fallen silent, western weapons were retrained on the Soviet Union, and a vicious Cold War was unleashed. This 'new' battle wasn't simply, as is often told, waged against Stalinism or out of a desire for 'democracy' in the Soviet Union and Eastern Europe, but was an attempt to extirpate the very idea of an alternative society, to prevent further 'infection' of the capitalist-dominated western world. That is why the West, after the war, did its utmost to prevent the emergence of popular governments, including communists, in those areas under its own control, like Greece, Italy and France. If the aim had really been to encourage democracy in Eastern Europe, surely peaceful coexistence and invigorated trading relations would have had a more effective impact?

Even the notorious and oft-cited Nazi-Soviet Pact of 1939, concluded shortly before the outbreak of the Second World War, was only signed by Stalin after the British and French had dragged their feet over the signing of a friendship agreement with the Soviet Union to halt Nazism in its tracks. Western consensus, especially with increasing historical distance from the period of the alliance with the Soviet Union during the Second World War, is that Hitler's tyranny and Stalin's were two sides of the same coin – the two most evil totalitarian dictatorships of the 20th century.

While in no way wishing to diminish or dismiss the horrors and mass killings that took place during Stalin's rule, such an attempt to draw comparisons between the two 'isms' needs to be forcefully rebutted. Nazism was based, from the very outset, on a racist, anti-humanitarian and aggressive ideology and involved the eradication of the Jews, whereas communism is based on the polar opposite – humanitarian justice, an end to exploitation and oppression and the pursuit of peace. The fact that Stalin usurped collective leadership of the Soviet Communist Party and made a mockery of its aims does not, in itself, make the two philosophies equivalent in any way.

It also needs to be underlined that many, not just those who opposed the socialist transformation of Soviet Russia, but also genuine communists and sympathisers were themselves victims of Stalin's tyranny. Rather, I wish to put these crimes in the context of the battle for world domination and capitalism's desperation to repel the rising tide of demands for fundamental change in international relations and for social justice and national independence.

A mere six months after Allied Forces had liberated German concentration camps, a military tribunal formed at Nuremberg set about prosecuting the Nazi war criminals. Some of the most dangerous were brought to justice – but not all. Over 4,000 former Nazis were immediately employed to work for the US government to help in its fight against the Soviet Union. Reinhard Gehlen, a top counter-intelligence officer for the Nazis, was taken on to head the US intelligence programme in West Germany to spy on the Russians. Werner von Braun, the man who was chiefly responsible for the rain of V1 and V2 rockets on London's civilian population during the Second World War, gained new celebrity status as the man behind the post-war space programme of the United States. Thousands of former Nazis, some of whom had committed atrocities, immediately began working for the United States government without the public's knowledge; they were put on the US payroll either as scientists or as intelligence agents in Europe. Others found refuge elsewhere, even in Britain.

At the height of the Korean War, US General McArthur was urging US President Truman to use nuclear weapons to bomb China and even Russia if the latter threatened to join in the war to help North Korea. These two examples alone demonstrate the extent of anti-Soviet and anti-communist hysteria and how the Cold War had become entrenched in Western diplomacy even before the Second World War was over. It is within this context that one has to examine the motivation of so many in signing up to the communist cause.

The long and dangerous Cold War period that stretched from 1945 until the demise of the Soviet Union in 1990 was, as we now know, based on a myth of a Soviet threat. Recently revealed CIA papers have demonstrated how Soviet defence capabilities were routinely exaggerated by the West throughout the Cold War period in order to maintain this myth and provide the alibi for increased armament production levels. Despite Stalin's dictatorial rule and the Soviet Union's possession of nuclear weaponry, there is no real evidence that the Soviet Union ever envisaged a pre-emptive attack on the West or that it had imperial ambitions beyond its East European sphere of influence. In fact, Stalin invariably took a very insular approach to foreign policy: he was concerned almost exclusively with defending the Soviet empire, but had no concrete ambitions to expand it. Even the imposition of communist regimes in Eastern Europe after the end of the Second World War were undertaken with the aim of protecting Soviet borders rather than for any greater imperialist aims. Stalin's whole political strategy was based on defence, and in view of the many demands made by leading Western figures for the elimination of Soviet communism, it is little wonder that the Soviet Union itself adopted an almost paranoid fear of a pre-emptive strike by the West.

On the other side, the US-engendered paranoia of communist subversion led to draconian internal policies to exterminate not only national communist parties, but any organisation or individual even loosely associated with communism, Marxism, the Peace Movement or friendship societies with the Soviet Union. Despite the thousands of lives ruined by the House Committee on Un-American Activities hearings and the McCarthy witch hunts in the United States, as well as the torture and killing carried out by Britain in its imperial colonies, all has been eclipsed, in the writing of history, by the focus on the Soviet Union as 'the real crucible of horror and oppression'.

It also needs to be remembered that it was the Soviet Union, not the US, Britain or any other western power that gave selfless support to national liberation movements throughout the world during its existence: to the Spanish Republic already in the 1930s, the ANC in South Africa, the MPLA in Angola, Frelimo in Mozambique and the Viet Minh in Vietnam and many others. The West, on the contrary, did all in its power to suppress these independence movements. Only recently are the atrocities committed by Britain in putting down liberation struggles in its own former colonies, like Kenya, being given an airing in the mainstream media in the wake of demands for compensation by some of its victims.

As many recent academic papers and books reveal, communism, as an idea and goal, is being given a new lease of life in the face of the ongoing world economic crisis and the apparent inability of capitalism to solve humanity's most pressing problems. That is why the search for an alternative way of organising society will continue. It is also why all on the Left, including communists and socialists themselves, need to properly evaluate the historical experience of attempts to build communist societies. Only in this way will we be able to separate the distortions and crimes of Stalin and his henchmen from the heroic and admirable deeds of many ordinary communists worldwide and to view the deeper communist experience over and beyond that narrow perspective of conflating communism with Stalinism.

One of the central strands in communist thinking and in communist activity has been a humanist one, but this has been invariably ignored by writers on communism. Only when the communist experience is examined separately from the Soviet model and experience will a fuller appreciation and understanding of the lives and loyalties of these individuals make sense. This book is an attempt to begin such an appraisal. In the succeeding chapters the Party's role in key areas of public life will be examined and evaluated.

Writers and the Battle of Ideas

'By this time, so many people of relative eminence were writing, speaking, or marching in one or another form of militant political expression that St John Clarke's adhesion to the Left was a matter of little general interest... as an elderly, no longer very highly esteemed writer such views may even have done something to re-establish his name. The younger people approved, while in rich, stuffy houses, where he was still sometimes to be seen on the strength of earlier reputation as a novelist, a left-wing standpoint was regarded as suitable to a man of letters, even creditable in a widely known, well-to-do author, who might at his age perfectly well have avoided the controversies of politics. However, St John Clarke himself apparently felt less and less capable, in practice, of taking part in the discussion of Marxist dialectic, with its ever-changing bearings. As a consequence of his laxity in "keeping up" he had lost ground in the more exacting circles of the intellectual Left. His name was rarely seen except in alphabetical order among a score of nonentities signing at the foot of some letter to the press...'

ANTHONY POWELL, CASANOVA'S CHINESE RESTAURANT (1960)

'The meeting began on time. It was quite a distinguished platform – an assortment of well-known Communists, and various hardly less-distinguished "fellow-travellers" – a well-known actress, a well-known poet, a distinguished cleric, authors, male, female and intermediate. The chairman, a party member, rattled off a set piece about the struggle of the Spanish people against Franco being part of a world-wide struggle... the struggle of the forces of progress against the forces of reaction... class struggle between rich and poor, exploiters and exploited... call upon... distinguished poet... read translation he has made of one of the poems of a distinguished Spanish anti-fascist poet... The distinguished poet, clad in classy tweeds, heaved up languidly from his chair and in a bored, classy tone murmured that he would first read the perm [sic] in the original Spanish...'

ETHEL MANNIN, COMRADE, O COMRADE (1947)

'Who was Tristram Abberley? What manner of man was he? Sportsman; idler; intellectual poseur; spendthrift; communist; homosexual; womanizer; traveller; wastrel; husband; father; soldier; poet'.

ROBERT GODDARD, HAND IN GLOVE (1992)

Three novels – high-brow, middle-brow and low-brow – written in different decades with very different purposes, but each employing the idea of the Communist writer as dishonest, a knave and a fool. Communist writers have a special place in the popular demonology of British communism. Variously dismissed as power-fantasists, neurotic scions of the ruling-class, intellectual elitists, cynics in love with violence or hopeless idealists, they are expected to bear a special responsibility for the crimes and failures of the communist idea. As writers they had a duty to tell the truth. Instead they betrayed their country – and their art – for a sinister and foreign ideology which they knew to be based upon cruelty and injustice:

'between the October revolution and the Stalin-Hitler Pact, numberless men of letters, both in Europe and America, were attracted to Communism... Their conversion therefore expressed, in an acute and sometimes in a hysterical form, feelings which were dimly shared by the inarticulate millions... The intellectual in politics is always "unbalanced" in the estimation of his colleagues. He peers round the next corner while they keep their eyes on the road; and he risks his faith on unrealized ideas, instead of confining it prudently to humdrum loyalties. He is "in advance," and in this sense, an extremist.'[9]

Or as George Orwell once put it,

'They take their cookery from Paris and their opinions from Moscow. In the general patriotism of the country they form a sort of island of dissident thought. England is perhaps the only great country whose intellectuals are ashamed of their own nationality... All through the critical years many left-wingers were chipping away at English morale, trying to spread an outlook that was sometimes squashily pacifist, sometimes violently pro-Russian, but always anti-British.'[10]

An interest in Russian opinions or a taste for French food – it is difficult to tell which seemed most treasonable to Orwell ('the patriotism of the deracinated,' 'the kind of person who is always somewhere else when the trigger is pulled,' 'playing with fire by people who don't even know that fire is hot').[11] This is what the writer on espionage Andrew Boyle has called the 'climate of treason', a literary intelligentsia composed of 'rebellious and discontented idealists' who were easy targets for Soviet intelligence.[12] For the US writer Stephen Koch, the Communist conspiracy in Britain operated on two levels, connected by 'the language of the democratic elites and the language of revolt'. Culture – more specifically literature – was the 'point of intersection between propaganda and espionage', a meeting place of knaves and fools:

'On the public level, the move to Stalinize Bloomsbury taste was led by Otto Katz and the Münzenberg apparatus, using British fronts such as the Left Book Club and its many appendages. Covertly, the process was led by Blunt and his gofer, Burgess, guided by Maly and by Ludwik's Recruit in the London offices of the Secret Intelligence Services (SIS), silently sustained by the talent-spotters throughout the universities and in the Münzenberg-Gilbarti propaganda network, and tied to the Soviets through a dual NKVD-Comintern network running through Amsterdam, Berlin and Paris.'[13]

For Koch, the fact that the most famous British recruits to Soviet Intelligence numbered left-wing writers among their friends – Anthony Blunt (Louis MacNeice), Guy Burgess (Rosamund Lehmann), Michael Straight (John Cornford) and Kim Philby (Graham Greene) – confirms the suspicion that the cultural campaigns of the Popular Front years were a cover for something else. Recent revelations that Orwell later provided British Intelligence with lists of suspected CP members and fellow-travellers (including several notable writers) has only served to underline his claims that the Communist Party and its writers were up to no good.

The idea that British communist intellectuals were all either knaves or fools is found in British fiction, where they usually appear either as humourless, dishonest, bookish and uncompanionable zealots – for example, George Orwell's Coming Up for Air, Evelyn Waugh's Unconditional Surrender, Aldous Huxley's Point Counter Point – or as sad and solitary figures caught up in espionage – C.P. Snow's The New Men, Graham Greene's The Human Factor, John le Carré's The Spy Who Came in from the Cold.

Considering the importance of these caricatures to popular anti-communism, historians have paid curiously little attention to the facts of the Party's literary life. If communist writers are remembered these days, it is either despite their communist attachments (Patrick Hamilton, Sylvia Townsend-Warner, John Lehmann, Cecil Day Lewis, Nancy Cunard), or because of their subsequent anti-communism (Doris Lessing, Edward Upward, Stephen Spender).

Most histories of the Party, like Henry Pelling's, The British Communist Party, Willie Thompson's The Good Old Cause: British Communism 1920-1991 and Keith Laybourn and Dylan Murphy's, Under the Red Flag: A History of Communism in Britain attend rather more carefully to the Party's relationship with the Soviet Union, to its industrial struggles and its anti-colonial and peace campaigns than to its cultural achievements. Of the six volume official history of the Party, only John Callaghan, Cold War, Crisis and Conflict: the CPGB

1951-58 pays any serious attention to the Party's 'cultural workers'. And yet the Party's literary culture may prove to be one of its most enduring achievements. For over seventy years the British Communist Party conducted a sustained, concentrated educational and imaginative intervention in British literary life, quite out of proportion to either its size or political influence.[14] No British political party ever contained within its ranks so many distinguished writers as the CPGB. Kingsley Amis, Brendan Behan, Robert Bolt, Elizabeth Bowen, Lewis Grassic Gibbon, Patrick Hamilton, Hamish Henderson, Doris Lessing, Ewan MacColl, Hugh MacDiarmid, Olivia Manning, Iris Murdoch, John Prebble, Stephen Spender (joined the Party in 1937 but only stayed for a short time), E.P. Thompson, Sylvia Townsend Warner, Arnold Wesker and Raymond Williams (joined 1940) were all Party members at one time or another. Cecil Day Lewis, Poet Laureate in the 1960s, was one of the Party's most public literary figures in the 1930s.

Dylan Thomas used to call himself a Communist. E.M. Forster once said that he would have joined the Party if he had been younger. Graham Greene (who was briefly a Party member while he was a student in the 1920s) told Salvador Allende that he was 'forever searching for Communism with a human face'.

Despite the disadvantages which inevitably accompanied a party card, a remarkable number of professional novelists were once party members (or so close as to make no difference), most notably Edward Upward, James Barke, Ralph Bates, Robert Briffault, Arthur Calder-Marshall, Ralph Fox, Yvonne Kapp, Margot Heinemann, Jack Lindsay, Olivia Manning, Iris Morley, Edith Pargeter, Maurice Richardson, John St John, Montagu Slater, John Sommerfield, Philip Toynbee, Arthur Ransome and Geoffrey Trease.

Among the Party's published poets were Valentine Ackland, Jack Beeching, Maurice Carpenter, John Cornford, Nancy Cunard, Charles Hobday, Geoffrey Matthews, Frances Moore, Arnold Rattenbury, Edgell Rickword, Roger Roughton, Hugh Sykes-Davies and Randall Swingler. Even in the last years of crisis and decline, the Party's ranks included poets like David Craig, Julia Darling, Jackie Kay, Jackie Litherland, Wendy Mulford and Chris Searle. In the early 1970s Searle attracted national attention when he was dismissed from a school-teaching job for publishing a book of poems by his pupils, and the children went on strike in protest.

From the early 1930s to the early 1990s, Communists were responsible for producing an almost unbroken line of literary and critical magazines – Storm, Viewpoint, Left Review, New Writing, Left Book Club News, Poetry and the People, Our Time, Seven, Theatre Today, Arena, Circus, Day-light, Fireweed, Artery, Fires, Red Letters – as well as hundreds of locally produced magazines and poetry anthologies.

Left Review was the second-best-selling monthly arts magazine in late 1930s London. The Party's publishers Lawrence and Wishart first published the ground-breaking journal New Writing (which later became the long-running Penguin New Writing). By 1939 there were twenty poetry-groups around Britain attached to Poetry and the People. The magazine Seven – a war-time publication devoted to writing from the Forces – sold 60,000 copies a quarter. Our Time, which ran from 1940 to 1950, sold 18,000 copies a month. The radical paperback publishing company, Fore Publications, sold over half a million books in its first twelve months. Poetry readings were a regular feature of Party Congresses from the early 1950s to the last Congress in 1991. The first London musha'ara (an Urdu poetry-reading) was initiated by the Communist Party, and the Notting Hill Carnival came into being as a direct result of the initiative of Caribbean Communists living in London, under the able leadership of Claudia Jones.

The Sunday Worker, the Daily Worker and the Morning Star always devoted generous space to reviewing contemporary fiction, theatre and poetry. The Party's long-running weekly, World News and Views used to carry a regular poetry-supplement. The theoretical journals Modern Quarterly and Marxism Today were frequently enlivened by literary criticism and controversy. The magazine Arena published for the first time in English new work by writers like Neruda, Aragon, Pasternak, Éluard, Cassou and Hikmet.

Why was the CPGB so interested in literature? Why did such a tiny, hard-pressed, over-stretched and often defensive organisation take literary culture so seriously? What could it possibly hope to gain? And what did it achieve? First, Marxism was a totalising ideology. There was no aspect of living in which communists were not supposed to be interested. The Party's 1945 Congress declared that 'it is essential that our members take a lively interest in all questions in which the people are interested, including social, art, music, literature, entertainment and sport. We must strive to end the feeling, which undoubtedly exists, that members of the Communist Party should be interested only in politics.' If the Soviets took literature seriously, then it was clearly the duty of British communists to do the same. Lunacharsky's writings on education and culture were available in Britain in the early 1920s; Trotsky's Literature and Revolution was first published in Britain in 1925.

Being part of an international movement the Party was encouraged – if not expected – to imitate the examples of more successful Communist parties. In the early 1920s, communists tried to import the ideas of the Soviet Proletkult into Britain (via the magazine Plebs and the National Council of Labour Colleges). The Party's publishing house Martin Lawrence translated a number of Soviet and German writers into English.

During the Third Period, the Party's cultural initiatives were more closely modelled on those of the KPD (German Communist Party), the Worker's Theatre Movement self-consciously imitating the work of the German Volksbühne and the Rote Sprachrohr. There was even a bold attempt to reproduce the success of the Arbeiter Illustrierte Zeitung with the short-lived Workers Illustrated News. After the Second World War, Communists were responsible for publishing the first English translations of writers from the East European socialist bloc like Fucik, Vitezslav, Mickiewicz and Vaptsarov. During the Cold War the Party's cultural apparatus made some unconvincing attempts to introduce Zhdanovism into the Party's internal literary life with the stage-managed 'Caudwell Controversy' in Modern Quarterly.[15] From the late 1960s onwards, the Party increasingly looked to the Italian Communist Party for its strategy and to Gramsci for its theory. The Party's 1977 People's Jubilee at London's Alexander Palace (attended by over 11,000 people) was expressly modelled on the Festa dell'Unita and the Fête de l'Humanité.

Second, the Party was the inheritor of pre-1917 working-class and radical political traditions – particularly the Socialist Sunday Schools movement, the Chartists, the Independent Labour Party (ILP) and the Labour College Movement – in which literacy and literature had always been central preoccupations (Walt Whitman had a special place in ILP iconography). Britain was the first mass-literate society, with the first literate working-class. The Party's first generation leaders were the products of a skilled trade-union autodidact culture which respected books. The Communist MP Willie Gallacher (the chapter titles of his memoirs were all quotations from Shelley) once published a book of poetry, Palme Dutt wrote a play about Dimitrov and Wal Hannington (see section on the Party and trade unions) a semi-autobiographical novel. When Tommy Jackson collected some of his essays from the Daily Worker about the English Realist novel, he gave pride of place not to Defoe, Fielding, or Dickens, but to 'the incomparable' Jane Austen.

Lewis Jones, unemployed leader in South Wales and a delegate to the Seventh Congress of the Comintern, published two novels. Tom Wintringham, one of the twelve Communist leaders gaoled for 'sedition' in 1925 and who later commanded the British Battalion of the International Brigade in Spain was a widely published poet. Ralph Bates was a railway-worker who served as a Political Commissar with the International Brigades. He also wrote a biography of Schubert and a great many novels, including two set in Spain Lean Men (one of the very first Penguins) and The Olive Field, which earned Bates comparisons with Malraux, even Tolstoy.

Lawrence and Wishart published the first unabridged edition of Robert Tressell's The Ragged Trousered Philanthropists. In the late 1930s and again in the early 1950s they encouraged the development of a native, working-class Bildungsroman. The British Communist Party may have attracted some distinguished and well-known writers, but more significantly it encouraged young working-class writers to write. A remarkable number of these went on to be published – Brian Almond, Charles Ashleigh, Fred Ball, George Chandler, Alexander Baron, Dan Billany, Simon Blumenfeld, Robert Bonnar, Max Cohen, Len Doherty, Willy Goldman, Frederick Harper, Harry Heslop, William Holt, Lewis Jones, Dave Lambert, Julius Lipton, Jim Phelan, Charles Poulsen, Herbert Smith, Dave Wallis, Bert Ward, Ted Willis, Roger Woddis. Several of these were successful enough to make careers as professional writers – Willis and Baron in television, Doherty in journalism, Blumenfeld as a theatre critic, Woddis as the New Statesman's resident satirical poet. The film rights to Dave Wallis's novel Only Lovers Left Alive were bought by Mick Jagger (though the film was never made). In the 1970s and 1980s individual Communists were heavily involved in establishing and maintaining the Federation of Worker Writers and Community Publishers.

Third, cultural activity was understood by Communists to be a valuable and necessary bridgehead on the mainland of British life. For such a small political party, with little or no access to the mainstream media, literature was a particularly effective way of communicating, popularising and naturalising its ideas and values to a public well beyond its natural audience.

Virginia Woolf and J.B. Priestley wrote for the Daily Worker. Alan

Sillitoe wrote for the Morning Star (Arthur Seaton votes Communist in Saturday Night and Sunday Morning). Sean O'Casey sat on the editorial board of the paper for many years. During the Spanish Civil War, Randall Swingler and Nancy Cunard published a questionnaire about the war in Spain, Writers take Sides in which almost all the most famous writers of the day declared their support for the Spanish Republic. The polymath Jack Lindsay wrote over two hundred books of poetry, fiction, science, translation, history, archaeology and art-criticism. He once filled Trafalgar Square with a performance of his Mass Declamation On Guard for Spain. During the Second World War the poet Montagu Slater – a founder editor of Left Review – was head of film scripts at the Ministry of Information. Slater later devised and scripted Britten's Young Person's Guide to the Orchestra and wrote the libretto for Britten's opera Peter Grimes. Dirk Bogarde starred in the film of one of Slater's novels. Randall Swingler once packed the Albert Hall with a musical pageant starring Paul Robeson and set to music by twelve of the most distinguished contemporary composers, including Vaughan Williams, Elizabeth Lutyens and Alan Rawsthorne.

Literature was also a two-way process, by which the Party saw itself reflected in the public imagination. In Goodbye to Berlin, Christopher Isherwood (who was then very close to the Communist Party of Germany) based Sally Bowles, the most famous character in 1930's English fiction, on the Daily Worker film-critic Jean Ross. The distinguished Communist scientist J.D. Bernal appears in C.P. Snow's The Search. The character of Guy Pringle in Olivia Manning's Balkan Trilogy is based on the legendary 'Red' BBC radio producer Reggie Smith. The NUWM leader assaulted by the police in Walter Greenwood's best-selling Love on the Dole was the young Communist Eddie Frow, later AEU Manchester District Secretary, bibliophile and historian. Arthur Seaton in Sillitoe's Saturday Night and Sunday Morning attends a factory-gate meeting addressed by John Peck – later a Communist councillor in Nottingham. National Organiser Dave Cook is one of the main characters in Alison Fell's Tricks of the Light. The gamekeeper in the first draft of D.H. Lawrence's Lady Chatterley's Lover is secretary of a Party cell in Sheffield...

Even in the worst periods of self-immolation (1929-33, 1940-1, 1949-1958) Communists demonstrated an extraordinary ability to keep open lines of communication with mainstream literary life in London. They often shared the same agents and publishers – and pubs – as non-Communist writers, who could usually be persuaded to

BRITAIN'S COMMUNISTS: THE UNTOLD STORY

contribute a poem, a story or a book-review to the Party's publications. At the height of the Cold War, Edith Sitwell and George Barker – who could never have been accused of having Communist sympathies – were published in Swingler's Key Poets series. The poet and folk-song collector Hamish Henderson, expelled from Italy (after pressure from the US), where he was lecturing on folk-song, won the Somerset Maugham Prize for his collection Elegies for the Dead in Cyrenaica. The Scots poet Hugh MacDiarmid rejoined the Party in 1956. Two of Patrick Hamilton's plays were filmed by Hollywood studios in the Cold War years, Rope (starring James Stewart) and Gaslight (starring Ingrid Bergman). The Australian-born British writer James Aldridge settled in London from 1938 and wrote over 30 books. His A Captive in the Land was made into a film by blacklisted Hollywood writer, John (Jack) Berry.

Fourth, because this was an organisation at ease with literary controversy, organisational and ideological debates were often mediated through arguments about books. An apparently arcane debate in Marxism Today in 1957 about the relationship between literature and ideology was actually a coded discussion of the Dr Zhivago affair. When, ten years later Marxism Today held a similar debate around the Party's statement on Questions of Ideology and Culture, the discussion about the relative autonomy of culture may be seen as sublimated disagreements over the Party's emerging Eurocommunism.

During the late 1920s the popular books-pages of the Sunday Worker were marked by a series of fierce and coded debates about D.H. Lawrence, the Workers Theatre Movement and Shakespeare. Some readers objected to the paper carrying any arts coverage at all, in a way that can have left no-one in any doubt that the debate was really about the party's relationship with its allies in the national left-wing movement and to the rest of British society. Not for the first time, anti-intellectualism proved to be a useful tool in disciplining the Party's own writers. When one of the editors, Tommy Jackson, ridiculed the arcane and sectarian language of the Third Period, the Comintern EC took the opportunity to overhaul the British Party leadership; the left-wing movement was liquidated and the Sunday Worker closed down.

Almost two years before the Seventh Congress of the Comintern, the establishment of the Writers International in Britain anticipated the Popular Front by calling for the broadest possible alliance of writers, artists and intellectuals to defend the 'best achievements of human culture' against fascism. The 'left' opposition, arguing for the class-basis of language and literature, was swiftly defeated in the pages of Left Review.

The situation was reversed again in 1950, when Jackson was the subject of another furious correspondence in the Daily Worker about cultural 'snobbery'. His argument that 'there is no such thing as 'bourgeois' or 'capitalist' culture... only our common cultural heritage' was clearly incompatible with the Cold War 'Battle of Ideas'. This was followed by a series of critical rows in the paper around the magazine Arena and the Key Poets series. Although they were ostensibly about Modernism and 'bohemianism', they may be seen as coded attempts to control the intellectual loyalties of the Party's best-known writers in the worsening political climate.

Because of the shoe-string nature of the Party's finances, few of the cultural publications with which it was identified were actually owned or controlled by Party Centre. The Party did not really try to organise its writers before 1947 (and then without much success). On the other hand, communist writers could not rely on the Party for subsidy or for a sufficiently large readership for their books and magazines. Instead they had to negotiate the market. British Communist writers thus enjoyed a degree of autonomy which was probably unique in the Communist world. The consequences of such freedom were complex and not always advantageous. When Communist writers were blacklisted at the BBC during the Cold War, their work attacked by reviewers or rejected by publishers, the Party's largely unpaid cultural infrastructure was unable to provide alternative sources of professional employment or satisfaction.

On the other hand, British Communist writers were able to develop a native radical literary tradition, almost entirely independent of theoretical developments elsewhere. The vicious literary controversies that disfigured other, bigger Communist parties (the 1947 row between Aragon and Garaudy in France, for example, the controversy over Picasso's Stalin portrait, or the Lukacs-Brecht polemic in Germany) went largely unreported in the Party's literary magazines. The reports in Left Review of the 1934 Soviet Writers Congress barely mentioned the notion of Socialist Realism. Even Zhdanov's assault on Akhmatova and Zoschenko was disingenuously referred to, at least at first, as 'the Soviet Literary Controversy'.

Few of the most imaginative and enduring interventions made by British Communist writers owed anything to the Party's 'international' commitments. During the 1930s, for example, Communist novelists breathed new life into generic fiction, particularly the historical novel (Lindsay, Townsend-Warner) and the detective-thriller (Day Lewis and the fellow-travelling Eric Ambler). Montagu Slater and Randall Swingler (working with the Communist composer Alan Bush) re-invented the mass theatrical pageant in the 1930s and 1940s. The work of Ewan MacColl, Charles Parker and Reggie Smith effectively shaped radio documentary and drama for a generation. The early years of British TV drama were heavily influenced by Unity Theatre writers.

Above all, British Communists were able to develop a home-grown, popular Marxist literary criticism. Between them, the group of writers who dominated the Party's literary culture during the years of its ascendancy in the middle decades of the century – Montagu Slater, Edgell Rickword, Jack Lindsay, Alick West, Randall Swingler, Christopher Caudwell, George Thomson, Ralph Fox, Tommy Jackson, Leslie Morton and A.L. Lloyd – created an extraordinary body of criticism and literary history. Some of this was published in book form – notably West's Crisis and Criticism and The Mountain in the Sunlight, Fox's The Novel and the People, Caudwell's Illusion and Reality, Lindsay's John Bunyan ; Maker of Myths, Jackson's Charles Dickens : the Progress of a Radical, Lloyd's The Singing Englishman, Morton's The English Utopia. But most was published as essays and reviews, a developing, informal and accessible critical corpus (only George Thomson of the older generation was employed by a university), celebrating the English realist tradition in fiction and the English romantic tradition in poetry. While this may have dovetailed with the political requirement of the Popular Front (and later of the Cold War) to promote radical national traditions, it nevertheless helped to mitigate the destructive effects of Soviet literary politics on the Party's intellectual life. Moreover, the work of this group was crucially influential on a group of younger Communist writers – principally E.P. Thompson, Christopher Hill, Raymond Williams and Arnold Kettle – who after the Second World War were responsible for the development of cultural studies in post-war adult education and later the Open University.

In European terms, none of this may seem remarkable. But in the context of British political life it is a unique and extraordinary record. The Conservative Party has occasionally included writers among its parliamentary leadership (Disraeli, Churchill; Enoch Powell; more recently Jeffrey Archer, Edwina Currie, Anne Widdecombe and

Douglas Hurd). Labour Prime Minister Harold Wilson's wife Mary used to write poetry; the novelist Melvyn Bragg is a very public Blairite. But British political culture is generally afraid of the arts, as British artistic culture is hostile to politics. Economism and electoralism leave little room for the imagination. The Labour Party – like the British ultra-left sects – has never been famous for an interest in the arts. Labour Party conferences do not include poetry readings. The Labour Party has never, of course, published any literary magazines. The Labour Party's only response to the first Edinburgh People's Festival (the forerunner of the Edinburgh Festival Fringe) was to declare that – because it was organised by Communists – attending the Festival's poetry-readings and ceilidhs was incompatible with membership of the Labour Party. Glasgow Unity Theatre was also one of the Fringe's initiators.

In comparison with other Communist Parties, the CPGB never possessed the resources to create a literary culture of its own able to compete with the dominant literary culture or to compensate those writers who found themselves – because of their Communism – excluded from its rewards. Joining the British Communist Party (as opposed to leaving it) was never a good career move. Not all the books written by British Communists will last, although many still deserve to be read. It was a long-term, educational project to debate and popularise ideas about the relationship between understanding and action, between culture and politics, writers and readers, literature and society. The Party's efforts were always under-funded, sometimes ill-considered and often self-defeating. But no one could ever argue that it did not take literature seriously or that individual Communist writers did not create a remarkable body of literary criticism, history and theory, fiction, drama and poetry.

ANDY CROFT

Addendum

Andy Croft, above, has more than adequately demonstrated the significant role the Communist Party played in the literary life of Britain during the thirties and forties. It is, though, worth noting that this tradition, even if diminished after the forties, still continued.

One writer who does deserve mention in this context is Robert (Bob) Leeson who was for many years the Daily Worker/Morning Star's literary editor, before becoming a full-time writer. Alongside studies in trade union history, he wrote an impressive array of popular adventure stories for younger readers, always in strong social or historical settings. He also wrote five novels inspired by the BBC TV series, Grange Hill, in collaboration with its producer, Phil Redmond. In the 1980s Leeson was elected chair of the British Writers Guild and played a vital part in negotiating minimum terms agreements with leading British publishers.

As far as attracting writers was concerned, the heyday for the Party was undoubtedly the thirties, but some were still joining right up until shortly before its demise in 1991. One of these was Nigel Williams. Talking with Rob Cowan on BBC Radio 3 on 14 January 2014, Williams told him he had been a member of the Communist Party during its 'Eurocommunist' phase. After graduating he had joined the BBC as a general trainee, and worked as an arts producer, eventually becoming the editor of Omnibus and Bookmark.

He related to Cowan how he went to a meeting at King Street (CPGB headquarters) and asked how he could best promote the revolution among his colleagues at the BBC, and was told by a Party official: 'Nigel, you are the only one there'! He was clearly unaware of the BBC blacklist and the BBC appeared to be unaware of his new allegiance, and, in this case, it didn't seem to hinder his career.

Williams's first novel, My Life Closed Twice won the 1978 Somerset Maugham Award., and he has won a television BAFTA. His most successful work has been the script for the 2005 TV drama Elizabeth I, for which he was nominated for an Emmy Award.

Bill Ash[16] was a novelist whose own life reads like a dramatic novel. He arrived in Canada from his home in Dallas, Texas in 1941, and asked to join the Royal Canadian Air Force, as he wanted to fight fascism. On enlisting in the RCAF, he lost his US citizenship. 'I tried to explain that I was not so much for King George as against Hitler,' he said, 'but they didn't seem to care much at the time.'

From Britain, he flew Spitfires with 411 Squadron, but after crashing in France and being hidden by a sympathetic French peasant family, was caught and imprisoned by the Gestapo. He was tortured but refused to divulge the names of those who had helped him. His numerous escapes became famous – he went over the wire, through it with cutters, and out of the gates disguised as a Russian labourer, but it was as a tunneller that he won most renown. Among his co-escapees was Richard, the father of the one-time Conservative leader Ian Duncan-Smith, and the future MP Aidan Crawley. His autobiographical reminiscences of that period, as recounted in his book Under the Wire, are among the most riveting and heroic of stories of wartime survival. He had three spells in Stalag Luft III and his escape attempts provided one of the inspirations for Steve McQueen's character, the 'cooler king', in the 1963 film The Great Escape. After the war, he was made an MBE, became a British citizen and studied politics and economics at Balliol College, Oxford. In the early fifties, when Bill joined the BBC, his colleagues included Tony Benn, who became a lifelong friend. His spell in India changed his outlook fundamentally and, back in Britain in the late 1950s, his politics became solidly Marxist, and that frightened his employers. The BBC didn't renew his full-time contract, but he continued to work for it as a freelance radio script reader. He applied to join the CPGB in the late sixties but was rejected (probably being considered as too pro-Chinese), so, together with engineering trade unionist Reg Birch, co-founded the Communist Party of Britain (Marxist-Leninist). Throughout the 1970s he edited the paper of the CPGB (ML). He wrote several novels and a best-selling autobiography, and became mentor for a generation of theatre and radio writers.

His novels include The Lotus in the Sky, Choice of Arms, and The Longest Way Round (described by Anthony Burgess as the work of 'a very considerable novelist'), Ride a Paper Tiger (1968) and Rise like Lions (1998), a rather hectoring political lecture in the form of a novel. In 1988, he published Marxist Morality. 'As far as I'm concerned, anyone who is one pay cheque ahead of disaster is working class,' he said. In the seventies and eighties, he chaired the Writers' Guild of Great Britain, and encouraged a new generation of writers through his work at the BBC and, later, as literary manager at the Soho Poly theatre in central London. His 1985 book The Way to Write Radio Drama is a standard text.

The Communist Party always attracted a strong following of poets. Andy Croft deals with some of the big names from the pre-war period, but many others took up the baton. Hugh MacDiarmid in Scotland, remained a communist most of his life, even though an unpredictable one; the Caribbean-born poet Peter Blackman brought a new perspective to bear on concepts of colonialism, race and internationalism, but much of his work was never published; Andy

Croft himself is a poet of some distinction and a publisher of poetry, through his directorship of Smokestack Books; the teacher and poet Bob Dixon was a quirky, humorous rhymer of agit-prop; and Chris Searle who won wide admiration for his promotion of poetry by the children he taught in London's East End (The volume of poems written by the children, Stepney Words, sold over 15,000 copies), is an outstanding poet in his own right. He has also been a strong promoter of Caribbean literature, a committed campaigner against racism and fascism and dedicated teacher; and the performance poet, Atilla the Stockbroker is still treading the boards. These are just a handful of poets who belonged to the Party or were sympathisers.

Communist literature and the Left Book Club

Perhaps one of the Communist Party's least appreciated influences is how it has encouraged reading. No other political party has come anywhere near to the publishing output of the CPGB – many hundreds of books, pamphlets and leaflets in runs of from one thousand to hundreds of thousands. Every Party branch used to have its own 'Literature Secretary' responsible for taking orders, promoting and selling literature. Many semi-literate workers began reading through these publications. My own father, who left school at 14, barely able to read, was introduced to writers like Bernard Shaw, Jack London and Edward Bellamy as well as the works of Marx and Engels as a result of his joining the Party. Most branches would have an Education Secretary, too, whose responsibility it was to organise classes, usually in Marxist philosophy or economics.

John Gorman underlines this educative role of the Party in his autobiography, Knocking Down Ginger, when he writes, 'my reading was dominated by Party pamphlets, but there is no doubt that many who had no previous habit of reading were introduced to the world of books upon joining the Party'.

Only one year after its founding, the Party established a bookshop at its headquarters, and in 1927 this became the 'Workers' Bookshop'. In 1939, the Party set up Central Books as its main retailer, wholesaler and distributor of books, magazines and pamphlets. By 1945, the Party had 32 bookshops up and down the country, even in such unlikely and unrevolutionary places as Cheltenham, Stroud, Kings Lynn and Caerphilly. Central Books stayed in business until 1999. An offshoot, still retaining the name of Central Books, but no longer with direct connections to any political party, is still in business as a wholesaler of progressive and left-wing titles.[17]

After being set up in 1947, the Party's National Cultural Committee initiated a campaign for 'factory libraries' to encourage dissemination of Marxist literature and socialist classics. Although little came of this initiative it is symptomatic of the Party's emphasis on the empowering force of literature.

This intellectual ferment during the thirties also led to the establishment of the famous Left Book Club, mentioned above. A scheme was devised, with the help of John Strachey (who regularly wrote columns for the Daily Worker, but left the Party in 1940 to join the Labour Party and later became a government minister), to set up a selection committee to choose left wing books from any publisher's list and then to recommend them to working people. Only Victor Gollancz, of all the publishers approached, replied, so the idea for the scheme was dropped, however, Gollancz decided to go it alone and begin his own scheme. This became the Left Book Club, publishing affordable editions of key works on social and political issues: literature, science and the arts. It became a huge success and opened up the opportunity for a whole generation of ordinary people to obtain books to which they would otherwise have had no access. Its declared aim was 'for the service of those who desire to play an intelligent part in the struggle for World Peace and a better social and economic order, and against Fascism.' Those who were interested in the proposal were asked to send a postcard to Gollancz – the response was overwhelming.

Although the Left Book Club was certainly not a Communist Party operation, it was, as Andy Croft writes,

'usually denounced as such ('it was how Stalinist opinion was "networked" in England' according to one historian). The LBC was a real success story, publishing 260 titles and selling millions of books in its thirteen-year life. It had 40,000 members by the end of the first year; by 1939 it had a membership of 57,000 and 1,200 local and specialist LBC discussion groups, including groups for London taxi drivers, architects, teachers, railwaymen, lawyers, accountants, poets, cyclists, musicians, puppeteers, scientists, postmen and sixth-formers.'

The first book in the series was published in 1936 – France Today and the People's Front by Maurice Thorez, General Secretary of the

French Communist Party. Not long after, Left Book Club discussion groups had mushroomed around the country to discuss the current month's choices – rather like the book clubs of today. In these groups Labour Party members joined communists and other left-wingers. Some of the groups also became activist, particularly in the cause of aid for the Spanish Republic, and giant rallies were held around the country calling for support for the Republic. On the platform of such rallies left-wing Labour leaders like Bevan and Cripps spoke alongside communists. Clement Attlee, then leader of the Parliamentary Labour Party sent a message of encouragement to the Club's first Albert Hall rally in 1937. However, his attitude was not shared by many in the leadership of his party or by the TUC who viewed the Left Book Club as just another 'communist conspiracy'. There is no doubt, though, that the Club played a key role in the political and social education of a whole generation and helped significantly to create a more 'informed democracy'.

During the thirties it could be said that the Party exercised a virtual hegemony over left-wing intellectuals and very much set the agenda of debate. Even those who didn't actually join the Party often worked closely with it or with communists in their area of work. The Party was invariably looked to for political leadership by many of those on the left. Even at branch level culture was taken seriously. It was not unusual, for instance, for Party branches to have their own cultural or-ganisers who would be responsible for organising activities, or for comrades to listen to and discuss pieces of classical music.

Honor Arundel was one of the best known Communist children's authors. She was a Daily Worker film critic, and was married to the actor Alex McCrindle (see chapter: Film – 'The Most Important of the Arts').

Honor (Morfydd) Arundel was born in North Wales in 1919. She had a passion for poetry and writing. As a result of her interest she became heavily involved in the development of the Left Book Club's Poets Group, established in 1937; its London section met at Honor Arundel's flat in Belsize Park.

Under the initiative of the Communist Party, The Left Book Club Poetry Group was re-established in July 1938. The group produced a monthly newsletter, Poetry and the People. Its first editors were John Ongley, John Isserlis and John Manifold. Poetry and the People was an attempt by the Communist Party to build on the relative success of Left Review which reached sales of around 5,000 but had little broad appeal beyond the Party. However, not everyone in the Party felt that Swingler, Arundel and the other Communist Poets were necessarily spending their time productively. Maurice Cornforth, in the Daily Worker, wrote that there was 'no point in treating communist poets as tender shoots which wilt at the first wind of critical comments from the working class'.

With the collapse of the Left Book Club at the beginning of the Second World War, Swingler and other Communist writers took the decision to establish a new 'more professional' publication, Our Time, which would include architecture, medicine, education, art and literature. The first edition appeared in February 1941 and incorporated Poetry and the People. The editors were the writer, Randall Swingler, artist James Boswell and newspaperman Allen Hutt, and later Honor Arundel.

By 1943, Honor Arundel and Peter Phillips became editors of Our Time. Initially, sales hit the 5,000 mark, the maximum possible due to paper shortage and war time distribution restrictions. But the Forces' demand for cultural magazines was such that by the end of the war it was selling 18,000 copies. In the immediate post-war period sales began to fall, largely as a result of a political re-trenchment, and Our Time folded in 1949.

The home of Arundel and McCrindle became a hub of Communist Party activity and organisation. Doris Lessing notes in her autobiography,[18]

'In a garden on the canal known as Little Venice, now very smart, then dingy and run down, there were held ceilidhs, where Ewan MacColl sang [...]. The house belonged to Honor Tracy (sic) [Arundel], an upper-class young woman whose education had destined her for a very different life, and her husband Alex McCrindle ... who was in a radio series of immense popularity. There were people from the worlds of radio, music, and nascent television, and of course, women with children. Most of them were communists, but none of them were communists ten years later, except for Alex. And Ewan MacColl, the communist troubadour and bard.'

Arundel, as with so many writers who were members of the Communist Party, was also concerned about rural issues and as such was a regular contributor to the Country Standard, as well as being involved in the National Agricultural Workers Union. She was the

Communist Party candidate in 1958 for the West Stirlingshire, Scotland constituency.

As the Daily Worker's film critic during the forties and fifties, Arundel attended the 1949 International Film Festival at Marianske Lazne, Czechoslovakia, where she met photographer and filmmaker, Paul Strand. He was there to present his film Native Land. A life time friendship developed and, she accompanied him on a visit to Uist prior to the making of his acclaimed photography study on Tir a'Mhurain /Outer Hebrides (1962) about life on the Scottish islands.

Arundel's children's books, many of which were set in Scotland became quite popular, and included: Emma's island, Emma in Love, The Longest Weekend, A Family Failing, Girl in the Opposite Bed, The amazing Mr. Prothero and Terrible Temptation.

Arundel also wrote: The Freedom of Art edited with Maurice Carpenter and New Lyrical Ballads in1945.

Unity Theatre

Inspired by the Russian Revolution and the cultural upsurge that followed in its wake, a Council for Proletarian Art was formed in Britain in 1924. Two years later the name was changed to the Workers' Theatre Movement (WTM). Groups then sprang up around the country, mainly in the big cities were there was high unemployment and they took on rather bombastic names like the Red Magnets in Sunderland, Red Front Troupe in Dundee, Red Dawn in Southampton and Red Megaphones in Salford. There were around 300 left-wing theatrical groups at the height of this movement. It made important contributions to the changes that took place in British theatre after the war, like winning the struggle for public subsidy for the theatre, as well as widening the repertoire and stimulating the resurgence of regional theatres.

The transition from WTM to Unity Theatre came mainly through the work of the Rebel Players, which, as the WTM disintegrated, began to absorb members from other groups. Some WTM members pursued their own special interests and set up groups like the Workers' Music League, forerunner of the Workers' Musical Association; a dance/drama group was set up, as well as a film section that became Kino, a left wing film distribution company, involved in setting up the Workers' Film and Photo League. All of these groups maintained links with Unity Theatre, which was, from 1936 to 1975, effectively the Party's theatre in London.

It was a collective of theatrical semi-professionals and amateurs (the company briefly turned professional in the late 1940s).

Unity also offered a hectic social and recreational life; at one time or another there was a choir, an orchestra, a film club, a camera club, folk club, poetry club, a soccer team, exhibitions in the foyer, a Unity magazine and various other social events. This world was a nursery for the nation's cultural talent. Many of its members went on to work professionally in the theatre and media spheres.

The twenties and thirties were very much characterised by communal activity. After the war, a steady increase in affluence and the rise of mass entertainment led to more passive and individualised leisure activities and a concomitant demise of much local cultural activity. Unity Theatre could only arise and flourish based on a fervent commitment of many volunteers and enthusiasts. Men and women would think nothing of coming straight from a hard day's work in the office or factory to rehearse, paint scenery or build props, and to repair and refurbish the theatre building. They willingly took upon themselves arduous tours in old busses to perform their plays and cabarets in uncomfortable venues outside London, because this work not only gave them an adrenalin buzz, but it also very much strengthened their conviction that they were contributing to social change.

Unity Theatre was not simply a fixed theatrical space, but presented countless mobile touring shows, on top of mounting more than 250 productions at its own theatre, over half of which were new plays, many specially written for Unity, and a third of which contained original music. This is an astonishing productivity for an amateur company. Its example spurred the setting up of a number of regional Unity theatrical groups too.

In Manchester there was a direct link between the Red Megaphones in Salford, through Theatre of Action to Theatre Union and, after the war, to Theatre Workshop. (Joan Littlewood and her first partner, Ewan MacColl were to adopt this name for their theatre in Stratford)

Unity nurtured many actors and others who became nationally-known, including the actors Michael Gambon, Bob Hoskins, Alfie Bass, Lionel Bart, Warren Mitchell, Maxine Audley, Harry Landis, Mark Dignam and Bill Owen, the playwright Ted Willis, film director Ken Hughes, the painter and set designer Lawrence Gowing, Walter Lassally, later renowned as an Oscar-winning cinematographer, who was the lighting technician on several productions, and the classical musician James 'Jimmy' Gibb who played piano for Unity's musicals and reviews. Others; like the radio comedian Arthur Askey and the actor David Kossoff were on Unity's management board.

Unity staged British premieres of works by playwrights like Brecht, Sartre, Adamov and Frisch. Productions also involved other creative professionals, like the composer Alan Bush, writers Randall Swingler and Montagu Slater, as well as artists who designed and painted sets. Unity maintained an extensive network of regional amateur theatres, too, including Glasgow Unity, which also tried to go professional after the Second World War.

Slater was involved, with Britten and W.H. Auden, in many of the John Grierson documentaries, such as Coal Face. He wrote the strike drama Stay Down, Miner (1937) with music by Benjamin Britten and scripts for several films, including The Brave Don't Cry (1952), about a mining disaster. Britten dedicated his Temporal Variations for oboe and piano and his Ballad of Heroes to Slater, who also wrote the libretto for one of Britten's best loved operas, Peter Grimes.

It was a crucible for theatrical talent of every description as well as being a focus for innovation and experiment. A list of those who supported it, and, at times, worked with it, reads like a theatrical Who's Who of the theatre at that time: Michael Redgrave and his wife, Rachel Kempson, Sybil Thorndike and Lewis Casson, Beatrix Lehmann, Vida Hope, John Slater and Hattie Jacques, apart from those already mentioned above.

In its heyday, Unity had considerable attraction for left-leaning actors and others active in the theatre and the arts. Paul Robeson, at the height of his popularity turned down an offer of a starring West End role to appear in a strike play at Unity as just another member of the anonymous cast. Unity's popular musical Winkles and Champagne appeared live on BBC TV, as well as enjoying a long run at the theatre.

There were also some depressing incidents during its turbulent life. Already in the thirties the theatre was visited often by plain clothes policemen, some of whom tried to purchase tickets as non-members which would have broken the club's rules and make the theatre open to prosecution. One policeman did eventually manage to obtain a ticket from a trade union official (who had nothing to do with the theatre's box office) and this led to a successful prosecution of the management under the Theatres Act (a relic from the time of Charles II and the

WRITERS AND THE BATTLE OF IDEAS

restrictive patent laws!). Despite its high standing in the theatrical profession and beyond, Unity was deemed by the establishment to be a 'communist front organisation' and anyone associated with it automatically came under suspicion.

Unity's attempt to put on the German playwright Ernst Toller's play Pastor Niemöller in a 1939 production by Lewis Casson was considered to be 'too anti-Nazi' to be granted a licence by the Lord Chamberlain's office .

On another occasion, in 1951, two policemen and an official from the Lord Chamberlain's office arrived on its doorstep in a clear attempt to censor and even close down the company after the government had come under pressure from the US embassy. On two other occasions, during the forties and fifties the theatre received visits by officials from the US embassy as well as a number from MI5, when it was again accused of 'anti-Americanism', on the basis of some satirical episodes in its widely-praised production Here Goes!

Although witch-hunts against communists in Britain were much less severe than in the USA, they did take place. Robert Gorley, an actor with Unity, but not a member of any political party or even a trade union, was banned, as an 'undesirable', from emigrating to Canada even though he had a job there. Other former Unity members found themselves blacklisted in the United States on the basis of their former association with the theatre.

As a result of the government's anti-communist paranoia, civil servant, Beryl Lund, who sang in one of Unity's revues, was purged from her job as a clerical officer in the Ministry of Supply, as was Leonard Peck, who had worked in the Civil Service for fourteen years, on the same grounds as Lund. Anyone associated with Unity was deemed to be a communist and thus a danger to the state. Liverpool City Council even went so far as to ban Merseyside Unity from using any of its halls.

Unity was the only British theatre to keep playing throughout the war years, and it continued touring and performing at outside venues, including in tube stations that were being used as temporary air-raid shelters during the war. It also toured and performed at many factory workplaces. After the war it also performed for squatters who had taken over empty buildings in London as there was a desperate housing shortage.

In 1939, it launched the radical theatre magazine New Theatre. Colin Chambers writes that, 'New Theatre was an attractively produced and illustrated forum for thoughtful and polemical debate...and its list of contributors reads like a roll call of theatre's leading lights,'[19] including Peter Brook, Arthur Miller Bertolt Brecht and Peter Ustinov who was its theatre critic.

Its productions achieved a popularity rare for amateur or semi-professional troupes. Graham Greene, writing in the Spectator about its 1939 political pantomime, Jack the Giant Killer said; 'The strength to non-Communists lies in its humour more than in its idealism; but the idealism, even if we disagree with its details and distrust the blind belief in modern Russia, is young and fresh'.

In 1946, Unity organised a conference, 'Theatre and the People' which called for, among other things, government subsidy for the theatre, the inclusion of drama teaching in schools and the setting up of subsidised local repertory companies – revolutionary ideas that were later taken up and implemented when Jennie Lee became Minster of Arts under the 1964 Labour government.

It did, though, suffer a series of financial crises but was rescued by its many members and supporters, like Sidney, later Lord, Bernstein, Stafford Cripps and Oscar Lewenstein, communist and keen Unity participant, who went on to become one of Britain's top theatre and film producers, helping create some of the leading British theatre and film productions of the 1950s and 1960s. Perhaps not surprisingly, it also went through a number of ideological crises and there were con-tinuous heated discussions about its programming, its focus, whether it should remain an amateur troupe or go professional, its goals and its relationship with the Communist Party.

One person whose name was intimately associated with Unity over most of its lifetime deserves mention, and he is the actor/director André van Gyseghem, who became a key and influential figure in the development of British workers' theatre. He directed several productions at Unity and became its first president in the late 1930s. He was also a director of several of the popular mass pageants of the period, both in South Africa (where he helped found the Bantu People's Theatre) and in Britain, including a 1939 May Day event which involved some 6,000 people in three South Wales mining valleys celebrating the centenary of Chartism.

He had a distinguished professional career as an actor with three major British companies and was the first artistic director of the Nottingham Playhouse. In January 1934, alongside Miles Malleson, Ina de la Haye, Lionel Britton and Barbara Nixon, he was a founder of the professional left Theatre Company that put on plays in the West End on Sunday evenings. He remained a communist all his adult life. When Bertolt Brecht visited London in 1934/5 for a short stay, he lodged with Jean and André van Gysegham at their Abbey Road home.

Lionel Bart, the lyricist and composer, was another notable alumnus of Unity. He started out as John Gorman's partner in a small screen printing business they called GB Arts. Both joined the communist Party as young men, recently demobbed from their National Service in the late forties.

Bart's first professional musical was produced in 1959, Lock up Your Daughters, based on the 18th century play Rape Upon Rape, by Henry Fielding. Following that, Fings Ain't Wot They Used T'Be produced by Joan Littlewood's Theatre Workshop in Stratford East, was notable for encouraging the use of authentic Cockney accents on the London stage. A number of Unity actors also went on to work for Theatre Workshop. Bart's Oliver! (1960), based on Dickens's Oliver Twist was a huge hit from the beginning, becoming the first modern British musical to be transferred successfully to Broadway.

GB Arts was associated with a number of progressive organisations and individuals. It printed posters for the Daily Worker, Marks and Spencer, Joan Littlewood's Theatre Workshop as well as for the Royal Shakespeare Company, going on to win many awards for its top quality poster designs.

While working with John Gorman in their small printing office, Bart soon became involved with Unity Theatre, based in Mornington Crescent, behind St. Pancras station. He began writing songs for the theatre's productions, as well as acting, designing and painting scenery, as members of the company were expected to do. His immersion in Unity led to his association with other communists working there, and to his becoming a member of the Party in the early fifties. One of those with whom he worked closely was the biochemist Barnet 'Barney' Woolf, who was a keen and talented lyricist as well as an excellent medical research worker.

Bart was among those to change the British theatre scene profoundly by introducing working class slang, humour and accents to the stage, and he helped to create a new genre of musical. Beforehand actors spoke in clipped, received English accents, as if class didn't exist and ordinary people's lives were hardly considered worthy of more than walk-on parts in the majority of plays.

Arnold Wesker was another communist from London's East End Jewish community who profited from Unity's pioneering work and went on to become a talented playwright, placing ordinary working people centre stage in his plays – something we take for granted today. His trilogy of plays, beginning with Chicken Soup with Barley was largely autobiographical and Sarah, the feisty communist mother at the centre of the play, is based on his own mother, Leah who was a militant East End communist.

Unity pioneered new forms of performance like its, 'Living Newspapers documentary pieces as well as satirical pantomimes. It certainly challenged the Lord Chamberlain's censorship and introduced new writers both British and international: presenting the first Brecht play in Britain (Señora Carrar's Rifles in 1938) and premieres of Sean O'Casey's The Star Turns Red (1940) and Jean Paul Sartre's Nekrassov (1956).

Unity also had a strong core of women, but their work has invariably been eclipsed by the men. During the war, when many of its male actors and staff had been called up, the women came into their own and formed a short-lived women's mobile troupe called 'The Amazons' which kept going until 1944. It was very popular, particularly in the hospitals where the war wounded were treated and where they often performed.

During the sixties, London Unity became a venue for the new Left-wing theatre then emerging in Britain. Companies like 7.84, CAST, General Will and Belt and Braces all performed there. It was also the venue for new plays by people like Edward Bond, John Arden and Margaretta D'Arcy; new, young directors like Charles Marrowitz, Clive Barker and John McGrath worked there.

In 1975 Unity's theatre building was burned down, but a series of fundraising events, to which the great and the good – from people like David Frost, Vanessa Redgrave to Frankie Howerd – contributed their talents to help keep the company going. It eventually folded in 1988 during the Thatcher era.

In his book The Story of Unity Theatre,[20] Colin Chambers paying tribute to Unity, writes that 'it changed the face of British Theatre' and 'could justifiably claim to be the leading amateur theatre in Britain and, during its 40 year history, rose to national and international prominence.'

Its influence on Britain's theatrical scene was indeed profound. It introduced a whole number of budding actors from working class backgrounds to the public, it put on the sort of politically committed plays rarely seen before in the country and it also pioneered the use of regional and working class accents as a norm. Joan Littlewood and her Theatre Workshop, in Stratford, East London, were to take these iconoclastic concepts even further. It also nourished the talents of writers from its own ranks. The Communist Party's direct influence on Unity helped bring the real lives of ordinary working people and their problems onto the stage, in stark contrast to the stuffy middle class plays on offer in the West End. Many of its plays also prefigured the 'kitchen sink' dramas of the late fifties and early sixties, epitomised by the plays of writers like Arnold Wesker.

With all its shortcomings, Unity was to be an example of a type of socialism in practice, anchored in working class activity. As a political theatre of the Left, like the political parties of the Left, it was subject to the ebbs and flows of the movement itself and to the pressures and conflicts within it. 'Whatever the theatre's record,' Colin Chambers writes, 'it is communists who, in the main, bear the burden of both the successes across nearly half a century and of its ultimate failure to renew itself.'

Although not directly connected with Unity Theatre, a number of other talented theatre people found inspiration in the Communist Party for their work. Margery Mason, was a founder of the Actors' Company, before joining the Royal Shakespeare Company. She later played a key role in theatrical management in a number of cities. As an actor, she also appeared in productions for television and film, including roles in Midsomer Murders and Harry Potter. During the Second World War she toured with the Entertainments National Service Association throughout the Middle and Far East. She became a lieutenant in the army.

Buzz Goodbody was a young director of much promise at the Royal Shakespeare Company during the seventies, where she directed several experimental productions. She joined the Communist Party as a teenager. She was the moving force behind the establishment of the company's The Other Space studio stage, where she directed the young Ben Kingsley in Hamlet. 'Reviewers fell off their seats in shock' after seeing her Hamlet, wrote Andrew Dickson in the Guardian. The Times's Irving Wardle, said 'It is a long time since I've been so gripped'. Sadly, she took her own life at the age of 28 before her talent could fully unfold. The RSC's deputy artistic director said, 'She changed us for ever'.[21]

Culture – an ideological battlefield

In the continual struggle against communism, symbolised by the Soviet Union, the West, to begin with, dealt with its cultural influence and cultural exports largely by means of censorship and suppression. However, with the increasing influence of Marxist and left-wing ideas in the wake of the Spanish Civil War, the rise of fascism and the alliance with the Soviet Union during the Second World War, there arose a new interest in culture, by establishments on both sides of the Cold War divide, as a key aspect of the ideological battle. In the post-war era, culture became a vital ideological battleground and much attention was devoted to promoting a 'western culture' to counter that emanating from Eastern Europe, as well as indigenous left-wing culture itself. In this battle, the CIA played a significant role and was able to recruit, wittingly or unwittingly, leading British cultural figures to help them wage that struggle. The whole saga deserves a chapter of its own, but other writers have more than adequately dealt with this subject, so I will only mention it here. The book by Frances Stonor Saunders, Who Paid the Piper?: The CIA and the Cultural Cold War, is a good study of this fascinating issue.

Despite the British Party's lack of resources, the United States, certainly on a European level, clearly feared what they perceived as a left-wing dominance of cultural and intellectual life. As a response, throughout the period between around 1950 – 67 the CIA expended much time, effort and money. It set up a Congress for Cultural Freedom in Berlin and promoted a whole range of publications, exhibitions, conferences etc. to counter what it saw as communist infiltration. It also funded the cultural magazine Encounter, founded in 1953 by poet Stephen Spender and journalist Irving Kristol. It avidly promoted ex-communists like Orwell, Koestler and Douglas Hyde, whose book, I Believed (1950), tells of his disillusion with communism and conversion to Catholicism – and which became a bestseller. As part and parcel of these efforts, the CIA also used its financial clout to 'buy' collaborative journalists who were willing to ensure that all bad news about the Soviet Union and Eastern Europe was given continuous negative coverage in the media.

Influence among Professional Workers

*'To condition people to accept the inevitability of injustice
and misfortune is the final achievement of the tyrant.'*

EILIS DILLON

*'The Communist Party in the 1930s found itself in the
vanguard of culture, and its achievements were real and
lasting.'* [22]

FRANCIS BECKETT

The continued growth of the Party during the late twenties and thirties
brought with it a new section of people into membership. It became
increasingly attractive to those who were not members of the working
class, and there was a steady influx, not only of students, but
professional workers, as well as artists and intellectuals. Many of those
joining were also very young. They not only made a contribution by
taking on their share of mundane tasks like canvassing and selling the
Daily Worker, but their skills were of great practical help too. Both in
refining the propaganda work and in developing movements on
specific issues, their input was significant. Party architects and lawyers
played key roles in the tenants' movements; Party doctors campaigned
against malnutrition and for a prophylactic approach to health, in the

late thirties they helped organise medical aid to Spain and, importantly, campaigned vociferously for a national health service. Scientists like the eminent bio-chemist and geneticist J.B.S. Haldane, and leading physicist J.D. Bernal also campaigned against food poverty and were active in the agitation for protection against air raids once the war began. Party writers, actors, musicians and artists (see chapter: Writers and the Battle of Ideas) fostered the growth of a new kind of entertainment and helped develop more creative ideas for propaganda, education and the organisation of large public events.

In 1947, the Party established a National Cultural Committee and under its auspices the early post-war years saw a proliferation of specialist Party groups being set up, including ones for architects, psychologists, scientists, writers, artists, musicians, economists and historians, as well as an educational advisory committee, made up largely of teachers. It was hoped that these groups would help harness the specialist expertise of the membership and assist in the formulation of appropriate policies in all areas of public life from a Marxist perspective. The educational advisory committee, for instance, advocated full implementation of the 1944 Education Act and began campaigning for the introduction of comprehensive schooling long before it was introduced by a Labour government in 1965.

In December 1945, the Party relaunched Modern Quarterly, a journal for Marxist discussion. Among those who contributed articles to the journal over the coming years were, the physicist, J.D. Bernal, the mathematician, Hyman Levy, the economist, Maurice Dobb, the historians, Christopher Hill, Leslie Morton and Rodney Hilton and writers such as Randall Swingler, Edgell Rickword and Alick West.

Maurice Dobb became a Fellow of Trinity College in 1948 and Reader in 1959, holding this post until his death. He was widely published and his works were translated into a number of languages. Political Economy and Capitalism (1937) and Studies in the Development of Capitalism (1946) are perhaps his best known works. After their completion, he collaborated for many years with Piero Sraffa on the latter's comprehensive edition of the works of David Ricardo.

Academics

As well as endeavouring to use their skills in the service of the Party and the wider movement, communist intellectuals also sought to involve their fellow professionals, and made efforts to establish a Marxist theoretical approach towards their own subjects. A whole number of books were written by such intellectuals as part of this effort. The philosopher John Lewis wrote A Textbook of Marxist Philosophy, Hyman Levy wrote A Philosophy for a Modern Man, J.D. Bernal The Social Function of Science.

Bernal and the mathematician Hyman Levy were instrumental in reviving the Association of Scientific Workers which, after war broke out, grew to 11,000 members and was affiliated to the TUC. Also, largely on the initiative of Bernal, a Cambridge Scientists Anti-War Group was formed in 1936, consisting of around 80 members.

The Party's historians have been particularly influential, having a profound impact in their specific field. Kevin Morgan writes that the Communist Party 'nurtured as brilliant a school of historians as any this century'.[23] Figures such as Eric Hobsbawm, E.P. Thompson, Christopher Hill, A.L. Morton, George Rudé and Raphael Samuel all helped develop a Marxist approach to history that continues to resonate today. Their approach to history has had its impact on later historians, such that, still today, historians are often crudely categorised as 'Marxist' or 'non-Marxist'. Before Marx and Engels history had been very much written as a collection of 'facts' to be sorted chronologically and, primarily, as a narrative of military exploits, monarchic dynasties and leading, influential personalities. Marxists introduced the idea of a history 'from below' and of class and class struggle as being keys to a proper understanding of history as a process, and with economic relations as a central motor. Hobsbawm is undoubtedly the most renowned of the group, with his now classic works on modern European history translated into many languages. Hill is most famous for his work on England's Civil War which he, rightly many believe, characterised as a 'revolution' – the world's first bourgeois revolution. Historian and Labour MP, Tristram Hunt, said of him: 'In his generosity, wisdom and tangible feel for the significance of the 17th century, Christopher Hill stands as the finest of guides to the man [Oliver Cromwell] of the times.' [24]

Professor George Thomson was born in Dulwich, London in 1903. He graduated from Cambridge, and went on to become professor of Greek at Galway University before moving back to England in 1934, returning to King's College, Cambridge. He became a professor at Birmingham University in 1936, the year he joined the Communist Party. Thomson pioneered a Marxist interpretation of ancient Greek drama. His outstanding books, Aeschylus and Athens and Marxism and Poetry both garnered international acclaim. Martin Bernal, the son of J.D. Bernal, has also made a controversial but stimulating contribution to our understanding of ancient Greece, with his book Black Athena: the Afroasiatic Roots of Classical Civilization, which argues that Greek classical culture was born in Africa.

The archaeologist Gordon Childe was a flatmate of leading communist theoretician, Palme Dutt, at Oxford. While he never joined the Communist Party as far as is known, he remained close to it. In 1927, Childe accepted the newly created post of Abercromby Professor of Archaeology at Scotland's University of Edinburgh, but in 1946 left to take up the position of Director and Professor of European Prehistory at the Institute of Archaeology in London. He was the first archaeologist in the West to use Marxist theory in his work.

In the more recent period, Mary Davis certainly deserves mention. She has been a leading activist in the Communist Party of Great Britain and its successor, the Communist Party of Britain for much of her life. She was editor of the latter's theoretical journal, Communist Review, for several years and was on the CPB's Executive Committee. She was until 2009 Professor of Labour History at London's Metropolitan University, where she occupied the posts of Deputy-Director of the Working Lives Research Institute and Head of Centre for Trade Union Studies. She was an executive committee member of her union, the University and College Union (UCU) and an elected member of the TUC Women's Committee. She was also a founder and initiator of the recently established Charter for Women Campaign.

She has broadcast frequently on radio, television, and in addition to her research she also contributes non-academic articles to various journals and is a regular speaker at public events involving the Left and women. She has done extensive research on women's history, in particular on Sylvia Pankhurst. She was one of the founders of a campaign to erect a memorial statue of Sylvia Pankhurst on College Green, Westminster, which has attracted extensive sponsorship and aroused widespread interest.

Her book of essays, Class and Gender in British Labour History has become a classic volume. It examines the 'making' of the other half of the working class – women as workers, trade unionists and political activists – and seeks to weave together intricate relationships between class and gender. Davis argues that despite the enormous contributions made by Marxist historians to our understanding of class, the failure of Labour and Marxist historians to acknowledge the role that women and black workers have played in class formation, trade union struggle and political action, has resulted in an incomplete and gender-blind analysis of class and capitalism. In these essays Davis seeks to rectify that omission and document the valuable role played by women in the UK as workers, trade unionists and political activists.

Medics

In the medical profession the Party attracted doctors like Joan McMichael, Madeleine Sharp, Hugh Faulkner, Julian Tudor-Hart and the eminent orthopaedic surgeon Lippman Kessell. Most doctors in the Party, if not all, also belonged to the Socialist Medical Association (now Socialist Health Association – SHA). A number of these also belonged to the Sigerist Society, which was set up in 1947 by a group of doctors who felt the need to discuss the theoretical and social aspects of medicine from a Marxist point of view. The society folded in 1955.

The SHA was founded in 1930 and was set up to campaign for a national health service. It has been very influential, not only in helping to persuade the 1945 Labour government to actually set up a National Health Service, but in continued campaigning for free and equal health care for all, for a prophylactic approach to healthcare and in establishing links between society, poverty and ill health. The Association was also active in campaigns against the introduction of NHS charges, and on smoking, tuberculosis and for placing an emphasis on adequate nutrition as the basis for good health, for the establishment of a network of health centres and for salaried GPs. It changed its name in 1980 to the Socialist Health Association to reflect increased interest in public health. It is associated with the campaigns against health inequality around the Black Report, and is a socialist society affiliated to the Labour Party.

Hugh Faulkner was a leading figure in the Socialist Medical Association, and practised in North London. He was a leading figure in both the Medical Practitioners' Union and the SHA, and made a key contribution to the development of the 1966 Doctor's Charter.

Julian Tudor-Hart,[25] the son of Alex Tudor-Hart who worked as a medical doctor in Spain, was a communist for many years. He studied medicine at Cambridge and London, before working for 30 years as a general practitioner in Glyncorrwg, South Wales where his partner was Dr. Brian Gibbons, later minister of health in Wales. He has always been a passionate advocate of the NHS and was President of the

Socialist Health Association. At the Practice many of his patients were miners or ex-miners from the surrounding collieries and his research and dedication to their health led to his developing pioneering ways of diagnosing and treating their work-specific illnesses.

In 2006, he was awarded the inaugural Discovery Prize by the Royal College of General Practitioners as 'a general practitioner who has captured the imagination of generations of GPs with his groundbreaking research... His practice in Glyncorrwg, Wales, was the first in the UK to be recognised as a research practice, piloting many Medical Research Council studies. He was also the first doctor to routinely measure every patient's blood pressure and as a result was able to reduce premature mortality in high risk patients at his practice by 30%. Graham Watt, Professor of General Practice at the University of Glasgow, who nominated Dr Tudor Hart for the award, said:

'His ideas and example pervade modern general practice and remain at the cutting edge of thinking and practice concerning health improvement in primary care. His work on hypertension showed how high quality records, teamwork and audit are the keys to health improvement. His life-long commitment to the daily tasks of general practice has always given his work and views a salience and credibility with fellow general practitioners. Julian Tudor Hart has been and will remain an inspiration to health practitioners and the communities they serve.'

Dr Joan McMichael was born in India, in a tent, on February 8th 1906 and delivered by her own father, who was to become the Inspector General in the police of the Indian Raj. Much to her disapproval, he was to arrest Mahatma Ghandi on several occasions.

In the early 1920s, she went to Edinburgh University, being one of the first women medical students to study there. In spite of having had no previous scientific training at all, she graduated as a doctor in 1929. Like many of her contemporaries, she became aware of politics during the 1926 General Strike, having treated strikers who had been physically assaulted by police; this contributed to radicalising her views enormously. Some years later, she joined the Labour Party and then the Communist Party in 1936, remaining a staunch, even leading, communist for the rest of her life. During the Spanish Civil War, she was involved in Medical Aid for Spain and then went on to set up organisations to deliver Medical Aid to China and Vietnam.

At the beginning of the Second World War, she worked for the blood transfusion service in Slough, later becoming Medical Officer for Health in West London, where she was noted for her dedication to occupational health. She was also an early champion of children's and workers' health rights and was instrumental in carrying out Britain's first industrial mass X-ray screening for tuberculosis. After the war, she became Medical Officer for Health with London County Council, working especially with children with disabilities in the Fulham and Hammersmith areas, a field in which she remained involved well into the 1970s, writing a book on the subject.

Joan certainly wasn't satisfied working simply within the confines of her surgery and became a leading activist in the post-war squatters' movement, which enabled families living in appalling conditions to move in and occupy empty luxury dwellings. In 1947, she was elected one of three Communist councillors to Westminster Borough Council, where a particular interest of hers was in fighting for better housing and conditions for working people. She was also, for a time, a member of the Party's Executive Committee.

She was even more widely known for setting up Medical Aid for Vietnam (MAV) in 1965, following a visit to the World Congress of Women in Moscow 1963, as chair of a group of some fifty women delegates from Britain. She had listened, spellbound, to accounts of horrifying terror and torture that the Vietnamese people were enduring. This so moved her that she dedicated the remaining 24 years of her life to the cause of peace in Vietnam. She became close friends of the head of a hospital in Hanoi, the director of the Vietnamese Institute for Medical Research and the Minister of Health. Twice, she was able to hold discussions with Ho Chi-Minh about the medical needs of the country, and how supporters in Britain could help. She raised some £2.5 million to send penicillin, anti-malarials and other drugs; even blood donated in Britain for the Vietnamese people was reduced to serum and transported across the world by MAV. Towards the end of the war in Vietnam, Joan poured her efforts into raising funds for a completely refurbished and re-equipped hospital in that devastated country. This dedication was recognised by the Vietnamese government in 1980, when it awarded her the Order of Friendship.

Dr. Madeleine Agnes Sharp[25] was born in Newcastle upon Tyne in 1920. Her parents could not afford to pay for her to train as a doctor, so she served during the Second World War in Queen Alexandra's Royal Army Nursing Corps. Had the founder of the NHS, Aneurin

Bevan, not made grants available for the poor to train as doctors, Madeleine Sharp would have remained a nurse. An NHS grant enabled her to graduate from Edinburgh University Medical School. She became a GP at an inner-city practice in Coventry for over 30 years. She was also one of those early pioneering women who stormed the barricades of male privilege in the medical profession.

Sharp was never afraid to stand up for the poor and downtrodden, whether it was fighting for better food in hospitals or in opposing production-line maternity wards where babies were routinely induced to make life easier for the consultants. I cannot be certain that she actually held a Party card, but she was certainly very close to the Party, working with local communists in the city and regularly reading the Morning Star and contributing letters to the paper.

Like Joan she took up the cause of Vietnam and worked tirelessly over many years to send vital medical assistance to that war-ravaged country. She worked closely with the Vietnamese government to reduce the high rates of infant mortality, improve medical training and investigated how traditional treatments could work alongside Western medicine. She was the long-serving Secretary of the Medical and Scientific Aid for Vietnam, Laos and Cambodia Society which grew out of MAV. She was, over many years, also a leading figure in the Coventry Committee for Peace and Reconciliation and in the Cyrenians. In 2002 she was awarded an MBE for her work on human rights and humanitarian causes in Southeast Asia.

Lipmann Kessel MC, FRCS was born in Pretoria, South Africa, but after coming to the UK he joined the Communist Party in 1938, and remained a member until his death. Kessel joined the Royal Army Medical Corps as a surgeon during the Second World War, serving in the western Sahara. In 1944, he was parachuted into Arnhem to work on the wounded at the frontline hospital. He developed a special technique for saving wounded soldiers on the battlefield, based on an approach originated by the Red Army. Amongst the many he saved was a Brigadier commanding the 4th Parachute Regiment. Kessel himself was taken prisoner at Arnhem, but escaped and surprised the comrades at his Party branch in Acton when he suddenly turned up.

In the post-war period, be became an eminent surgeon, and was appointed Professor of Orthopaedics at the University of London. According to his wish, he was buried at Arnhem's Osterbeek cemetery. His life is told in more detail in his autobiography, Surgeon at Arms, published in 1958.

Architects

Berthold Lubetkin (1901-1990) was undoubtedly the foremost architect to have been in the Party and whose work was very influential. He was a Russian émigré architect who pioneered modernist design in Britain during the 1930s.

He practised in Paris in the 1920s in partnership with Jean Ginsburg, with whom he designed an apartment building on the Avenue de Versailles. In Paris he associated with the leading figures of the European Avant Garde including Le Corbusier. He continued to participate in the debates of Constructivism, designing a trade pavilion for the USSR in Bordeaux and participating in the Palace of the Soviets competition, for which his entry was shortlisted.

Emigrating to London in 1931, Lubetkin set up the architectural practice Tecton. He joined the Communist Party of Great Britain in that same year. The first projects he undertook included landmark buildings for London Zoo: a gorilla house and a penguin pool. Tecton was also commissioned by London Zoo to design buildings for their reserve park at Whipsnade and a completely new zoo in Dudley consisting of twelve animal enclosures that represented a unique example of early Modernism in the UK. According to the 20th Century Society: 'Encapsulated in the playful pavilions at Dudley is a call to remember the higher calling of all architecture, embracing not just material needs but also the desire to inspire and delight.'

Tecton's housing projects included private houses in Sydenham one of the UK's few modernist terraces and most famously the Highpoint apartments in Highgate. Highpoint One was singled out for particular praise by Le Corbusier.

Eventually, Tecton's plans for a housing and a health centre development in Finsbury were adopted by the Labour and Communist councillors of Finsbury, an inner-city borough since absorbed into the London Borough of Islington.

The Labour council in Finsbury was a major patron of Tecton, commissioning the Finsbury Health Centre, which was completed in 1938. Lubetkin and Tecton's particular achievement in Finsbury was to unite the aesthetic and political ambitions of Modernism with the radical municipal socialism of the borough. The health centre resolved the tension between three key modernist ideals. First: a social function; universal access to healthcare, free at the point of delivery, for the borough's residents (a decade before the NHS was to be established). Second, the political: no longer was social good to be achieved through charity or hope, instead it was to be provided by a democratically elected and accountable municipal authority, funded through local taxation. And third, the element which made Tecton's work unique, was the aesthetic. The building's tiled facade shone above the surrounding slums, its rational conception, it was felt, asserted the ideal of a socialist future as the rational endgame to progress; in Lubetkin's words the architecture 'cried out for a new world'. Lubetkin's modernism – 'nothing is too good for ordinary people' – laid down a challenge to the class bound complacency of thirties Britain. But Tecton's plans to replace Finsbury's slums with blocks of modern flats were frustrated by the onset of war in 1939.

Paradoxically the war would move Lubetkin's work from the radical fringe to the mainstream. The post-war Labour victory was built on the promise of modernism as pioneered by Tecton. The Finsbury Health Centre became a model for the new National Health Service. To confirm the significance of Lubetkin's vision, Aneurin Bevan, Minister of Health, laid the foundation stone to Tecton/Finsbury's Spa Green Estate in the winter of 1946. For most of these projects Lubetkin and Tecton worked closely with the Anglo-Danish, Ove Arup, as structural engineer. Arup's innovative concrete 'egg-crate' construction at Spa Green gave each flat clear views unobstructed by internal pillars, and his aerodynamic 'wind roof' provided a communal area for drying clothes and for social gatherings.

He also designed a modern housing complex at Cruikshank Street, London WC1. It is built on the site of the bomb-destroyed Holford Square in Finsbury. The group of buildings as a whole reflect Lubetkin's respect for the pre-existing urban environment, a characteristic that makes his work stand out from that of many modernist architects of his generation.

Post war austerity imposed far greater budgetary constraints than in Tecton's housing showpiece Spa Green Estate, forcing Lubetkin to strip the project of the basic amenities he had planned; there were to be no balconies, community centre or nursery school. Instead Lubetkin focused his energies on the social space. Fusing his aesthetic and political concerns he created a stunning constructivist staircase – a social condenser that forms the heart of the building.

It occupies the site of a house where Lenin lived during his exile in London (1902-03) while editing the Russian socialist newspaper Iskra

(Spark). In honour of the former Soviet leader, the building was initially planned to be named Lenin Court. In addition the building was to incorporate Lubetkin's memorial to Lenin, which had been located on the site of Holford Square since 1942. However British fascists repeatedly vandalised the memorial, to the extent that it required a 24-hour police guard.

In 1947, Lubetkin was commissioned to be master planner and chief architect for the Peterlee new town. And in 1982, he was awarded the RIBA Royal Gold Medal. He was also the subject of a Design Museum exhibition in 2005. His daughter, Louise Kehoe, published an award-winning memoir in 1995 which included previously unknown details of Lubetkin's early years.

He remained a Communist Party member to the end of his life. In 2009 East Durham Houghall Community College, based in Peterlee, named its theatre after Lubetkin in honour of the vision he had for the town. The Lubetkin Theatre was officially opened by his otherb daughter Sasha Lubetkin in October 2009. At the opening she said:

'I'm immensely proud that this beautiful theatre has been named after my father and that his work is remembered in spite of the brutal way it ended. He had such dreams for Peterlee, he wanted to turn it into the miners' capital of the world. His respect and admiration of the miners made him want to create something really special that didn't exist anywhere else but unfortunately that wasn't possible.'

The other 'big' communist architectural figure was Ernő Goldfinger, who died in 1987. He was a Hungarian-born architect and furniture designer, moving to Britain in the 1930s, where he became a key member of the architectural Modernist Movement. He is most prominently remembered today for designing residential tower blocks, some of which are now listed buildings.

During his stay in Paris, in the twenties, he was, like Lubetkin, strongly influenced by the publication of Le Corbusier's Vers une Architecture. After the war, Goldfinger was commissioned to build new offices for the Daily Worker. He also built Alexander Fleming House in south-east London for the Ministry of Health.

In an attempt to solve the huge shortage of housing in the country following the Second World War, in which nearly 4 million houses had been destroyed or damaged, the British government began to see high-rise buildings as a solution, and Goldfinger rose to prominence in England as a designer of tower blocks. One of the most 'notorious' of such blocks was Trellick Tower in North Kensington – a prime example of Brutalist architecture.

He was also a controversial figure and could be extremely autocratic. Ian Fleming appropriated his name for the villain, Auric Goldfinger in one of his James Bond novels. Fleming had been annoyed by the pre-war demolition of cottages in Hampstead, which had been removed to make way for Goldfinger's house. This was Fleming's way of exacting revenge.

Communist local architects Bill Evans and Julian Tayler, while not in the same league as those architects mentioned above, both worked for many years in leading positions in a number of local government architectural departments, and made attempts to influence local authority design and planning so that it truly served the people and the communities for which they were intended.

Legal profession

There were a number of Party lawyers, like Bill Sedley and his son Stephen, now a QC, Sigmund Seifert and his son Michael, Barry Amiel, Jack Gaster, John Bowden, Tess Gill and John Hendy QC. D.N. Pritt and John Platts-Mills, both leading defence lawyers who became QCs, were never members of the Party but remained very close throughout their lives..

Most, if not all, of these lawyers belonged to the Haldane Society of Socialist Lawyers which was founded around 1930, after a small group of barristers set it up to provide legal expertise of a progressive nature to the government, trade unions and the Co-operative Movement. The Society was named after Viscount Richard Haldane (J.B.S Haldane's uncle), who, as a Liberal, had been Asquith's Lord Chancellor from 1912 to 1915, but was hounded out of office by the attacks on him by the then, as ever, xenophobic Daily Mail. Ever since, the Haldane Society has been a legal thorn in the side of every government, lobbying for law reforms, civil liberties and access to justice for all; supporting national liberation movements against colonialism and campaigning against racism and all forms of discrimination. It was affiliated to the Labour Party but its members have always included Labour, left-wing and Communist Party members.

As might be expected, communist lawyers readily took on briefs and cases concerning trade union rights and individual cases of injustice involving government or official bodies. They also often gave free legal advice and represented progressive organisations and individuals who couldn't afford large legal fees. D.N. Pritt and Platts-Mills, as leading barristers and QCs, were also in the forefront of defending individuals involved in the early colonial liberation struggles. These lawyers have also made a significant contribution to efforts to democratise the legal system and make it more accessible to ordinary people. John Hendy, in particular, has been one of the chief defenders of trade union rights, since the introduction of draconian anti-union legislation under Thatcher, and he remains a vociferous opponent of such legislation.

Musicians

The composers Rutland Boughton and Alan Bush were the most noted Party composer-musicians and both, together with Aubrey Bowman, played leading roles in the formation of the Workers Music Association in 1936. However, another Party musician of note was James (Jimmy) Gibb,[27] a versatile and accomplished pianist, who played at the Proms, at Wigmore Hall and abroad. He was a prominent member of the post-war British Communist Party until he resigned in 1956, after the Soviet invasion of Hungary.

Despite his radical views, Gibb shared a piano teacher with the future Queen, sang Beethoven on the D-Day crossing to France, and spent many years teaching at the Guildhall School of Music and Drama. He used to wonder, relates Andy Croft, whether his piano teacher, Mabel Lander, ever suspected how many of her pupils were members of the Communist party. While she was giving lessons to the princesses Elizabeth and Margaret, she was also teaching Jimmy Gibb, Geraldine and Mary Peppin, David Ellenberg and Alan Bush, all members of the Unity Theatre orchestra and active in the Hampstead Communist Party branch in the late 1930s and early 1940s.

According to Jimmy, at one point there were so many musicians in the Party that 'it got around the profession that it was not a good thing to be outside the party if you wanted to get on, so they put me on a cadre committee to vet musicians who were applying to join the party!' It was, he thought, the only time in history that membership of the Communist Party was dependent on passing an audition.

Communists were also a dominant political presence in the 30,000-strong Musicians Union, which set up a Jazz Appreciation Society in the late fifties. Those in the Workers' Music Association, alongside A.L. Lloyd, also did much to help the folk song revival during the late fifties and sixties and were involved in organising the first big Folk Song Festivals with such prominent figures as Ewan MacColl and Ian Campbell. Ewan MacColl, together with producer Charles Parker went on to devise the highly popular and award-winning BBC Radio Ballads, even though the programmes elicited some disapproval among the very staid BBC's governors.

The Topic Records label which began as an offshoot of the communist-led Workers' Music Association in 1939, selling Soviet and left-wing music by mail order, took on a new lease of life with the upsurge of interest in folk music during the sixties onwards, becoming a leading record producing company and seen as almost synonymous with folk music itself.

A.L. Lloyd is widely recognised as 'the father' of English folk music and was a key figure in the folk song revival during the fifties and sixties. After working for a time in Australia, he returned to Britain in 1935 during the Great Depression. In the absence of a permanent job, he pursued his interests in studying folk music and social and economic history, doing much of his research at the British Museum. He was quoted as saying that there is 'nothing like unemployment for educating oneself'. Joining the Communist Party in the thirties, he became strongly influenced by the writings of the Marxist historian, A.L. Morton.

In 1938 the BBC hired him to write a radio documentary about seafaring life, and from then on he worked as a full-time journalist and singer. He was also commissioned by the BBC to produce a series of programmes on the rise of Nazism. Between 1945 and 1950 he was employed as a journalist by Picture Post magazine but quit the job in an act of solidarity with one of his victimised colleagues.

By the 1950s he had established himself fully as a professional folklorist. Later, when the English folk revival was dominated by young people, wearing jeans and pullovers, Lloyd was rarely seen in anything other than a suit and a wide grin. Ewan MacColl described him (with affection) as 'a walking Toby Jug'. In 1959 he collaborated with Vaughan Williams on the Penguin Book of English Folk Songs.

The 1956 film, Moby Dick, directed by John Huston featured Lloyd singing a sea shanty as the Pequod first sets sail.

He also became associated with Arnold Wesker's cultural project, Centre 42, which arose from Resolution 42 of the 1960 TUC, concerning the importance of arts in the community. Centre 42 organised a touring festival aimed at devolving art and culture from London to other working class towns of Britain. It was led by Arnold Wesker, with MacColl and Lloyd providing the musical content and Charles Parker producing. Centre 42 was important in bringing a range of folk performers to public attention: Anne Briggs, the Ian Campbell Folk Group, The Spinners and The Watersons. Lloyd went on to publish many books on folk music and related topics, including The Singing Englishman, Come All Ye Bold Miners, and Folk Song in England. He was a founder-member of Topic Records and remained as their artistic director until his death.

The Artists International Association and the Communist Party Artists' Group

The Artists International Association (AIA) was another example of a successful left-wing professional organisation that came into being as a result of the struggle against fascism and war. Originally called the Artists International (AI), it was founded in 1933 by a small group of left-wing artists, many of them communists. It added the word Association to its name when it was reconstituted in 1935, and continued until 1971, abandoning its original objectives in 1953, thereafter existing as an exhibiting society only.

The group wanted to publicise, through their art, their commitment and resistance to the 'Imperialist war on the Soviet Union, Fascism and colonial oppression'. Its aim was a 'Unity of Artists for Peace, Democracy and Cultural Development'. The Artists International and its successor the AIA provided a forum for regular discussions on socialism and the arts. It managed to attract the participation of a number of leading non-communist progressive artists, including Robert Medley, Paul Nash and Henry Moore. Its inaugural exhibition was entitled 'The Social Scene', and a subsequent exhibition was entitled 'Artists Against Fascism and War' for which many of Britain's top artists lent works; it attracted around 6,000 visitors.

The AIA supported the Republican side in the Spanish Civil War (1936-39) through exhibitions and other fund-raising activities. It also attempted to promote wider access to art through travelling exhibitions and publicly accessible mural paintings. In 1940 it published a series of lithographs known as Everyman Prints in large and consequently low-priced editions to provide an opportunity for ordinary people to own examples of contemporary works of art. By the end of World War II, membership numbered over a thousand and in 1947 a gallery, founded by the AIA central committee, was established at 15 Lisle Street, Soho, London. Distinguished foreign artists also occasionally exhibited work at AIA exhibitions, including Fernand Léger and Pablo Picasso.

It is hardly possible today to imagine the artistic ferment there was in the twenties and thirties in response to the Russian revolution. It galvanised artists from every branch of culture who threw themselves into the struggle to build a better society. They put their art at the service of the 'common good', becoming involved in a whole variety of popular events. There were workers' theatrical groups, particularly Unity Theatre in London, pageants and musical performances were organised in support of anti-fascist and progressive causes, and for which enormous backdrops were designed, banners painted, posters printed, many by leading artists; books and magazines were also published in support of these causes. For a short time artists became again directly connected to the society in which they lived. The sculptors Barbara Hepworth and Henry Moore contributed works to exhibitions organised by communist-led groups, as did many other top artists. The Cold War destroyed that link through the worldwide ideological polarisation that resulted from it.

Cliffe Rowe, a young communist artist travelled to the Soviet Union on holiday in 1932 and managed to get a job as a graphic artist in Moscow. On his return in 1933, and on the urgings of his Soviet friends, he was instrumental in setting up the British nucleus of the Artists International. The aim of the AI was to be a forum for progressive artists and offer them a channel for political and social expression. It was not intended to be a communist artists group per se, even though it espoused Marxist ideology, and the majority of its membership was not in the Communist Party. A specifically Communist Artists Group, was formed later, and was for Communist Party artists only and, although most of its members would also have been in the AI and AIA, its role was different. It grew out of what used to be the Hogarth Club, a grouping of radical artists, mainly communists, which was formed in the twenties and took William Hogarth as an example of a socially critical, great British artist.

The Party, from the thirties onwards, had around seven different cultural groups, from writers to actors and film-makers and they had an enormous influence on British cultural life during that period. The organisation of the AIA was loose and although it had around a hundred Communist Party members, they were the minority in it. Not being an adjunct of the Party the AI/AIA was thus not constrained by Party policies on art. It was, from the beginning, a socio-political rather than stylistic group of artists which was thus able to accommodate most of the styles of the period.

David Elliott, former Director of the Museum of Modern Art, Oxford, said in his foreword to the catalogue for an exhibition about the AIA there in 1983: 'It says much for the breadth of its support as well for its flexibility that it continued until 1971.' Although its real demise took place in the early fifties after an acrimonious split between its communist members and those who had become disillusioned with the Soviet Union and communism.

Cliffe Rowe was a modest, but very talented man who could have been a renowned artist if he'd had the time to devote to it instead of having to earn a living as a commercial graphic designer. Geri Morgan, one of the early members of the AIA along with Rowe, recalls walking with him up Primrose Hill. They were discussing the merits of Picasso's work and Rowe said: 'What Picasso achieved was like an Olympic champion diving from the top board. He dived, though, without being certain that there was any water to dive into. I have no head for heights and wouldn't have had the nerve to do it anyway and, on top of that, I had to earn a living.'

Another of the early members of the AIA was the painter William Coldstream, later to become head of the Slade School of Fine Art, who, in this context, commented that: 'The 1930 slump affected us all considerably. Through making money much harder to come by it caused an immense change in our general outlook...Two very talented painters who had been at the Slade with me, gave up painting altogether, one to work for the ILP, the other for the Communist Party. It was no longer the thing to be an artist delighting in isolation.' This comment sets the framework of those times.

The founding members of the AIA had grown up in the twenties and had responded to the deepening economic and political crisis by acting collectively to form the organisation. There had been many occasions in the past when artists had collaborated around particular artistic programmes, but there had never been a group of artists brought together solely by their sense of social responsibility and the urgent need to prevent the spread of fascism.

The founding meeting of the Artists International took place during

BRITAIN'S COMMUNISTS: THE UNTOLD STORY

the autumn of 1933 in Misha Black's studio and among its founding members were James Boswell, a New Zealander, James Holland and James Fitton – known collectively as the three Jameses and several others – about six people in all. Francis Klingender (the author of *Art and the Industrial Revolution*) was also involved, as was his partner, the art critic and art historian Millicent Rose, and the artist Pearl Binder. Black later became the first professor of Industrial Design in Britain, at the RCA. They were all communists at the time. In the AI's first manifesto published in the Artists' International Bulletin in 1934 its aims were stated as:

1. The uniting of all artists in Britain sympathetic to these aims, into working units, ready to execute posters, illustrations, cartoons, book jackets, banners, tableaux, stage decorations etc.
2. The spreading of propaganda by means of exhibitions, the press, lectures and meetings.
3. The maintaining of contacts with similar groups already existing in 16 countries.

It goes on to record in more detail how this programme was to be implemented.

Writers International, a parallel writers organisation was founded in April and the two organisations worked closely together. One of the members of the latter was Virginia Woolf who, in 1937, wrote an article for the Daily Worker arguing the case for artists to be politically active.

In 1934 the AI's first success in attracting attention beyond the various anti-war and revolutionary groups, was the Social Science Scene exhibition in London in 1934. It included paintings, sculptures, photos by such photographers as Edith Tudor-Hart, and a wall of poster montages contrasting the housing plans and achievements between capitalism and socialism, and realised by the architects' group. Eric Gill commented on the exhibition as follows, 'I visited the exhibition, rather expecting to find many anti-God paintings, as I had been told I should do, but in half an hour's walk round I could see none. All I saw were various works depicting the hardship of the proletariat, the brutality of the police, the display of armed forces against street demonstrations, orators, starving children and slum conditions generally.' [28]

By 1935, responding to the calls for a Popular Front, The Communist Party adopted a new policy in line with the new more-inclusive politics. The AI responded in similar manner by adding 'Association' to its name and adopting a new rallying call: 'For the unity of artists against fascism and war and the suppression of culture'. There was widespread and growing support at the time amongst all democrats for a broad coalition to defeat fascism which became known as the Popular Front movement.

The AIA organised regular discussions on Socialist Realism, about content and form, abstract art, Russian art and experiments for a new socialist art. It worked together with the Marx Memorial Library and the Workers' School in organising lectures and exhibitions. Following in William Morris's footsteps, the AIA also represented a new and concerted attempt to break down traditional barriers between commercial art and fine art and to place art at the service of working people. It had its own regular newsletter which was edited first by James Boswell then Paul Hogarth and later by Ray Watkinson. It had premises in Charlotte Street in Soho, which were also used as a gallery.

The AIA received a real boost during the Spanish Civil War, which gave it a focus and purpose as an 'international' organisation. The list of artists it attracted, included virtually all the renowned artists of the era, among them, Eric Gill, Laura Knight, Henry Moore, Augustus John, Barbara Hepworth, Ben Nicholson, John Piper and Herbert Read, the anarchist art critic – the cream of the British art world. One rather unlikely member of the group was Viscount (Jack) Hastings, later the Earl of Huntingdon. He, along with Clifford Wight, had worked with the Mexican muralist, Diego Rivera on the Chicago murals and was much influenced by the latter's politics. There is a rather crude example of Hastings' mural work that can still be seen in the Marx Memorial Library.

At this time the AIA boasted almost 1,000 members. The artists forming the AIA were a mixed bag and, as with any group of artists, there were huge differences of approach between them, also much individualism and self-promotion, but despite this, it did still manage to function as a unifying organisation and made its mark.

The AIA organised a number of very successful anti-fascist art exhibitions in aid of campaigns such as help for the Basque children who had been made refugees by the Spanish Civil War. In 1939 it also launched the 'Everyman Prints' scheme – cheap art prints which ordinary people could buy – the art equivalent of the paperback. I have very clear memories of a number of these prints from my school days, as they were hung on the walls in many of our schools. A number of

London-based AIA artists also worked closely with Unity Theatre and helped produce backdrops and scenery, design programmes and posters; the AIA also organised exhibitions in the theatre's foyer.

The Artists for Peace group, which grew out of the AIA after the war, held three exhibitions in 1951, 1952 and 1953. It provided a link with the pre-war role of the AIA, and included many artists who had been associated with the AIA. At the third Artists for Peace Exhibition organised in London in 1953, its sponsors included the artists Jacob Epstein, Henry Matisse, Pablo Picasso, Augustus John, Stanley Spencer, Fernand Léger, Jean Lurçat and the critic John Berger.

A committee was set up by artists like Stan Young, Geri Morgan and Peter de Francia. The latter invariably supported the Party Artists Group and their initiatives but was never a member of the Party.

With the end of hostilities with Germany and Japan, and the hardening of the new Cold War divisions, the AIA became a victim of these changes. Those forces which had brought about the expansion of the AIA in the pre-war period were also the ones which brought about its demise in the post war period. The rapid escalation of the Cold War, the rise in anti-Communism and Stalin's autocracy led to a steady drift of intellectuals and artists from the Party. The CIA was also increasingly active in Europe after the end of the war and targeted what it perceived as communist-front organisations. Any progressive artist or cultural organisation which showed sympathy with socialist ideas or with the Soviet Union was deemed suspect.

A grouping crystallised within the AIA which advocated a distancing of the organisation from militant politics. It wanted politics taken out of the AIA's constitution. A ballot was held and this faction lost, but ballot boxes had apparently gone missing and this caused a minor furore, contributing to the organisation's disintegration. Its political objectives were eventually abandoned in 1953 and with the drifting away of many of its leading lights, it lost its raison d'être. It managed to limp on as an organisation until 1971 but only as an artists' run exhibiting society.

A fundamental split had already occurred in the AIA shortly after it had organised an exhibition, The Mirror and the Square, in 1952. The exhibition attempted to show the range of art practice at the time, but the arguments over formalism and realism at the height of the Cold War, which were reflected in the exhibition, in the end tore the AIA apart. Abstract art became synonymous with freedom; realism and social commitment were tarred with the brush of communism and

Stalinist oppression. During the Cold War artists were, irresistibly, consciously or unconsciously, co-opted into the armies of the Cold War – abstract artists were drafted onto the side of capitalist freedom and figurative ones were placed on the side of communist 'dogma'.

An exhibition, Art for Society, was organised in 1978 at the Whitechapel Gallery forty years after the big AIA exhibition to demonstrate the 'Unity of Artists for Peace, Democracy and Cultural Progress' and was a kind of homage to politically committed artists. It was organised by Nicholas Serota and Martin Rewcastle and was one of the very few post-war attempts to take 'political art' at all seriously. Ken Sprague was among the artists exhibited and the Sunday Times art critic, William Feaver, in his review of the exhibition, said of his work: "Ken Sprague, the most practised and efficient image maker of them all, shows a school of fish organising themselves to devour a big predator and, in a couple of water colours, reveals himself to be something of a humane Burra."

Sprague, being of a slightly younger generation than most of the artists who set up the AIA, became involved in the mid-fifties when it was already in decline and then joined, together with some of those who remained loyal to the politics of the AIA, the Communist Party Artists Group. He was, though, clearly influenced by this tradition.

'We used to meet at the Garibaldi Restaurant once a week when I came to London in 1954,' Sprague relates. 'Cliffe Rowe, one of the founding members of the AIA, was the leading figure of the group. Rowe was a good artist who also produced a lot of work for the labour movement and was commissioned by the Electrical Trades Union to paint five murals for the union's college. His finished panels are a celebration of labour movement history and a classic example of realist mural painting.'

Even among Party artists, however, there were divisions. The group was characterised very much, as Sprague puts it, by a divide between the 'fine artists' or 'easel painters' and the graphic designers. Artists like Harry Baines and Ern Brooks, who came from an industrial, printing background, like Ken himself had different aspirations from the others. They were more practically minded and more in touch with working people and were more prepared to do the mundane work of banner painting and poster making.

By the time Sprague became active in the group most of its energy had been expended. Some artists had already been expelled, others had left. But even up to the end of the fifties and into the sixties many artists were still donating paintings to its annual art exhibition and later to art shows in support of progressive causes, like the Campaign for Medical Aid to Vietnam, organised largely by the Party Artists Group. The exhibitions were supported and opened by non-communist progressives like John Berger. Berger was, for a long time, closely associated with the Communist Party artists' group, but he was never a member of the Party as far as is known.

The Communist Party Artists' Group never actually formulated policy on the arts or produced manifestos, but was a loose discussion group. In practical terms its main contribution was the production of banners, posters and designs for Party publications. In its early days this involved an enormous amount of work, as demonstrations, pageants and meetings were organised on a regular basis. There were also numerous book covers and leaflets to design. There also existed a number of local Party artists groups, some of which were very active, like the West Middlesex Artists Group set up and run by artist Muriel Young and her husband, the painter, Stan Young.

In Britain, there had never been a close or easy relationship between artists or intellectuals and working class organisations. However, in 1945 the Amalgamated Engineering Union became the first ever union to sponsor an art exhibition in Britain, to commemorate its silver jubilee, titled: The Engineer in British Life. The exhibition was organised by Francis Klingender, a member of the AIA, who used it as a basis for his classic treatise, Art and the Industrial Revolution.

The AIA was undoubtedly the most influential and broad artists' organisation to be created in Britain during the 20th century. It drew artists together, encouraging them to become politically engaged, and to join the struggle against fascism and war. It played little role in determining stylistic genres or in promoting a particular style of artistic expression, even though it did, in its early years strongly promote the concept of socialist realism, under the influence of Soviet art. A commemorative 50th anniversary exhibition on the AIA was mounted in Oxford in 1983 which later came to London.

In 1934 a British section of the Writers' International was also formed on the same model as the Artists International. It issued Viewpoint, 'a revolutionary review of the arts' which then morphed into Left Review. This was followed shortly afterwards by the formation of the Workers' Music Association which is still in existence.

A few communist artists were still at work into the 21st century, but they no longer belonged to any broad artists' organisation. In the seventies a small group around Desmond Rochfort and David Binnington attempted to initiate a British-based public mural movement, inspired by the Mexican one, and they produced some memorable examples, including the Cable Street mural and one, sadly later destroyed, at the TUC Education Centre in Crouch End. The sculptor Ian Walters produced a number of public monuments, including one, on London's South Bank, commemorating those who fought in the International Brigades in Spain and the two sculptures of Nelson Mandela, one of which stands in Parliament Square and the other alongside the Festival Hall.

The role of communists in the development of education policy

In the 1920s, little more than a handful of those who joined the Party had been to university and most members were ordinary workers. This was not unconnected with the emphasis placed on the 'proletariat' as the revolutionary force in society. The middle classes, so-called professionals or white-collar workers and particularly intellectuals were seen as marginal to the struggle. However, in the thirties, with the rising awareness of the dangers of fascism and the fact that it was the Communist Party that was in the forefront of that struggle against fascism, the Party began to draw in a wider spectrum, including significant numbers of intellectuals. Teachers, particularly, began to take an interest in communism and looked to the Party to give a lead on educational reform.

When communists were elected onto Lochgelly town council in Scotland in the 1940s, they played an influential role on the Education Committee, and immediately restricted the use of the strap, introduced improved school meals and declared May Day a holiday!

One of those who played a prominent role in the Party's educational group was G.C.T. Giles (who became president of the NUT in 1944). Granville Trelawny Courtney, always known as G.C.T. Giles, was an old Etonian, fond of recalling that Tory Prime Minister, Harold Macmillan, had been his fag at school and that he, Giles, had, in the meantime, become head of one of the first comprehensive schools in the country. A Cambridge scholar, he served in the army in the 1914-18 war. In its aftermath he served in disabled servicemen's resettlement for the YMCA and then worked in journalism, before he joined the

Teachers Labour League (later Educational Workers League) in the 1920s. His experiences in the First World War seem to have influenced him first towards the Labour Party and then the Communist Party, which he joined in 1926. He was also an executive member of the Educational Workers International, and became headmaster of Acton County School, where he remained from 1926 to 1956.

From 1931, Giles played a significant role within the Communist Party's Teachers' Advisory. His particular advocacy of a struggle for a decent basic scale of pay as the main road to professional status evoked massive support. He was, year after year, unanimously elected as leader of the Middlesex Teachers' Panel, effectively a negotiating forum. He was one of several communists who also played a leading role in developing British education policy at the time.

Perhaps the most renowned of those influencing educational policy was, however, Professor Brian Simon. Simon was widely regarded as one of the most influential figures to have worked in the field of education during the second half of the twentieth century. He was also one of the most vociferous advocates of comprehensive schooling. While it is impossible to say who or which individuals were instrumental in bringing in Comprehensive Education, Simon was certainly one of the most influential in developing the thinking behind the concept.

Comprehensive schools were introduced in 1965 by Anthony Crosland, Education Secretary in the Labour Government of the time. Beforehand, students sat the 11-plus examination in their last year of primary school and were then allocated a place at a Secondary Modern, Secondary Technical or Grammar School, depending on their perceived ability. The idea for comprehensive schools, where children of all backgrounds and abilities would be educated in a single school, went back to the 1920s. 'The idea was there before the war,' said Simon. 'It had strong proponents. For instance, the London County Council took a decision to go comprehensive when they could, back in 1936.' [29]

After the Second World War a strong momentum for change grew as parents increasingly revolted against the 11-plus examination. Also, many new teachers had greater expectations for education than could be achieved under a system that divided children at the age of 11, sending one group to Grammar Schools from which they could continue to university and beyond, while the others – much the larger group – went to Secondary Moderns from whence opportunities were severely limited. At the same time there was increasing criticism of the grammar school system. Working-class children and their parents had been alienated by the ethos of such schools. Consciousness was also growing about the enormous wastage of ability among working-class children, particularly girls, in the old school system.

Brian Simon was emeritus professor of education at the University of Leicester and will be best known in educational circles for his four-volume history of the English education system from 1780-1990, and his life-long advocacy of equal secondary opportunities for all through comprehensive schooling. His history has become a standard text, and among the most translated of the 40 or so books he wrote.

He campaigned vigorously for comprehensive education and inspired many of the country's best comprehensive school teachers during the 1960s and 1970s. Above all, Simon was, to many who knew him and his work, a humane and perceptive voice, but he was also strongly criticised and even reviled by opponents of comprehensive schools, as an upper-class intellectual who misunderstood the needs of working-class children. He was also attacked as the education spokesman for the Communist Party, which was campaigning in the 1950s and 1960s for the end of intelligence testing.

He did indeed come from a privileged background. His parents were celebrated civic figures in Manchester. His father, Ernest Simon, head of the family engineering firm, was made Lord Simon of Wythenshawe for his contribution to public services, which included a long spell on the city council and serving as lord mayor, during which he campaigned for – among other things – a smokeless city and better housing. He also had a passion for education, and even managed to persuade the leader of the Hallé Orchestra and leading Old Trafford cricketers to give lessons to his boys.

Brian Simon's mother, Shena, to whom he was always very close, was on Manchester's education committee for 50 years, working to improve the state system. Among close family friends was R.H. Tawney [the historian], also strongly committed to secondary education for all. Simon remembered, as a young lad, being told by him in a moment of exasperation with central government that the only good parliamentarian was Guy Fawkes.

As Anne Corbett wrote in her Obituary of Simon:

'At Trinity College, Cambridge, he was part of the concerned generation which, horrified by fascism, turned to communism. Some of this group became infamous, but allegations that Simon recruited Guy Burgess to the KGB were refuted by him. His communist beliefs, unlike those of many of that generation, survived the war and the 1956 Soviet invasion of Hungary.

While at Cambridge, Simon became involved in international student politics and met his future wife, Joan Peel – a direct descendant of the 19th-century prime minister, Robert Peel. In 1939-40 he was president of the NUS, and in 1943, at the age of 27, wrote A Student's View Of The Universities, a critique of the university system.

But this gently elegant man did not want to go into full-time politics. His aim was to become a teacher, and he trained at the London Institute of Education. Then, after war service with the Corps of Signals and GHQ Liaison Regiment (Phantom), he taught in Manchester and Salford. Five years later, in 1950, he was drawn to Leicester University School of Education, where academics were doing field work devising a comprehensive school system.' [30]

Simon stayed at Leicester for the rest of his professional life, retiring in 1980. In 1970, with Caroline Benn, he co-authored a research study on comprehensive reform, Half Way There... He had also been writing a definitive history of the British educational system, which was uncompleted at his death. An autobiography, A Life In Education, was published in 1998.

Corbett concludes her obituary by suggesting that, 'had Simon lived in a culture more tolerant of communist intellectuals, his educational thinking would surely have been recognised as mainstream earlier.'

Nan McMillan was another leading communist educationalist, but from a very different background. She, too, made a significant contribution to the reform of our educational system, if not on such a broad canvas as Brian Simon.

She was born in 1906, the sixth of 12 children, into a working class family in Bermondsey, south London. Exceptionally talented, she won a Junior County Scholarship to St Saviour's and St Olave's Girls Grammar School. She was persuaded to borrow £20 – then a considerable sum – from her secondary school's fund to equip herself for teacher training college and was eventually to repay the debt from winnings in an international essay competition.

She trained as a teacher at Furzedown College in London and, on graduation in 1926, she was offered a secondary school post, specialising in English. In 1927, she met David Capper, a founder member of the Communist Party and a lecturer, who had just led a delegation to the fledgling Soviet Union.

They met at a Labour League for Youth dance and began living together. If they had married then, the bar on woman teachers marrying would have meant not only her having to give up her job but also her certificate of teaching, neither of which she would countenance. At a time when co-habitation was strongly frowned upon, she and David did exactly that; although Nan told her mother that they had married in secret. Fortunately, her headteacher was supportive and covered for her.

She became particularly active in campaigns against the marriage bar in the London County Council area. When the bar on employing married women was lifted in 1947, Nan and David married, but it was then too late to have children.

In 1963, she became President of London Teachers Association, and at the age of 59, was appointed Head of the large and ethnically diverse Sarah Siddons Comprehensive School for girls in Westminster where she spent six years before retiring in 1971.

A staunch proponent of comprehensive education and opportunities for working-class girls, she abolished caning, declaring that 'it plants the seeds of hatred in children's hearts', and developed a broad curriculum for children of all abilities. She attributed her pedagogic successes with her working-class intake to her commitment: 'I was on their side'.

At the same time as running a large school she continued her union work. Once equal pay was finally conceded in 1955 (though not implemented until the 1960s), she relinquished membership of the by then shrinking NUWT and threw all her energies into the NUT. An outstanding conference speaker, she was also a local activist, being elected to the presidency of the London Teachers Association in 1963. She subsequently became one of the first teacher members elected to the Education Committee of the Inner London Education Authority.

Nan McMillan's fierce commitment to causes in which she believed lasted throughout her life. During the War she campaigned for the implementation of the 1944 Education Act as a move towards full comprehensive education, and was the first chair of the London Women's Parliament, the sessions of which were recorded and broadcast to troops overseas.

She retired from teaching in 1971, and in her long 'retirement', was active in the Dorset Against the Cuts Campaign, CND, the

Christchurch and District Women's Group and her local Pensioners Group. Her energetic campaigning on a range of local and national issues attracted the attention of the local press, which ran articles on her life under headlines such as 'Still campaigning at the age of 83' and 'Former head teacher who lived in sin!' She was also sought out for television programmes such as 'School Rules' and 20/20 Vision's 'History of Education'. She died at the age of 96 in 2002.

Norman MacKenzie[31] was another educational pioneer who played a key role in planning and setting up the Open University. Although he was only a member of the Communist Party briefly, he remained a man firmly on the left for all his life.

Professor Harold Rosen, father of the poet and former Children's Laureate, Michael Rosen, was also an influential figure in the educational field. A veteran of the battle of Cable Street, and a feisty campaigner for comprehensive education and a school teacher before he embarked on a long-term career in teacher education.

My own mother, Marguerite Morgan, was a dedicated teacher and deeply interested in educational ideas. Shortly after completing her teacher training as a mature student in the fifties, she was offered a job in a large girls' secondary modern school in Coventry. Before she began, the headmistress called the staff together and warned them 'that a communist would be joining the staff' and that they should be 'vigilant because communists were very persuasive'. My mother went on to win not only the respect of the staff, but particularly of the students. She was told by the Head that the girls were the failures who hadn't made it to grammar school, so were not academic material. When Marguerite said she wished to take some of them on to 'O' and eventually 'A' levels, she was ridiculed, but was eventually allowed to try. Several of her pupils obtained good grades and went on to university – unheard of for Secondary Modern students in those days. Forty years' later, some of her former pupils organised class get-togethers in her honour.

One basic approach that characterises all communists involved in education is their rejection of the idea that children's abilities and potential are circumscribed by their genes. The latter attitude was encapsulated in the now notorious 11-plus IQ tests designed by Cyril Burt (since shown to be based on fraudulent evidence) and which stigmatised generations of school students. Communist educationalists were of the opinion that, irrespective of genetic inheritance, all children should be given the best opportunities for the full development of their potential, and that appropriate nurture is vital because it is that aspect of human development that can be most easily influenced.

The Party's Education Advisory Committee and its journal Education Today and Tomorrow, edited until recently by retired teacher, Tony Farsky, ensured that communist and Marxist ideas were continually under discussion.

The Party not only had several leading educational theorists like those mentioned above, but it also had a whole number of teachers on the ground who carried a Marxist approach to education into the classrooms directly; this meant viewing the world dialectically, as a complex unity of contradictions. Such an approach was based on helping children obtain the best out of their education in order to help them reach their full potential. It is based on the idea that all children and young people have something worthwhile and creative in them and need to be given the opportunity for developing these. It also involves viewing education as a joint voyage of discovery by teacher and pupil, of encouraging students' curiosity and questioning.

Film – 'the Most Important of the Arts'

'Film for us is the most important of the arts.' [32]

LENIN

In Britain, although communists never managed to play a large role in the film industry or in television, they did play a decisive role in the only national film trade union (ACTT) over many years.

There are multiple reasons for the lack of involvement of communists in the top levels of film production, but the two main ones have been lack of financial capital and blacklisting by government institutions and employers. Nevertheless, a number of communists were excited by the way the young Soviet Union was using film, and saw its potential as both an educative and propaganda tool in the UK. They made a concerted effort to ensure that these films were made available to British audiences.

Certainly in the early years of the film industry – the twenties and thirties – making films was not only, even then, a very expensive business, but was also technically complex, requiring large studios, cumbersome lighting equipment, heavy cameras, expensive film stock and laboratory access for development, cutting rooms for film assembly and sound studios for dubbing – a prohibitive exercise for all but the moneyed. With the advent of television in the fifties, communists were, from the very beginning, excluded from employment by a vigorous vetting process, just as they had already

BRITAIN'S COMMUNISTS: THE UNTOLD STORY

been in radio. The ruling establishment felt that these media were too vital and influential to have communists being granted any access to them.

In the early years of the film industry, a number of film technicians were communists or joined the party later and continued working in the industry. Also, because of the party's emphasis on trade union work, it is hardly surprising that the fledgling film technicians' union soon had communists in prominent positions.

The union was founded by technicians at the Gaumont Studios in 1933 as the Association of Cinematograph Technicians (ACT). It elected George Elvin, a left-wing member of the Labour Party, as its first General Secretary. He was followed by Alan Sapper (whose elder brother Laurie, a communist, was General Secretary of the Association of University Teachers) and on the union's executive, over the years, were a number of communists, including Ivor Montagu, Sid Cole and Ralph Bond.

Where the Communist Party did have some influence was in the documentary field. Making documentaries was a lot cheaper than making features, and documentaries were also seen as representing real life more directly and honestly, being more suitable for reflecting social and political issues. Certainly the leading documentarists of the thirties and forties, while not necessarily communist party members, had communist sympathies and made very left-wing, socially-critical films. John Grierson was perhaps the most famous of the group. Returning to Britain after a stint in the USA, he became a tireless organiser and recruiter for the government's curiously titled Empire Marketing Board EMB, enlisting a stable of energetic young left-wing filmmakers into the film unit between 1930 and 1933. Those enlisted included Basil Wright, Edgar Anstey, Stuart Legg, Paul Rotha, Arthur Elton, Humphrey Jennings, Harry Watt and Alberto Cavalcanti (a Brazilian-born communist who made some notable films in the UK). This group formed the core of what was to become known as the British Documentary Film Movement.

What characterised communist and such left-wing film makers as those mentioned above, in contrast to their many colleagues, was that they viewed film, in the first instance, as a 'Bildungs' medium. They were more interested in film's educational and informative roles and saw it as a means of promoting human betterment.

Where communists did become centrally involved early on was in setting up workers film societies in the twenties as a means of creating opportunities for working people to watch progressive and Soviet films. Ralph Bond, a foundation member of the Communist Party, published in the Sunday Worker – a forerunner of the Daily Worker – an appeal for interested parties to get in touch to facilitate the setting up of a London Workers' Film Society, and the response to this appeal surpassed all expectations.

The Soviet director, Sergei Eisenstein's film Battleship Potemkin had an unprecedented impact on audiences everywhere with its revolutionary montage techniques and searing imagery. This was followed by other, equally powerful and iconoclastic films from the Soviet Union. However these films were banned for public showing in many countries, including the United Kingdom, as they were deemed too inflammatory and seen as dangerous communist propaganda.

The first workers' film societies were set up to provide a means of showing such films (and they were also seen as a way of getting around the censor). The first, founded in London in 1925, had as its object the 'showing of films of artistic interest, which could not be seen in ordinary cinemas'. Such societies had already been active on the continent of Europe. However, before the new film society even got off the ground it was already involved in skirmishes with the London County Council (LCC) over permission to show their selected films. The LCC was London's licensing authority for film screenings under the 1909 Cinematographic Act.

After the setting up of the London society, several others soon appeared, and an attempt was made to create a national federation of film societies to facilitate easier access to films, better distribution and co-ordination. The Federation of Workers' Film Societies (FOWFS) was founded in the autumn of 1929 and led to the creation of a network of local workers' film societies all over Britain.

In 1928, the LCC banned the showing of Battleship Potemkin and then also banned Pudovkin's The Mother. Leading many progressive individuals, including J. M. Keynes, Julian Huxley, Sybil Thorndike, Bertrand Russell and George Bernard Shaw to protest, but even they failed to have the ban rescinded.

On the London Workers' Film Society's first attempt to show two Soviet-made films at the Gaiety Cinema in Tottenham Court Road in November 1929, the cinema owner refused the booking at the last minute after pressure from the London County Council. Such run-ins between the LCC and the LWFS became regular occurrences.

While the LCC adhered to its bans on the Soviet films mentioned above, it relented as far as permitting the LWFS to put on Sunday shows in the West End.

The Labour Party itself had shown no interest in setting up workers' film societies but with the success of the London Society, it became highly suspicious of its activities and denounced the society as being merely a communist propaganda vehicle.

Communists were, indeed, active in the management committees of most of the local workers' film societies, and the founders had the clear aim of using film as a means of political education. However, this strong communist participation in the societies made the Labour Party and the right-wing-led trade unions even more suspicious of them and they distanced themselves from any official involvement.

In 1930, the Atlas Film Company, in collaboration with the Federation, took the momentous step of making newsreels under the title: Workers' Topical News. Newsreels at the time, before the advent of television, were instrumental in shaping the opinions of a large number of people on political and world affairs. In 1930, the Federation (FOWFS) took the decision to launch its own production fund 'with the purpose of producing films based on the lives of the workers in this country.'

It wasn't only in London that such film societies had trouble with the censor. The Salford Workers' Film Society made several applications to the local Watch Committee for permission to show uncensored films privately to its members, but was refused. One of the films it wished to show was Pudovkin's Storm over Asia. During a council debate on the issue, Tory Alderman J. Bratherton silenced his opponents who kept referring to the artistic qualities of the film with a profound comment: 'From start to finish Storm over Asia is Bolshevik propaganda...' [33]

The Salford Workers' Film Society was later involved in making its own short film about a large textile dispute in Burnley. This was included as an item in a Workers' Topical News report. And, in 1931 another film, titled simply, 1931, was produced as part of the Charter Campaign movement and modelled on the Chartists' campaign in the 19th century. It agitated for better labour conditions and unemployment benefit. This was the first example of a film specially produced to support a campaign by a working class organisation. It was a cooperative undertaking between the FOWFS, LWFS and Minority Movement (see chapter: Trade Unions – the Main Focus) set up by communists to campaign on employment rights and unemployment benefits.

The film societies in Salford and Manchester eventually merged to become the Manchester and Salford Workers' Film Society, with their first screening in November 1930. The main organiser was Reg Cordwell who was to remain at the centre of operations for the rest of his active life. In 1937 the name was shortened to the Manchester and Salford Film Society.

Ewan MacColl, who was growing up in Manchester during this period commented:

'This was the era of the growth of Hollywood, the era of the first international stars, the age of the comedians, the celluloid sweethearts and the tough guys. As the lines of unemployed grew longer and longer, so the gigantic baroque palaces of Hollywood's new art form grew more and more sumptuous and the lines of high-kicking chorus girls more and more desirable. The Hollywood film of the late twenties and early thirties was the staple diet of the vast army of unemployed and I would venture to suggest that it provided the main art fare for the entire working class. It was certainly one of the most important artistic influences in my life up until late 1929.

In the autumn of that year the Deansgate cinema ran a season of Russian films. This was long before the art-cinema concept first appeared and it must have been a financial flop for I remember going there for several weeks and sitting in splendid isolation as the great epics of Pudovkin, Eisenstein and Dovzhenko unrolled on the screen. It was, I think, Eisenstein's October and Pudovkin's End of St Petersburg which started me on the road I was to travel for the next twenty years.

When, in 1930, the Salford Workers' Film Society was formed, I was among its foundation members. It was, I believe, on the Labour Party's list of proscribed (communist) organisations and every Sunday morning, in a small flea-pit on Oldfield Road, it presented the cream of the world's best films.

There, in the space of the next few months, I saw Storm over Asia, The New Babylon, Pabst's Kameradschaft, Dziga Vertov's Man with the Movie Camera, Aaron Room's Bed and Sofa and The Ghost that Never Returns, Fritz Lang's Metropolis and Dovzhenko's Earth. The opportunity of seeing films of such stature compensated for some of the deprivation experienced by an ill-educated adolescent who faced the bleak prospect of trying to earn a living in the arid desert of 1930.' [34]

The FOWS eventually folded in 1932, but the Workers' Theatre Movement (WTM), forerunner of Unity Theatre, came to the rescue, by including film in many of its agit-prop productions. It was founded in 1926 and utilised the experience of agit-prop theatre in the Soviet Union and Germany as its guide, and was very keen to use film in an innovative way. It was also closely associated with the Communist Party from the very beginning. Charlie Mann (the son of the famous trade unionist Tom Mann), who had been active in the Rebel Players theatre group, was instrumental in setting up the WTM and had a particular interest in film. After visiting Moscow for the Workers' Theatre Olympiad, he returned determined to do something similar in Britain. He and a number of other comrades set about putting 'Propaganda in Pictures' into practice. They got hold of a 16mm projector and a van with a screen and held showings on the streets of London, as well as in community halls, which were highly popular. Charlie Mann and other comrades then, in 1933, set up Kino (the Soviet word for cinema) as a production company, based in Soho. In the years that followed, Kino became the most important distributor of left-wing films on 16mm in the UK.

In June 1948, Jack Woddis, Secretary of the Party's International Department, warned readers of the Communist journal World News and Views that 'American imperialism is conducting an ideological drive alongside its general economic campaign.' [35]

The British film industry had become famous with its wartime productions but was, after the war, on the brink of yet another slump, largely due to the import of cheaper Hollywood light entertainment films. Woddis's claim about this new domination of the British cinema industry by Hollywood was clearly no fantasy. The Communist Party then began a campaign to reform the film industry and theatrical exhibition system. It called for a 'fourth circuit' of government-owned and operated cinemas, or alternatively municipally-owned and operated ones, to help establish an outlet for British-made films, and thus offer protection to the industry from Hollywood's cultural dominance.

Ralph Bond was a founding director of ACT Films, the production company the union set up in 1949 to make films and to offer its members work. He served as its first Production Supervisor and General Manager. Throughout his working life, Bond was a committed trade unionist: he had joined the Association of Cine Technicians in 1935, was elected to its Executive Committee in 1936 and served as its Vice-President from 1942 to 1974. John Grierson had earlier given him a role at the GPO Film Unit, and during the war, he directed films for the Ministry of Information and other official bodies, but afterwards spent more time as a producer in the documentary sector and on distributing and exhibiting left-wing films. In the 1970s, Bond taught at the London Film School, guiding young filmmakers in documentary techniques; and right up to his death, was still participating in trade union meetings.

Ivor Montagu was also a founder member of the Cine technicians' union alongside Bond and would undoubtedly have gone on to map out a distinguished career for himself in the film industry, but for his politics. He was the third son of the second Baron Swaythling – and thus another 'traitor to his class'. He was a pupil of Westminster School and went on to King's College, Cambridge, where he contributed to Granta. With Sidney Bernstein he established the London Film Society in 1925, the first film club devoted to showing art and independent films. He undertook the post-production work on Alfred Hitchcock's The Lodger in 1926 and was hired by Gaumont British in the 1930s, to work as a producer on a number of the Hitchcock thrillers. His 1928 silent slapstick movie Bluebottles (slang for police) is included in the British Film Institute's History of the Avant-Garde – Britain in the Twenties. The story was written by H.G Wells, and the stars of the film were Charles Laughton and Elsa Lanchester.

Montagu later went to the Soviet Union and worked with the renowned Soviet director, Sergei Eisenstein. In 1930 he accompanied Eisenstein to New York and Hollywood; later in that decade he made a number of compilation films, including Defence of Madrid (1936), on the Spanish Civil War, and Peace and Plenty (1939) for the Communist Party, about the betrayals of the Chamberlain-led Tory government. During the Second World War, he also made a film for the Ministry of Information. After the war Montagu worked as a film critic and reviewer, becoming the first film critic on The Observer and then the New Statesman. In 1933, he became a founder member of the Association of Cinematograph and Technicians (later the Association of Cinematograph and Television Technicians), holding various positions in the union until the 1960s.

In early 1951, as the Cold War began in earnest, the new Labour government Foreign Minister, Herbert Morrison, considered using government powers to ban the import of films from 'behind the Iron Curtain'. The Establishment was concerned that 'propaganda' from Eastern Europe would have a corrupting influence on the youth of Britain. One of the films they were particularly worried about came from the GDR (East Germany): Immer Bereit (Always Prepared) about the youth movement there. It had been presented to the National Union of Students by Erich Honecker, General Secretary of the FDJ (Free German Youth Movement). Morrison, an avid anti-communist, was worried about its effect on 'immature persons who have not the political wisdom to see through it'. Much valuable time was wasted in Cabinet discussing the issue, but in the end the government was reluctant to use a huge mallet to kill a flea, so dropped the matter. Later that year, another East German film Council of the Gods, about the role of the big IG Farben chemical conglomerate in collaborating with the Nazis to produce the poison gas used to exterminate the inmates of the concentration camps, was to be shown in Britain, but was refused an import licence. Finally, a year later, the ban on the film was lifted.

Despite the Party having two MPs – Phil Piratin and Willie Gallacher – in the immediate post-war parliament, the BBC refused it air time for electoral broadcasts. It was also virtually impossible for the Party to find distributors willing to show progressive films, which led to it attempting to set up its own, modest distribution structure. In 1951, Plato Films was created, under the directorship of Stanley Forman and with the help of Ivor Montagu. Although not a Party organisation as such, it collaborated closely with the Party's leadership and was the company was run by communists. Among its shareholders were Eva Reckitt, (communist and founder-owner of the famous Collett's Bookshop in Charing Cross Road – now long gone), and the composer, Alan Bush. It soon established its own film projection service, to enable Party branches, trade unions and other groups to hire films and have them shown anywhere in the country.

Shortly before the establishment of Plato Films, two young film technicians, Peter Brinson and Tony Simmons, had become so frustrated by what they perceived as a lack of initiative shown by the Party in using the film medium that they set up a new workers' film society, the New Era Film Club. It began showing films in 1950, and shortly afterwards New Era began producing its own films. The two men managed to persuade a number of other ACT film technicians to join them and work for free. One of their first films was about the London May Day march of 1950, which had been banned by the Labour Home Secretary, but which went ahead, despite brutal police attempts to prevent it. The resulting film, May Day 1950 was premiered in June of that same year. Among the communist film technicians who worked with New Era were established film technicians like the cameramen, Lewis McLeod, Manny Yospa and Walter Lassally who was not a member of the Party.

Plato had hardly begun operating, however, when it faced competition from an unexpected source. Charles Cooper, another Jewish communist who had been active in Kino and the Film and Photo League during the thirties, had emigrated to the US, but because of his politics was forced to return to the UK once the McCarthy witch-hunt began in earnest. He returned to London in 1950 with a collection of American Labour films, Soviet and other classics he'd been distributing in the USA through his company Contemporary Films Inc. In the spring of 1951, he set up Contemporary Films Ltd., based in London, and he resumed his distribution activities. Plato and Contemporary eventually reached an amicable agreement that Charles would stick to features and Stanley would take on documentaries, so establishing separate niches for each other and avoiding what could have degenerated into acrimonious competition.

In Ian Christie's obituary of Charles Cooper he wrote:

'He was a movie enthusiast whose Contemporary Films opened new horizons for British cinema audiences. His early interest in film had led Charles to become, in 1933, secretary of the Kino group, an association of left-wing film enthusiasts who were determined to circumvent Britain's draconian film censorship, which was especially aimed at the new Soviet cinema. Kino organised 16mm screenings of Eisenstein's Battleship Potemkin for trade union and Soviet friendship groups, as well as producing a "workers' newsreel" and agitational films such as Bread, in which a starving, unemployed worker is harshly treated by police and magistrates.

This early experience of taking films to motivated audiences, often in the teeth of official hostility, proved crucial when Charles and his wife found themselves stranded in the United

States at the outbreak of war in 1939. They had planned to cycle to Mexico to film the work of Lázaro Cárdenas's revolutionary government but, having to find work, set up a film department of the International Workers' Order in New York, promoting welfare and socialism among minorities throughout the war. Back in England, the Coopers threw themselves into creating a new distribution company, Contemporary Films, which cooperated with Stanley Forman's Plato Films in sharing the business of maintaining links with the eastern bloc while trying to expand Britain's cinematic vision.

It is hard now to evoke the heady mixture of political and aesthetic excitement that surrounded the new cinema movements of the 1960s, which Contemporary helped to launch in Britain. In rapid succession, films from Poland, the USSR and Czechoslovakia were followed by the French new wave, a new generation of Japanese directors, Buñuel in Mexico, Bergman in Sweden, and – among Contemporary's proudest achievements – the discovery of the Indian director Satyajit Ray. There were classic revivals too of such auteurs as Jean Renoir, who was virtually unknown in Britain until Contemporary promoted La Règle du Jeu, and, keeping the memory of early Soviet cinema alive, regular Eisenstein reissues.

Before being distributed to film societies and the emerging circuit of British Film Institute regional film theatres, new movies had to be launched in London, and the Academy Cinema on Oxford Street was a main venue for Charles's films, but Academy soon found other suppliers, so Contemporary moved into exhibition, becoming partners in the Paris Pullman cinema, in South Kensington, in 1967, and later adding two Phoenix cinemas, in Finchley, north London, and Oxford.

But even as the cultural impact of imported "art" cinema spread, Charles Cooper remained true to his campaigning roots. He helped produce the first British anti-nuclear weapons film, March to Aldermaston, in 1958, working with the film technicians' union and Lindsay Anderson (later renowned for such films as If which won the Grand Prix at Cannes in 1968), and he continued to support radical initiatives with non-sectarian zeal, distributing important films about Vietnam in the 60s, and the Greenham Common protest film Carry Greenham Home (1983). He also remained optimistic about gathering the independent film sector into a coherent grouping, patiently organising a short-lived Independent Film Distributors Association in the 1970s, even as new entrants loudly asserted their own independence.' [36]

Ted Willis was one of the few, with a communist background, to make it to the top in the film and television industry. He grew up in a poor, largely illiterate family, and became very active on the political left during his youth, before he went on to become a leading television dramatist. He was Chairman of the Labour League of Youth during the thirties, but in 1941 became General Secretary of the Young Communist League. He was a charismatic personality and an excellent public speaker, and often spoke at meetings in favour of opening a second front during the Second World War in order to help the Red Army which was bearing the brunt of the Nazi onslaught.

Willis was very involved in amateur theatre and journalism – he was drama critic for the Daily Worker during the 1940s. For Unity Theatre he wrote a number of plays during the war years – Buster (1943) among them – and he worked with such talents as Alfie Bass, Bill Owen and Vida Hope, who helped sharpen his theatrical sense. His passion for drama was first manifested in plays he wrote for Unity Theatre during the war.

He was the pioneer of British soap opera on television, becoming best known for writing the television series Dixon of Dock Green which ran, from 1953, for more than twenty years. Dixon of Dock Green was the first police series to appear on television and was the pioneering template for many police series that were to follow. The Adventures of Black Beauty (an acclaimed series, produced by Sidney Cole) and Z-Cars. Willis became Chairman of the Writers' Guild of Great Britain and served from 1958 to 1964. In 1963 he was awarded a life peerage and took the title Baron Willis, of Chislehurst, on a Labour Party nomination.

Sid Cole, who died in 1998, was, alongside Ivor Montagu and Ralph Bond, the third of the communist trio who were among the founding members of the cine technicians' union. He went on to become a successful film and television producer and editor, but blacklisting because of his politics and trade union activism meant work was often hard to come by.

Cole was a longstanding friend of director Thorold Dickinson, and edited Dickinson's The High Command (1936) and Gaslight (1940) as well as Alberto Cavalcanti's Went the Day Well? (1942). Cavalcanti was 'a joy' to work with, he said, and later in his life he remained pleased with his work on the film, stating that it was 'very tightly edited by me'.

For most of his career he worked as a producer, initially credited as an associate producer, for Ealing Studios (where he was employed for eleven years) and the television production company ITC. For ITC he produced Danger Man (1964–67) and Man in a Suitcase (1967–68). Later he supervised the productions of The Adventures of Black Beauty (1972–74) and Dick Turpin (1979–82) for London Weekend Television. Sidney Cole was politically engaged throughout most of his career. He was involved in making documentaries on the Spanish Civil War with Dickinson, and employed blacklisted American writers on The Adventures of Robin Hood, a television series (1995-60) whose executive producer, Hannah Weinstein, had also found exile in London as a refugee from McCarthyism.

In 1978, the Communist Party allowed a TV film crew to produce a three-part fly-on-the-wall documentary on the Party's deliberations on a redraft of its manifesto, The British Road to Socialism, and the run up to its congress as well as the congress event itself. It was broadcast as: Decision British Communism and made by the renowned documentary film-maker, Roger Graef. This was the first time the Communist Party had been given any in-depth coverage by the mainstream media. And, significantly, it was being made by Granada television, which was also responsible for the hard-hitting political magazine series, World in Action.

Sidney Bernstein, founder and first managing director of Granada TV, when first applying for one of the new commercial television licences in 1954 for Granada was accused by Tory MP Kenneth Clark of being a former member of the Communist Party. And was seen as a subversive character by many Tories, one of whom accused him of 'providing employment for Jews, Communists and queers'!

He was indeed a fervent socialist whose political activities and association with communist agitators in the early 1930s had even led to his being watched by the security services. Whether intentional or not, his decision to establish his television empire 200 miles from London within a few yards of the Manchester Guardian led to a political alliance between the two organisations that, half a century later, would play a significant role in the successful tarnishing of the Conservative government of John Major.

Born the son of a wealthy immigrant, Bernstein had made his own fortune from establishing a successful cinema and theatre chain. But despite the joys that his Granada cinemas brought to the masses, prior to bidding for one of the new broadcasting licences Bernstein had actually supported the Labour Party's opposition to the introduction of commercial television, such was his left-wing idealism. This was acknowledged by the Guardian itself following Bernstein's death on 5 February 1993, in an obituary by Dennis Barker entitled: Granada's hard core:

'When the Tories got wind that a "socialist" was applying for a television licence, Lord Woolton summoned the Chairman of the Independent Television Authority to his office and told him "Sidney Bernstein is a communist, now we don't want a communist running our new television network do we?" "Certainly not, replied the Chairman. You have a copy of his Communist Party membership and all your secret service files on my desk tomorrow morning, and I will see that he is disqualified immediately".' [37]

Needless to say, no files were forthcoming, so Bernstein got his franchise. What followed in terms of programming at Granada was therefore perhaps not fortuitous: it pioneered the first real working class television soap opera, Coronation Street, and produced the powerful, left-leaning political news magazine, World in Action.

While it would be inaccurate and hubristic to claim that communists played a central role in the British film world, their influence was certainly significant. The early workers' film associations and the importance of Plato and Contemporary in introducing British audiences to foreign film classics and East European cinema were inspirational for a number of progressive film makers, like Lindsay Anderson, Karel Reisz and Ken Loach, to name but three.

A whole number of thespians who were at one time members of the Communist Party, also made contributions to Britain's film culture, even if not in highly prominent roles. One of these was the Scottish actor, Alex McCrindle who was born in Glasgow. He was one of the founders of Scottish Equity, the actors' trade union, and was married to Honor Arundel, the communist children's author (see chapter Writers and the Battle of Ideas). He began his acting career in 1937 starring in minor roles in UK television. From 1946 to 1951 he played the role of Jock Anderson in Dick Barton – Special Agent on radio. In 1951 he starred in his first film in the US, The House in the Square. From there his acting career took off. He then did five more films: I Believe in You (1952), The Kidnappers (1953), Trouble in the Glen (1954), Geordie (1955) and Depth Charge (1960). From 1962-1974 he went into television acting. In 1976 he was cast as General Dodonna, leader of the Rebel Alliance in the first Star Wars film. He once again went back to minor roles on TV, including the role of the eccentric veterinarian Ewen Ross on All Creatures Great and Small. His life concluded with two last films and a TV appearance: Samson and Delilah (1985), Comrades (1987), Taggart (1988).

Another was the prolific actor Mark Dignam (1909–1989). Born in London, the son of a salesman in the steel industry, Dignam grew up in Sheffield and was educated at a Jesuit College, where he appeared in numerous Shakespearean plays. He became one of the first members of Equity, the actors' union, founded in 1929. Very soon afterwards, he joined the Communist Party, in which he remained until his death. A superb supporting actor, he played Buckingham, Claudius, Malvolio, Polonius, and similar roles alongside leading stars of stage and screen. Dignam was the Laird in the film The Maggie (1954), the prosecuting attorney in Carrington, V.C. (1955), and Merlin in Cornel Wilde's Sword of Lancelot (1962) and many other films.

The stage and screen actor, André van Gyseghem, about whom I've written in the section on Unity Theatre, also played a number of film and television roles. He was one of several 'Number Twos' in the 1960s cult classic television spy series The Prisoner. He also appeared in a memorable episode of The Saint in 1968 with Roger Moore.

Other actors who were never members of the Party but were associated with a number of its cultural undertakings and sympathised with its ideas were the comic actor and writer Miles Malleson, Dame Sybil Thorndike and the actor and theatrical director Bernard Miles. These individuals were also very much involved in Unity Theatre, which had an ongoing relationship with the film world. A group of Unity actors appeared in Ivor Montagu's film Peace and Plenty made for the Party's election campaign during 1939 for the general election due in 1940.

Unity set up its own short-lived film unit, Crescent Films, planned to be a counterpart to the theatre company. It made only one film, Century of Song, based on unity's show Winkles and Champagne, written and produced by Alec Bernstein. The film's director, Alberto

Cavalcanti, was also a leading member of Unity's Film Society, as was the television playwright, Charles Wood (who wrote the treatments for the recent television drama films The Charge of the Light Brigade and Tumbledown). The latter had been a scene painter at Unity. Oscar Lewenstein, another luminary of Unity, went on to set up Woodfall Film Productions which was responsible for some of the iconic British films of the sixties and seventies, including John Osborne's Look Back in Anger and Tony Richardson's Tom Jones. The artist and AIA member Lucien Amaral who had helped design sets and illustrated the programmes at Unity, became a scenic artist with Associated Pictures. Until it burned down in 1975, Unity Theatre, was also the venue for the showing of many classical and left-wing films, including, in 1965, Peter Watkins's The War Game, which had been commissioned then banned by the BBC.

Film-making, before the feminist movement erupted during the seventies, was very much a male preserve, apart from background jobs in costume departments and cutting rooms or, if you were photogenic enough, as actresses in front of the cameras, they hardly featured. So it is salutary to be able to feature one woman, Kay Mander, who bucked the trend. I am grateful for this information to Peter Frost whose article on her in the Morning Star alerted me to this extraordinary woman film-maker.[38]

Kay Mander has been outrageously overlooked in most histories of British film-making. The fact that she was an outspoken communist and a woman undoubtedly compounded her eclipse, despite the fact that she was one of the pioneers of the drama documentary and one of the first women film directors.

She became interested in film-making while living in Germany, where she worked as a translator at the 1935 Berlin international Film Congress. Back in Britain she found work at Alexander Korda's London Films company as an interpreter. There she worked in publicity and continuity, becoming one of the first women members of the film union ACCT. Her big break came during the Second World War when many experienced male colleagues joined the armed forces. She took a job as a production assistant at the Shell Film Unit and it was there that she made her directing debut.

By 1943 Mander was involved in shooting home-front propaganda films on subjects like the fire service and civil defence. However mundane the subject, her direction was characterised by a deep humanity and clarity of message.

In 1943 she was invited to make a short documentary about the government-subsidised Highland and Islands Medical Service, but instead she scripted, produced, directed and even acted in what turned out to be one of the first drama documentaries to be made. The film, titled, Highland Doctor, used professional actors and local people to bring a dramatic story alive. The film was not only popular and successful but it was also one of the most powerful arguments in the battle to promote a socialist ideal of a national health service.

In her 1945 film Homes For the People, she had ordinary, working-class women speak bluntly about terrible housing conditions. At this time Mander and her husband, the documentary producer R.K. Neilson Baxter, were shooting educational and promotional films for government and industrial sponsors. Neilson Baxter was also associate editor with Roger Manvell of the Pelican classic annual review of British film-making, The Cinema. In 1949 Mander's French-language films for the Ministry of Education La Famille Martin won a British Film Academy award.

With the end of the war, many male film-makers returned to their former jobs and her work started to dry up. No doubt, the fact that she was a deeply committed and outspoken member of the Communist Party and that she made no attempt to hide her political views didn't enhance her career prospects.

Lacking suitable work in Britain, she went out to Hollywood, but was only able to find work in the continuity department. There she worked on a whole range of features including From Russia With Love, The Four Horsemen of the Apocalypse, Fahrenheit 451, Tommy, and The Heroes of Telemark. On the set of Telemark she met and had a brief affair with actor Kirk Douglas. She remained passionate and committed to film despite all the hindrance and frustration she encountered.

Another example of a film-maker having problems with blacklisting is that of Jeff Perks. He was one of the first graduates from Britain's National Film School. He joined the Communist Party in that era of student radicalism. He sent a detailed and well-presented proposal for a documentary to the editor of BBC Omnibus, Barrie Gavin. Gavin remembered his work as a graduate director at the British Film Institute, and found Perks's proposal – about the poster maker Ken Sprague – interesting and exciting. He agreed to make the programme, and a three-month contract was passed to the personnel office for approval. the MI5 unit at the BBC tried to prevent Perks working for the BBC but were, unusually, overruled by Gavin. Three weeks later Perks was given a contract, and his film, Posterman, went on to secure the highest ratings of any Omnibus programme that year. Head of Arts at the BBC, Humphrey Burton also liked it. 'That was a very good film,' he remarked to Gavin. 'I think you should pursue this combination further.' So, in December 1976, Gavin asked Perks and Sprague to make a series of pilot programmes for Omnibus. But once again MI5 objected. A Personnel Officer told Gavin it was not possible to use him. MI5 objected to Perks for a simple reason. He had been a member of the Communist Party since 1971. But to Gavin this did not make him a legitimate target: 'The Communist Party is not a proscribed or illegal organisation. And anyway, the notion that the modern Communist Party is revolutionary is laughable.' Perks would also have been put on MI5's files in 1973 after making a film with Michael Rosen at the National Film School about the 'Shrewsbury Three', three building workers who had been jailed for picketing offences during a strike. Part of the film was shown on Thames Television's This Week, and caused a storm of protest from Tory MP's in the Commons. In the end Perks and Sprague went on to make a follow-up series for Channel 4 – Everyone A Special Kind Of Artist (1986). Perks left the Communist Party in 1977.[39]

The late 1960s and 1970s saw an upsurge of small documentary film collectives in the UK that attempted to address the burning political issues of the day. They developed radical forms of independent film production and distribution prior to digital or the web and produced a large body of work, from short agitational cinetracts to sophisticated features.

The introduction of the new television channel – Channel 4 – in 1982 also provided such new independent film-makers with an outlet and audience for their films. Channel 4 came under the auspices of the Independent Broadcasting Authority, but is now owned and operated by Channel 4 News Corporation, and has long since lost its initial radical edge.

During that period, filmmaking collectives such as the Berwick Street Collective, Cinema Action, Newsreel Collective, Amber Films, Liberation Films, the London Women's Film Group, Black Audio Film Collective and Four Corners Films promoted socialist, feminist and anti-racist ideas. Most, if not all, of these groups were set up by young left-wing activists, many from the spectrum of the Trotskyist left. While communists played little role in their formation, several were involved in their work and the Party certainly gave qualified support to them. John Green and Georgia Kalla were involved in the production of several of Cinema Action's films, as part of the location team, and the artist, Ken Sprague, made graphics for an animated sequence in an agit-prop film, Fighting the Bill, made as part of the campaign to combat the Industrial Relations Act of 1971. The group was also given support by Stanley Forman of ETV (formerly Plato) Films and Charlie Cooper of Contemporary Films.

The collective, Cinema Action was formed in the wake of the student rebellions in Paris in 1968, in which several of its founding members took part. The group began by organising showings in factories of a film about the French student uprising of that year. With a handful of core members – Ann and Gustav 'Schlacke' Lamche, Marc Karlin and Eduardo Guedes – the group pursued its collective methods of production and exhibition for nearly twenty-five years.

Its work stands out from its contemporaries' in its makers' desire to co-operate closely with their working-class subjects. By the beginning of the seventies, Cinema Action also began to receive small grants from trades union branches and, latterly, from the British Film Institute.

The group's approach was to let those directly involved express themselves without commentary. The films were designed, the group avowed, to provide an analysis of struggles, which could encourage future action by unions or political groups.

As indicated above, with the establishment of Channel 4, a valuable source of additional funding became available and it provided a new outlet for Cinema Action Films such as So That You Can Live (1981) and Rocking the Boat (1983) which were consciously made for a wider national audience. In 1986, Cinema Action made its first fiction feature, Rocinante, starring John Hurt. The group's documentary, Arise Ye Workers (1973), about the imprisonment and freeing of the Pentonville 5 dockers won a Silver Dove prize at the Leipzig Film Festival and was screened by the jailed dockers on the anniversary of their release from jail. And its two films on the Upper Clyde shipbuilders work-in, UCS1 and Class Struggle – Film from the Clyde were shown again at the big 40th anniversary commemoration in 2013.

Platform Films is another radical film making group, set up by former members of Cinema Action, and includes communists in its team. It produces films, DVDs and on-line web videos for trade unions, the public sector and campaigning organisations. It has made films for RMT, NUT, UNITE, UNISON, GMB, the NHS, Amnesty

International, the CPB, the Morning Star and the Green Party. Recent productions include a film for the GMB encouraging members' political involvement, a history of the RMT to coincide with the centenary of the NUR, a promotional DVD for the Morning Star, a campaign film Justice for the Shrewsbury Pickets, on-line reports on NUT pensions action and a film promoting children's centres for Tower Hamlets NHS.

The London Socialist Film Co-operative that is still going strong after 21 years, organises regular screenings of classic features and documentaries, including many contemporary ones, primarily on social, political and peace issues. At the screenings discussions are held with film makers and experts on the subject matters. Several of its organisers, like Nicola Seyd, founder member, treasurer and membership secretary, have been members of the Communist Party. It is one of the few remaining organisations that screen small budget left-wing films.

How the Hollywood blacklist impacted on British cinema

Although the stories of the blacklisted Hollywood film makers – many of them communists – are not directly related to British communists, the lives of a number of them did cross and several also managed to escape unemployment and destitution by working on British-made films and television productions, making a significant impact.

Joseph Losey is probably one of the most notable of the US communists who came to Britain in the wake of the Hollywood blacklist and who had a strong influence on British film making. A number of his films, particularly those in which he collaborated with Harold Pinter who wrote the screen-plays, have become minor classics. The Servant with Dirk Bogarde, The Go-between with Julie Christie and Alan Bates and Accident also with Bogarde and Stanley Baker, all used screenplays by Pinter.

Losey had worked earlier in the USA with the playwright Bertolt Brecht, directing the premiere of his play Galileo there, and he collaborated on two early films with the composer Hans Eisler, both of whom were in exile in the United States during the Hitler period. They were both soon blacklisted and expelled from the country.

Losey's first wife was the iconoclastic fashion designer and later union organiser, Elizabeth Hawes, who was also close to, if not a member of the US Communist Party.

Bernard Vorhaus was another US-born director who had moved to

Britain much earlier – in the late twenties – and made several films at Twickenham Studios, using a number of innovative techniques, including employing ordinary people as actors. He gave the character actors Margaret Rutherford and Stanley Holloway their first film roles and was inspirational for the young David Lean (later director of Lawrence of Arabia, Doctor Zhivago, Ryan's Daughter and other features) who was given his big break working as editor on his first feature film with Vorhaus. Lean says Vorhaus was a major influence on his career. He spent his days observing Vorhaus directing on the set and then carried out his editing work at night. That's how he picked up the basics of directing.

When the depression hit the British film industry, Vorhaus returned to the States in 1937. There he made several films with actors like John Wayne and the young Ronald Reagan, before serving in the army during the war. After being 'named' before the committee by director Edward Dmytryk while away filming in Italy, he realised there was little point in returning to the States to seek work, so came back to the UK. He was, however, unable to find his feet in the film industry again and ended up renovating and selling flats in London as work in the film industry had just dried up. His wife, Hetty Vorhaus, who was from Wales, had never lost her British citizenship even though she had become naturalised in the US. After moving back to the UK, she became one of the most important activists in the anti-Vietnam War movement, arranging for the playing of the tape of the Winter Soldier Hearings before the House of Commons and organising demonstrations in front of the US Embassy.

Hannah Weinstein became one of the key figures finding employment for her fellow black-listed compatriots. She moved to London in 1952 to escape the anti-Communist persecution raging in the US at the time, and became a producer, establishing her own television production company, Sapphire Films, and made several series for Britain's commercial ITV network.

In Britain the blacklisting of communists and leftists was not as draconian as in the USA and that's why several refugees, fleeing persecution by HUAC, were able to find work in the country. Weinstein is best known for having produced The Adventures of Robin Hood series for ATV (television) in the 1950s on which she was able to employ at least 22 blacklisted writers, including Waldo Salt, Ring Lardner jr. (writing under the pseudonym Lawrence McClellan), Ian Hunter, Robert Lees and Adrian Scott who were often forced to use pseudonyms, and institute elaborate security measures to ensure that their true identities remained secret. On that series she worked closely with the British producer Sidney Cole. Adrian Scott's wife, Joan LaCour Scott, like her husband, also worked in England on several films as a writer, but both returned to the USA after a short time.

The success of Robin Hood led Weinstein to create a further four television series, The Buccaneers (1956–57), The Adventures of Sir Lancelot (1956-57), Sword of Freedom (1958-60) and The Four Just Men (1959) (as Hannah Fisher). The film makers Tony Richardson, Karel Reisz and Lindsay Anderson, were among those whose first assignments as directors were on this series, but they were probably unaware of who really wrote their scripts. Weinstein returned to America in 1962, and resumed her involvement in left-wing politics.

In 1971 she founded the Third World Cinema Corporation to produce films with members of African-American groups. In 1974, she produced the Oscar nominated film Claudine, featuring an all-black cast in a story about an Afro-American family struggling through hard times and racism. She later produced Greased Lightning (1977) and Stir Crazy (1980) starring comedian Richard Pryor.

In 1982, she was awarded the Women in Film Crystal Award for outstanding women who, through their endurance and the excellence of their work over their lifetime, have helped to expand the role of women within the entertainment industry. In a letter that was read at the award dinner in Santa Monica, Hannah Weinstein's friend, Lillian Hellman, the playwright, said that 'one of the most remarkable things about Hannah is that in this shabby time when either nobody believes in anything or has long given up hope, she does believe and she does carry out what she believes in.' Weinstein also received the Women in Film Life Achievement Award from the Hollywood-based Women in Film organisation in 1982.

Weinstein knew that the FBI acted as the HUAC's investigatory and enforcement arm, and by 1955 the bureau had Weinstein in its sights. She was categorised as a 'concealed communist', a member of the CPUSA whose name was not kept on the membership's rolls, and the bureau believed that this omission was due to Weinstein's 'clandestine activities with other communists'. The FBI's director, J. Edgar Hoover, charged the bureau's agent at the American embassy in London to put Weinstein under close surveillance. Despite all the harassment, she kept her nerve and displayed courage at a time when Hollywood featured few real-life heroes or heroines.

After the blacklist collapsed in the mid-1960s, Ring Lardner explained that a TV series about an outlaw [Robin Hood] who takes from the rich to give to the poor provided him 'with plenty of opportunities to comment on issues and institutions in Eisenhower-era America'. Within the scripts for the series there is a significant theme that recurs: the probability that Robin Hood or one of the outlaws will be betrayed, and this would have certainly resonated with those associated with the HUAC betrayals.

Another, fascinating woman who had strong links to both the US and British film worlds is Betsy Blair Reisz. She began her career as a night club dancer on Broadway and then, after meeting Gene Kelly, they married and went to Hollywood. She applied to join the Communist Party but was discouraged from doing so by the leadership who told her she could have more influence by remaining a non-member, and this would also avoid jeopardising Kelly's career. Kelly was, as she defined him a 'social-democrat' but was sympathetic to communist and progressive causes.

Blair won a Best Actress Award in Cannes and was Oscar nominated for her film roles. She moved to France in the 1950s and then to England after being blacklisted. In Britain, after divorcing Kelly, she married the film director Karel Reisz (who had also, much earlier and co-incidentally, become best friends with a student colleague, Peter Worsley, who was already then a member of the Communist Party, later becoming a renowned sociologist (see chapter: The Enemy Within).

Ben and Norma Barzman were typical recruits to the US Communist Party from the intelligentsia during the 1930s and 40s. They were Jewish college graduates radicalised by the Great De-pression. Both were Hollywood screenwriters and Ben worked on a number of films with Joseph Losey. Although Ben was born in Canada, he worked in Hollywood for a number of years before fleeing first to Paris and then to Britain to escape the McCarthy witch-hunt. They had close working and social relationships with leading European filmmakers and actors such as Carlo Ponti, Vittorio de Sica, Sophia Loren, Yves Montand and Simone Signoret, as well as many other leftwing artists and writers, including Picasso. In the UK, Norma also managed to obtain work for a number of other blacklisted writers, to tide them over. While her husband was an established screenwriter, she felt that the blacklist had nipped her own burgeoning career in the bud.

The accidental collaboration between US communist film makers and their British colleagues was entirely due to a quirk of history, which was, at the same time, a very painful experience for the victims of the witch hunt and, for the USA as a whole, a deeply shameful episode. The Cold War and the hysteria whipped up, largely by the United States, in its demonisation of communism, sucked into its vortex the whole Western alliance and forced the rest of the world to 'take sides' in its misguided crusade. A minor consolation for those who managed to salvage something of their careers, is that they have bequeathed us some fine 'British-made' examples of their filmic expertise.

Trade Unions: the Main Focus

*'Those who swim with the current won't change the way
the river flows.'*

The National Unemployed Workers' Movement

As a central tenet of Marxist theory propounds that the working class
is the revolutionary force in society, the Communist Party, immediately
after its foundation, put all its weight into building up its working class
membership and focussing activities on the working class and the trade
unions. Its first big organising challenge arose very soon after its
foundation in 1920: the General Strike of 1926.

The General Strike not only frightened the Conservatives and their
business allies, it also shook the Labour Party and trade union leaders
who were, in those days, invariably very right-wing. The former were
worried that such a mass movement of working people could
jeopardise capitalism in Britain and even usher in a Soviet-style
revolution; the latter were also concerned about being outflanked on
the left by grass-roots action and the demand for more revolutionary
policies.

Although the Communist Party was still very small – it had only
been founded six years earlier, and at the close of 1926 it had less than
8,000 members –its influence was significant, even then. However, the

117

General Strike did not erupt because of Communist Party agitation or influence, even though individual communists played leading roles at grass-roots level in many parts of the country. The strike had been called by the General Council of the TUC, in response to pressures from the grassroots, determined to show their solidarity with the miners who had been threatened by the employers with wage reductions. It didn't really envisage the strike actually taking place, but thought the threat would be sufficient to force the government to reverse wage reductions and harsher working conditions that had been imposed on the miners, 800,000 of whom had been locked out in a bitter showdown with the owners. Some 1.7 million workers answered the strike call, especially those in transport and heavy industry.

Before the General Strike, the Party had already begun to win influence through the grass-roots organisations it had been instrumental in setting up. There was the Minority Movement, aimed at bringing trade unionists together in a campaign for more militant policies and to counter the collaborationist and soft-reformist approach of the union leaders. The other influential organisation it helped create, in 1921, was the Unemployed Workers' Committee, which helped organise the thousands of workers who were without jobs, around the slogan: 'work or full maintenance'. These organisations played a central role in helping to set up local strike committees, picketing and public meetings during the General Strike.

After only ten days, the TUC General Council capitulated, believing that the government and coal owners would be unwilling to make further concessions, and the strike was called off, leaving the miners to fight on alone. It had never been intended to challenge the existing order, and a continuance of the strike would have had such a consequence.

During the Depression of the 1930s unemployment reached 70% in some areas (with more than three million out of work nationally) and many families depended entirely on dole payments from local government. The scheme only paid out according to levels of contribution made, rather than according to need, and was only payable for 15 weeks. Anyone unemployed for longer had to rely on Poor Law relief – a variable sum – paid by their local authority. Millions of workers who had been too low paid to make contributions, or who had been unemployed long term, were left destitute by the scheme.

Wal Hannington, like many of those working class men and women who joined the Communist Party in this period, was a bright boy, but with no chance of a proper education. He was born in 1896 in Camden Town, London into a large family; his father was a bricklayer. Apprenticed to a toolmaker at 14, he joined the Toolmakers' Society during the 1914-18 war, and became a founder member and life long Communist Party member. He and his comrades saw the poverty and unemployment around them and felt strongly that there was something very wrong with a world in which such a situation was tolerated and appeared to be the norm. But unlike those who sought escape from the deprivation by forging their own individual career paths, and by working the system successfully to join the privileged classes, Hannington saw the solution as the liberation of his class, rather than just himself. The philosophy of Marxism offered a ready-made explanation and reasons why poverty, unemployment and social injustice existed; and it also offered a utopian solution to it. The Communist Party was seen as the means of implementing that philosophy. Individuals like Hannington threw themselves selflessly into the struggle, believing socialism was on the horizon.

Made unemployed during the 1921 slump, he helped found the National Unemployed Workers' Committee Movement (NUWM), which organised the hunger marches and other activities to draw attention to the consequences of unemployment. Hannington was National Organiser of the NUWM from its formation at the International Socialist Club, City Road, Hoxton, in April 1921. He spent a number of spells in prison as a result of his politics and activity on behalf of the unemployed.

The Unemployed Workers' Committee was renamed the National Union of Unemployed Workers Movement (NUWM) in 1929 and was to become the largest movement of the unemployed the country had known. It continuously led agitation against unemployment and its effects between the two world wars. It was tenacious and effective, giving it a high profile not only nationally, but internationally too. It was founded by Hannington and led in Scotland by Harry McShane, also a leading communist.

The Party's own makeup in the thirties very much reflected the situation in the country. In November 1930 when membership had reached its lowest level, at 2,555, no less than 845 – a third – were unemployed. A year later when membership again shot up to around 6,000, the majority of recruits were still from among the unemployed.

No one had attempted to organise the unemployed before, but the Party threw its weight behind this new organisation. Throughout the interwar period the NUWM, was the body chiefly responsible for mobilising the jobless and organising resistance to hunger and persecution. The redoubtable Wal Hannington who was also on the Party's Central Committee became its national organiser. Arthur Horner, another communist, was the leader of the Miners' Minority Movement and a renowned figure in the South Wales Miners' Federation.

The NUWM showed incredible resistance to all outside attempts to destroy it – both the Labour Party and the TUC had proscribed it as a 'communist organisation' and it suffered continual harassment from officialdom. Ironically, it gained widespread support precisely because the official Labour Party and the TUC were doing so little to give succour to the unemployed. At its height the NUWM had a dues-paying membership of around 50,000. Its activists would hold open air meetings outside Labour Exchanges or on street corners, standing on chairs or boxes, and, as many of these were communists, they were invariably experienced open-air speakers and their words fell on sympathetic ears. It organised marches and demonstrations to pressurise local authorities to provide benefits on the highest scale. At a time before the Citizens' Advice Bureau (CAB) had been thought of, it also gave vital guidance and advice to individual members on their rights. It was, though, not just active on the purely political level, but put on football matches between teams of the unemployed, brass band events and organised children's Socialist Sunday School activities. On the Clyde it organised children's outings, on one occasion raising over £100 (a large sum in those days) to take 5,000 Clydeside children on a day out to a local park.

The Daily Worker of 20th October 1933 pointed out that 'while the working class the breadth of Britain was looking to the hunger marches, the Labour candidate for the Skipton by-election, [John Percival Davies], said they "got the workers nowhere, they did no good, and only served to make certain people notorious."' And that 'he omitted mention of the Notts and Derby march which had managed to force the local authority to provide "free meals for school children" or how the last Lancashire march "had levered from the most hostile authorities the doubling of children's allowances."'

Interestingly, although it is the Jarrow March that is always mentioned in the history books and it has come to epitomise the situation of the unemployed during the thirties, much more significant and influential were the activities and hunger marches organised by the NUWM, but they have been largely elided from official history. The reason the Jarrow March was given all the publicity and the NUWM movement largely ignored was that the former appealed largely to public sympathy and government compassion whereas the latter was making concrete demands. During the period 1929-36 five such large hunger marches to London from the depressed areas were organised by the NUWM, the largest in 1932. It is clear that the relentless struggle by the NUWM did manage to secure considerable concessions from government as well as changes to government policy which would not have been forthcoming without such a strong and well-organised national movement.

In 1932 Welsh miners' leader Arthur Horner and 28 comrades were sent to prison on a charge of 'unlawful assembly and incitement to riot' for trying to prevent the eviction of a worker from his home in Maerdy for rate arrears. Horner was given the harshest sentence of 15 months' hard labour. In November Wal Hannington was given three months for a speech 'likely to cause disaffection among London police' and in December renowned trade union organiser, Tom Mann, was arrested for 'disturbing the peace' in connection with his work on behalf of the NUWM.

Again, in 1933, a number of leaders of the Wales NUWM were arrested under a 14th century Gagging Act and were summonsed for taking collections on behalf of hunger marchers and making speeches 'likely to provoke a breach of the peace'. Among those arrested was Lewis Jones, later to become a well-known novelist, and local councillor Jim Thomas.[40] Miners in the country were based largely in tightly-knit communities and were traditionally very militant as a response to the harsh working conditions, poor pay and intransigent owners. In 1932 more that half of all British communists lived in the Scottish and South Wales coalfields. Three places with particularly high concentrations of communists who dominated local politics, were known as 'Little Moscows': Maerdy in the Welsh Rhondda Valley, together with the Vale of Leven and Fife in Scotland.

Despite hostility at national level by the Labour Party and TUC, the big march on London in 1932 experienced warm welcomes en route from both trade union and Labour Party members in the towns through which it passed. It did however suffer continuous police harassment and violence, and these culminated in baton charges by mounted police in London, where many were injured. The NUWM headquarters was later raided and four of its leaders – Wal Hannington,

Sid Elias, Emrys Llewellyn and Tom Mann – were all arrested. By the time the hunger marches of 1934 and '36 had taken place the police became more restrained – the authorities probably realising that such harass-ment and brutality were counter-productive. For the 1936 march a crowd of over a quarter of a million was present in Hyde Park to welcome it.

In January 1935 the government introduced much harsher terms for benefit recipients, but by February, as a result of the mass demonstrations held in all the big industrial cities organised by the NUWM, it was in full retreat and issued a Standstill Order, which ensured that benefit applicants would not be treated more harshly. The NUWM suspended activities in 1939 at the outbreak of the Second World War and was eventually dissolved in 1946.

There is no doubt that the Communist Party's determined efforts to assist the unemployed and their ability to organise on a national level for meaningful demands gave it a high profile in many working class communities, where neither the national and local authorities, nor the Labour Party or TUC had taken any meaningful action.

During the thirties the Party continued to consolidate its influence in the trade unions, albeit largely at grassroots level, as the union leaderships were still extremely hostile to communists. In 1934 the TUC had issued what became known as the 'Black Circular' forbidding Trades Councils (its organisation at local level) of accepting communists as delegates from union branches. However, the trade union movement itself was slowly changing, despite virulent opposition from the top leadership to communists. This was reflected at the Thirteenth Party Congress in 1935 when out of 294 delegates, 234 were trade unionists and of these 34 were national or district officials of unions and 82 were branch officials.

Organising in industry

Despite its still relatively small size, the Communist Party, by the beginning of the thirties, found itself leading a whole number of industrial disputes, not because it had surreptitiously infiltrated the movement, but because the official unions were extremely tardy in taking any determined action at all on behalf of their members, and communists were setting a more militant example.

In the spring of 1930 there was a big strike in the Yorkshire woollen mills. There, about 250,000 workers – 60% of them women – were working in the mills and many were not in trade unions. The Party made the area a focal point for its activities during the strike. It sent in its best organisers, including two women: Lily Webb and Isabel Brown both from Tyneside. Many meetings were held outside the mill gates, but they were often broken up by the police with considerable brutality and a number of Party organisers, including Isabel Brown were arrested.

Isabel Brown was another of those charismatic women who were among the founder members of the Party. born on Tyneside, she attended the Party's first congress in 1921 and went on to become its National Women's Organiser during the Second World War. She captivated audiences with her fiery rhetoric and inspiring speeches.

In 1931 around 75 per cent of those employed in the country as a whole were manual workers and most Communist Party members came from that section: miners, engineers, furniture workers, building workers, shipyard workers, railwaymen and dockers. In the 1931 general election, of the 26 candidates the Party fielded, five of them were sitting in jail for activities related to helping the working and unemployed poor. In total the Party's candidates received 75,000 votes between them.

Another of the big strikes during the early thirties in which the Party played a leading role was that against the Bedaux system (a time and motion system imported from the USA that was intended to intensify productivity) at the Henry Hope window manufacturers in Smethwick which Tom Roberts, the Birmingham Communist Party Organiser, helped run. There was a six-week long strike in 1933 at the big Firestone tyre factory in west London, led by London Communist, Ted Bramley with support from Abe Lazarus. And the Party was also involved in the leadership of a strike against wage cuts at the Ford Motor Works in Dagenham.

In 1934 when a strike broke out at the big Pressed Steel company works at Oxford, a deputation of strikers went of its own accord to the local Communist Party premises to ask for help; they clearly lacked confidence in the official union leadership to fight for them. Abe Lazarus, the district Party organiser, emerged as acknowledged leader of the strike which ended in victory and with a factory 98 per cent unionised thereafter.

The Party's basic units of organisation had been of two kinds: factory or workplace groups and residential street or area groups. Workplace groups were, unsurprisingly, the main focus, as it was among workers that the Party strove to build up its base. It was very active in setting up shop-floor organisations and building the burgeoning shop stewards' movement into a powerful grass-roots force in order to challenge the, invariably, right-wing and collaborative leaderships.

One of the big campaigns in the engineering industry during the thirties was the apprentices' strike of 1937. Beginning in Scotland, it focussed on demands for better training and pay, as well as job security in the Clyde shipbuilding and engineering industry, and within a week the apprentices there were joined by 13,000 young engineers. Young communists were at the forefront of this movement. After four weeks the employers agreed to negotiate and several had already conceded some of the demands. The movement later spread south to Manchester, Coventry and other big cities.

The Party's main industrial strength had always been in the mining industry, from where many of its leading figures over the decades have been drawn. The United Mineworkers of Scotland, based in Fife, chose well-known communist Abe Moffat as its General Secretary. At this time the miners' unions were organised on a company, area or county basis and each had total autonomy. Communists campaigned ceaselessly for a unified, national miners' union, so that the employers could be confronted with a united force, but this was consistently resisted by the regional officers. There were also the so-called company unions, based on the individual employers for whom the miners worked. These were necessarily weaker than the county unions and the leaders were often putty in the hands of the mine owners. In South Wales, particularly, communists fought such company unionism, and there the communist Arthur Horner played a leading role.

One of the most dramatic struggles against company unionism was in the Nottinghamshire coalfield where a right-wing Labour MP, George Spencer, in agreement with the coal owners, had set up a breakaway union after the General Strike of 1926. In most pits only those men who agreed to join a 'Spencer union' would be offered jobs. Interestingly a similar tactic was used by Margaret Thatcher during the big miners' strike of 1984 when a separate 'independent' anti-strike union was also formed in the Nottinghamshire coalfield and was used quite effectively to undermine the national strike.

The Spencer union tactic came unstuck at Haworth colliery, Nottinghamshire, where the men had voted by 1,175 to 145 to join the Nottinghamshire Union of Mineworkers. The branch secretary at

Haworth was the well-known communist Mick Kane. A strike was called over checkweighting, and the union told the men to return to work pending negotiation, but the owners refused to let them back unless they agreed to join the Spencer union. They refused, whereupon over 100 police were drafted into the village to escort scab labour to the pit. The dispute came to an end only after the Mining Federation of Great Britain (MFGB) threatened a national mining strike. The sequel was that 11 miners and a miner's wife were charged with 'unlawful and riotous assembly'. They all received very harsh sentences and Mick Kane was given a prison sentence of two years, although it was later reduced after much protest. This was yet another example of 'class justice' and the draconian treatment of those who opposed an unjust system.

During the early thirties, the Party, due to its committed activity on the ground, undoubtedly made a major contribution towards building up trade union membership. 'Over one hundred of our members have been presented with the Tolpuddle Medal for recruiting...' the Central Committee reported to the CPGB's 14th congress in May 1937.

The Party's attitude to trade unions had been one of 'revolutionary pragmatism', and the success of this policy can be put down largely to two men, the Party's General Secretary, Harry Pollitt and the editor of the Daily Worker, Johnny Campbell. By 1945 the Party's goal of making the Communist Party an important force within the trade union movement had been achieved. Within the strong post-war shop-stewards' movement, communists were dominant, as they were in many of the lay bodies. The role they played within the trade unions and in the economic struggles between 1933-45 represented a significant contribution to the revival and wartime expansion of British trade unionism. These achievements have been largely ignored by trade union and academic historians.

The impact of the Cold War

The war years between 1939 and 1945 were a testing time for the Communist Party. In those early years of the 'Phoney War' and as a result of the Party's policy, following Comintern instructions, of condemning it as an inter-imperialist war, it was subjected to considerable state harassment and accused of sabotaging the war effort. However, once the alliance with the Soviet Union had been belatedly established, and all efforts were then concentrated on defeating the

Nazis, the Party suddenly found itself socially and politically acceptable even by the establishment. With the successes of the Red Army on the Eastern Front, its profile rose considerably by association. The Party's strong representation in the trade unions at grassroots level was also utilised during the war to help raise production and to maintain industrial peace. The war was hardly over, however, before a return to the traditional animosity and demonisation of communists was firmly back on the agenda.

Since communists were tireless activists in the workplace, they were now increasingly being elected to official union positions and this was worrying employers and the government. The Labour Party frequently accused communists of obtaining elected positions by dishonest means. It was an ongoing accusation that the Communist Party could not win electoral endorsement in national elections, but gained positions in the unions by underhand methods. Prime Minister Attlee underlined this when he addressed the TUC in 1940, where he said: 'Democracy is becoming a much abused word. It is often used by those who have never understood or practised democratic principles, to mean the achievement of power by hook – or more often by crook – by the Communist Party'. Despite this visceral animosity to the Party and its members, communists continued to work with the Labour Party at grassroots level and gave critical support to the government.

Although communists have always been blamed for fomenting industrial unrest, they have rarely been praised for their efforts in maintaining production or in solving disputes without resorting to strikes, particularly during the war. In January 1947, during the coldest winter on record and with coal stocks at an all-time low, the Party sent a congratulatory letter to two members in South Wales for 'their magnificent work in getting nine pits in the Rhondda working emergency shifts on a Sunday'. There was though for a brief period during the war, once an alliance had been forged with the Soviet Union, there was a let-up in the anti-communist tirade for reasons of expediency.

Although the Party gave critical support to the Labour government, it found itself at odds with the government over its plans for nationalising the coal mines. In its Britain for the People manifesto it urged that nationalisation must include 'adequate representation of workers in management and control', but this did not take place. The Party's main gripe with this process of nationalisation was that the Labour government had appointed too many former colliery company directors to national and divisional boards. The Party also baulked at the generous compensation paid to former owners which meant money flowing out of the industry far into the future, and paid by the industry itself, not the government.

Individual communists were, even if offered the chance, reluctant to serve on managerial boards for this reason. Arthur Horner, the Welsh miners' leader, refused to join the National Coal Board when former TUC General Secretary, Lord Citrine left. Abe Moffat, the miners' leader in Scotland also refused a board position. Jock Kane from Nottingham did, though, accept one. Most Communist Party activities were carried out openly and publicly and few communists hid their allegiances, but because of harassment and persecution by the state some of its deliberations and tactics were kept within the confines of the Party itself. However, unlike the Militant Tendency in the sixties and seventies, which attempted to infiltrate the Labour Party using entrist methods, the Communist Party made no secret of its wish to affiliate to the Labour Party or of its role within the unions. To accuse it of 'intrigue' and 'infiltration' was tendentious and largely inaccurate.

Most of the Communist Party's male members had been trade unionists before joining the Party, and it was their work within the trade union movement and their direct experience of working alongside those who were already communists that encouraged many to join. Bill Jones, a communist and member of the Central Bus Committee of the Transport and General Workers Union (TGWU), maintained that, 'Communist strength in the unions depends on their ability to give leadership to the members'.

It was undoubtedly true that many of those trade union leaders closely linked to the Labour Party were often reluctant to lead militant action or to vigorously stand up for workers' rights out of fear of 'embarrassing the Labour Party leadership'. It was certainly untrue, as the right-wing maintained, that communists 'manipulated' their way into union positions or 'sneaked in' through the back door; they had to stand in open and transparent elections for office like everyone else. Also the suggestion that communists thrived on the apathy of the unions' members was hardly something that could be laid at their door; they were among those most engaged in encouraging workers to join unions and to take an active part in union activities.

In the face of such continued attacks, the Communist Party continued to build up its strength in the trade unions and its influence was a continuing worry for the right-wing Labour leadership. In

December 1947, a circular from Morgan Phillips, then Secretary of the Labour Party, was sent to every affiliated organisation and it stated: 'Now is the time to go on a great campaign against communist intrigue and infiltration inside the Labour movement'.[41] But this was a campaign that actually back-fired. Shortly after the circular had been issued, there were elections in Birmingham for the Trades Council executive. The local Labour Party encouraged its members to turn up and vote for Labour Party candidates and oust the communists. In the end more communists were elected on to the committee than there had been beforehand and there was an all-time record attendance of 257 delegates! The same pattern could be seen in elections to other Trades Councils. Phillips's greatest setback was in the TGWU where Walter Citrine was making frantic efforts to undermine communist influence. In ballots for the union's executive council, eight communists were reelected, several with higher votes than previously. Even in some local council elections this policy also back-fired. In a by-election in Spitalfields, East London, a former Labour ward, a communist, A.C. Steinberg, was elected, giving the party 12 councillors in the area.

At the Party's 20th congress, held in 1948, there were 762 delegates whose average age was 33. Peter Kerrigan, the Party's National Organiser, challenged the myth perpetrated in the mainstream press that the Communist Party was controlled from Moscow: '...we challenge any other organisation to hold a gathering so widely representative of Britain's mines, factories, shops, offices, professions and houses,' [42] he declared.

Towards the end of the forties, the country was again going through an economic crisis: wages were stagnating and there was price inflation, leading to rising anger among working people. In the summer of 1948 an unofficial dock strike took place in response to a dispute over 'dirty cargo' money and led to the suspension of 11 dock workers. In the end 30,000 came out on strike on be-half of their sacked colleagues and the government proclaimed a state of emergency. Predictably the strike was denounced as a 'communist plot' although in the strike committee of over 40, only five were communists and 19 were Labour Party members.

Throughout the coming decades the struggle for ascendancy between the left and right in the trade union movement continued unabated and the right-wing invariably used the Communist Party as the scapegoat in struggles over principles. While Florence Hancock, president of the TUC in 1948 used her inaugural speech to attack communists for 'trying to provoke industrial struggles' she was then obliged to award a Congress Gold Badge for outstanding services to the movement to Rose Carr, chief shop steward at Carreras tobacco factory and member of the Tobacco Workers Union, who was also a communist. At the same congress, unofficial strikes were denounced as 'disloyal activism' and a motion to nationalise the steel industry (which did eventually happen in 1967) was rejected on the basis that three of the speakers who spoke in favour were communists.

In 1949, the TUC issued two pamphlets, Defend Democracy and the Tactics of Disruption, in its attempts to counter communist influence in the trade union movement. It characterised communist influence as 'interference' in trade union matters, despite the fact that at this time the Conservatives, Liberals and the Roman Catholic Church all had their own distinct organisations within the trade unions.

The worst setback to the Party came in 1949 when the TGWU – Britain's largest union with over a million members – passed a motion to ban communists from holding office in the union and this was only reversed in 1968. However, the union's then general secretary, Arthur Deakin, was not satisfied with this success, and went on to encourage the government to take legislative action to outlaw the Communist Party.

In 1948, after a perfectly orderly, but huge May Day march, Home Secretary Ede imposed a temporary ban on all political processions in London. The pretext was the 'depleted state of the police', but this hadn't stopped the government deploying large numbers of them to protect meetings by British fascist leader Oswald Mosley who was attempting to resuscitate his party after the war. The ban was re-imposed in 1949 on the grounds that a fascist attempt to march through north London had led to 'disorder'. The traditional May Day march, held for the previous 60 years, had to be abandoned, so instead participants made their own way to Trafalgar Square and, despite their facing continued harassment from mounted police, turned it into the largest May Day demonstration for many years.

Again in 1949 the government sent in troops as strike-breakers to overcome a London dock strike in solidarity with Canadian seamen who had been out on strike. Strikes in support of other workers, whether in Britain or abroad, had been a traditional form of solidarity among trade unionists. However, yet again, this strike was used to heighten the anti-communist campaign. Six out of seven of the strike leaders, including the legendary dockers' leader and communist Jack Dash[43] were suspended from union office.

Even after the end of the war, the workplace still remained the Party's chief focus and target of recruitment. One Irish shop steward in a Coventry car factory recruited 50 new members within a few months. The building industry, now in full swing with the post-war building boom, was another area where the party successfully organised. Party building workers launched a new monthly paper called New Builders Leader and its stated aims were to create one union for the building industry, rather than the several small craft unions that pertained at the time, as well as to win improvements in wages and conditions and a reduction of wage differentials between craftsmen and labourers. It also campaigned for the introduction of direct labour schemes by public bodies in place of private contractors. In the following years that is what came about, with many local councils introducing their own direct labour schemes.

The Party also saw the campaign for equal pay for women as another of its priorities. This fight had become much harder after the war ended, with men now demobbed and replacing women in the workplace. In the February 1946 edition of The Propeller (the progressive rank-and-file engineering journal), Dorothy Coulthard, a communist shop steward at CAV described how employers were sacking women on men's rates and then offering their jobs back at the lower women's rates. This practice appeared to be widespread, and in June of that year 500 women from 22 factories assembled outside the Ministry of Labour to protest, and several weeks later, women from 40 factories marched through London with banners. As a rank and file trade unionist, Coulthard was one of the most active and influential campaigners for women's equal pay in the trade union movement over many years.

Where communists have particularly distinguished themselves throughout the history of the Party is in their consistent and determined struggle for equality and against all forms of racism both in the workplace and in the trade union movement itself. Individuals were often subject to attack and abuse for the stance they took, but this deterred few, if any, from continuing to publicise the issues and to demand justice.

Trade unions remain the chief focus

In 1965 Bert Ramelson was appointed the Party's Industrial Organiser and held the post from 1965-77. He was a remarkable man, the sixth of seven children born into a Jewish family in the Ukraine. The family emigrated to Canada, where Ramelson studied law, before going off to work on a kibbutz in Palestine and later fighting with the International Brigades in Spain, where he was twice wounded. Shortly after settling in Britain in 1939, he joined the British Army and fought as a tank commander during the Second World War, but was captured at Tobruk and interned in a prisoner of war camp.

His main contribution during his time as Industrial Organiser was the establishment of good relations with most of the leaders of the trade unions and a strengthening of the Party's influence within the movement. The late sixties saw leadership elections in the two biggest unions – the AUEW and TGWU – result in a transfer of power to the left-wing in the form of Hugh Scanlon, as general secretary of the former and Jack Jones in the latter. Both were former members of the Communist Party and were still ideologically close to it; Jones had been a secret member, who fought in Spain and had strong left-wing credentials. He left the Communist Party to join the Labour Party, it is believed, sometime in the early forties. Both men were elected with the full backing of the loose broad-left alliance which communists had been actively promoting.

The influence of the Party during the late sixties and seventies in the trade union movement could be seen right through to the Labour Party itself. Communists, through their trade union membership and thus affiliation to the Labour Party, were able to influence motions to Labour Party conference and thus to a certain extent Labour Party policies. Ramelson underlined this role when in 1971 he declared that:

'We have more influence now on the labour movement than at any time in the life of our party. The Communist Party can float an idea early in the year. It goes to trade union conferences as a resolution and it can become official Labour Party policy by the autumn. A few years ago we were on our own but not now.'

The Party's economic policy as developed in its Alternative Economic Strategy during the late sixties was another attempt to unite the broad left on the need for fundamental economic change. It was eventually adopted by a number of trade unions and parts of it found their way into Labour Party conference motions.

The Party had always put its main focus on the working class and trade union movement, as this class was, according to Marxist ideology, the revolutionary force that would lead the country to a socialist revolution. However, working in this area meant that much of the Party comrades' time was, of necessity, taken up dealing with the day-to-day issues of wages and working conditions rather than the essential goal of politically educating the workers and creating the basis for a socialist society.

The British tradition of pragmatism, rather than philosophical introspection or revolutionary militancy, has always been reflected in the trade union movement and political sphere as well as in other areas of society. This makes the work of any ideologically-motivated organisation a difficult if not impossible task.

The Party has often been criticised by the far left for its 'dereliction of political radicalism' and favouring industrial militancy instead. Its trade union 'loyalism' and its willingness to work with the trade union leaderships (the 'trade union bureaucracy') were seen as 'selling out'. However, the Party leadership saw this type of work as essential if it were to be successful in building broad left unity in the trade union movement.

During the sixties and seventies, the Party's industrial work under Ramelson's able leadership was largely responsible for the establishment of unity on the broad left within the unions and this also helped the Party become more integrated into the mainstream of British trade unionism.

During a national seamen's strike in 1966 the Party found itself once again the focus of government ire. As is the case in the overwhelming majority of strikes, genuine grievances among seamen were the reasons for taking action. The strike aimed to secure higher wages in a notoriously low-paid industry and to reduce the working week of seamen from 56 to 40 hours. It was widely supported by union members and, for its duration, caused great disruption to shipping. However, that genuine cause of the strike didn't deter Labour Prime Minister Harold Wilson accusing 'a tightly knit group of politically motivated men' and the 'whole formidable power of the Communist Party's industrial apparatus' for being behind the strike. While there were several communists on the NUS strike committee, and Bert Ramelson was providing active support and advice to the strike leadership, it was inane and inaccurate to suggest that the strike was fomented or organised by the Party. Wilson's intervention, though, fulfilled its purpose by providing the mainstream press with lurid headlines and red-baiting articles.

In this connection, it is interesting what John Gorman writes in his autobiography:

'The idea [so often projected] of the Communist Party as a disciplined, efficient and dedicated force that could mobilise for action within hours, was largely a myth, but there is no doubt that in its heyday the Party could bring experience, organisation and energy and flair to any campaign in which it engaged'.[44]

Probably the most successful of the Party's attempts to organise the left in the trade unions during this period came about with the setting up of the Liaison Committee for the Defence of Trade Unions (LCDTU). It was formed to help counter the Labour government's 1966 Prices and Incomes Bill which was aimed at curbing the unions' freedom to negotiate wages, and as a means of keeping inflation down. The LCDTU was a genuine rank and file movement formed to galvanise the trade unions into taking concerted action to prevent the Bill becoming law, and to protest against any form of incomes policy; it was not envisaged as an alternative, or in opposition, to the official union leadership, but more as a pressure group. It became very effective as an organising vehicle at the grassroots level and was crucial in delivering victories in a series of industrial struggles during 1967-9. Its Chair throughout its 47-year existence was Kevin Halpin, a blacklisted engineering worker, long-time communist and militant activist. The Campaign for Trade Union Freedom was established in 2013 following a merger of the LCDTU and the United Campaign to Repeal the Anti-Trade Union Laws.

The LCDTU also played a key role in campaigning against Barbara Castle's (Secretary of State for Employment and Productivity) 1969 White Paper 'In Place of Strife'. This policy proposal was another attempt to regulate union powers and prevent strike action by enforcing obligatory negotiations and strike ballots. It was withdrawn in 1969 as a result of determined opposition from the trade unions, thus vindicating the Party's position.

The dividends from Ramelson's industrial strategy were, in the late sixties, paying out in the successes of communists in elections to union leadership positions, at national and regional level. Among those elected to top regional positions were John Tocher, Reg Birch, George Wake, Dick Etheridge and Cyril Morton (AEU), Mick McGahey, Arthur True, Jack Dunn and Sammy Moore (NUM) and Lou Lewis (UCATT). Ramelson was succeeded as the Party's industrial organiser in 1978 by Mick Costello who continued to build on his legacy and also won widespread respect.

For a brief period between the late 1960s and mid-1970s there was a lively debate about industrial democracy within the official labour movement instigated largely by the Institute for Workers' Control (IWC) which had been set up in 1968 by Ken Coates and Tony Topham. The Communist Party had no role in the setting up of the organisation, although Coates was a former member. He became leader of the International Marxist Group, before becoming an MEP and then Chair of the Bertrand Russell Peace Foundation. The IWC was, as Seifert and Sibley say, 'a somewhat eclectic movement, stretching from a syndicalist approach to advocating socialist revolution to moderate demands for workers' participation in management structures of private companies as well as nationalised industries.' [45] For a time, during its short existence, it represented an ideological challenge to the Communist Party, as it proposed alternative strategies of struggle.

Another similar initiative was the Lucas Plan, to convert arms factories to peaceful production, which was masterminded by ex-communist Mike Cooley, who had been a member of the Communist Party for many years, but left over ideological differences. His initiative was controversial within his own union, TASS, at the time, although the Party gave it tacit support. The Lucas Plan won considerable publicity as well as vocal support in the Labour Party and in leftist circles.

Mike Cooley was a senior designer at Lucas Aerospace, and chaired the local branch of the technical trade union TASS. His was a radical strategy to avoid workforce layoffs by converting production at Lucas from armaments to civilian products. The vision of the plan was to replace weapons manufacture with the development of socially useful goods, like solar heating, artificial kidneys and new intermodal transportation systems. The goal was not to simply demand job reten-tion, but to design work so that the workers would be motivated by the social value of their activities. The proposals of the alternative plan were not accepted or taken seriously by the Labour Party or by Lucas management and, in 1981, Cooley was dismissed.

In 1971, Tory Prime Minister, Edward Heath, attempted, once more, to bring in legislation to curb union power with his government's Industrial Relations Act. The Liaison Committee for the Defence of Trade Unions again played a key role in the major industrial battles of the period which were also, implicitly, demonstrations of opposition to the Act, which, nevertheless, came into force. The Act obliged unions to register if they wished to have legal recognition and protection. The Party called on unions to refuse to register and to boycott the Industrial Relations Court, set up to oversee the Act's implementation. At the 1971 TUC, despite recommendation from the platform to go along with the legislation, Congress voted against and the motion was defeated, largely due to avid lobbying by Communist Party trade unionists.

The Tory government's decision, in 1972, to arrest and imprison five London dockers under the Act for 'contempt of court' after they had called for a boycott of certain road haulage firms in protest against 'containerisation', led to one of its most ignominious defeats.

The case of the 'Pentonville 5' as they became known has gone down in trade union history. Two of them – Bernie Steer and Vic Turner were communists – and the Party pulled out all the stops to obtain their freedom. Immediately their imprisonment became known, trade union activists and shop stewards began calling workers out on strike in protest, and even the TUC was obliged to threaten a general strike over the case. This was enough to force the government to backtrack. It discovered a get-out by instructing the Official Solicitor, of whom no one, until then, had heard, to order the men's release before the week was out. Mike Power, a Party print worker in Fleet Street, recalls Ramelson giving instructions to call out all Fleet Street's print workers 'by the end of the week', and that is what happened.[46]

In 1974 the newly elected Labour government offered the trade unions a deal whereby it would repeal Edward Heath's Industrial Relations Act (1971) in return for a 'Social Contract' between employers and unions.

The government went ahead, and introduced its Employment Protection Bill, incorporating the concept of a 'social contract'. With this legislation, the Labour government hoped to persuade the TUC to cooperate in a programme of voluntary wage restraint. Bert Ramelson called it 'a social con-trick, pure and simple' and orchestrated a campaign throughout the trade union movement against it. In the end, there was just too much opposition from ordinary trade unionists and the policy was dropped.

Certainly, during the Ramelson era the Party's influence in the trade unions was considerable. Francis Beckett in his book, Enemy Within, writes that, 'In the sixties and seventies the CP gave the unions much of their flavour, stability and sense of direction.'[47]

Upper Clyde Shipbuilding Work-in

The Upper Clyde Shipbuilding work-in, more than any other industrial action, served to refute the charge against the Communist Party that it was only interested in industrial militancy and not in the ideological role of politicising workers.

In 1971 the Tory government refused to give any further subsidy to keep Scotland's shipyards on the Clyde working. This would have meant the closure of most, if not all, of the yards, resulting in massive redundancies. Rather than going on strike – the traditional method of opposing employers' or government policy – the workers decided, on the initiative of the yards' local union leadership, to carry out a 'work-in' instead. Three of the main leaders of the work-in were communists: Jimmy Reid, Jimmy Airlie and Sammy Barr. Reid was the former national secretary of the Young Communist League and it was very much his vision and his leadership which gave the work-in its organisational strength and vision. It is perhaps difficult to imagine today how a localised industrial struggle in the north of the country fired the imagination of many workers in Britain and inspired tens of thousands to support the shipbuilders. Jimmy Reid toured the country to gain support, talking to packed meetings everywhere – I heard him in Ealing at a rapturous meeting of over a thousand at the town hall. Here was a communist who, because of his honesty, rhetorical flare and clear commitment to his community, overcame many ordinary people's deeply-held prejudices about communists. His famous phrase that 'the rat race is for rats not people' struck a chord with many. The 'work in' continued until February/March 1972 when the government reversed its decision not to support UCS.

Bobby Starrett was also one of those actively involved in the work-in. Because of his locally renowned skills as a graphic artist, he became the official cartoonist of the struggle. His brilliant and acerbic cartoons chronicled the work-in with humour and keen perception. His memoir of that time, written in the form of anecdotes and short stories, had a foreword by Sir Alex Ferguson for whom Bobby had painted a mural in the days when he was a humble publican in Glasgow before going on to manage Manchester United over many successful years. He wrote:

'His loyalty to the working class is the badge he has worn all his life. There is no better root for Glasgow humour then the shipyards, but also it is a place to capture the human frailties of a

Glasgow man's enduring endevour and determination, and his capacity to laugh at himself. Bob captures these traits derived mainly from his own experiences.'

This new method of protest was followed in 1972 by another work-in and eventual workers' take-over of the engineering company Fisher Bendix in Kirby, Liverpool, in the face of threatened redundancies and closure. The workers there sent a delegation to the UCS workers in Scotland, seeking advice. After occupying their factory, the workers under the able leadership of convenor Jack Spriggs, a Labour Party member, attached a huge notice in letters two feet high to the railings near the main gates which said: 'Under New Management'. Other, similar actions were undertaken around the country: the workers at the Triumph Motor Cycle works at Meriden near Coventry took over the factory and set up a cooperative in 1977. The Lucas Aerospace plan for workers' control was formulated the same year, and this was followed by the occupation of the Bathgate plant of Plessey Capacitors in 1982, which provided an interesting example of collective action taken by a mainly female workforce against their multinational employer; then, much later, in 2003, there was an occupation of Appledore Shipbuilders, in Devon.

Those early factory occupations very much influenced the writing of the Labour Party manifesto of 1974 which called for 'a radical extension of industrial democracy in both the private and the public sectors'.

Building workers victimised

The Shrewsbury 24 were trade unionists who took part in a successful national strike of building workers in 1972 to back up their demands for better pay and conditions and to campaign against LUMP labour (i.e. unregulated employment practices). In view of the success of the strike action, the Tory government instructed the police to investigate alleged picketing incidents that had taken place in Shrewsbury, where unions were poorly organised and where they hoped they could make an example by arresting some activists.

A whole year later, in February 1973, the first six of twenty four pickets were arrested, under the Industrial Relations Act, tried at three separate trials and six of them were sent to prison. The longest sentences – three and two years respectively – were imposed on Des

Warren, a leader of the strike in the north-west and a member of the Communist Party, and Ricky Tomlinson, later to become a well-known actor, for 'conspiring to intimidate people to abstain from their lawful work' and for the lesser charges of affray and unlawful assembly.

The 24 pickets were split up into three groups and tried in separate trials. This was highly unusual given that the charges against them all arose out of the same set of circumstances, on the same day, on the same building sites in Shrewsbury. Importantly, the conspiracy charges against the pickets were centred on a joint union meeting held on 31 August 1972 in Chester which many of the 24 arrested had attended.

Labour movement protests, in which the Communist Party was centrally involved, at the time of the trial of the 'Shrewsbury Two', as they had become known, focussed on the anachronistic use of the 1875 Conspiracy Act and on the judge's advice to the jury that conspiracy could be proven even if there was no evidence that the accused had ever met together and had reached a decision as a result of having a conversation or had expressed anything in writing – it could be done 'with a nod and a wink'. Throughout 1974 and 1975 there was a labour movement campaign for the release of the 'Shrewsbury Two' but, despite the best efforts of their supporters, both Warren and Tomlinson served their time. John Platt-Mills, the QC who represented Des Warren at Shrewsbury Crown Court, wrote in his autobiography *Muck, Silk and Socialism*:

'The trial of the Shrewsbury Pickets is the only case I know of where the government has ordered a prosecution in defiance of the advice of senior police and prosecution authorities...

Still today, the government is refusing to release official papers surrounding the trial, which many on the left are convinced was government-instigated to 'teach the unions a lesson.' [48]

The period between 1968 and 1979 witnessed one of the most intense waves of industrial unrest for a long time, with a whole series of strikes – both official and unofficial – and thousands of working days lost. These culminated in the public service strikes (in response to the government's unpopular attempts to control inflation at the expense of workers' wages) during the 'winter of discontent' in 1978/79. Largely because of the extremely negative and 'union-bashing' coverage in the media, this led to the defeat of the Labour government in the 1979 election, ushering in Margaret Thatcher's reign and, with it, the eventual destruction of Britain's manufacturing and heavily unionised industries.

The Heath government suffered two debilitating national miners' strikes in 1972 and '74 over pay – the first since 1926. The 1974 one led to the government declaring a national emergency and to Heath's calling an election over 'who ran the country', which he subsequently lost. In both those strikes communists in the National Union of Mineworkers played crucial roles, particularly in Scotland, Wales and in Kent – the most militant areas. Local Party groups also made crucial contributions, particularly to the now famous picketing of the big coal depot at Saltley, led by the young Arthur Scargill. There Frank Watters, the Party's district secretary was able to call on workers from Birmingham's factories and workplaces to support the miners' picket and turn it into a mass demonstration of working class strength. It was the key battle in winning that strike.[49]

Ironically the seemingly terminal decline of the communist movement in Britain coincided with the last great and decisive industrial dispute of the century – the miners' strike of 1984-85. Although the Party and the Morning Star, particularly, gave support to the miners, there were deep divisions within the Party leadership about the wisdom of supporting what some saw as a lost battle and wrong tactics by the leadership of the NUM under Arthur Scargill (a former activist in the YCL and still very close to the Party). Even among communist miners, while maintaining their loyalty to the union and the strike, there were severe misgivings about the way things were going.

Despite the continual accusations that communists were 'infiltrators' or used underhand means to penetrate the unions, the factual evidence presents a different story. Communists offered organising ability, courage and leadership. Only by being seen to be honest and incorruptible were communists able to gain the confidence of ordinary trade union members who were willing to elect them to positions of responsibility.

The unique case of ballot-rigging in the electricians' union (ETU) elections in 1960, in which leading communist ETU officials were involved, was a catastrophic blow to the Communist Party and its reputation. Although the members implicated were subsequently expelled from the Party, the case gave the government and media a perfect weapon with which to hammer the Party. It was, though, the only case of proven communist subterfuge and, although completely unforgivable, there were certainly mitigating circumstances for the action of these union officials. The ETU had, over the years, been able to secure relatively high levels of pay and good working conditions for its members, and the union's effectiveness had infuriated the big employers who were keen to break its hold; in the run up to the election of the big guns of the media were discharged and a concerted national campaign to break the communist hold on the union was unleashed. Fearing defeat in the face of this onslaught, the leaders resorted to ballot rigging. This played straight into the hands of their enemies.

In discussing the Communist Party's influence on life in Britain, there is no doubt that its role in the trade union movement has been the most effective and continuous. Largely due to its efforts, what began largely as a movement of skilled male workers, organised in small craft unions, developed into a much broader-based movement, encompassing people from all sections of the workforce.

The trade union movement's early leadership had been overwhelmingly conservative and protective of the privilege and status of its skilled membership. During the twentieth century there was, though, a gradual erosion of right-wing dominance, accompanied by the rise of communist or communist-backed union officials playing more prominent roles. The unions that, pre-war, had been almost like an integral section of the Labour Party, became more autonomous, more determined to protect their members' interests, even if that meant in opposition to Labour government policy. This change came about largely as a result of communist pressure and an increase in the number of left-wingers in union leaderships.

Communists were also very much a driving force behind the union amalgamations that took place during the sixties and seventies, in order to consolidate their strength and provide a more effective tool to combat the power of the employers. However, running parallel to that process was the government's new determination to curb union power.

Under Margaret Thatcher's governments during the seventies the country experienced a steady destruction of Britain's manufacturing base and the disintegration of those traditional working class communities associated with it. This was accompanied, almost automatically, by a parallel decline in trade union power and with it the Communist Party and its influence.

The relationship between the Communist Party and the trade unions has been an often stormy and uneasy one. While the Party saw the trade unions as central to any potential socialist transformation of society and the working class as its true base, the trade union leaderships, particularly during the first half of the 20th century, viewed communists as irritating and disruptive outsiders. It was a long, hard struggle for communists to gain recognition and widespread respect for their efforts. Undoubtedly the chief role communists played was to encourage a more militant defence of workers' wages and working conditions, and indeed in those industries where they were most active and influential wages and conditions were invariably better than elsewhere. In its attempts to reinforce a genuine class consciousness among working people and to promote a Marxist understanding of class relationships and the workings of capitalism it has had little success. The working class has invariably been prepared to fight for pragmatic bread-and-butter demands but rarely for abstract concepts of radical social change.

During virtually the whole of the 20th century the Communist Party gave leadership and spearheaded a continuous attempt to ensure working people were properly represented and their interests addressed. Party activists were invariably among the most effective organisers of industrial and economic struggles.

The Party fought relentlessly against restrictions on unions' freedom to organise and for an extension of rights at work. While it was in many specific cases successful in these efforts, it has to be recognised that in the long term it has failed. In today's Britain working people have fewer rights at work than many of their European counterparts and the restrictions on trade unions' freedom to organise are the most draconian in Western Europe. It needs to be stressed, though, that the failure to consolidate trade union achievements and to build on those of the post-war Labour government has not been the fault of the Communist Party, but more that of an over-cautious or pusilanimous Labour Party and TUC.

Hundreds of communists have worked in various rank and file capacities within the official trade union movement, over the years, many making exemplary contributions to the ongoing struggle for rights at work, but their names are too many to list here. They readily took on the work of representing their work colleagues and, to use a cliche, which is nevertheless apt, were prepared to put their heads above the parapet when others preferred to keep theirs down. They were always the first in the firing line when redundancies were made, and were otherwise victimised because of their activist role. A number of them, though, did go on to occupy leading positions at national and regional levels, and hundreds at local level in all of Britain's trade unions, particularly before the big union amalgamations of the latter part of the twentieth century. The following are some of the best known: Ken Gill (General Secretary of DATA, then AEW-TASS, later to become the first communist Chair of the TUC General Council), Harry Francis (General Secretary of the Musicians' Union), Arthur Horner (General Secretary of the NUM), John Horner (General Secretary of the FBU) Laurie Sapper (General Secretary of the Association of University Teachers), George Guy (General Secretary of the National Union of Sheet-metal Workers, Coppersmiths, Heating and Domestic Engineers, and he also served on the TUC General Council), Bob Crowe (RMT), Frank Haxell (General Secretary ETU), Ken Brett (Assistant General Secretary of the AEU), Bill Ronksley and Alex Gordon (both presidents of train drivers union ASLEF), Graham Stevenson (a member of the Executive of TGWU/Unite and President of the European Transport Workers Federation), Reg Birch and Jimmy Airlie (both members of the National Executive of the AEU); the following all became presidents of their unions: Max Morris and Marian Darke (NUT), Dave Bowman (NUR), Harry Landis (Equity), Anita Halpin (NUJ), Eric Paice (Screen Writers' Guild), Ralph Bond (Vice-President of ACTT). Others edited union national journals: Ken Sprague, followed by Mike Pentelow (TGWU/Unite), Paul Olive and David Whitfield (NALGO/UNISON), Peter Avis (ACTT), Nick Wright (RMT), Gus Brain (UCATT), and Jim Tait (Scottish NUM). In addition there were general secretaries like Alan Sapper (ACTT), Ray Buckton (ASLEF) and Ken Cameron (FBU) who were all very close to the Party.

It is also worth being reminded that although TUC leaderships continuously railed against communist influence in the unions, they relied on Party members very much to recruit and to serve as lay activists at grassroots level.

Of the thousands of trade unionists who have at one time been members of the Communist Party, it is impossible to choose one or even several quintessential individuals to represent them all. But I have selected one who perhaps best exemplifies those qualities that characterised a generation of self-educated workers, particularly during the first half of the 20th century, who were passionate about knowledge, as well as committed to the struggle for justice and workers' rights. He will have to stand in for all the others.

Eddie Frow was born into a farming family in Lincolnshire in 1906, then served his time as a toolmaker in Wakefield, where, among the workers there he met a number of older socialists, and very soon found himself drawn to the ideas of communism.

In 1924, after reading Lenin's book, State and Revolution, he joined the Communist Party and remained a member until the 1980s. Moving across the Pennines, he rapidly made his mark on the party in Lancashire and in 1930, still only 24, was sent to Moscow to work with the Communist International.

Although a highly skilled worker, it was inevitable that a 'Bolshy' worker like Eddie would find it almost impossible to find work in those years of mass unemployment. This enforced 'idleness' gave him time to devote to politics and to reading. He became active in the Salford Unemployed Workers' Movement, and in October 1931, he received a broken nose and a five-month prison sentence after being involved in a confrontational demonstration with the police, later dubbed the Battle of Bexley Square. The event provided the novelist Walter Greenwood with a template for an episode described in his 1933 novel, Love on the Dole. In it, Eddie is portrayed as 'a finely featured young man... heaping invective upon all with whom he disassociated himself in the social scale'. Kevin Morgan, in his obituary of Eddie Frow, writes:

'In later years, he may perhaps have lost a little of his youthful intransigence, but never the passion for social justice that underlay it. With the beginnings of economic recovery in the mid-1930s, Frow resumed work in the engineering industry and until his retirement in 1971, his main activities were focused on his trade union, the Amalgamated Engineering Union. As a shop floor activist, a shop stewards' convenor, an AEU national committee and TUC delegate and eventually a full-time union district secretary, there was little in the world of engineering trade unionism with which he did not become acquainted. As a succession of oral historians can testify, few could expound as lucidly as he on the dynamics and constraints of industrial militancy. Books, that were to become his passion, soon took over his life. Whatever he did, there were always books involved, and he also developed a fervour for working-class education. In his teens, already secretary to Wakefield Labour College, Eddie began wrestling with the new world of Marxist ideas, Lenin's Materialism and Empirio-criticism causing him a particularly furrowed brow. Increasingly, though, it was British working class and radical history that occupied his thoughts. When he met Ruth, his wife-to-be, in the 1950s, they eyed up each other's bookshelves and this meeting of minds and spirits led to a memorable, life-long partnership. These were the days, before E.P. Thompson's The Making of the English Working Class and the academic vogue for labour history. Trailing round England with a tent, later a caravan, the Frows were thus able to scour book-shops countrywide for the bargains that radical literature then provided. By the late 1960s their book-lined house in Old Trafford was acquiring a semi-legendary status, encouraging the further building up of their collections through donations and bequests. Many distinguished historians will have warm memories of the library, but there wasn't a student, political activist or trade union branch that didn't receive exactly the same welcome. In the library itself, now housed and maintained by Salford City Council as the Working Class Movement Library that tradition lives on. With Frow's death, we lost one of the last and finest representatives of an extraordinary generation of working-class autodidacts and agitators. His library survives as a memorial both to the man himself and to the rich plebeian culture which produced him.' [50]

Edmund Frow and his wife Ruth will best be remembered as the founders of that Working Class Movement Library, which is a fitting legacy of their life and work and is, still today, a valuable resource for academics and others researching working class history.

The Daily Worker and the Morning Star

*'If you don't read the newspaper, you're uninformed. If
you read the newspaper, you're mis-informed.'*

MARK TWAIN

It was Lenin who stressed the vital need for a newspaper to put forward
communist ideas and to help educate the workers. He knew that an
organisation could never communicate its ideas to a wide section of
the population without its own journal. Of course, there had been a
strong tradition already in Britain of political leaflets, pamphlets and
newspapers produced by radical groups and organisations, these
flourished particularly during the Chartist campaigns in the mid and
late 19th century.

Immediately after the Party was founded in 1920, the aim of
publishing its own newspaper became a priority. The new weekly
paper called The Communist was launched and publication began
on 5 August 1920, just four days after the completion of the
convention which founded the Communist Party, and publication
continued without interruption until its 131st issue, on 3 February
1923. It was in many ways a direct continuation of the British Socialist
Party's The Call, retaining the same look and style, the same editor, and
even continuing the serialisation of articles begun in the earlier
publication. Its first editor was Fred Willis, former editor of the BSP's
weekly, assisted by Raymond Postgate.[51] It was replaced by the

Workers' Weekly, established in February 1923, which was the first
official newspaper of the CPGB. That publication was succeeded by
Workers' Life in January 1927, following a successful libel action
against the paper by J. H. Thomas MP. Workers' Life was in turn
replaced by the Daily Worker in early January 1930.

The decision to launch a daily newspaper was not taken without
heated debate in the Party. Many members thought it a foolhardy
undertaking under British circumstances. To launch a national paper,
even in those days, cost an enormous sum of money. The failure of the
Labour movement to maintain its own daily and the financial collapse
of the Daily Chronicle, a left-leaning, Liberal paper, with a circulation
of 900,000, were certainly not good auguries.

The first Communist Party daily newspaper was the Daily Worker,
and it was launched towards the end of December 1929. The first issue
was planned to come out on January 1st 1930. Its first editor was
William 'Bill' Rust, later to be replaced by Johnny Campbell.

The launch went ahead under almost unimaginably adverse
circumstances. That first issue was produced in a grimy and dingy east
London office by candlelight and in freezing temperatures, three days
later than planned, on January 4th 1930. The Daily Herald rang the
paper on the day of its first issue and asked if it were true that it
wouldn't be coming out again. It and its successor title the Morning
Star have now been going continuously for over eight decades.

Its first editorial board consisted of the journalist Walter Holmes
who had worked on the Daily Herald and been editor of the Sunday
Worker alongside Tom Wintringham, an Oxford educated writer and
poet; others were Frank Brennan Ward, a former miner from Durham,
Bill Shepherd, a woodworker, and one woman, Kay Beauchamp, a
former teacher, who was put in charge of the Women's Page. The
paper's launch was greeted outside the Party with widespread
scepticism, few believing it would last beyond its first edition.

Immediately the first issue was published it faced attacks, harassment
and suppression. The Times led the onslaught and demanded
immediate government action against this 'flagrant piece of Bolshevik
propaganda'. Three and half weeks later when it became clear that the
Daily Worker was not going to die a premature death, concrete steps
were taken to throttle it. The Provincial Wholesalers Federation (that
distributed most newspapers) took the decision to boycott it –
undoubtedly action that was not legally enforceable – but it meant that
the paper had to set up its own distribution system. Any other paper

would have folded within weeks in the face of such a boycott. However, what it did achieve was to help establish close and unbreakable ties between the paper and its readers. The selling of the Daily Worker became a regular task for the Party members.

The wholesalers' boycott lasted 12 years, but when it failed to kill the paper, other methods were instituted. Police raids, censorship and libel suits followed and members of its staff were jailed. Already in the summer of 1930 the paper was in the High Court charged with contempt. The paper's business manager received a sentence of 9 months in prison and two partners involved in publishing the paper were also sentenced.

Despite these problems, after an encouraging start, the paper settled down to a stable circulation of about 11,000 – nowhere near as much as hoped for, but a good base to build on. By the end of 1932 it had achieved a circulation of 20,000, with 30,000 on Fridays and 46,000 on Saturdays.

By 1934 the paper was beginning to recruit some talented journalists like the legendary Claud Cockburn, and Wilfred Willett,[52] the naturalist and communist, who wrote the weekly Nature Notes, and there were regular articles by the renowned scientist J.B.S. Haldane[53] and others.

By 1935 daily circulation was 30,000 with weekend sales of up to 100,000. It functioned as a mobilising force, not only for the Party, but for working people everywhere, keeping them up-to-date with what was happening on the industrial front in the country and covered international affairs very differently from the mainstream press. Many, who were far from being communists, read the paper because it was virtually the only way of finding out what was really happening in the workplaces and the trade unions. It was a paper that made no effort to hide the seriousness of its content, its educational aims or its politics.

Despite its relatively tiny circulation the authorities regarded the paper as a dire threat. Throughout the thirties the paper was subjected to continuous police surveillance, numerous court cases and the arrest and imprisonment of its staff. It was for this reason that, at the time, the name of the chief political editor was never made public.

In September 1931 the paper was again prosecuted under the Incitement to Mutiny Act, over its support for the Invergordon mutineers (see chapter: The 'Enemy Within'). The police raided the paper's office and censorship was imposed by the police. Two leading members, Frank Priestly and Frank Paterson were arrested – both had already served prison terms on behalf of the paper – Paterson received two years in prison and Priestly three years penal servitude. On the night of the police raid two thousand workers marched on the office in east London in solidarity with the paper. From then on it was under constant surveillance by Special Branch, which scrutinised every person who went into the office. The paper's staff were hauled up to face legal proceedings on a regular basis over the following years. Kay Beauchamp, managing director, of Utopia Press, which printed the paper, spent five months in prison after being unable to pay a fine imposed, once again, for the paper's 'contempt of court'.

After the paper moved its base to Cayton Street in 1934, the staff would regularly use the local Eagle pub. The paper's columnist, Claud Cockburn[54] wrote that, 'there were rarely less than three plain-clothes men from the CID putting their whisky down to expenses' sitting in the pub with ears pricked to pick up any subversive comments in the conversations.[55]

In 1942, the wholesalers' ban on distributing the Daily Worker was finally lifted. Throughout the intervening 12 years, it had relied on its readers, many Party members, to take on the distribution burden. Even now that it no longer faced a wholesalers' boycott, party members still engaged in massive door-to-door and street sales of the paper. Weekend sales averaged 49,000 in addition to the daily sales figures. This compares with the Party's then membership of 35,671, around half of which was concentrated in London, Wales and Scotland alone.

On top of the wholesalers' boycott, there has been a continuous boycott by advertisers, with the consequence that the cover price and donations have to cover publishing and printing costs. All other newspapers are sustained largely by their advertising revenues and can thus hold their cover prices down.

The paper's news reporting had, from the very beginning, been characterised by a strong coverage of international issues, particularly colonial and imperial affairs. Already in the early thirties, the paper was waging a campaign against Japanese warmongering in China, reporting on the terrible bombardment of Shanghai and calling for a ban on weapons shipments to Japan. Few other papers were covering this brutal colonial war. The paper had its own war correspondent, Walter Holmes, in Shanghai, and he later reported from Abyssinia on Mussolini's invasion of that defenceless country in 1935. It argued that these events presaged a rise of fascism and of a new world war. It was already sounding a warning that the world economic crisis was giving birth to fascism and that the German ruling class was preparing to bring Hitler to power. Such suggestions were either poo-poohed or the fascists given outright support by their allies and apologists in the country, like Lord Rothermere in the Daily Mail who wrote in 1933 that, 'Hitler has converted a despondent and embittered nation into one radiant with hope and enthusiasm' and even the Labour-supporting Daily Herald consoled its readers by telling them that the Nazis were really 'socialists' as well as 'nationalists' and would challenge big business and landlords!

In 1936, the paper became the clarion of the movement to stop Mosley and his fascists from marching through London's East End. Under the headline; 'They Shall Not Pass!' it took up the baton and helped rouse opposition to Mosley. The response was so enormous that it is estimated that a quarter of a million people gathered at Aldgate and Cable Street to prevent Mosley marching. The Labour Party had advised people to 'stay indoors'! After the police failed to open the way for the fascists to march and Mosley was forced into an abject retreat, his journal later said 'the government had openly surrendered to Red terror'. Members of his blackshirt organisation later attacked the offices of the Daily Worker, damaging cars and breaking a window, but vigilant staff prevented any further damage.

In 1937, the paper was again in court for publishing details of correspondence between the Economic League[56] and the TUC. The correspondence revealed apparent assistance the League had been giving to leading Labour Party and trade union figures to help them in their fight against communists.

At a time when all daily newspapers were communicators of lightweight news, gossip and entertainment (as is still very much the case today), the Daily Worker pioneered the use of features on science in order to help educate and popularise scientific endeavour. Its chief feature writer on science was J.B.S. Haldane, whose columns attained great popularity among its readership. It did something similar also with its coverage of the arts, literature and social issues in an attempt to make the paper not only a paper with news but also an educational journal. In one of his columns in 1939, Haldane wrote about uranium and how nuclear energy could be harnessed for human good, but he also added, prophetically, that 'doubtless uranium will be used for killing in some way'.

By 1939, the Daily Worker was riding a wave of popularity, largely because of its clear anti-fascist campaigns. In April of that year it announced that it had gained 10,000 new readers in the first three months of the year. On the basis of increased contributions it was able to invest in a new rotary press which would speed up printing and make possible several editions. A new editorial board was established with some notable personalities on it, including professor Haldane as Chair, the Irish playwright Sean O'Casey, R. Page Arnot, the writer and Marxist scholar, and Councillor Jack Owen, a veteran militant engineer. However the Chair of the new editorial board felt obliged to issue a statement immediately accusing the authorities of going to systematic lengths by using the police to intimidate sellers of the paper on the streets and newsagents who stocked it.

On May 1st the first edition was printed on the new press. Even Gracie Fields, the nation's favourite music hall star, sent a good luck message to the editor: 'Reit good luck to t'DailyWorker – reit good luck, laad.Tell 'em I'll be reit glad when there's more work i' Lancashire'.[57]

In that same year the paper mounted a concerted campaign for the removal of Neville Chamberlain and his fellow appeasers from government and for a new government determined to combat fascism. It announced a 'Crusade for the Defence of the British People'. Undoubtedly this campaign found ready support and helped speed Chamberlain's eventual departure from office. The paper gave full support to Sir Stafford Cripps's People's Petition campaign warning of the war danger and in defence of living standards. At the same time, Chamberlain continued negotiating with Hitler and was, in fact, actively collaborating with the Nazis.The paper called for the formation of a new government headed by Attlee and wrote: 'The house is burning, and the Fire Brigades are in league with the fire-raisers who are only interested in drawing the insurance – which for them means the establishment of fascism in Britain'.

In late 1940, the paper was again leading a national campaign, this time for the setting up of a 'People's Convention to demand a people's government and a people's peace'.While this movement was gathering strength the demands in Parliament by right-wing MPs for the paper's suppression were becoming more vocal. In spite of the paper's support of the Nazi-Soviet pact, its influence was still strong and throughout 1940 it was causing the government acute embarrassment by campaigning against Keynes's 'deferred pay' scheme, which was then withdrawn, it also campaigned on the seven day week and the Factory Acts, arguing that munitions output would drop, which was later admitted and the Acts were amended; and it continued to campaign for proper protective measures for civilians and to force the opening of the tube stations as air-raid shelters.

In early January 1941, Home Secretary Herbert Morrison issued a formal ban on the paper under the Defence Regulations. That same evening, a posse of Special Branch men descended on the paper's offices, supported by uniformed policemen who surrounded the building. All papers and documents were seized and the paper's printing press sequestered for 20 months. Never before in British history had a newspaper been kept out of action for so long by a mere ministerial diktat – the ban was only lifted in September 1942.

Perhaps unsurprisingly the ban brought the paper a wider sympathy throughout the country. It was felt that direct suppression of a newspaper was not the 'British way of doing things'. Leading MPs and personalities demanded an end to the ban, including Bernard Shaw, H.G. Wells, the Bishop of Bradford, J.B. Priestley, Augustus John, professor Barriedale Keith, an eminent authority on constitutional law, and Lord Ponsonby. Shaw wrote that the Daily Worker and The Week 'were suppressed, not for saying the things that all other papers were saying as well, but for very wisely grasping that a good understanding with Russia is all-important to us, for a war between the USSR and the British Commonwealth would make every intelligent Briton a defeatist'.[58] Even Lloyd George was infuriated and stated that 'the continued suppression of the Daily Worker is an act of stupid and wanton partisan spite and of sheer despotism. No wonder there still remains a trace of suspicion in Russia as to the wholehearted genuineness of our cooperation'.

To get around the ban, the paper's staff began issuing a daily news bulletin under the title Industrial and General Information, with the aim of maintaining a link with its readership. Very soon after the ban had come into force, in that same year, 1941, the offices publishing the new bulletin were also raided and searched but nothing transpired. The success of this bulletin, was also, in large part, due to the fact that the publishers were able to make good use of the Daily Worker's many 'worker correspondents' who were the paper's invaluable 'eyes and ears' on the factory floor. The staff journalists were then able to work up these reports from around the country's industrial heartlands and produce excellent stories that no other paper was able to.

Although the ban was originally imposed ostensibly because of the Communist Party's objection to the 'Phoney War', it was kept in place for a further 14 months after the Party changed its policy to one of support for the war, once it became clear that the government was willing to collaborate with the Soviet Union to defeat Hitler fascism. No specific charge was ever made against the paper and it was not brought to trial.

Once the ban had been lifted and the paper was rolling off the presses again, it immediately returned to its outspoken campaigning. One of the big issue this time was the demand for proper shelters in the cities to protect the civilian population. Then there was the demand to open up a second front in the war. A second front demonstration in Trafalgar Square in July 1942 brought together over 60,000 Londoners to demand action, and a national deputations day to lobby MPs on the issue, became one of the largest mass lobbying events ever seen, with around 1,500 delegates from nearly 350 constituencies.

Despite the paper's support for the war, the government of the day still refused to provide accreditation facilities to the paper's war correspondent, so denying it the opportunity of reporting from the front.

Six months after its reappearance, a conference was organised to discuss how the paper could best contribute to the war effort. In London's Central Westminster Hall 1,169 delegates from trade unions and other organisations gathered, representing a membership of almost 540,000. The conference agreed to add new individuals onto the editorial board: the 'Red' Dean of Canterbury, the Rev. Hewlett Johnson, and the celebrated actress, Beatrix Lehmann, together with three trade union leaders.

The paper played a vital role in encouraging working people everywhere to intensify their efforts at work to help the war effort and speed the defeat of fascism. This was not without effect. The president of the NUM at the time, Will Lawther, noted that 'the redder the pit, the greater was the output'.

With the wartime collaboration between the Soviet Union and Great Britain as well as the extensive cooperation on the ground in the country between all progressive forces in the prosecution of the war, the Communist Party felt it would be opportune to apply, once again, to affiliate to the Labour Party. There was also, within the trade union movement growing support for affiliation. The dissolution of the Communist International in May 1943, and thus the Party's direct ties to Moscow, was also seen as removing an obstacle to affiliation. Needless to say, the Labour leadership once again rebuffed the approach.

History certainly demonstrates that on all the above burning issues, the Daily Worker was correct, but it was a lone voice, even though it vocalised what many people at the time felt. Already before the end of the war, it had been campaigning for a post war government 'of the people' with a socialist programme. With that in mind, only a few days after VE-Day in May 1945, it organised a conference in Shoreditch Town Hall to discuss plans for the paper in a post-war Britain. It was one of the most successful conferences the paper had yet organised. There were delegates from trade unions and other organisations representing nearly two million workers, and they enthusiastically endorsed the paper's proposals. Typical of the broad character of the conference was a friendly and constructive message from the author and playwright, J.B. Priestley, who wrote:

'We want a paper that in size, in improved technique, in popular content and appeal, in its features, its news stories, its sport presentation, its woman interest, and in its art of writing…that in all these things will compete with and go one better than the millionaire Press of this country.'

The most radical proposal put forward at this conference was to convert the paper into a cooperative, and in September 1945 the paper did become a readers' cooperative, the People's Press Printing Society, which operates on a one-vote-per-shareholder basis. Its editorial policy has always been that of the Communist Party – first that of the CPGB and thereafter of the CPB, but control of the paper's finances and elections to its managerial board are rested in the hands of the shareholders who meet annually. This change was made to facilitate the paper's aim of becoming the 'daily paper of the left', rather than just of the Communist Party. It remains the only national daily paper wholly owned by its readers. No individual shareholder was permitted to own more than £200's worth of shares to obviate the danger of wealthier shareholders taking a controlling interest. One of the first to buy his full quota of shares in the paper was George Bernard Shaw, and in its first six months the Society reached a membership of over 14,000 and raised over £100,000 of capital.

In 1948 the paper found itself in a much healthier financial position and was able to move to new premises in Farringdon Road, just off Fleet Street, and to purchase new presses. The first issue of the paper from the new premises was greeted with great enthusiasm. The staff were particularly proud to receive a message of congratulation from the village of Tolpuddle, signed by George Loveless, a descendent of one of the 1834 Tolpuddle Martyrs. The message read: 'Today is a proud day for all of us. That is what our ancestors fought for. Long live the People's paper!'

The Daily Worker and its successor the Morning Star (from 1966 onwards) continued to play a central role in communicating communist ideas, and was read not only by Party members and sympathisers, but by many trade union leaders and Labour Party supporters, of the right as well as the left. It was widely recognised that if you wished to know what was really going on in the industrial arena, you had to read the Worker. The mainstream press either ignores that area altogether or gives it coverage from an employer and government perspective.

The work of the Communist Party was transformed by having a daily paper – it was a cam-paigning and propaganda organ, a daily weapon vital for an effective struggle. But it has only been kept going by its fighting fund which over the years has raised thousands upon thousands of pounds each month to help defray the costs of production. Interestingly, one of its early fighting fund organisers was Violet Lansbury, daughter of George Lansbury, the renowned Labour Party leader, who was a Communist Party member.

What also distinguished the Daily Worker from most of the other daily papers was its in-depth coverage of international affairs. And sometimes this coverage put it in hot water with the government of the day. Its journalists covering the Korean War in the fifties, for instance, were accused of treason – a hanging offence at the time.

When British troops were sent to quell the Malaysian independence struggle which lasted from 1948-60, the paper reported on atrocities committed by British forces. It published a photo of British soldiers holding up the decapitated heads of soldiers of the Malayan People's Liberation Army, decapitated by Dayak head-hunters the government had imported from Borneo as mercenaries. This photo caused a furore in establishment circles and the paper was accused of fabricating the evidence and of treason. Such attacks were part of a regular fusillade the paper had to endure. Sometimes a more surreptitious line was taken, as in the seventies when the security services under Prime Minister Edward Heath made arrangements to have the offices of the Morning Star bugged in connection with the miners' strike.

The paper has consistently supported liberation struggles worldwide. It gave wide coverage and support to the Vietnamese people's wars against colonial and imperial domination. In more recent decades it has taken a strong editorial line against military intervention in Yugoslavia, Iraq, Libya and Syria. It has also continually championed demands for women's equality, for lesbian and gay rights, as well as for all minorities, it has also been in the forefront of anti-racist campaigning. In this sense, on all levels, it has played an exemplary role.

Now that the archives of the Daily Worker and Morning Star are accessible online, it is much easier to examine the paper's news coverage over its lifetime. In doing this, it would be difficult to argue that most of its reporting was false or incorrect. Certainly with hindsight, it also has to be recognised, by friend and foe alike, that the demands made in its pages have invariably been more than justified by subsequent developments. Only in its reporting on the Soviet Union and the communist countries of Eastern Europe was its coverage very often one-sided and rose-tinted, but it could be argued that this offered a perhaps necessary corrective to the bias and distortion in the other direction as demonstrated by the mainstream media.

The last edition of the Daily Worker came out on Saturday 23 April 1966, to be re-launched as the Morning Star, the first edition of which appeared the following Monday, 25 April 1966. An editorial in the final issue declared:

'On Monday this newspaper takes its greatest step forward for many years. It will be larger, it will be better and it will have a new name. During its 36 years of life our paper has stood for all that is best in British working-class and socialist journalism. It has established a reputation for honesty, courage and integrity. It has defended trade unionists, tenants, pensioners. It has consistently stood for peace. It has always shown the need for socialism. Let all Britain see the Morning Star, the inheritor of a great tradition and the herald of a greater future.'

The paper's birthday rally, three years later, at London's Festival Hall in 1969 was addressed by such luminaries as Michael Foot, later to become leader of the Labour Party, and the comedian, Spike Milligan, both supporters of the paper. And it continued to have support from individuals on the left in the Labour Party and the trade unions. Today, it carries regular feature articles by Labour MPs like Jeremy Corbyn, Kelvin Hopkins and Michael Meacher, and many trade union general secretaries also write for it. During Ken Livingstone's London mayoralty, he had a weekly column in the paper.

It has regular articles by leaders of the Green Party, the Scottish and Welsh Nationalists and by journalists who are politically independent. In recent years it has become even more of a broad church than ever in its attempt to be recognised as the daily newspaper of the left as a whole.

The Daily Worker/Morning Star has also been the training ground for a whole number of journalists who went on to establish distinguished careers elsewhere. Many of the editors of trade union journals cut their teeth as reporters or sub-editors on the paper. Others went on to develop their careers with other Fleet Street papers. Noll Scott was one of those.

'He was an aficionado of Latin America, journalist, traveller, boy chess champion and computer expert. He also combined a range of talents in a way that is rare among journalists – he was skilled at newspaper production, an intelligent and thoughtful editor, a brilliant foreign correspondent and regional expert, who was a pioneer in the use of new technologies and who played a critical part in the expansion of the Guardian and the Observer on to the internet. Before joining the Guardian, he spent several years working for Prensa Latina in Cuba. He died at the height of his career in a car crash in Brazil, aged 51... Here [at the Morning Star] he honed his journalistic skills and his political passions took shape, although he remained remarkably free of dogma – retaining his anarchic, mischievous spirit... Before leaving again for his beloved Latin America, Noll Scott developed the technology used to produce the Guardian and Observer digital editions... He was a joy to work with, always in a good mood, and ready to find space for the funny and the unconventional, as well as the detailed, intelligent examination of a place rarely explored. His political interests were in social justice and ordinary people's struggles – a value system which came from his parents. He was also a man of great charm, whose often dishevelled appearance betrayed a brilliant mind and a superb ability to communicate,' wrote Victoria Brittain and Paul Webster.

The Daily Worker/Morning Star's demise has been foretold many times since its first issue, but the doomsayers have been proved wrong. In the face of almost total silence about its existence – for instance it is rarely, if ever, featured in the BBC's round-up of daily newspapers or in discussions of the press – it is, in its own words, a veritable 'daily miracle'. With so many newspapers gone to the wall, others struggling to survive and costs of publishing and distribution continually soaring, it is a phenomenon that the paper has been able to survive at all.

Despite its always small circulation the paper, certainly during the thirties and forties, has had an impact far beyond what its modest circulation figures would indicate. In the pre-Thatcher days when Britain still had a large manufacturing base, it was essential reading for all those, on the left or right, who wished to know what was happening in industry. It has been the only British daily paper to consistently offer a different narrative and perspective on national and international events from that of all the other media. It and its successor title the Morning Star have now been going continuously for over eight decades and is also still coming out. It is struggling, as always, and is still dependent on its fighting fund to survive and no longer has the income from sales to the Soviet Union and Eastern Europe to help keep it afloat. However, at a time when the unions themselves are today struggling for survival in an inclement economic and political climate, it is perhaps ironic that their links with the paper are probably stronger today than they have ever been, and the unions are a vital source of financial support for the paper, as the paper is an ideological support for them.

Internationalism – a Cornerstone of Communist Policy

'For a colonised people the most essential value, because the most concrete, is first and foremost the land: the land which will bring them bread and, above all, dignity.'

FRANTZ FANON

The early anti-colonialist struggle

One key element of communism that has always frightened or discomforted the ruling elites is its internationalism. Communists have always felt themselves to be part of an international fraternity and sorority. This corresponds to the age-old trade unionist motto: 'an injury to one is an injury to all' as well as to the Christian idea that we are all 'our brother's keepers'. In this sense struggles against oppression and for justice everywhere were the natural concern of communists. From the outset the Party was deeply involved in the campaigns for colonial freedom and gave vital support to trade unionists abroad and those struggling for liberation and independence. This internationalism was also a gift for those who wished to accuse the Party of 'lack of patriotism and national pride' and, of course, of being a 'foreign agent'.

The establishment of the Comintern in 1919 represented an attempt by the international communist movement to emphasise international worker solidarity over national and racial divides. The logical consequence of this was also to oppose colonialism and to support anti-colonial struggles.

Because of the Party's overt internationalism and its support for all struggling nations, it is hardly surprising that it became a first port of call for many politically active foreigners and exiles arriving in Britain. They found little sympathy or support for their nationalist aspirations in the mainstream political parties or official organisations.

Already, in 1918 leading figures in the young Communist Party were involved in the 'Hands off Russia' campaign to help stop further foreign intervention in that country. They also immediately took up anti-imperialist work, assuming what they saw as their 'international responsibility' to help organise revolutionary movements in Britain's colonies. The Party sent emissaries, first to India – seen as the Empire's Achilles Heel – where there had been a number of nationalist rebellions in the wake of the First World War. It called for Indian independence right from the beginning, and very quickly developed a strong influence over Indian students in the United Kingdom. Communists could often be seen at meetings on the platform alongside Jawaharlal Nehru, Subhas Chandra Bose, Krishna Menon and other visiting nationalist speakers.

In 1923 British communists took part in a conference in Berlin that set up the Indian Labour Bureau, which began the process of establishing trade unions on the Indian sub-continent. British communist MP Shapurji Dorabji Saklatvala was prominent in the work of the Bureau. During the twenties the Party was already making efforts to establish links with revolutionary groups in a number of the colonies or helping set up such groups. James Crossley was sent by the Party to Egypt and Palestine in 1925 and helped establish an Egyptian communist party. In the same year the Party established its own Colonial Committee. The Labour Party's International Department, by contrast, did not employ a single permanent official to specialise on colonial affairs until 1949.[60]

By 1924 the Party was also already making links with Indian student societies in Oxford and Cambridge in order to establish contact with young intellectuals who would return to their country to play prominent roles.

After the end of the war, from 1945 onwards, there was a greater influx of black people from the colonies to Britain; prior to that most West Africans living in the country had been seamen or students from the colonies. However, already by 1925 West African students had established a West African Students' Union (WASU) in London. In the late twenties it contacted the communist MP, Saklatvala, and also Reginald Bridgeman and his League against Imperialism (LAI) to win support. The Party recruited its first West African, J. Desmond Buckle, in the thirties and he remained a member all his life. In the fifties, he became editor of the Party's Africa Committee's Africa Newsletter. Buckle went on to work for the National Council for Civil Liberties and in the peace and trade union movements. Later, close links were established with the West African Secretariat, formed by Nkrumah (who went on to become the first president of independent Ghana in 1957), and the Sierra Leonean trade union activist and communist politician, Wallace-Johnson, as well as others who were, at that time, highly sympathetic to the Party and to the Soviet Union. In 1947 the Party held a conference of communist parties of the British Empire which, unsurprisingly, came out unequivocally for independence and self-determination for all peoples.

In 1948, Emile Burns, one of the Party's leading theoreticians, organised a class on Marxism for around 40 West African students and in that same year he was enthusiastically received at WASU's annual conference. Several leading young Nigerian nationalists made contact with the Party on their arrival in Britain, looking for support and advice. The Party itself did pay Nigeria a great deal of attention, particularly during the fifties. At this time there was a large influx of Nigerians to London and 150 joined the Party. It was even argued that a separate Nigerian branch should be created. In the end, they were not immediately incorporated into ordinary branches but put into their own special 'Robeson branches'.[61] This is perhaps one of the earliest examples on the British political scene of a 'self-organised group', so in that sense alone it was significant.

On returning to Nigeria later, these young and largely inexperienced ex-students found themselves confronted with a very different set of local circumstances to the one they had experienced in Britain; most very soon settled down to further their careers and put radical politics behind them.

In 1951 the African and West India Advisory Committee of the Party began publishing its own monthly paper, the Colonial Liberator. The Party also supported and helped organise African and Caribbean seamen, especially in Cardiff and Liverpool, where there was a concentration of foreign-born seamen, and a Colonial Defence Association was set up, producing its own paper, The Coloured Worker.

In West Africa itself the communist movement was countered with severe repression by the colonial administration and this was intensified during the Cold War. Communists were hounded out of the trade union and independence movements and barred from government employment. This pattern was replicated in all the colonial countries, thus stifling any burgeoning communist, trade union or left-wing movement.

During the 1929-31 Labour government many Communist Party members were imprisoned for activities connected with their support for colonial liberation. Members of the Party had always taken an uncompromising stand for the liberation of all colonial peoples. However, this policy was not widely popular at the time, as generations had been brought up to believe in Britain's 'civilising' and essentially liberal influence in the colonies, and many felt pride in 'our great empire, on which the sun never sets'. Communists were very much in a tiny minority in their dedication to the struggle for colonial freedom and in their belief that all peoples should have the right of self-determination. They also felt it was correct to give full support and direct help to liberation movements in the colonies. Various Party members went out to India to help build up liberation organisations, where growing discontent with imperial rule was already building up by the twenties.

Most Indian workers were unorganised and some of the communists who went out there attempted to assist in the setting up of trade unions on the British model. Among the first who went out to India were Guy Horniman and George Allison.

In 1928, there was a six month long strike in the jute mills in Bombay in which Indian communists, alongside their British comrades, played a leading role. In 1929 both Horniman and Allison were among 31 trade unionists arrested on charges of conspiracy. Later another Englishmen, Lester Hutchinson, a left-wing journalist, who had offered his services to the trade unions in India, was also arrested. Guy Horniman and George Allison were deported from India, after being charged with sedition. Shortly after their deportation, two other members left for India to help organise the unions there. The latter two were Ben Bradley and Philip Spratt. Bradley was a member of the Amalgamated Engineering Union and on the London District Committee of the Party and Spratt was an ex-Cambridge graduate. They were also arrested and charged, but the proceedings to prosecute dragged on for nearly four years, during which time the prisoners were held in appalling conditions. When finally found guilty in 1933, on a charge of 'seeking to deprive the King-Emperor of his sovereignty over India', sentences of extreme severity were handed down. Spratt was given 12 years transportation and Bradley 10 years. This meant being taken to the notorious penal settlement of the Andaman Islands.

The sentences provoked such international outrage and led to big public demonstrations that, on appeal, the prisoners were eventually acquitted. All this happened under a Labour government.

Even under conditions of tremendous oppression, as in India and South Africa, communists have always stood unwaveringly for racial equality, and this fact alone won them deep respect and trust in those countries.

Another interesting individual, who was very much involved in colonial liberation, was Reginald Bridgeman, mentioned above. He was educated at Harrow and Cambridge and had a distinguished career in the Civil Service. Then, after a visit to India in the early twenties he left the service, horrified by what he saw of British imperialism there, and he began a close association with the Communist Party.[62] He was directly involved in setting up the British branch of the League Against Imperialism (LAI) in 1927, an organisation that played a key role in the early struggles for colonial liberation.

The League Against Imperialism was established at a conference in Brussels in in 1927 with support from the Comintern, but very soon established non-European branches in many colonial nations, from Cuba, Nicaragua to Mexico and South Africa. Indian's future prime minister, Nehru, was one of those actively involved in the organisation in those early years. The LAI immediately incurred the wrath of imperial governments, like Belgium, France and the UK, of course, as well as the Labour and Socialist International (LSI).

It was the first organisation to attempt to coordinate the nationalist liberation struggles throughout the colonial countries. During its existence it included a number of communist, Labour Party and nationalist leaders from Asia, Africa and Latin America. It provided an organising centre to aid co-operation with, and solidarity, between colonial nations. It called unequivocally for full independence of all nations, as well as stressing the equality of all peoples, irrespective of colour or race.

There had been insurmountable difficulties in even organising this first conference as well as subsequent ones with most countries refusing visas to delegates. A number of those who attended its deliberations were arrested and imprisoned on their return home. Among early members of the LAI executive were ILP Chair James Maxton, Labour MPs George Lansbury and Ellen Wilkinson, Reginald Bridgeman and Helen Crawfurd, a leading British Communist.

The second congress was held in Frankfurt-am-Main in 1929. Among the delegates was the Trinidadian activist George Padmore as well as Jomo Kenyatta and the West Indian Marxist scholar C.L.R. James.

In the wake of this congress, the ILP leader James Maxton was expelled from the League for refusing to follow instructions to publicly distance himself from the British Labour Party's 'imperialist' policy, despite his clearly stated rejection of those policies. He described his expulsion as 'final proof of the impossibility of working with Communists while they remain in their present state of mind, except upon terms of absolute subservience to their narrow and stupid ukases'.[63] He was no doubt driven to express such anger because of the Communist Party's very narrow and sectarian attitudes at the time, largely at the behest of the Comintern.

At this congress in Frankfurt, the LAI discussed 'the negro question' and took the decision to organise an international congress of 'negro' workers involving such black militants as George Padmore,[64] Jomo Kenyatta (in 1963 Kenya's first post-independence prime minister and later its president) and others from countries like Nigeria, Sierra Leone and Gambia. Kenyatta became the representative of the Kikuyu Central Association in London and depended on LAI for financial and political support. Both Padmore and Kenyatta contributed articles to Labour Monthly, a Communist publication, semi-independent of the Party itself, but edited by one of the Party's leading intellectuals, Raji Palme Dutt, as well as to the Daily Worker. The League also established the Negro Welfare Association in 1932, with Bridgeman as chairman.

A British section of the League was set up at the House of Commons in April 1927. The Labour Party's Fenner Brockway was one of the moving lights on the Executive of the British section, alongside MPs Ellen Wilkinson and John Beckett, and several communists. Only a short time later, both the Labour Party and TUC distanced themselves from the League completely, because of what they saw as communist dominance. This intransigent position became in many ways counter-productive because the League was seen by most nationalist leaders at the time as the only forum that took colonial liberation seriously.

The LAI was undoubtedly an invaluable help to nationalists struggling to establish viable organisations in their own countries and in providing organisational support and solidarity. The League also gave invaluable practical help and encouragement to African nationalists at a time when both the national and labour movements were struggling to establish themselves.

In 1931 the London Negro Welfare Association (NWA) was founded under the auspices of the League. It undertook community work among London's black population, organising social events such as annual summer excursions for the children. This was at a time when racism in the country was endemic and discrimination against black people the norm. One of its spokespersons was the West Indian communist Peter Blackman who was on the Coloured People's (LCP) executive board and edited its journal, The Keys.

It is difficult to fully evaluate the extent to which such organisations and activities were effective in accelerating the process of colonial liberation, but they did provide a forum for discussion and co-ordination for the various groupings of left-wing and nationalist leaders from a number of countries in the Empire who were actively pushing for independence. The Brussels Congress was certainly seen as the 'turning point' in Nehru's political development, and the durability of the League's relationships with African nationalists are also evidence of its impact. The League also helped mould the political thinking of a whole number of future leaders in the colonial countries.

Its activists were undoubtedly a thorn in the side of complacent government, too, and kept the issues of colonial liberation and racial equality in the public sphere. Bridgeman himself provided unswerving commitment to the anti-imperialist cause, often acting as the conscience of the left and ensuring that it remained an integral part of its political ideology.

The Communist Party, as a central motor of the League, was also seen as a source of vital information for interested trade unionists or Labour Party members about the situation pertaining in those countries making up the Empire, because they were unable to obtain such information from their own organisations. And the LAI was certainly assiduous in exposing the realities behind the widely purveyed image of benign imperial rule.

By pushing the issue of decolonisation and liberation for Britain's colonial peoples, the Communist Party certainly won no popular support, but in fact the opposite: it was an uphill struggle to gain understanding among working people. John Callaghan writes, 'Given the prevailing climate of ignorance and indifference, the communists had their work cut out simply in pressing the issue of colonialism before audiences of organised labour.' [65]

The Labour Party was no different from the rest of the establishment in its Euro-centric assumptions in terms of social evolution and racial hierarchy and was certainly very pro-empire. In its election manifesto of 1918 it could still talk about 'the moral claims upon us of the non-adult races'.[66] Against the conventional wisdoms, the Communist Party insisted that political independence was the only basis on which economic independence could be founded. Party leaders spoke regularly on the same platforms as visiting nationalist leaders like Nehru and his intimate political ally, Krishna Menon, together with Subhas Chandra Bose during the thirties, and it worked closely with Krishna Menon's India League. Menon was considered by MI5 to be a communist and 'serious menace to security'. He later became Minister of Defence and Indian ambassador to the UN, after India gained its independence in 1949.

While unrest in India was spreading during the late twenties, British armed forces were sent out to quell the disturbances and strikes. In response, the Communist Party issued an appeal directly to British soldiers not to allow themselves to be used against their fellow workers. This was, in effect, a call to mutiny, and was a red rag to the government of the day. Predictably, it turned nasty: two communists were arrested and charged with 'maliciously endeavouring to seduce soldiers from their duty' under the 1797 Incitement to Mutiny Act. The Party leaflet they were caught handing out was headed: 'We must not murder the workers and peasants of India'. The two arrested were 44-year-old Arthur Eyles, an unemployed miner and widower with four children and 28-year-old John Ryan, an unemployed labourer. The two decided to plead guilty to the charges, but the judge couldn't believe that they had acted out of pure conviction and distributed the leaflets for no monetary gain; he was convinced they must have had mercenary motives. Eyles was given 12 months hard labour and Ryan 8 months. A similar case came up later in Aldershot, where 35 year old electrician, Edward Thomas, was arrested and charged. He came up before Mr. Justice Swift, a former Conservative MP who had in 1925 tried and sentenced 12 communist leaders on a charge of seditious conspiracy. Thomas was found guilty and given 18 months hard labour.

The Daily Worker's report on the trial was headlined: 'Eighteen months hard labour for fighting war,' and the article described the judge as a 'bewigged puppet' and referred to his 'strong class bias'. For these words the paper was summonsed for contempt of court, and three of the paper's staff were sentenced to terms of imprisonment. This pattern of harassment, arrests and sentencing continued over the years to come.

The Party had, over considerable time, attempted to break down the barriers between 'workers in uniform' and those in industry. It produced a pamphlet The Soldiers' Programme to be distributed outside barracks. However, those Party members who took part in this work were invariably arrested and often fined.

Defending the Spanish Republic

The clearest indication of the Party's strong sense of international solidarity was demonstrated by the thousands of volunteers who went to fight on the side of the Republican government in Spain against the fascist military uprising in the 1930s. However, well before that, in the twenties, a number of working class communists had gone to Russia shortly after the revolution to help build what they saw as the new socialist society

From 1935 onwards the Daily Worker campaigned vociferously for the setting up of popular front governments in Europe to counter the growing threat of fascism. Predictably this call for unity was ignored by the western powers, thus leaving Europe and the world to suffer the consequences.

The election of a progressive Spanish Republican government in 1936 should have been seen as a positive signal, but the governments of Britain, France and others were relaxed about allowing a fascist coup to topple that democratically-elected government, and thus giving fascist Italy and Germany the green light for further military adventurism.

In the summer of 1936 a group of Spanish army officers led by General Franco staged a rebellion against the democratically elected republican government of Spain. To begin with there appeared every likelihood that the Spanish government and the Spanish people, left to their own devices, could have defeated this coup attempt. However, once Mussolini's fascist forces and then Hitler's Nazis waded in on the side of the coup leaders, the battle became a very one-sided affair between European democracy and fascism; it was also viewed by the fascists as a testing ground to see how far the other non-fascist western powers would let them have free reign. In essence the 'non-interventionist' policy of the other Western powers vis-à-vis Spain's 'civil war' gave the fascists a green light for their expansionist aims in the rest of Europe and made the Second World War inevitable.

Spain captured the imagination not only of communists but progressives of different shades everywhere. It was seen as a clear struggle between a legitimate, elected republican government and a right-wing military uprising supported openly by the fascist states of Italy and Germany. Those who supported the republican government realised that the outcome of this struggle would impact on subsequent developments in Europe as a whole. This was borne out with Hitler's consolidation of power and the outbreak of the Second World War. The Party's general secretary, Harry Pollitt addressing a meeting in Clydebank, Scotland at the outbreak of the civil war, prophetically told his audience: 'If you don't stop the bombs falling on Madrid, they will soon fall on Clydebank.' [67]

Between 1936-39 thousands of communists and progressives from around the world formed international brigades to help fight the fascists in Spain. 2,500 of these volunteers came from the United Kingdom, and 500 of them were killed on the battlefield.

Despite widespread calls for Britain and other western European countries to give support to the legitimate Spanish government, they preferred to stay aloof and pursued a strict policy of so-called non-intervention, denying the Spanish government even the right to buy arms or supplies of any sort. In fact many in the British establishment – Conservatives, the Catholic Church, the business class and assorted right-wing groups – were avid in their lobbying on behalf of Franco and the fascists. They viewed Franco, as they did Hitler, as a crusader 'against the red menace', even though there were no communists in that first Spanish republican government. On the left, many realised that the outcome of the battle in Spain would determine Europe's future: whether it would be fascist or democratic. That's why so many volunteered to fight with the International Brigades to try and prevent the country and consequently Europe tipping into the abyss. By far the majority of those who volunteered for Spain were communists – men like Bert Ramelson, Tom Wintringham, Bill Alexander – but there were also a number of Labour Party left-wingers and other progressive individuals who were members of no party, like the writer George Orwell.

Mass meetings throughout Britain were organised on the initiative of the Communist Party, calling for aid to Spain and the lifting of the ban on the country's right to buy the supplies it needed to repel the fascists. In 1936, in London, the Albert Hall was packed with 7,000 people in support of Spanish Medical Aid; in Leeds 2,000 assembled in the Town Hall and resolved to set up a Spanish Aid Committee. The campaign around the Spanish Civil War mobilised probably the most widespread support on such an international issue that had been seen in the country, and it united the Left as nothing had before. It brought together working people, intellectuals, artists and professionals in unprecedented numbers. It galvanised a generation into taking political action on an issue not directly related to Britain as no cause before or since has been able to. There was undoubtedly widespread sympathy throughout the country for Spain's struggle.

Among those Party members who went to Spain there were a significant number of medics, like Dr. Colin Bradsworth, a GP from Saltley in Birmingham, who worked behind the lines bringing out the wounded and treating them, and Dr. Reginald Saxton, a GP from Reading, who stayed in Spain for two years. There were also trained nurses, like Mary Slater of Preston and Margaret Powell, together with Nan Green who served at the front in a nursing capacity; Winifred Bates (the wife of novelist and International Brigadier, Ralph Bates) reported from the front and became personnel officer for the British Medical Aid Unit.

At a packed send-off meeting at Shoreditch Town Hall for a shipload of food for republican Spain, Young Communist League Secretary, John Gollan, informed the audience that the food would be despatched from Southampton and that dockers loading the ship had pledged to donate all payment for the work towards a second boat of supplies.

Spanish aid committees were set up in many of Britain's industrial areas on the initiative of local communists, but although the latter were invariably the driving force behind these committees, the aim was to make them representative and to involve as broad a section of the population as possible.

Of course, the most significant contribution made by communists to Spain was the formation of the British Battalion. One of the first to join the International Brigade was in fact a woman, the artist Felicia Browne, who happened to be in Barcelona when the military uprising erupted. She was the first British volunteer to be killed in

Spain by Franco forces in Aragon in August 1936.

One of the earliest moves to organise a British group was undertaken by two East London garment workers, Sam Masters and Nat Cohen. Nat had previously been deported from Argentina after organising workers there. The British Foreign Office, however, declared the enlistment of men and women to fight in Spain illegal under the Foreign Enlistment Act. This meant that anyone wishing to fight had to make their own way and enter the country illegally. It increased the difficulties for those wishing to help Spain in this way. In the end around 2,500 volunteers managed to reach the country and join the International Brigades, most making the hazardous crossing by foot over the Pyrenees. Around nine in ten of the volunteers were industrial workers.

Bill Alexander,[68] one of seven children of a rural carpenter, became the commander of the British Battalion. Later, in 1940, he was recommended by the 'red' Duchess of Atholl for a commission at Sandhurst, where he finished top of his year. He later served in north Africa, Italy and Germany during the Second World War, rising to the rank of captain, even though the promotion board made it clear they knew his history and political background.[69] In retirement Alexander devoted a great deal of his time to the International Brigade Association, which was set up to commemorate the contribution made by the International Brigaders and to become a source of information and education for future generations.

The Spanish Civil War has been covered by numerous writers, and includes several biographies by some of those who took part. For those interested in reading about this period in more detail, there is a wealth of available material.

**The Second World War and its impact on
empire and colonial liberation**

The Second World War involved the deployment of significant numbers of soldiers from the British colonies who were encouraged to join the fight against fascism and for democracy. Many of those who enlisted and fought alongside British troops wondered if this 'democracy' shouldn't apply to them too and perhaps their own countries should also be free and independent.

In August 1941 Churchill and Roosevelt signed a joint declaration known as the Atlantic Charter, which stated that their countries 'respect the right of all peoples to choose the form of government under which they will live.' However, Churchill afterwards declared that this would not apply to the British Empire.

In late 1941, the Communist Party published a pamphlet by Ben Bradley entitled: India: What We Must Do, calling for Indian independence; the Left Book Club published the book India Today by R. Palme Dutt and Penguin the Problems of India by a member of the Party's Colonial Committee, D. Shelvankar. These books were banned in India by government dictat even though Hitler's Mein Kampf could be found prominently displayed on bookstalls there.

The Indian National Congress had already been actively campaigning for self-rule, but the British government remained intransigent, supported in its stance by a subservient TUC and Labour's National Executive.

Michael Carritt, who worked for the Indian Civil Service, joined the Communist Party over the government's refusal to move on Indian self-government and he kept in close contact with the Rev. Michael Scott, Chaplain to the Bishop of Bombay (later to become a leading anti-apartheid activist and, along with Bertrand Russell, a prominent member of the Committee of 100[70]). The Party's Clive Branson held frequent briefing meetings with leading Indian Communists on the state of the struggle, and the Daily Worker devoted a number of articles to convey a sense of the appalling conditions prevailing in India.

In March 1946, Raji Palme Dutt, one of the Party's leading theoreticians and editor of Labour Monthly, was able to visit India himself although his passport had been marked 'not valid for the British Empire'. There he met many leaders involved in the struggle for independence and reported back to the Party on the ferment he found.

In other colonial countries the situation was not dissimilar. Ben Bradley, secretary of the party's colonial committee, which issued a monthly bulletin, Inside the Empire, commented that measures being taken in India, Burma, Nigeria and elsewhere bore 'all the hallmarks of Tory imperialism'.

In February 1947, a special event took place in London: a six day Empire Communist Conference at which representatives from communist parties from all parts of the British Empire participated. This conference provided a vivid picture of what was actually happening on the ground in these countries. At its conclusion the conference declared that, 'the democratic right of self-determination of all peoples is the cardinal principle of communist policy'.

Although India was a focus, the Party also took a clear stand on de-colonisation in other parts of the world too. This work was co-ordinated through its Colonial Information Bureau, set up in 1937 and, during the forties, the work of the Party's Colonial Committee was much extended. It consisted of 16 members, including Reginald Bridgeman,[71] pre-war secretary of the League Against Imperialism, who had, in the meantime, been expelled from the Labour Party because of his work with communists, the Indian author, D.K. Shelvankar, Desmond Buckle from West Africa, E. Pappianou from Cyprus (later to become general secretary of AKEL in Cyprus), Desmond Greaves a life-long campaigner for Irish independence, Arthur Clegg, a prominent member of the China Campaign Committee, Daily Worker journalist, Malcolm McEwen, Maud Rogerson, a north London activist and George Rudé, the historian and, later, author of the best-selling The Crowd in History.

The Party issued a pamphlet called Colonies: The Way Forward and argued that the victory over fascism presented the most favourable climate for colonial liberation. Today such undertakings and attitudes may sound rather tame and obvious, but at that time they represented still very much a minority and 'extremist' viewpoint in the country. The political establishment, all the mainstream media and much of the population were still very gung-ho about the Empire.

In 1946, while on a tour to the United States, Deputy Prime Minister Herbert Morrison declared: 'We are friends of the jolly old empire...we are going to stick to it'. And, in the same year, Foreign Secretary Ernest Bevin, revealingly, told the House of Commons that, 'I am not prepared to sacrifice the British Empire... I know that if the British Empire fell... it would mean the standard of life for our constituents would fall considerably'.[72]

People from the underdeveloped world, particularly those of a different skin colour, who were the overwhelming majority, were still widely deemed as being inferior to white Caucasians. However, the issue was not only one of colonial liberation but also one of tackling endemic racial discrimination in Britain itself. Again, at that time, such discrimination was widely accepted as normal. When war broke out the number of black people living in Britain was quite small, but as the war continued many more came to Britain, not only from the West Indies, but also black GIs with the US forces.

In October 1943, Marx House in conjunction with the Daily Worker published an issue of its fortnightly journal, Educational Commentary, with the heading: The Colour Bar – A Barrier to Progress. It rejected the argument that white people were basically superior, and quoted professor Haldane's study on the subject in which he wrote emphatically that blacks were not inferior to whites either mentally or physically. It concluded by emphasising that expressions of racial and colour prejudice had to be fought vehemently wherever they occurred.

During 1944 and '45 the Daily Worker continued to draw attention to the colour bar question and it quoted a young, black serviceman who protested about the treatment of those black men, British subjects, who had helped defeat Hitler. However, it was not until the 1960s that the first official attempts were undertaken to introduce legislation to curb racial discrimination.

In 1958 the murder of Kelso Cochrane, a black carpenter from Antigua, sparked the notorious Notting Hill riots in London and laid bare a festering sore of underlying racism in the country. Notting Hill was at the time a stronghold for Mosley's fascist Union Movement and Colin Jordan's White Defence League. Mark Olden, who wrote an investigative book about the killing, cites the Daily Worker of the time, which took a very strong position on the need to eradicate racism for good, and he gives Communists like Claudia Jones due credit for their stance against racism.[73] Also, in his book, he illustrates how the Conservative government of the time, in cahoots with the police and right wing Caribbean Uncle Toms, attempted to smear the left rather than damn the right over Kelso's death.

During the fifties the Party had its own West African branch and West Indies Committee that played key roles in the Party's anti-colonial work. Claudia Jones, a Trinidadian-born communist, who was forced to leave the US because of its persecution of communists, arrived in Britain in 1955 and became an active member, working closely with local members of the Caribbean community. She was elected onto the Party's International Committee and became editor of the West Indian Gazette. As a result of her pioneering work, Claudia Jones received abusive and threatening letters from racist organisations like the self-styled 'Ku Klux Clan of Britain'. She was one of the founders of the Notting Hill Carnival, first established as an answer to the then prevalent racism and as a celebration of Caribbean life and culture. Jones identified the need, as she put it, to 'wash the taste of Notting Hill … out of our mouths' (see chapter: The Struggle Against Fascism).

She suggested that the British black community should have its own Caribbean carnival. The first was held in St. Pancras town hall in 1959. Jazz guitarist Fitzroy Coleman and singer Cleo Laine performed and the event was televised by the BBC. Funds raised from the event were used to pay the court fees and fines of young black men convicted in the riots. Today Notting Hill is far more renowned for the huge street carnival than for the racist riots that erupted in that hot summer of 1958.[74]

As part of her efforts, Jones also brought together members of the black British community, as well as various international leaders, including Cheddi Jagan of British Guiana (the first Marxist to be freely elected as prime minister of an English-speaking country, only to be ousted by British intervention), Norman Manley of Jamaica and Eric Williams of Trinidad and Tobago.

A forerunner of all these Caribbean activists was The Jamaican poet and communist activist, Claude McKay, who came to Britain following the First World War and in 1917 became the first black British journalist, to write for the Workers' Dreadnought, first founded by Sylvia Pankhurst and the Workers' Socialist Federation as the Women's Dreadnought, one of the earliest socialist newspapers.

The Barbadian poet, Peter Blackman, was another leading black communist. He had studied theology at Durham University, but then worked as a railway engine fitter (and was the only member of his NUR branch who could read Greek and Latin!). Being black and a communist meant that a post in academia was virtually impossible to obtain. He became one of the early pioneers of black British poetry.[75]

Winston Pinder,[76] a youth worker in North London, and also originally from Barbados, experienced extreme racism as a young man. He joined the Communist Party to help fight such racism, and played a leading role in the Camden Committee for Community Relations. He was instrumental in setting up safe homes for young black youths in Camden. All these black activists, like most of their compatriots, were subject to a continuous stream of hatred, abuse and threats. Trinidadian, Trevor Carter and Jimmy Barzey, from Montserrat, were two other leading black community activists who joined the Party. Carter was recommended to receive an MBE from the Queen but declined on three counts: Britain no longer had an Empire, his work on the education of black children was not truly valued by the Prime Minister, and he was still a Communist. These black communists often worked closely with other renowned non-communist black activists like Jessica and Eric Huntley, former members of the People's Progressive Party in Guyana, the political and cultural activist, John La Rose, and the educationalist Gus John.

The Movement for Colonial Freedom

The Movement for Colonial Freedom (renamed Liberation in 1970) was set up in 1954 on the ini-tiative of the left-wing Labour MP Fenner Brockway and was actively supported by a number of left-wing MPs like Barbara Castle, Harold Wilson, Tony Benn and the composer Benjamin Britten. Communists were involved in the organisation from its early days and played leading roles throughout its existence and also subsequently after its renaming as Liberation in 1970. The organisation gave strong support and publicity to liberation and independence movements throughout the British colonies as well as to those of other nations. Tony Gilbert, a former volunteer in the Spanish International Brigades, a rail worker and active member of the NUR, played a prominent and courageous role in combating racism and a colour bar in the railway industry during the fifties. He later became a leader of Liberation, where he and his wife, Kay Beauchamp, continued their active campaigning against racism in all its forms.

During the fifties, particularly, discrimination against black workers was endemic in Britain, but Communist Party members like Tony Gilbert played an exemplary role in fighting racist attitudes. In 1955 alone the Party distributed 100,000 leaflets calling for 'No Colour Bar for Britain'. In response to a ban imposed by white bus drivers on employing black drivers in Bristol in the early sixties the Bishop of Bristol's Industrial Mission made a statement saying that only two types of trade union members had opposed the ban in the city – 'Christians and Communists'.

As a knee-jerk response to perceived public disquiet about immigration, whipped up by an irresponsible media, the Conservative government introduced its Commonwealth Immigration Bill, in 1961 (It was aimed at restricting the immigration of black Commonwealth citizens). This Bill was immediately denounced by the Party as 'clearly a colour bar measure'. It became law in 1962 and all political parties, except the Communist Party and other small left wing parties, readily capitulated to its measures.

Leading communist activists on the London docks also strongly challenged those dockers who came out on strike and marched in support of Enoch Powell, after his notorious 'rivers of blood' speech in 1968. His stance had considerable support among certain sections of the white working class. Those communist and left-wing trade unionists who actively opposed such hatred, like the docks shop stewards Jack Dash, Bernie Steer and Vic Turner, were subject to considerable abuse and even threats of violence.

Racism has always been used by ruling elites to foment divisions among working people; the best way to counter demands for better working conditions and pay is to set one ethnic or religious group against another. There are myriad examples of such policies: In India, between Muslims and Hindus, in Ireland, between Catholics and Protestants and in Guyana, between those from an African and those from an Indian background; the list is long. The Communist Party has, since its establishment, been consistently and continuously in the forefront of anti-racist campaigning and struggle.

The Jamaican Richard Hart also deserves mention here, because he has been very influential in terms of helping to educate succeeding generations through his lectures and writing on the Caribbean. He was born in the year of the Russian Revolution in 1917 in Kingston and gained prominence for the enormous contribution he made to progressive Caribbean politics, but also for his work on behalf of the Caribbean community in Britain. Although the Caribbean was the focus of his political life, he also spent long periods in Britain, where he died at the close of 2013 in Bristol.

He became a leading historian of the Caribbean, solicitor and politician. He was a founding member of the People's National Party (PNP) and one of the pioneers of Marxism in Jamaica. He served as Attorney-General in Grenada under the People's Revolutionary Government in 1983. He is also the author of several seminal books on the Caribbean.

He played an important role in Jamaican politics in the years leading up to Independence in 1958, before going to Guyana where he edited The Mirror newspaper which supported Cheddi Jagan and the People's Progressive Party. In Jamaica he was imprisoned without trial by the British colonial government for his political activities.

On leaving Guyana in the early sixties, Hart moved to London, where he worked as a solicitor to a Local Government Authority from 1965 to 1982. In 1974, he was a founding member of Caribbean Labour Solidarity (CLS), together with Cleston Taylor (1926-2010), Lionel Jeffrey (1926–93) and others. He was a widely acknowledged authority on Caribbean affairs and was awarded honorary degrees by the universities of the West of England and of Hull for his contribution to Caribbean history, politics and culture.

Aiding South Africa's struggle for liberation

Nelson Mandela, soon after his release, became every politician's and celebrity's favourite hero. During the life he spent fighting for justice and the 27 years he languished in an apartheid jail only very few such people showed any interest in him at all or were supportive in any way. He and the liberation organisation he belonged to, the African National Congress (ANC), were vilified as 'terrorists' and 'communist subversives' by western politicians like Margaret Thatcher, Ronald Reagan and other leaders of the 'free world'. 'The African National Congress,' declared Margaret Thatcher in 1987, 'is a typical terrorist organisation. Anyone who thinks it is going to run the government in South Africa is living in cloud-cuckoo land.' Just two years after that hardly prophetic prediction, a young David Cameron, then a rising star of the Conservative Party research department, accepted an all-expenses-paid trip to apartheid South Africa. It was organised and funded by Strategy Network International (SNI), a firm that had been specially set up with the sole aim of lobbying against trade sanctions on the apartheid regime.

Only four years later, once he'd become president of a new South Africa, but now too old to play an active role anymore, Nelson Mandela was feted as a dignified elder statesman. He was no longer the dangerous militant; he had become the iconic political leader alongside whom everyone wanted to be photographed.

In his autobiography Mandela emphasises what he and the struggle owe not only to the South African Communist Party and its comrades, but also to communists worldwide as well as to the Soviet Union and Cuba, in particular, for their unstinting support during the hard years of struggle. Many leaders of the ANC were also communists, as Mandela was according to SACP sources, and many were killed or incarcerated for long periods in response to their efforts to build a non-racist South Africa. Communists have always viewed racism not only as a denial of our common humanity but as a means of dividing oppressed peoples, and it should therefore be no revelation that they were very active in helping combat apartheid in South Africa.

What was not known until the recent book, London Recruits: The

Secret War Against Apartheid, edited by Ken Keable,[77] is what sort of secret role British communists played in the struggle for freedom in South Africa.

During the long, harsh years of oppression, many black and white comrades sought exile in Britain, from where they continued the struggle as far as it was possible. But even in their UK 'safe haven', the ANC offices were broken into and documents stolen by the South African secret service (BOSS) and individuals' homes were bugged and spied upon with the tacit connivance of the British secret services. The British secret services certainly co-operated with BOSS and were to some extent complicit. It has since been revealed that the British also spied on the Anti-Apartheid Movement in Britain whose general secretary over many years was Mike Terry, who had joined the Party as a student.

In 1960 when the ANC called on all countries to institute a boycott of South African goods, the Communist Party took up the call immediately and used its strong links with the unions to try and co-ordinate action to ensure that the issue would be raised also at Labour Party conference.

One of those who became involved early on in solidarity work with the oppressed of South Africa was Nan Berger. She was particularly concerned with the situation of black women there, and in 1962, she joined the renowned South African anti-Apartheid activist, Helen Joseph, on a visit to make contact with banned women activists in South Africa. Nan Berger[78] was co-author of the feminist book, Woman – Fancy or Free? and a Penguin handbook on women's rights in 1973.

After Nelson Mandela and other leaders of the African National Congress were jailed at the Rivonia trial in 1964, almost all ANC members who were not in prison or under severe internal restriction were forced into exile, if they were to evade arrest and torture. The problem they then faced was how they could continue the struggle under such circumstances. How could they demonstrate to the South African people that the ANC was not defeated? The ANC's four-man London leadership dealing with underground activities soon found an answer. They began recruiting young, white, non-South African men and women, unknown to the regime, who could enter South Africa without arousing suspicion. These were the 'London Recruits'.

Ronnie Kasrils,[79] (a South African communist and exile, later to become head of military intelligence for MK, the ANC's armed wing, and then a minister under Nelson Mandela and Thabo Mbeki in the post-apartheid democratic government) enrolled at the London School of Economics, where he quickly found suitable recruits among left-wing students, including members of the Intenational Socialists, forerunner of the Socialist Workers' Party. Others were recruited in various ways, but by far the main source was the Young Communist League. A meeting was held (involving the Party's International Secretary, Jack Woddis) at which it was agreed that the London District Secretary of the YCL would play the role of recruiter. George Bridges and his successor, Bob Allen, performed this role, recommending selected members to Ronnie Kasrils.

These London Recruits (who, Ken Keable estimates, numbered at least 60 in all) took on an amazing variety of tasks. Some posted letters or packages in large numbers; some planted 'leaflet bombs' – harmless devices that blasted hundreds of leaflets into the air in crowded places in the big cities, usually during the after-work rush hour – often accompanied by street broadcasts of speeches and songs, using amplified cassette players. Over the period between 1967 and 1971, the London Recruits carried out such activities each year, often hitting South African cities simultaneously. Some arranged for banners to be unfurled from high buildings, with slogans such as, 'ANC lives' or similar. Some smuggled weapons, assisted ANC fighters to enter the country, did reconnaissance work, or carried messages to individuals. In 1972, a number of seamen, recruited through the Party's Merseyside Area organisation, sailed from Somalia on the yacht Avventura in an abortive mission to land MK fighters and their weapons on the South African coast. This was the 'Mother Project', known to the Soviet agencies involved as 'Operation J'. In order to be better equipped in carrying out such dangerous tasks, some of the London Recruits received training in Cuba and the USSR.

Three non-British recruits – Dublin-born Sean Hosey (of Islington YCL), Party member Alex Moumbaris and his French wife Marie-José – were arrested and tortured. Marie-José, who was pregnant, was released after four months, but Sean Hosey served five years in prison (in addition to pre-trial time, including eight months in solitary confinement). Alex Moumbaris, after seven and a half years of a 12-year sentence, dramatically escaped along with two other white ANC members. They had managed to fabricate 14 wooden replica keys in the prison workshop.

Sean Hosey, like all the others who were contacted by Ken Keable

BRITAIN'S COMMUNISTS: THE UNTOLD STORY

while compiling material for the book, had no regrets about what he did, despite his appalling fate. They are all proud of the contribution, however small, that they were able to make to the overthrow of the iniquitous apartheid system, which ended with the election of the first freely-elected and non-racial government in 1994.

As Pallo Jordan (former Minister of Arts and Culture in the first post-apartheid government) says in the book cited above:

'They were drawn from different backgrounds and political formations of the left. What they shared was a readiness to risk life and limb in the struggle of another country. Working in self-contained cells that were unaware of each other, under the guidance of a small unit operating out of London, these dedicated women and men helped the liberation movement to rebuild its capacity inside South Africa at a time when repression had all but extinguished the embers of resistance.'

Besides Ronnie Kasrils. the ANC unit in London that masterminded the activities of the London Recruits included Joe Slovo, Dr. Yusuf Dadoo and Jack Hodgson, assisted by science lecturer Dr. Ron Press in Bristol. All were members of the South African Communist Party as well as the ANC. Hence it was the official relationship between the SACP and CPGB that made the selection of London Recruits much easier than it would have otherwise have been. In addition, most (or perhaps all) of the leaflets that the Recruits distributed inside South Africa were printed by Farleigh Press, a printing firm set up by the Communist Party.

The South African regime was so blinded by its own racial stereotyping that young white people travelling to South Africa from London rarely raised suspicions. The security services were initially totally baffled by the appearance of leaflets and evidence of other oppositional activity in the country when they were convinced they had destroyed the underground ANC.

Ronnie Kasrils, who sent most of the London Recruits on their missions and who wrote the introduction to the above mentioned book says: 'The impact of those daringly subversive actions on rush-hour workers who loathed the apartheid system was electric.' He also asks the interesting question: 'what drives individuals to engage in struggles for a just cause in distant lands at considerable personal risk?' Clearly each individual had their own personal motives; there was also an element of romanticism and adventure, Kasrils admits, but for most, if not all, the over-riding factor was the wish to demonstrate their sense of international solidarity and to help others win justice, just as Byron was motivated to help the Greek struggle for independence or Bolivar was in devoting his life to Latin American independence, both during the early in the 19th century.

'The context,' Kasrils writes, 'was the heady days of student and worker occupations and protest around the world; the anti-Vietnam War; the 1968 events in France; the mobilising work of the Anti-Apartheid Movement. All these formed part of the tapestry.'

London became a centre for ANC activities as many of those driven from their homeland by the apartheid regime's brutal oppression settled there. These exiles, though, were concerned not to jeopardise their temporary residence status by embarking on military training or armed activities. It was in the Soviet Union, Cuba and East Germany (GDR) where the military wing of the ANC (Umkhonto we Sizwe) obtained its training. The ANC's monthly journal Sechaba was printed and published in the GDR and became a vital instrument of international mobilisation and an organising tool.

These are just some of the many examples of the role played by communists in assisting and supporting liberation struggles in other countries. I am unable to enumerate every individual by name or detail the roles each played, but such information can be found in the many autobiographies and biographies that have been written or in the archives of organisations like Liberation or the Spanish International Brigades Association.

Communists in Ireland

This subject doesn't really fit under the heading of the international role played by the Communist Party of Great Britain, but I feel it would be remiss not to include a few paragraphs on the Irish communists who have made significant contributions to political life in Ireland – a country that has been so intimately connected and intertwined with Britain for centuries. Ireland's struggles have had a significant impact and influence on the British Isles as a whole, and are deserving of mention. They fit in better here than elsewhere, I feel.

Ireland is home to one of the oldest Celtic civilisations in Europe, but Britain has claimed sovereignty over it since the 12th century. Since that time, the country has experienced a continuous struggle for independence, marked by many uprisings and their brutal suppression. Ireland's demand for independence has, during its long occupation by Britain, attracted support from many charismatic figures, both within the country and from outside.

In the more recent period, one of those who gave his life for Irish liberation was James Connolly. He is also undoubtedly Ireland's most famous communist, even though Scottish-born.

He was a communist and Marxist theoretician already before the Irish Communist Party was founded (in 1933). Connolly was a staunch Republican and was made Commandant of the Dublin Brigade during the Easter uprising in 1916. After his capture, he was sentenced by the British government to death by firing squad, aged 48. That Easter Uprising led eventually to Ireland's partial liberation and, in 1921, its partition into the Irish Free State and Ulster.

Another early communist who deserves mention here is Jimmy Gralton. The director, Ken Loach made a film about his life, Jimmy's Hall in 2014. Gralton was born at Effernagh, near Gowel, Co Leitrim, in April 1886.

Like so many Irish people he was forced to emigrate, first to Britain and later to the United States, where he took out US citizenship. It was there that Gralton first became involved in the labour struggles of the time. Never breaking his links with Ireland he was active in the Connolly Club in New York which also counted among its members Jim Larkin, Nora Connolly and Liam Mellows. The battle for Irish independence drew him back to Leitrim, where soldiers of the British occupying army, the Black and Tans, had burned down the social hall in Gowel. This galvanised Gralton to respond, erecting a large replacement hall on his parents' land, which he named the Pearse-Connolly Hall in honour of the Socialist and Republican leaders of 1916.

The hall became a very popular centre for both social activities and political study. It also became the base for the Direct Action Committee which Gralton had set up to help tenant farmers regain lands from which they had been evicted. Gralton and his supporters drove cattle on to the property of large estate-owners and settled former tenants on the land. Eventually, the frequent cattle drives onto the big estates, the Arbitration Courts held in the hall and the land takeovers gave the district the name of the Gowel Soviet. It was not long before Gralton became the target of the local landowners' and clergy's wrath. The more popular the activities in the hall, the greater became the attacks on its founder. In June 1922, with his authority considerably undermined by constant clerical condemnation, Free State troops came to arrest him. But he escaped and returned to America.

There he became active in the Communist Party and immersed himself in the work of the American Labour movement, and with a number of other Irishmen he played a leading role in the formation of the powerful Transport Workers' Union. In 1932 he returned once more to Ireland.

Gralton re-opened the Hall and took up the land agitation once again, but the local establishment and clergy were furious. He was, though, not easily put off. Stories about him and his run-ins with the clergy have lived on in local folk memory. One is about Canon McGraver, who in his sermon during mass in Kiltubrid, denounced the hall as a den of iniquity and said he would put horns on Gralton and on anyone who attended events there. Some days later Gralton presented himself on the priest's doorstep 'to have his horns fitted'.

He joined the Revolutionary Workers Group and spoke at numerous anti-eviction gatherings and at meetings of the National Unemployed Workers Movement. He addressed Leitrim County Council on the issue of road workers and along with his cousin Packie Gralton, and other comrades, he organised a series of cultural and political activities in the hall.

However the local political establishment colluded with the local gombeen men and the clergy to whip up another campaign of opposition to him. On one night in November 1932 a dozen shots were fired into the hall, and finally on Christmas Eve 1932 the Hall was burned down in an arson attack.

A massive Red Scare now gripped both the country and county Leitrim. A deportation order was issued by the new Fianna Fail Government in 1932, ordering Gralton – 'an undesirable alien' – to leave Ireland. He went on the run, but was eventually captured and deported to the USA in 1933.

The Leitrim Socialist was never allowed to return again. He spent the remaining days of his life in the American Labour Movement and was a candidate for the US Communist Party in the Borough elections in Manhattan. He again became involved in the Irish Workers Clubs in New York, reprinted Connolly's pamphlets, raised funds for the International Brigades in Spain and participated in the many campaigns of the period. He died in New York in December 1945.

Ireland also sent a number of communists to fight in Spain on behalf of the Republican government, among them the Party's late general secretary, Jim O'Riordan.

Two of the country's well-known dramatists – Sean O'Casey and Brendan Behan – were also communists, although the latter only fleetingly. Behan was 'discovered' and made famous by Joan Littlewood and her Theatre Workshop. That other renowned Irish playwright, Bernard Shaw, was never a Party member, but was a life-long sympathiser and supporter of the Daily Worker.

The two-state solution imposed on Ireland in 1921 was always an uneasy one, and many Catholics living in the North who also invariably had strong Republican sentiments, continued the struggle for full Irish independence. Their struggle was given added impetus by the blatantly discriminatory policies of the Northern Irish government, which privileged the majority Protestant section of the community above the Catholic minority. It was grievances over such policies that fuelled the Civil Rights movement of the late sixties and seventies.

Madge Davison was a young activist from a Presbyterian background who became one of the most prominent leaders of the Civil Rights Movement in Northern Ireland. The movement had evolved in the early sixties and the Northern Ireland Civil Rights Association (NICRA) had been founded in 1966 to fight discrimination in the province. Although the Republican Movement was involved in setting up NICRA, it was largely invigorated by individuals from outside that Movement, including leading communists like Betty Sinclair, who became its first Chair. It organised petitions, meetings and lobbying as well as mass demonstrations to underline its demands.

Bernadette Devlin, a young student from Queens University, Belfast, had been instrumental in setting up the Peoples Democracy (PD) movement, and in January 1969, it organised a 'Long March' from Belfast to Derry modelled on Martin Luther King's civil-rights march to Montgomery, Alabama. In the meantime members of PD had been joining NICRA en masse and this led to the organisation being pushed into a more extreme and confrontational position. Many PD members were very young, predominantly students, with a determination to force through change at any cost, but with little political experience. Madge Davison and Edwina Stewart, together with a number of leading trade unionist and other supporters in NICRA managed to bring it back from the brink and, while maintaining a radical stance, ensured that it once again became a responsible organisation, firmly based in the given political realities of Northern Ireland.

The brutality of the Royal Ulster Constabulary and their insensitivity in dealing with such peaceful protests encouraged the IRA to resort, once again, to armed violence. To quell this escalating violence, British armed forces were sent over in 1969, but the situation only deteriorated further. Despite everything, the Civil Rights Movement continued to press its demands in a peaceful manner.

After becoming general secretary of the Connolly Youth Movement (the youth branch of the Communist Party of Ireland), Madge Davison threw herself full-time into the Civil Rights struggle, alongside her fellow comrades, Edwina and Jimmy Stewart and others. But the dedicated work of Madge and Edwina, in particular, won widespread respect from all sides. By the 1970s Madge had become a full-time assistant organiser of NICRA. When the organisation folded in 1977 and she finished working for it she began studying law and became a barrister, but died tragically young, aged only 42, in 1991. She was a courageous young woman who feared neither British soldiers nor intimidation by the RUC, the IRA or UDA. She was an outstanding orator, and excellent organiser. During her short life she took part in many struggles and activities for justice and equal rights. She taught typing in Twinbrook and law in the Falls Road Women's Centre; she was an active member of the Irish Anti-Apartheid Movement, and an adviser to the Rape Crisis Centre (Belfast), as well as a member of the Northern Ireland Women's Rights Movement.

In the North, Betty Sinclair and her fellow communist trade unionist, Andy Barr, were prominent in the trade union movement over many years, Betty as long time secretary of Belfast Trades Council and Barr in the shipbuilding and engineering industry; he was a member of the Irish TUC executive council and president of the Confederation of Shipbuilding and Engineering Unions. Both fought unremittingly against the religious sectarianism that had dogged union organisation and sown social division in the province for so long. They worked untiringly for working class unity across the religious divide.

The 1998 Good Friday Agreement brought peace to the North for the first time since the emergence of the Civil Rights Movement in the late sixties, and the deployment of British troops who had been waging a protracted struggle against an armed Republican movement.

The Struggle against Fascism

'The womb from which it emerged is fertile still.'

BERTOLT BRECHT

The infamous 'Class against Class'[80] policy imposed by the Comintern in 1928 did tremendous damage to the communist movement worldwide and made cooperation between communists and social democrats virtually impossible. Partly as a result of that inane policy Hitler's road to power in Germany was eased – the last thing most people, including communists expected. In 1933, in Britain, this 'class against class policy' was belatedly abandoned and a policy of promoting alliances on the left and the formation of Popular Front governments was given priority. The Communist Party proposed a united front to the Labour Party, the TUC, Co-operative Party and the Independent Labour Party as the best way of combating the rise of fascism. The first two rejected the overtures emphatically. In fact, in its rejection response the Labour Party equated communism with fascism. The ILP responded positively and later disaffiliated itself from the Labour Party, largely as a result of the latter's negative attitude.

Originally a great deal of anti-fascist activity was focussed around the Relief Committee for the Victims of German Fascism, set up in 1936. At the Committee's first delegate conference Labour peer, Lord Marley took the chair and Ellen Wilkinson, (a founder member of the Communist Party, a former Labour MP and at this time, its

parliamentary candidate for Jarrow) was on the platform. Two months
later, at a mass meeting in London's Kingsway Hall 2,500 queued to
get in to hear leading Communist and Labour speakers. At its next
public meeting in September 1933, the audience numbered 4,000.
Only a short while later, however, the Labour leadership declared the
Relief Committee for the Victims of German Fascism an 'organisation
ancillary or subsidiary of the Communist Party', thus forbidding
Labour Party members from associating with it. The Labour leadership
also stifled any debate or activity around the notorious Reichstag fire
and the Nazis' attempt to blame the communists for it.

This latest proscription meant that there were now eleven
organisations proscribed by the Labour Party, as communist: The
League Against Imperialism, the Left Wing Movement, Minority
Movement, Workers' International relief, National Unemployed
Workers' Movement, Friends of Soviet Russia, National Charter
Campaign Committee, International Labour Defence, British Anti-
War Council and the European Workers' Anti-Fascist Congress.

It is little wonder that many Labour Party members and supporters
had begun to question how serious the party was in its claims to defend
working people and combat fascism. The Labour leaders were so
alarmed by the positive response to the Communist Party's call for
unity against fascism that they themselves issued a pamphlet, The
Communist Solar System, warning members against any association
with 'Communist auxiliary organisations'. This stubborn rejection of
unity in the face of the fascist danger led many to look to the
Communist Party for leadership. Dennis Healey, a minister in
successive Labour governments, told an audience at a seminar held at
Gresham College in 2013 that, as a young man, this was the main
reason he joined the Communist Party, rather than any other.[81]

The alarming rise of Oswald Mosley's British Union of Fascists
during the 1930s, with the support of Lord Rothermere's Daily Mail
and London's Evening News and Sunday Despatch, was also a factor
demanding urgent action. Mosley had organised giant rallies at
London's Albert Hall and at Olympia and he encountered little
opposition apart from small groups outside the venues distributing
anti-fascist literature. The Communist Party argued that such rallies
should be banned. It invited the London Labour Party, Trades Council
and the ILP to join in a protest demonstration at Olympia. The Labour
Party ignored the invitation and at a meeting of the London Trades
Council a motion to participate was ruled out of order. In the end

2,000 people did march on Olympia but were met by a large force of police, protecting the fascist rally. Mounted police made a number of charges into the demonstrators, but no police were inside the hall where an audience of around 12,000 including 2,000 uniformed Blackshirts, had gathered to hear their 'Führer' Mosley. A few protesters had been brave enough to enter the hall and heckle, but they soon became victims of fascist brutality, ending up badly beaten and thrown onto the pavement outside.

Mosley, soon after, announced that he was going to march through the East End of London, which had a dense Jewish population (almost half of Great Britain's Jews lived there). Despite urgent attempts to persuade the Home Office to ban the march as provocative, including a petition with 100,000 signatures, it was allowed to go ahead and a massive force of police was on hand to give the fascist marchers protection and to ensure that the march went ahead successfully. The Labour Party advised its members and supporters to stay away from the area on the day of the march, but a call was issued by the Communist Party and the Independent Labour Party with full support of the Jewish Ex-Servicemen's Association to join in the counter demonstration under the slogan: 'They Shall Not Pass'.

It was only the combined action and organisational skills of local communists and the largely Jewish community that stopped Mosley in his tracks and delivered his first defeat. A number of books and numerous essays and articles have been written about this episode, so there is no need to elaborate here. Suffice to say, that the 'Battle of Cable Street', as it came to be known, went down in history as one of the decisive setbacks for fascist ambitions in Britain.

Because the Communist Party was the only political organisation that appeared to take the struggle against the fascist threat seriously and because it was prepared to take decisive and militant action, it won widespread admiration and support. Three of the organisers of the East End counter-demonstration were communists: Phil Piratin (later a communist MP), Ted Bramley and John Mahon. For the Party this success against the fascists marked a new stage of struggle. From then on those who wanted to participate in the anti-fascist struggle found themselves, unavoidably, either in or associated with the Party.

Aubrey Morris[82] was one of those who took part in the Battle of Cable Street alongside others like Harold Rosen, the father of the Children's Poet Laureate Michael Rosen and the Stepney councillor, Max Levitas. Morris, like many of his fellow East enders, grew up in a family of Jewish immigrants from Eastern Europe, alongside such luminaries as Arnold Wesker, Alfie Bass and Lionel Blair. He joined the Communist Party because he felt it was the only organisation committed to fighting fascism. And, despite becoming a millionaire travel agent and having left the Party, he remained a socialist all his life and was a founding supporter of the magazine Red Pepper.

Oswald Mosley was promptly released from his war time internment immediately the war came to an end, and it wasn't long before he was once again attempting to rebuild his fascist movement. Anti-Semitic slogans began appearing on walls and rallies were held. Here, once more, in the absence of any other effective action, the Communist Party became instrumental in mobilising opposition to ensure that his movement never got off the ground. The establishment didn't appear perturbed in the least by a resurgent fascist movement.

With the slow demise of Mosley's organisation, other fascist groups filled the gap. The League of Empire Loyalists was established in 1954, The National Front was founded in 1967, then there were Colin Jordan's National Socialist Movement and a renewed BNP, Combat 18 and the English Defence League today.

Maurice Ludmer, a member of the Communist Party, was a long time editor of the dedicated anti-fascist magazine, Searchlight, which was preceded by a newspaper of the same name, founded in the sixties by two Labour MPs, Joan Lestor and Reg Freeson. Searchlight has done so much to investigate and highlight fascist activities in the UK.

Although the Party continued to fight fascism, it was the Socialist Workers' Party which was to spearhead and lead the high profile and successful Anti-Nazi League during the late seventies and eighties with an imaginative campaign and large demonstrations. However, there is in my opinion little doubt that without the determination and self-sacrifice of many communists throughout the earlier part of the century the struggle against fascism would not have been so successful or effective.

It was even on the cards that it would not have been confronted at all and both Britain and other parts of the world could well have experienced fascism directly. After all, the Channel Islands were occupied by the Nazis and many there, particularly government officials, willingly collaborated. Certainly, well before the outbreak of the war, Oswald Mosley had been gaining traction among disaffected sections of the working and middle class, as well as enjoying the support of leading establishment figures. Without the Communist

Party's demands for action and providing courageous leadership to the struggle against the rise of fascism, the scenario would have been very different.

In their book Deadly Illusions,[83] about the British-born Soviet agents, Kim Philby, Guy Burgess and Donald MacClean, the authors relate how Philby manoeuvred himself into a position where he was readily recruited by the British Secret Service by first undertaking journalistic work for a British-based pro-Nazi German magazine and then reporting favourably from the Francoist side during the Spanish Civil War. It is clear, certainly then, that pro-fascist sympathies were deemed a good indication of potential loyalty to the British elite services.

The Party and the Second World War

*'I know not with what weapons World War III will be
fought, but World War IV will be fought with sticks and
stones.'*

ALBERT EINSTEIN

Italy invaded Abyssinia (now Ethiopia) in 1935 and the Communist
Party immediately campaigned for sanctions against the aggressor.
When the government refused to respond and the Labour Party
declined taking any action, it initiated direct action by workers involved
in making or supplying war materials to Italy. Already, in Cape Town,
South Africa, dockers had refused to load meat for the Italian army, in
Alexandria, Greece, seamen declined to handle Italian war materials,
French dockers took similar action. In Britain immediate action came
from an unexpected quarter: it was the National Union of Boot and
Shoe Operatives that instructed its members to stop handling orders
of boots for the Italian army.

Before the outbreak of the Second World War, fascist Japan had
already mounted an all-out offensive against China. While the rest of
the world looked on indifferently, workers in several parts of the
world, including Britain, decided to take action. British communists
successfully initiated industrial action to block exports to Japan. In
December 1937, a Canadian Pacific liner, the Duchess of Richmond,
arrived in Southampton carrying 200 tons of Japanese goods. At the

docks there was a very active Communist Party branch and when one of its members, Trevor Stallard, discovered where the cargo had originated, he called a meeting of the men and they agreed not to unload the Japanese cargo. The event made headlines. Years later Stallard was elected to the TGWU's executive council. The London Communist Party then distributed leaflets to London dockers, calling on them to emulate their colleagues in Southampton. In January 1938 stevedores in Middlesbrough refused to load a Japanese ship, the Haruna Maru, with a cargo of pig iron destined for Japan. The TGWU tried to persuade the men to change their minds and, when this failed, had even, without success, attempted to recruit casual labour to do the job.

In 1938, when Hitler was already threatening Austria, and Britain's government was still appeasing the dictator, British communists called for Prime Minister Chamberlain's removal. The London Communist Party immediately called for a mass demonstration and the setting up of a Council of Action to bring down the Chamberlain government. Its call met with a huge response, and 40,000 joined a protest march.

In March 1938, the Soviet Union proposed discussions between the French, British and American governments in order to plan joint action against Hitler and ensure European security. This overture was dismissed out of hand and Hitler, as we know, proceeded to threaten Czechoslovakia after his annexation of Austria. At the time the communist Daily Worker, was the only daily paper which consistently demanded that we stand by the Czechs in the face of Hitler's aggression. The Party organised around 3,000 'Stand by the Czechs' meetings up and down the country and it distributed 500,000 leaflets, entitled, Stop the Betrayal.

Only one MP in parliament attacked Chamberlain for appeasing Hitler and that was the communist Willie Gallacher who was barracked by his fellow MPs and his speech was barely mentioned in the press. He said:

'No one desires peace more than I and my party, but it must be a peace based upon freedom and democracy and not upon the cutting up and destruction of a small state... Whatever the outcome, the National Government will have to answer for its policy...'

Only a few months later the appalling results of Chamberlain's appeasement became apparent and the drums of war rumbled closer than ever.

Appeasement failed and, on the outbreak of war in 1939, the Communist Party published a manifesto:

'You are being called upon to take part in the most cruel war in the history of the world,' it began, 'one that need never have taken place. One that could have been avoided…had we had a people's government in Britain… We are in support of all necessary measures to secure the victory of democracy over fascism. But fascism will not be defeated by the Chamberlain government.'

After September 1939, with war now declared, the government and employers imposed disagreeable and at times unacceptable wartime working conditions across all industries, deemed vital for the war effort. These provoked much anger, but it was very often communist shop stewards who were instrumental in persuading the workers to accept many of these impositions as temporary and necessary measures to support the war effort.

During the thirties, the Party had been the driving force behind the shop stewards' movement in industry and so was in a key position to influence workers at the grassroots. It could easily have jumped on the opportunist bandwagon and lent full support to angry workers, fomenting strikes and work stoppages if they had been the cynical manipulators as so often caricatured.

In 1940, at a national engineering conference held in Birmingham, an Allied Trades Shop Stewards' National Council was set up to coordinate action and policies during the extreme circumstances of the war. It became an immensely powerful grassroots organisation, and its first national secretary was the well-known communist Len Powell. Every factory elected its own shop stewards who were the first direct link between management and the workers on the shop floor – they were often the key figures in factory floor negotiations and in maintaining industrial peace. Interestingly, and as an aside, the conference also called for a campaign within the Amalgamated Engineering Union to open up its ranks to women workers, although it took another two years before the union actually began admitting women into membership.

The Engineering union leadership felt very threatened by the rising strength of this shop stewards' movement and, after the 1940 conference, it summoned a number of stewards to the union's headquarters and threatened them with expulsion from the union for undertaking actions 'detrimental to the union and of attempting to form a new union and fomenting strikes.' [84] At least three of those threatened were leading communist shop stewards.

In April 1940 the 'phoney war' was overtaken by the real war; in May Chamberlain was forced to resign and Winston Churchill took over as prime minister. Nevertheless, behind the scenes, the government was still discussing whether or not to ban communist propaganda. At this time the Party had adopted a controversial anti-war position, because of the failure of Britain and France to cement an alliance with the Soviet Union. It characterised the war as an inter-imperialist one, in which British lives should not be sacrificed. It demanded instead a war directed seriously against fascism.

The Home Secretary of the War Cabinet proposed banning the Daily Worker, but other Cabinet members were worried about possible negative repercussions and raising alarm in the country about the suppression of free expression. In the end, though, the government did decide to ban the Communist Party leaflet, The People Must Act, which called on people to demand of the government that it pursue the war seriously by working with all anti-fascist forces. The government also issued a warning to the Daily Worker of a possible ban if it didn't stop publishing 'matter calculated to foment opposition to the prosecution of the war.'

Even before the government took action on the leaflet, communists up and down the country were already being harassed and arrested by the police. The Daily Worker wrote that this was all part of the government's attempt to suppress all criticism of the 'Men of Munich' who had supported Chamberlain's appeasement policies. This police action began by a harassment of those engaged in outdoor activities, but soon homes of Party members were being raided, ostensibly, in the search for leaflets. In some cases complete sets of Left Book Club books were removed as potential evidence of subversive activity! In a number of cases of those whose homes were searched, the residents were also arrested and questioned by police, following which, their employers were informed, with the aim of securing their dismissal from employment. My own mother was caught up in this wave of persecution. Some of her correspondence to the local Communist Party office had been opened by the security services and she was immediately summoned to her manager who told her openly that MI5 had demanded her dismissal because of her political affiliation. At that time, she worked for British Aluminium in Banbury as a minor secretary.

In the wake of such cases, a survey of the repressive action being taken by the police was compiled by the legal adviser to the National Council for Civil Liberties. It reported:

'Police broke into a closed branch meeting of a provincial Young Communist League and stopped the meeting. They took all the identity cards of those present and made lists of names and addresses from them and asked the names of employers. Several officials were taken to the police stations and interrogated for several hours. Afterwards they were told they might leave, but must attend no meetings in future of any kind. Shortly afterwards, the police visited various employers, and later members of this group were dismissed from their employment.' [85]

The pressures became so acute that the Party issued a pamphlet entitled: How to Defend Yourself: a Practical Legal Guide for Workers.

One wartime measure that appeared to pose a direct threat to the existence of the Communist Party itself was Defence Regulation 18B. This gave the Secretary of State the power 'to detain without trial the members of any organisation which was either subject to foreign influence or control...' This regulation had been used in 1940 to arrest British Union of Fascist members. In the event 18B was only used against a handful of communists, one of whom was T.E. Nicholas, a dentist and well-known Welsh poet, but his detention was clearly a blunder by over-zealous police. The worst case was that of John Mason, a shop steward and secretary of Mexborough Trades council in Yorkshire, and employed by English Steel. He was arrested and spent 11 months in an internment camp. Herbert Morrison, who in the meantime had become Home Secretary, stated that he upheld Mason's detention because he was involved in efforts to slow down production, but details of what Mason was actually accused of were never made public. A Mason defence committee was set up to demand his release. As with other 18B detainees, he was never brought to trial and after 11 months campaigning, was eventually released.

In September 1940, the German blitz on London began, with nightly bombing of residential areas of the city. Some two years before the outbreak of war the Communist Party had already been agitating for adequate air-raid protection and for the construction of bomb shelters. It was pointed out that these had been constructed for ministers and government officials, and had been installed in luxury apartments for the rich, but not for the poor. JBS Haldane, in his book, Air Raid Precautions, published in 1938, argued for a system of tunnel shelters for London and other big towns. An Air Raid Protection (ARP) Co-ordinating Committee of architects, engineers and scientists was then set up and chaired by Haldane, but government was extremely tardy in taking up the ideas they came up with. Experience in the Spanish Civil War had demonstrated clearly to those who had taken part that, given the state of weaponry and increasing use of aerial bombardment, effective bomb shelters were essential if civilian populations were to be protected. Shortly after its creation, the Labour Party Executive banned the ARP Co-ordinating Committee, as 'a subversive organisation'.

As a result of Chamberlain's futile and obsequious attempts to appease Hitler and bring 'peace in our time', the country was woefully unprepared for war and had taken few measures to protect the population from bombing or invasion. When the blitz began in 1940 the London District of the Communist Party issued 100,000 leaflets and 5,000 posters demanding the immediate construction of bomb shelters and the opening of tube stations as night shelters. The following week police raided various Party offices and bookshops and seized all the leaflets and posters they could find. Plainclothes officers often burst into premises associated with the Party using violent methods of entry, as if they were dealing with unscrupulous criminals, and refused to show search warrants, according to a Daily Worker report at the time. These raids were also accompanied by police action to close the tube station gates whenever an air-raid warning sounded, to prevent citizens using them as shelters. By the end of September, however, 79 Underground stations in Greater London were already being used as shelters for around 177,000 people.

Undaunted by police raids, the Party published and distributed another 20,000 leaflets, demanding the construction of bomb-proof shelters and the setting up of shelter committees, and many Party members were involved in these committees. Party members were also instrumental in campaigns to open up private shelters. In St. Pancras they picketed the Carreras tobacco factory, demanding that its shelter (capable of holding 3,000 people) be opened up to the public at night. The most spectacular of such actions was that led by Phil Piratin, at the time a local Stepney councillor, who mobilised around 70 people to occupy a deep shelter at the Savoy Hotel.

Herbert Morrison, in his first speech as Home Secretary, stated that the people who were demanding deep shelters were doing so for mischievous and political reasons. In private, he told the War Cabinet that it was essential to counter communist agitation but that one had to be careful about a possible negative side-effect of appearing to oppose the provision of shelters.[86]

On 3rd November, Morrison announced that deep shelters would be provided in London, a measure that should have been taken much earlier. John Gorman in his autobiography, Knocking down Ginger, describes vividly this situation for those living through the Blitz in London's East end.

Of course, communists were not alone in campaigning for adequate protection for the civilian population, but they did play, largely because of their organisational strength on the ground and ability to mobilise popular movements, a key role in forcing government to address this important issue.

In Coventry, where the Party was only 70 strong, it also played a significant role in getting the local council to take adequate measures. The day after the blitz on the city in November 1940, the Party distributed copies of the Daily Worker, the only paper on sale in the city on that day, and Bill Alexander, former commander of the British Battalion in the Spanish Civil War, was sent in to become the Party's full-time organiser in the city. Bill Warman, a communist shop steward at the Coventry Standard Motor Company, immediately called an emergency public meeting to organise action on housing and feeding those who had been made homeless, as well as calling for adequate protection for all citizens. As a result of these initiatives, Party membership in the city increased to 150 within a few months.

Incidentally, my grandparents' home in Stoney Stanton Road, in the city centre, was completely flattened in that raid on Coventry. Luckily, beforehand, they and my parents had taken refuge in Kenilworth, outside the city. Both my parents were already active in the local Communist Party.

Another contentious issue the Party took up, was that of pay and conditions for men and women in the armed forces. This issue was highlighted in October 1940 when a delegate to the annual TUC conference appeared on the platform in uniform and spoke in support of a resolution demanding improved pay and allowances for those in the armed forces. He was Harry Berger, a London communist. He pointed out that the men, in particular those who had wives and perhaps children to support, received totally inadequate pay and couldn't even afford to buy a packet of Woodbine cigarettes for 3½ pence. As a consequence of this apparent dissatisfaction in the forces, the Daily Worker began including a regular 'Soldiers' Page' as part of its coverage of the war effort. Partly as a result of this, the paper achieved a significant popularity among ordinary soldiers.

Tom Wintringham, though now no longer a member of the Communist Party – he was expelled in 1938 after refusing to toe Party instructions concerning his personal relations – became the key figure in setting up the Home Guard in 1940. He had fought and been decorated in the First World War and was commander of the British Battalion during the Spanish Civil War. He still considered himself a communist, although no longer a member of the CPGB.

This was still the period of the Phoney War and government was still dithering about what measures to take in Britain's defence. Wintringham was one of the best proponents of guerrilla warfare and do-it-yourself defence and he lost no time in setting up a home defence force training school to prepare for a possible Nazi invasion. He was a revolutionary patriot, becoming the founder and director of the Guerrilla Warfare Training School at Osterley Park in west London, out of which the Home Guard emerged. He saw the Home Guard as a new sort of army, a concept based on Oliver Cromwell's New Model Army. He wanted to see the formation of a genuinely democratic, people's army.

He was widely known as the 'Red Revolutionary' and because of his communist background was mistrusted by the War Office who proceeded to take over his training school and moved it out of London. He wrote about his ideas in Picture Post, the Daily Mirror and gave talks on the BBC about them. His two books, New Ways of War and Armies of Free Men set out those ideas in detail. Orwell said of him, that he was 'a notable voice in stemming the tide of defeatism'. He later went on to form the short-lived Common Wealth Party and was almost elected to parliament.

In January 1941, largely on the initiative of the Communist Party, a 'People's Convention was convened in Manchester. The aim of the Convention was to press the government to institute changes in the country to isolate the 'Men of Munich' and the powerful and wealthy friends of fascism – those whose policies had helped build up Hitler's power. It demanded a government truly representative of the people, a protection of living standards, for democratic trade union rights, adequate air-raid protection and friendship with the Soviet Union.

When the Manchester Free Trade Hall was unexpectedly destroyed in a raid, the Convention had to be relocated to London and attendance 'exceeded all expectations' according to one of its organisers. There were 665 delegates representing trade unions, 471 were from shop stewards committees, and the remainder from organisations like Labour parties, Co-operative Guilds and tenants associations. The Convention received wide coverage in the mainstream press, since there were clearly strong feelings among the population at large about the issues discussed at the Convention. However, most of the media took the opportunity to reiterate the usual mantra of 'communists exploiting the grievance of the people for their own sinister purposes'.

The Daily Herald's reporter (the Herald was generally seen as Labour's mouthpiece during this period) called it 'as clever a bit of political exploitation as I have yet encountered,' and that the organisers had 'exploited a situation which puts even the Labour Party at a disadvantage'.[87] No one asked why those in power were not addressing these grievances and that if they had done so, it would have taken the wind out of the sails of the communists. The Daily Mirror took a more objective stance and stated clip and clear that ninety per cent of the delegates were 'honest-to-God British citizens' with 'no wish to see Hitler victorious'. The government and establishment clearly feared that they were losing the initiative here and were determined to put a stop to communist agitation.

One week later the Daily Worker was banned by Morrison on the basis that it was undermining the war effort. At the same time he instigated the setting up of a special 'Committee on Communist Activities' in order to examine what further action should be taken. On 19 January 1941, two days before the ban was planned to take place, the Sunday Express (a strong supporter of Chamberlain's appeasement policies) carried a front page story under the headline: 'Government to stamp on Communist Trouble-Makers'. Special Branch and uniformed police immediately descended on the paper's offices and formally carried out the suppression, a day before Parliament had been formally informed of the ban. All this was taking place at a time when the country was supposedly concentrating on fighting the war against Hitler.

The Cabinet Committee set up to consider further action against the Communist Party held its first meeting in January 1941. At this and future meetings, it discussed banning the Party. It had received a report from the Home Defence (Security) Executive which argued that if further action was to be taken, 'it should be the proscription of the Party as an illegal organisation and the internment of a small number of leaders'.[88] The committee was chaired by Conservative MP, Lord Swinton, who had been closely involved in the notorious Zinoviev letter. The letter, purporting to come from Moscow and sent to the Communist Party of Great Britain, called for intensified agitation. It was published only days before the 1924 election and was designed to prevent the Labour Party winning the election. It has since been revealed as a forgery, probably concocted by the secret services in cahoots with right-wing establishment figures.

In the end the Committee took no action, as it feared the negative fall-out from such action could be considerable. It did, though, consider the banning of various Party publications, along with the Daily Worker; although there was already a ban in place on their export. In the end the only decision the Committee took was to stop the actual circulation of communist leaflets. The disappearance of the Daily Worker, the harassment and banning of leaflet distribution only meant that Party work became more difficult. However, if its declared aim was to undermine communist influence in the country, it failed singularly.

There was also a furore at the BBC after it decided not to employ People's Convention supporters as broadcasters, although these supporters came from a broad cross section of the population and included prominent individuals from the cultural scene. The BBC was forced to 'rethink' its ban as a result of opposition from a number of leading personalities. The renowned composer, Ralph Vaughan Williams, withdrew a choral work specially commissioned by the BBC because of its ban on the communist composer Alan Bush, who was also a leading figure in the Workers' Music Association. The writer, Rose Macaulay cancelled a broadcast; E.M. Forster withdrew all his services, and there were letters of protest from the great and the good, including J.B Priestley and David Low. It demonstrated once again that the Communist Party was not without considerable influence well outside its small circle of members. In the end, Prime Minister Churchill announced the lifting of the BBC ban.

When the Daily Worker was banned, the Party was forced to seek emergency means of communicating its ideas to its members and sympathisers, so it set up a 'news agency', under the nominal ownership of G.J Jones, a teacher, and Party member, called 'Industrial and General Information News Agency'. This agency proceeded to publish a daily duplicated bulletin every day to the press. It was also mailed directly to communist party offices, shop stewards and Party trade union officials. In this way the Party got around the ban on the Daily Worker. The government could hardly ban this 'industrial information' newssheet on the basis that it was undermining the war effort, however that did not stop Special Branch from raiding the agency's premises in March 1941 and taking away documents, but after two days the newssheet was coming out again and no prosecution of staff took place. This newssheet continued being published until the ban on the Daily Worker was finally lifted in 1942. In the meantime, over 800 organisations and numerous individuals had joined the campaign to demand an end to the ban.

Very soon after Nazi Germany invaded the Soviet Union in June 1941, Churchill announced that the UK would co-operate with the Soviet Union to crush Nazism. On the basis of that historical decision, the Party then also reversed its policy of not supporting what it had called an 'imperialist war' and now threw its whole weight behind the government. It was, of course, jeered by many for its 'somersault', but there had been justification for this attitude as the Soviet Union and communism had been lumped together with fascism as the common enemy by successive governments; that policy had now, it seemed, also changed.

The new allied coalition with the Soviet Union in the war against fascism brought about a big change in the Party's fortunes. Its membership showed a massive rise, from 22,000 at the end of 1941 to 53,000 only four months later. What was also striking was the youthfulness of the Party at this time: of the 1,323 delegates at its May 1942 conference, over 500 were in their twenties and another 500 in their thirties.

In order to ensure industrial peace and maintain or increase production levels during the war, Joint Production Committees (JPCs) of workers and management were set up in the big factories. This had been something for which the Party had also campaigned, and communists played leading roles in these committees.

Of course, many in Britain did not expect the alliance with the Soviet Union to last long; in fact those in government and the mainly right-wing media expected that country to collapse very quickly in the face of the German onslaught. When the Soviet Union defied all the odds and not only halted the German advance, but began a major counter-offensive in the winter of 1941-42 it provoked a dramatic change in political attitudes throughout the world, and Britain was no exception. Alone among political parties in Britain, the Communist Party had consistently stood for solidarity with the Soviet Union. As Branson put it in her History of the Communist Party (1941-51), communists were 'sneered at and derided by press and radio, they had been singled out for police persecution, and had received prison sentences for their activities.' The right-wing individuals who dominated the Labour Party and trade unions treated communists as untouchables. She relates that, 'At an open air meeting in Plymouth on Sunday 6 July – two weeks after the German invasion of Russia – the police acted according to previous custom and practice, and confiscated all copies of a Communist Party leaflet headed 'Solidarity with the Soviet Union.' The police action so enraged the 400 people present that they responded by buying up all the rest of the Party's literature still on sale. The local Chief Constable clearly hadn't realised that the political situation had now changed.' [89]

Many ordinary citizens in Britain realised that the Red Army's victories on the Eastern Front were also victories for them too, because it made a Nazi invasion of the United Kingdom's mainland less likely. This increased sympathy for, and interest in, the Soviet Union and the ideas of communism deeply alarmed the establishment, but there was little they could do about it at the time, as this would have appeared to undermine the anti-Nazi struggle and the war effort. Thousands around the country began attending Anglo-Soviet solidarity meetings and when Churchill's wife herself launched the 'Aid to Russia' appeal it met with an unprecedented response. Inevitably communist speakers were very much in demand at such events. Meetings were often chaired by local Lord Mayors and the platforms draped with the Union Jack alongside the Soviet flag; 'God save the Queen' sung along with 'the Internationale'!

In October 1942, a 50,000 strong rally, organised by the Communist Party, was held in Trafalgar Square calling for the opening of a second front in Europe. The communists were now waging an urgent campaign for the government to open up a second front in Europe to relieve the Red Army, then bearing the full brunt of the Nazi onslaught, but it would be another two years before that second front was opened.

In the inter-war years the Party's main efforts on the industrial front had been to campaign for better wages and conditions, but now with the war in full swing a new priority occupied its deliberations and that was the need to maintain and increase production of coal, steel, armaments and food. Here the shop stewards' movement that the Party had laboriously helped build up came into its own. A confidential Home Office memorandum in 1941 grudgingly admitted that, 'in industry, the Communist Party has obtained a representation among shop stewards out of all proportion to the strength of the party in the factories.' [90] Now that influence was directed towards solving production problems. From August 1941 onwards the Shop Stewards National Council began campaigning for the creation of joint production committees in the factories and mines.

At the Labour Party's annual conference in May 1942, Herbert Morrison suffered a spectacular defeat when conference supported a resolution calling for the ban on the Daily Worker to be lifted. In August he did lift the ban, almost certainly in order to avoid further humiliation and almost certain censure at the TUC congress later in the year.

Although bans on co-operating with communists or 'communist' organisations by the Labour Party were still in force, they were being flouted openly in many localities, where local parties were collaborating and working closely together on campaigns promoting Anglo-Soviet solidarity and other activities in support of the war effort. The Communist Party itself was still growing fast. And now had one member for every four individual members of the Labour Party. It was also a party of the young, whereas the Labour Party appeared to be ageing and was hardly attracting young people.

On the basis of this new close cooperation, at least at the lower levels, together with the tacit agreement that the Nazis were now the main enemy, the Communist Party, in December 1942, felt the atmosphere was more conducive for a new approach to the Labour Party on affiliation. In his letter to the Labour Party general secretary, Harry Pollitt the Communist Party's general secretary said that the Party was prepared to accept all the obligations of such an affiliation and would loyally accept all decisions carried at the Labour Party's annual conference. Again, the proposal was rejected.

During 1943, there was a sudden wave of strikes in the engineering industry and one of the longest was in Barrow-in-Furness at Vickers Armstrong, the big armaments manufacturer. The Communist Party found itself in the unusual and uncomfortable position of arguing against the strikes and emphasising the need to keep up production during the war. At Barrow it was George Crane, a leading communist, who was given the unenviable task by the AEW executive of sorting the problem out, which he managed to do. Many of the problems leading to these strikes were down to poor management and insufficient communication and co-ordination between unions and management.

In early 1944, with the end of the war already in sight, the Party became concerned about a possible victimisation of shop stewards once the war was over and things returned to 'capitalism as usual'. At a Shop Stewards National Council held in London in 1944, the opening statement was given by Scottish communist Finlay Hart who said:

> 'Let us firmly determine, along with our comrades in the armed forces, to make our voice heard now for the retention of vital controls after the war on prices, profits, distribution and commodities and investment of capital. Let us make our voices heard for the nationalisation of the land, mines, banks and other key industries, for a policy that will ensure jobs and security for all.'

With the more propitious environment in the country, communists were also now beginning to be elected to leading positions in many trade unions, particularly in the mining and engineering unions. Arthur Horner became president of the South Wales Miners and Abe Moffat president of the Scottish Miners. In the AEW Joe Scott was voted onto the Executive Council after several previous attempts and Wal Hannington, the legendary leader of the unemployed workers' movement, became national organiser of the union. Others took up leading positions in the Fire Brigades Union, the train drivers' and in the foundry workers union. In 1944, the first communist – the bus drivers' leader, Bert Papworth – was elected on to the TUC General Council. Bert had been expelled from his union in 1937 after the 'Coronation Strike' of 1937 and as part of the witch hunt launched by TGWU general secretary Ernest Bevin.

In a desperate last ditch attempt to stem the tide, the TUC General Council focussed on a new target: the Labour Research Department (LRD), a progressive research institute that provided important data and statistics on industrial and social issues, and still does so today. It was in fact an independent research body founded in 1912, by Beatrice Webb as part of the Fabian Society. The TUC won Labour Party support for its action and a joint circular was issued banning the LRD as it was 'to a considerable extent subject to communist influence and control.' For the following two years the TUC left the anti-communist crusade to the Labour Party alone.

After the Russians entered the war, an increasing number of those in uniform were applying to join the Party. According to King's Regulation 541, members of the army were not permitted to play an active part in the affairs of a political party. Not wishing to create serious problems for members, the Party refused to enrol those already in uniform and those who had joined before being called-up were told to leave their Party cards at home. Those members already in the forces still managed to make contact with others by word of mouth and were soon distributing leaflets and pinning up copies of the Daily Worker on barracks room notice boards, as well as actively participating in discussions laid on by the Army Education Corps and other army organisations.

One member in Catterick recalled how they made a YMCA discussion group their centre of activities until Intelligence got on to them.[91] Government secret services, of course, kept a tab on all suspected communists and most were prevented from taking on key roles and were denied promotion. One, though, who escaped that fate was the physicist J.D. Bernal who had been singled out for special responsibilities by Admiral Lord Mountbatten.

Although the armed forces were ostensibly fighting for democracy against fascist totalitarianism, the field of education became a controversial one. The War Office felt that educational activities for the forces would help boost morale and relieve boredom (particularly for the many still stationed in Britain and kicking their heels). On the other hand, some in the higher echelons of the army were perturbed at the idea of too much education and democracy, as potentially undermining their powers.

For a time, the communist philosopher, Dr. John Lewis was employed by the Army Education Corps as a full-time lecturer until those in charge got wind of him and he was promptly sacked. D.N. Pritt MP, who had been expelled from the Labour Party over his support of the Russians during the Finnish invasion, was another of those prevented from lecturing. Churchill himself is on record as saying, 'I do not approve of this system of encouraging political discussions in the army among soldiers'. So obsessed were the authorities about communist influence in the armed forces that they tried to prevent some from getting into the services at all. One of those was Phil Piratin, the Stepney councillor and later MP for Mile End, another was Henry Parsons who had been head of the Party's publishing firm, Lawrence Wishart.

Alan Winnington, later to become 'notorious' for covering the Korean War for the Daily Worker from the North Korean side, was accepted as a trainee fighter pilot in the RAF but after waiting three months, he received an official communication that 'his services were no longer required'. Clearly a blacklist was being operated, but despite all these efforts on the part of the authorities some members slipped through the net. One of those was Bill Alexander, former commander of the British Battalion in Spain, who during the war was a captain in the Reconnaissance Corps, but any further promotion was blocked from on high.

One of the Party's chief theoreticians and later editor of its journal Marxism Today, James Klugman, ran classes on fascism, the causes of war, dialectics and socialism on the troopship he was on and was given the sobriquet 'The Prof' by the lads. He was later parachuted into Yugoslavia as a liaison officer with Tito's partisans and eventually rose to the rank of Major.

Every effort was made to keep tabs on the 'reds' in the army and dossiers would be sent to commanding officers with names and details of who were to be watched and to be kept in the ranks. Clive Branson (the husband of Noreen Branson, who wrote two volumes of the series, History of the CPGB) also lectured to the Training Regiment of the Royal Armoured Corps, at the time stationed at Andover, and gave talks on Cromwell's army before the order came through to stop his lectures. Another of those blacklisted was R.J. Specter who, after the war, wrote a pamphlet for the National Council for Civil Liberties, called Freedom for the Forces. In contrast, and unsurprisingly perhaps, was the extreme lethargy of those in charge of security to investigate former fascists in the forces. For more details on this issue – see Branson's History of the Communist Party of Great Britain (1941-51), chapter: The Party and the Armed Forces.[92]

One of the high points of political activity in the forces was the so-called 'Forces Parliaments'. In Cairo the Army Education Corps had set up a cultural centre for leisure activities for the men stationed nearby. Those communists stationed out in the Middle East managed to contact each other and set up 'mock' parliaments, run on party lines, to debate the issues of the day and to discuss what form a post-war Britain should take. Similar 'Forces Parliaments' were set up in the Far East too. They also organised mock elections but, with the aim of

Labour-Communist unity, communists did not stand on a separate platform. Labour won overwhelmingly. These parliaments attracted around 500 participants, but in April 1944 the army top brass closed them down. When the Secretary of State for War was questioned about this by D.N. Pritt MP, he avoided a clear answer. Willie Gallacher MP suggested it was not so much a case of the troops discussing politics, but that they were discussing the wrong type of politics.

The landslide victory for the Labour Party in 1945 was in no small measure due to the votes of those in the armed services, and a small amount of credit for that should go to communists and others who organised such discussion groups and mock parliaments, encouraging their fellow soldiers to vote Labour.

By the summer of 1944, the Party had begun circulating its new draft programme for a post-war Britain. In doing so it was responding to the mood in the country for a fresh start and a widespread determination not to return to the hunger, poverty and unemployment of the thirties. It also produced a discussion document, Guiding Lines on Questions of Post-war Reconstruction, and set up a number of committees to look at specific areas of society, such as education, housing, agriculture, transport etc. All this culminated in a document titled: Britain for the People: Proposals for Post-war Policy. It emphasised the need to build on what had been achieved during the war. The programme also pointed out that central planning and state control during the war had been essential to ensure efficiency and proper management and distribution of resources, so why, it argued, couldn't this experience be carried over into peace-time.

Trade union membership was high and, as a result of the war and trade union recruitment efforts, most workplaces were better organised, and there had been a levelling up of wage rates as well as improvements of working conditions, despite all the war-time restrictions. Many working people felt a new sense of dignity and worth, and were proud of what they had achieved during the war.

In the changed economic and political circumstances and the widespread optimism of a post-war consensus, Party policy also changed from advocating Bolshevik-type 'revolution', to the idea of change through parliamentary means and a democratisation of the state machine. With that in mind, it also began advocating a voting system based on proportional representation, which was championed by the Party's lone MP, Willie Gallacher, in the House of Commons.

In 1945, having failed in its aim of achieving proportional

representation adopted, the Party then proposed local conferences of progressive organisations to choose local 'unity' candidates, to prevent splitting the anti-Tory vote. However, this idea was also rejected by the Labour Party. To prevent splitting the working class vote and perhaps letting the Tories in, the Party decided to reduce the number of its own candidates from 52 to 22. The election turned into a landslide for Labour, certainly in terms of seats, even though it only won 47.8 per cent of the actual vote, which clearly demonstrated the unfairness of the 'first-past-the-post' system. Of the 22 Communist Party candidates, only two were elected – Phil Piratin for Mile End and Willie Gallacher for West Fife. Other results, while not overwhelming, gave the Party a significant number of votes. Harry Pollitt, the Party's general secretary, who stood in Rhondda East, won 15,761 but was narrowly defeated by the Labour candidate. In local elections the Party made more gains than on a national level, even though these were still modest. By early 1946 the Party had increased its number of local councillors from 81 to 215.

The battle for decent housing – rent strikes, squatting and tenants' revolts

Communist strength in Stepney dated back to the foundation of the Party but it had been much boosted by anti-fascist action and taken to a whole new stage by its work amongst tenants, which was dominated by the boldness of working class women.

The first Communist candidate chosen to run for a borough council seat, in 1937, was Phil Piratin, who later became the MP for the area. East End resident Tubby Rosen was selected to stand in local elections in Mile End West, with Phil Piratin and Tom Rampling in Spitalfields East, Edward Kirby and Michael Shapiro in St George's North-West, Max Levitas and Queenie Weinberg in Whitechapel East, with Bill Carver and Fannie Goldberg in Mile End North. All these candidates had been active in the struggles for better housing. When the elections came, in November 1945, all ten Communist candidates were elected on to the council, three of them women. All of them, who included four non-Jewish men, won their seats in these predominantly Jewish neighbourhoods. Many observers at the time asserted that the communists could easily have taken 10-15 more seats had the Party not restricted the number it contested in the interests of left unity.

Immediately after the war the severe housing shortage was an acute problem. There had been a housing shortage before the war, but since

German bombing had also destroyed thousands of homes, the issue needed addressing even more urgently. Some 3.5 million men and women had been demobilised and many found themselves rejoining their families under intolerable conditions. Many of those in dire need decided not to wait for officialdom to start the ball rolling, and began squatting empty properties as an interim measure and to highlight their plight. Communists were to play an outstanding role in this movement.

Tubby Rosen was one of five Communist Party leaders arraigned at Bow Street magistrates court in 1946, charged with conspiring with others to trespass on property and aiding and abetting in directing such a trespass. The case arose out of the squatters' movement, and in particular the occupation of the Duchess of Bedford House, Kensington High Street in September 1946.

When the occupation began, The Times ran a headline: '1500 Squatters Occupy Luxury Flats –Audacious Operation in West End'. The Duchess of Bedford House in Campden Hill was invaded by some 200 squatters, after communist organisers had discreetly arranged for the flats to be 'opened' and available for ex-servicemen and their families. This was a block of luxury flats, half-way between Kensington and Notting Hill, with enormous accommodation, 'more space than the average house'. Within the next week or two, other mass squattings had taken place, at Fountain Court, Pimlico, and elsewhere, but, since the Duchess of Bedford squat was the first, it was regarded as a legal test case. Such squatting action was hugely popular in view of the severe shortage of sufficient housing.

The Ministry of Works had requisitioned the buildings to house Maltese building workers, who were repairing bomb damaged properties. They had all been moved on, and the place had been standing empty, but had not been returned to the original owners, possibly the Prudential Assurance Company, although, due to adverse publicity, the company denied all knowledge of the flats. Due to this confusion, the squatters were largely left alone by the authorities for weeks. Attempts to turn off utility supplies were thwarted by permanent picket duty rosters. Then writs were served and the squatters' own committee, which had been in negotiation to obtain other accommodation, decided to recommend that the squatters leave voluntarily. The Communist Party organised a band to accompany a march to a fleet of coaches, which took the families to the now empty Old Workhouse at Bromley by Bow. In time, all the squatters were rehoused. Clearly the squatters' direct action had forced the Labour government to speed up the rehousing programmes.

By the summer of 1946 there were already a number of empty army camps and these were targeted first by squatting groups. In Scunthorpe 48 families moved into two camps and a third camp nearby was taken over in the following week. The movement then snowballed to other parts of the country. In Scunthorpe the squatters were supported by their local MP. The War Office said it wouldn't evict the squatters if local authorities took responsibility. This appeared to give a green light, and by August of the same year, 45,000 people were occupying vacated camps. In many of the localities it was local communists who took the initiative.

In Birmingham, the Party announced publicly that it was looking for suitable camps and by August 257 families had been installed in 12 camps in and around the city. The Birmingham and District Squatters Association was chaired by the Party's district organiser, Sam Blackwell and its Secretary, Harry Chapman, was also a member. Bert Ward in Middlesbrough was another Party member who squatted with his wife and others, occupying a group of Nissen huts surrounding a former anti-aircraft battery. He recalled that the movement was led by another communist, Pat Durkin. Similar groups initiated by Party members were squatting in High Wycombe and at nearby Daws Hill which had been the HQ of the US Eighth Army.

These army camps were only looked upon as temporary accommodation until new housing could be built; the chief aim was to galvanise council house-building programmes. In London, too, there was great indignation at the number of empty blocks of flats and properties, when 500,000 families were waiting for homes.

Although councils had requisitioning powers to take over empty properties, they were often reluctant to use these. Tory controlled councils like those of Kensington, Chelsea and Westminster – in which there were many empty spacious and luxurious flats – were particularly reluctant to use their powers. So, on 6 September 1946, Ted Bramley, the Party's district secretary and a communist councillor on the London County Council, discussed the matter with the Party's organiser, Dennis Goodwin. That same evening they contacted members in various parts of London asking them, as a matter of urgency, to identify suitable empty dwellings. Once that had been done, the Party contacted local people to find out which families were in direst need and asked them if they'd like to join a squat. They arranged a time and date for the people to assemble and march on the identified properties. When they did this in Kensington, they were amazed at the number of people who turned up – literally hundreds, dragging suitcases and their small bags of possessions, as well as items of furniture.

The occupations were well organised and the flats soon occupied. News of the occupations was broadcast widely and this in turn helped spark off further occupations. Communist building worker Tom Durkin (later to be a leading organiser of the Grunwick strike picket) organised a squat in Willesden; Dr. Joan McMichael, who was on the Party's Executive, helped organise one in Westminster.

All over London Party branches were being approached by people in need of re-housing. The Communist Party London District then wrote a letter to Aneurin Bevan, Minister of Health, asking to meet with him to discuss the issue of emergency housing. On the day the letter was sent, the Cabinet met and decided to crush this popular, but unregulated, movement before it became an independent and alternative ministry of housing.

Initially much of the press had shown sympathy with the squatting movement, but after the Cabinet decision the mood changed. On 14 September 1946 four communist councillors – Ted Bramley, Joyce Alergant, Bill Carritt and Tubby Rosen, together with Party member, Stan Henderson, were all arrested and charged with 'conspiracy to incite and direct trespass', although all were released on bail. This was followed up with instructions to utility services to refuse supplies to the squats, as well as increased police harassment.

In October the case came up at the Old Bailey. Party solicitors, Jack Gaster and Bill Sedley were in charge of the defence (Bill was to become the father of the barrister, Stephen Sedley, who was also a member of the Party for many years before becoming a QC). They managed to secure the services of Sir Walter Monckton KC and eminent Conservative to act for the defence. The five were found guilty, but surprisingly the judge simply had them bound over for the following two years to keep the peace. The fact that in the coming months councils appeared to be much more willing to make use of their requisitioning powers, was not unrelated to this successful squatting campaign.

The Young Communist League
and the Student Movement

'It takes a very long time to become young.'

PABLO PICASSO

While the Party has always placed its main emphasis on the working class and the recruiting of working class members, students have, certainly since the thirties, also played a key role.

The First World War left a whole generation traumatised by the immense loss of life, particularly of young men. In its aftermath, invalid ex-servicemen could be seen begging on the streets of all the big cities; the end of the war was followed by the economic slump of 1919-21 and then the Great Depression of 1930-31, leaving thousands of people jobless and penniless. The clear inability of the governing classes to offer appropriate solutions to this deep social malaise, was clear, not only to those who were its victims, but to many individual members of the privileged sections of society. This is one of the main reasons for an upsurge of interest in communism and Marxist ideas during this period.

From the early thirties onwards, student communist groups began forming in a number of British universities, notably Cambridge. But most of the students who joined the Communist Party in the thirties felt that their main task was outside the universities, to involve themselves in working class struggles, to 'identify with the proletariat'. Students would willingly go out canvassing or selling the Daily Worker in working class areas. For most of these, overwhelmingly middle and upper class students, this activity brought them into contact with ordinary working people, often for the first time in their lives.

In 1932 a new Federation of Student Societies (FSS) was established by more radical students; it was seen as an alternative to the University Labour Federation that had been formed in 1920 and was affiliated to the Labour Party. The Communist Party leadership realised that winning more students to the Party was to be welcomed, but it didn't want students squandering their time on mundane Party work or focussing on 'joining the proletariat'.

So, in 1934, Willie Gallacher on behalf of the Central Committee told students that, 'We want people who are capable, who are good scientists, historians and teachers…We need you as you are; if you have a vocation, it's pointless to run away to factories…We want you to study and become good students.' Out of this came the slogan: Every Communist student a good student.

A new militancy was arising in the country during the 1930s, which also had an impact on students. There was an increasing awareness, particularly among left-wing and radical sections of the population, of the dangerous rising tide of fascism in Europe, and the urgent need to counter it. As an example of the new mood, at the Oxford Union debate in 1933, a motion 'This House refuses to fight for King and Country' was carried, to the horror of the establishment. And in 1939 Oxford elected its first communist president, Philip Toynbee, the son of historian Arnold Toynbee, and many of its students turned to communism in those years.

At the end of 1934, a British delegation of 90 students attended an international student congress against war and fascism in Brussels, and every British university was represented at this meeting. The Party students returning from it were full of determination to build a democratic student movement against war and fascism that would extend beyond the socialist society groupings and would include Christian and Liberal students and those belonging to the League of Nations Union.

In the wake of the Brussels conference, the FSS dissolved itself and affiliated to the University Labour Federation (ULF). John Cornford, a leading Cambridge communist (he was later to die in Spain) and Secretary of the FSS, was elected as vice-president of the new united organisation. Already by this time membership of the Party among students could be counted, no longer in handfuls, but in hundreds. A good number of those students went on to distinguished careers, a good many dropped out of the Party and left-wing politics altogether, and yet others remained sympathisers for a long time even if they no longer remained in membership. A tiny number decided to take the more radical step of becoming Soviet spies. Most, though, remained in the Party or retained sympathy with it throughout the thirties and the war years, but with the election of a Labour government in 1945 and the immediate onset of the Cold War, together with the information coming out of the Soviet Union in the wake of the 'show trials', there followed a steep decline in student as well as general membership.

During the fifties – the height of the Cold War – the Communist Party and its youth wing managed to maintain a presence in the country, but it was a severely inclement period for recruitment and effective public campaigning. In the colleges and universities, much of the impetus gained through the successful anti-fascist struggles of the thirties and forties had been dissipated.

The sixties in Britain, as in other developed western countries, brought about a period of profound social change. A new, self-confident and materially better off generation of young people was emerging, with its own identifiable culture and aspirations. There was a new radicalism and new social movements began to emerge. Class as the main identifier was giving way to a more egalitarian society, in which cultural allegiances were perceived as more significant than class. This period saw the emergence of student, feminist and gay rights movements. These social changes were also reflected, to some extent, in Party membership. There was also one significant individual breakthrough in the early sixties when mature student Mick Costello became president of Manchester University students union, beating future newscaster Anna Ford to become the first post war communist student union president.

In 1962, in an attempt to regain the initiative in student politics, the Party organised a Week of Marxist Thought, and in 1963 its Cultural Committee organised a 'Challenge of Marxism' Week boasting prominent speakers. Every attempt was being made to encourage renewed interest in Marxism and the Communist Party, particularly after the double blows of Khrushchev's revelatory speech on Stalin's terror and the 1956 uprising in Hungary which had repercussions far beyond Eastern Europe.

Perhaps somewhat surprisingly, given the rebelliousness of the new generation of young people and its anti-establishment ethos, the Young

Communist League (YCL), the Party's youth wing, gained new wind and was to play a key role on the left in the coming years. The YCL now sought to root its politics in popular cultural initiatives reflecting the generational change that was taking place in wider society.

It readily embraced rock culture, young people's hedonistic aspirations and a commitment to popular culture. As a result of this, the YCL's relationship with the older and more conservative Party was at times an uneasy one.

The YCL, despite the inclement factors mentioned above, began growing during the sixties and in many areas developed a significant political profile. There were new leaders and a renewed membership. Social events organised by the YCL were well-attended and fun was had by all; it had managed to discard the Party's perceived stuffy and Puritan image. For instance in Wembley, YCL membership rose from a handful to over a hundred between 1963-64 and its Rhythm and Blues Club became a popular focus for young people in the area, and it was to host the, as yet little-known, band, The Who, before the band achieved international renown. Pete Townshend, The Who's lead singer, was a member of both the YCL and CND at the time.[93]

Interestingly, the Party's general secretary, John Gollan, said that he'd never had to discipline the YCL, despite its often independent approach to issues. Unlike the Labour Party which had continual run-ins with its more left-wing and rebellious youth organisation, the Young Socialists.

From 1983, a series of moves by the Labour Party's National Executive and leader Neil Kinnock led to the expulsion of prominent members of the Militant Tendency which had virtually taken over its youth wing. This also led to the eventual loss of the Militant Tendency's two Labour MPs. These measures ended this Trotskyist organisation's influence, and presence, within the Party and led to the eventual disbandment of the Labour Young Socialists, to be replaced by an ineffectual Young Labour in 1993.

For many in the Young Communist League, the Soviet Union had long ceased to be a paragon or touchstone in terms of self-identity. And, when the Soviet Union sent troops into Czechoslovakia in 1968 the British Party condemned the action – a reversal of its position on Hungary in 1956 – and this also encouraged people, once again, to join the Party, as it had now clearly demonstrated its independence. But already by 1964 there were nearly 40 New Left clubs in the country, formed by those who had earlier left the Communist Party in the wake of the Khrushchev revelations and the invasion of Hungary, together with other Marxists and sympathetic left-wingers. The New Left severed all remnants of ideological adherence to the Soviet Union and East European communism, and sought instead a fuller understanding of the significant social and cultural changes that were taking place in Britain at the time. Largely because of this, it became attractive to left-inclined young people, particularly students.

On the other hand, during the sixties, the Party itself did begin a long road to recovery from the crisis years of the Cold War in the late fifties, and its membership rose from 28,000 in 1961 to 34,000 in 1963 in spite of the vote-rigging scandal in the Electricians Union in 1961 which dealt a severe blow to its integrity.

Undoubtedly, too, the relative improvement in the Soviet economy, its scientific achievements and the new policy of peaceful coexistence, had helped re-establish a degree of faith in East European socialism. Nevertheless, the Party had to face new challenges to its domination of the Left, not only from its own 'dissidents' in the New Left movement, but also from several Trotskyist organisations like the International Socialists, International Marxist Group, Socialist Workers' Party and the Workers' Revolutionary Party, which were particularly attractive to students and young people. These parties all had the advantage of carrying no 'baggage' – there had been no countries with Trotskyist governments – and they were also led by a number of charismatic leaders like Tariq Ali, Paul Foot, Tony Cliff and Vanessa Redgrave. However, these parties tended to function essen-tially as through stations for student activists who rarely matured into adult members, and invariably dropped out soon after leaving college. The Communist Party's influential position in the working class and trade union movement, on the other hand, remained quite unaffected.

An attempt to give political expression to the new, youthful energies in the Young Communist League was developed around 'The Trend is Communism' campaign in 1967. The YCL printed 10,000 leaflets, setting out how communist ideals would meet young people's aspirations. The culmination of the campaign was an international youth festival in May/June 1967, to which the Kinks and other leading bands were invited.

What have become known as the 'new social movements' were also beginning to have a profound impact on the Party. The anti-Vietnam War movement which was gaining momentum, particularly among students in the United States during 1964, had grown by 1968 into a world movement. Then came the campus rebellions of that same year which took the European Communist Parties by complete surprise and they were uncertain how to react – the working class was supposed to lead struggle, not students! This student movement was also, and significantly, led in the main by individuals from outside the party political mainstream, and they belonged, by and large, to various strands of Trotskyist, Maoist or Anarchist groups. Despite an initial lethargy, the Party in Britain did come out in support of the student movement and certainly put its weight and organisational strength behind the anti-Vietnam War Movement demonstrations.

In 1968, at the height of the widespread student rebellion, Trotskyist groups appeared to be more in tune with student thinking than the Party was, offering the notion of turning the universities into 'red bases'. Trotskyist students launched their Revolutionary Students' Federation in 1968, demanding an end to 'bourgeois ideology' in courses.

While the Party and the YCL had been somewhat left behind by the events of 1968, they did, belatedly, catch up and were to play a pivotal role in developing the 'Broad Left' alliances then emerging in the student movement and which were to dominate student politics from the seventies onwards.

Dave Cook became the Party's student organiser, taking over from Fergus Nicholson, and during his period in office, the Party's influence in the student movement reached its peak. The intellectual role communist students played, as well as the resurgence of Marxist ideas within the student movement, not least through the annual Communist University of London events, were at their height during the early seventies.

The National Union of Students, the body that represents all students in British universities and colleges, had been traditionally apolitical and right-wing, but that began to change with the formation of the Radical Students' Alliance in late 1966, which included Labour and Liberal as well as communist students. The leading communists in this Alliance were Martin Jacques, an activist at Manchester University (now a leading academic and journalist), and Alan Hunt at Leeds. This was the forerunner of the Broad Left Alliance (set up officially at Leeds in 1972) that was to dominate student politics throughout the seventies with the object of building a mass student movement and of engaging properly with the political process.

It began a campaign to change the leadership and policies of the official students' union, not least its 'no politics' clause. The breakthrough came in 1969 with the election of progressive candidate Jack Straw as NUS secretary (later to become a minister in the Blair government). He was followed in 1971-73 by communist Digby Jacks and, in 1977, by fellow member, Sue Slipman, who was elected as the NUS's first woman president. Judy Cotter also became a vice-president of the NUS, and featured in a BBC documentary on the Communist Party. Later she became an official in Liverpool of NALGO, the local government union. Slipman was followed in 1978 by Trevor Phillips (not a communist) as its first black president, also elected on the Broad Left ticket, and, in 1980-82, by the communist David Aaronovitch (now a right-leaning journalist).

In 1968 students at Hornsey College of Art occupied the Crouch End Hill campus in a sit-in. Communist Nick Wright, then President of the Students' Union, initiated the occupation, and one of the other students involved was the communist Kim Howells, later to become a trade union official and then, after having left the Party, a minister in the Blair government. The occupation was undertaken to force a discussion on the withdrawal of Student Union funding. The students installed their own temporary administration at the college, supported by sympathetic staff and visiting artists. They also put forward a principled critique of the education system at the time. However, the college was repossessed by the local authority at the beginning of the summer break.

1968 also saw the formation of the Revolutionary Students Federation (RSSF) which was a Trotskyist-led organisation, supported by a few Maoists, as part of a general growth of Trotskyist organisations like the International Socialists led by Tariq Ali. These groups with their more radical demands, readily rallied students to their banners and challenged the hitherto communist domination of left politics, eventually displacing communist influence in student politics altogether.

The RSSF grew rapidly to a strength of several thousands and at its Congress adopted an action programme around the Student Red Base concept – higher education as centres of opposition to the capitalist system – and concentrated on organising the big anti-Vietnam War demonstration in London in October of that same year.

One major outcome of what the Party saw as an urgent need to counter the rising influence of Trotskyism and increase communist influence in the student movement at the time, was the setting up of the Communist University of London (CUL) in 1969. This became an annual festival of Marxism which included series of lectures, discussions and workshops on politics, culture, sociology, economy etc. Although the attendance at the first CUL was only 159, that number increased considerably over the following few years. The impact of CUL did not go unnoticed in establishment circles. In 1977 the Institute for the Study of Conflict produced its 'Gould Report' authored by Julius Gould, the founder Chairman of the Social Affairs Unit and then a professor at Nottingham University, called The Attack on Higher Education: Marxist and Radical Penetration. This report alleged a Marxist penetration of British sociology and pinpointed Communist Party influence in higher education, prompting vigorous debate between left and right educationalists.

The year 1971 saw the first issue of Artery, an arts and cultural magazine, founded by four communist students at London's Royal College of Art, who used the school's mimeograph machine to print a small run of 100 copies. It was inspired by the second CUL and was published as a quarterly until 1984, helped over several years by a small amount of funding from the Arts Council. Its aim was to establish a Marxist discussion forum on the arts and it sought also to involve, not just artists, but trade unionists in its editorial discussions, in order to establish a worker-artist dialogue. However it never received official endorsement from the Party leadership. Those who wrote for it included John Lloyd (later to become contributing editor of the Financial Times, and a writer for The Times and New Statesman), the art critic Lynda Morris, artists Conrad Atkinson (since 1992 professor of Art and Art History at the University of California) and Desmond Rochfort (since 1999 professor, of Art Design at Alberta College, Calgary, Canada), the art critic and historian, Gen Doy, and the photo-montage specialist, Peter Kennard. Among other noted supporters were former communist, and stand-up comedian, Alexei Sayle, whose unique brand of comedy borrowed heavily from his communist family background, and the influential musician and former member of the Soft Machine, Robert Wyatt, along with his wife, artist and song-writer, Alfreda Benge.

It is always extremely difficult to assess what lasting impact any group or organisation has on society, certainly after such a short passage of time. So what can one say about the actual achievements of communist students? In terms of lasting influence, there is probably not much to chalk up on the scoreboard. Students are, of course, a rapidly shifting population and each new intake will reflect the wider social changes that have been wrought in society. Communists did, though, manage to help push student affairs onto the mainstream political agenda and, at the same time, demonstrate that students can and should play a more active social and political role in society. Perhaps the part played by former NUS secretary Digby Jacks, seen through the eyes of others, provides a partial answer to the above question.

Francis Beckett, NUS press officer under Jacks, said of him:

'I admired his energy, seriousness, hard work and courage. When he thought some student politicians (he would have called them head-bangers, or other, less repeatable things) were indulging in gesture politics, he said so in his address to the NUS conference. The conference condemned him for it, but he told me he would have still said it even if he had predicted the response.' [94]

Jacks was president while Margaret Thatcher was Secretary of Education and he once took her out to lunch at an expensive restaurants, and was attacked for doing so, but he felt it was important to establish a dialogue with the Minister responsible for education.

The Guardian's John Fairhall, 'grew to like and admire his [Jack's] seriousness and pragmatism' and the Daily Telegraph's then education correspondent, John Izbicki, insisting his newsdesk allow him to report Digby as the thoughtful man he was, rather than as a 'communist hot-head'.

Jacks led NUS opposition to Thatcher's proposals to restrict the finances and autonomy of student unions. A combination of quiet, serious argument and mass demonstrations produced the desired result: the proposals were shelved. He also negotiated an increase in the student grant, but then, at the NUS conference he faced calls from the far left to reject it and to campaign for more radical action instead.

In 1973, he was recruited to the Association of Scientific, Technical and Managerial Staffs (ASTMS) by Clive Jenkins, becoming a Divisional Officer. He later took some time out to write a book which set out his views on student politics – Student Politics and Higher Education,[95] published in 1975 – but then returned to trade union work. After retirement, and no longer a member of the Party, he served as a Labour councillor in Hounslow, West London.

Certainly during the period of the Broad Left domination of student politics during the seventies, communists provided a stable left leadership, based on a realistic understanding of pertaining social forces. It was a time when attacks on student grants and rights were just beginning and when an overhaul of higher education was widely seen as long overdue, but what students wanted and what the government of the day proposed were very different things. Communists provided the student movement with a more pragmatic and rational approach to issues, rejecting the ultra-left 'occupy the campuses' and 'establish red bases now' rhetoric, thus helping to keep lines of communication with government and college authorities open, as far as this was possible.

There are those on the far left, of course, who will argue that the communists were far too timid and 'unrevolutionary' and that they sold-out the students at a critical time. This is an oft repeated accusation made by those to the left of the Communist Party, but how far there is any truth in it is a debate that, no doubt, will be conducted by specialist historians for some time to come.

Socialist Sunday Schools and the Woodcraft Folk

Although the following short section doesn't strictly come under this chapter heading, it is nevertheless important to mention because of the role communists played in these two significant, independent educational organisations for young people, as well as the role the organisations played in influencing the political direction of many children who belonged to them.

Many early socialists and progressive secularists were very unhappy at the dominance of religion in the country's schools and the way that education was very much tied in with an elitist, ruling class outlook. Of course, even during the late 19th century, many working class children didn't even go to school or, at most, for a few years until they could work to support their families. This dissatisfaction led to the establishment of the Socialist Sunday School movement. The schools were set up as an alternative to Christian Sunday Schools, and arose in response to a feeling of the inadequacy of orthodox Sunday Schools as a training ground for the children of socialists and atheists, and of the need for some organised and systematic method of presenting the socialist point of view and of teaching the ideals and principles of socialism to young people.

The first Socialist Sunday School was set up by Mary Gray in 1892. She was a member of the Social Democratic Federation, some of whose members later helped form the Communist Party. She became involved in setting up a soup kitchen for the children of striking dockers during the big dock strike in 1889 and realised that those children had little, if any, education, so she took on the task of providing some education for them and making them aware of their socialist responsibilities. She started the first Sunday School with only one other child, apart from her own two.

In 1894, another Socialist Sunday School was created in Scotland by the trade unionist Tom Anderson (he was a member of the Marxist Social Democratic Federation and was the person responsible for establishing the Proletarian Sunday Schools in Glasgow. He was also a trusted political ally and close friend of the Clydeside revolutionary John Maclean, who had been appointed the Bolshevik representative in Scotland).

Socialist Sunday Schools were well established by the turn of the century, and by 1912 there were over 200 throughout Britain. In their early days they encountered vehement opposition from local authorities and politicians, who argued that they were subverting the minds of young people with unsavoury political and anti-religious doctrines and teachings. The schools played a key role in steering many, particularly women, towards communist policies. This was no doubt largely because the schools emphasised equality between the genders

The Independent Labour Party was also instrumental in promoting the movement in Scotland. A national movement, the National Council of British Socialist Sunday Schools Union, formed in 1909, traces its origin to a school opened in Glasgow by Carolyn Martyn of the ILP, and Archie McArthur. These schools worked in close harmony with the Labour Movement and were concerned with developing well-rounded, socially responsible students. One former pupil, Rose Kerringan, quoted in Neil Rafeek's excellent book, Women Communists in Scotland, says that the Socialist Sunday Schools, 'taught us not to...just accept things but to try and analyse them and try to see what was right and whether the truth was being told or whether things were just being hushed up.' [96] A socialist version of the Ten Commandments provided an excellent basis for establishing a non-Christian ethical outlook. [97]

The Socialist Sunday School movement was impeded by a lack of its own premises and met objections to hiring of suitable halls to the extent that in 1907 London County Council evicted five branches out of hired school buildings. A massive demonstration in Trafalgar Square ensued, which was addressed by Margaret McMillan (ILP) who, with her sister, campaigned for better education and health for poor children. The Socialist Sunday School movement did, though, play a central role for a number of working class children, many of whom would, as adults, go on to play active roles in the labour and socialist movement. The Schools continued into the fifties and even early sixties but then became defunct.

Just after the First World War one of the leading figures in the Scouting movement broke away from what he considered to be its militaristic approach and formed the Kindred of the Kibbo Kift. Kibbo Kift included people of all ages, not just young people, and was open to both sexes. John Hargrave, who founded it, believed the open-air life would help urban youngsters build a new world peace. However, not all members agreed with Hargrave's leadership and in 1924, led by 19-year-old Leslie Paul, some co-operative groups from South London broke away and set up their own organisation, calling it The Woodcraft Folk.

The Woodcraft Folk has always been closely associated with the Co-operative Movement, is another organisation based on similar principles and with similar goals. The organisation is run by thousands of volunteers and places great emphasis on cooperation, international solidarity and developing a healthy respect for the countryside and our environment. It was originally set up as a counter youth movement to the gender separated Scout movement, which was also deemed too imperialist oriented and based too much on military lines. It is certainly not an overtly political or even socialist organisation, but its strong international dimension and emphasis on collective activities undoubtedly influence children in a progressive direction.

The term 'Woodcraft' was used by the influential writer and naturalist Ernest Thompson Seton at the turn of the 20th century when setting up the American proto-scouting organisation Woodcraft Indians, and in this context it meant the skill of living in the open air, close to nature, like the indigenous North Americans – rather than implying the making of things out of wood.

Although the organisation was not set up by Communist Party members, on a local level they have continued to play active roles. A whole number of children raised in communist families have enjoyed the activities, camps and international get-togethers held under its auspices. Young people themselves also take an active role in planning and leading their own activities.

The organisation works in tandem with similar organisations

throughout the world and is part of the International Falcon Movement – Socialist Educational International (IFM-SEI) – a world educational movement that works to empower children and young people and campaigns for their rights. Woodcraft Folk members are given the opportunity to attend camps, courses and workshops abroad with children from many other youth movements. International friendship and cooperation is a cornerstone of Woodcraft Folk policy. Since its founding, the Woodcraft Folk has had close links with the Co-operative Movement, which still supports it financially.

Nine months before the outbreak of the Second World War, a rescue mission was launched to transport thousands of children – most of them Jewish – from Nazi Germany and the occupied territories of Austria, Czechoslovakia and Poland. The children travelled without their parents, and the mission became known as the Kindertransport. The United Kingdom took in nearly 10,000 children who were placed in homes, hostels and on farms, and many Woodcraft Folk members, including many communists, were involved in rescuing and taking care of many of these children.

Communists, specifically those with children, were attracted to both the Sunday School and Woodcraft Folk movements because they were seen to provide their children with something that was lacking in the formal educational system and in tune with their own internationalist outlook and concepts of socially responsibility. They have both had a strong influence on the children who belonged to them, and their emphasis on collective activities, strong community spirit and internationalism led many, certainly in the early period, to join the Communist Party as adults.

Although there are no Socialist Sunday Schools today, the Woodcraft Folk is still a vibrant organisation, even though its make-up has now become much more middle class and it has lost much of its left-wing essence.

The Peace Movement

*'The H-bomb has brooded like an evil genius over the lives
of two generations.'*

DORA RUSSELL

The euphoria that was unleashed, in 1945, over the winning of the war
against fascism and the vision of a new world of peaceful coexistence,
in which all countries would co-operate, was short-lived. In March
1946, Churchill gave his ominous Fulton Missouri speech where he
made it clear that the anti-fascist alliance with the Soviet Union had
only been an aberration and it was now back to facing the real enemy
once again. It was there that he also re-coined Goebbels's
scaremongering term 'Iron Curtain' to denote those eastern European
countries that had been liberated by the Red Army and were now cut
off and under Soviet domination.

In the meantime, the USA had acquired atomic weapons, whose
devastating power it had demonstrated on Hiroshima and Nagasaki,
and which were now to be targeted at the Soviet Union. In 1947, US
President Truman, in a speech on foreign policy, made it clear that
communism, indeed even socialism, was now once again the chief
enemy and he declared that freedom was more important than peace:
'better dead than red'. This new western consensus had enormous
repercussions around the world. Communists, in both Italy and France,
largely because of their courageous and selfless sacrifices in the struggles

against fascism, had won deep respect among the population and enormous electoral support in the first post-war elections. They were, though, kept out of government by collusion between their own indigenous right-wing parties and the USA, which funnelled enormous financial and logistical support to the anti-communist parties.

It was the horrendous experience of the First World War that led to an increasing concern about the destruction wreaked by modern warfare and the need to prevent such mass slaughter and destruction ever happening again. But it was only in 1934 that a national peace organisation was established by Dick Shepherd and other pacifists in the UK: The Peace Pledge Union (PPU). It is the oldest secular pacifist organisation in Britain, and has been campaigning ever since for a world without war. It launched anti-bombing campaigns during the Second World War, and is still protesting today against the use of remote controlled drone assassinations. Communists have not been involved in the PPU because very few, if any, were pacifists, although with the advent of nuclear and chemical weaponry, a pacifist outlook became ever more persuasive, and certainly provided a vital momentum to peace campaigners after the Second World War.

One of the British Communist Party's new post-war aims was to engender an international movement to obtain a ban on these terrible new weapons and it urged the immediate sharing of atomic secrets between the 'big three' – the USA, USSR and Great Britain – arguing that ultimate control should be vested in the Security Council of the United Nations. Such proposals were studiously ignored by both the USA and Britain. Behind the scenes, and without any public discussion, the British Labour government began developing its own nuclear weapons, while at the same time collaborating with the USA in an attempt to maintain a western monopoly on nuclear weapons.

The World Peace Council was set up in 1950, largely on the initiative of the Soviet Union to campaign, as its name implies, for world peace. With the establishment of NATO and a western determination to re-arm West Germany, the British section of the Peace Council led a strong campaign against German re-rearmament and called for the banning of atomic weapons. The Council's campaign against German re-armament won support from a number of Labour MPs, including Ian Mikado, Aneurin Bevan, Harold Wilson, Michael Foot and Fenner Brockway. By 1954 over 150 constituency Labour Parties had registered their opposition to their party's policy in support of German re-armament.

When NATO was launched in 1949, as a western military alliance to counter the Soviet bloc, it was followed by the birth of a world peace movement, determined to prevent the outbreak of a new world war. Its first congress was held in Paris in 1949 and it elected a permanent committee composed of Russians, French, British, US, Chinese and others from countries around the world. The Committee's president was the French nuclear scientist, professor Joliot-Curie. On its return, the British delegation set up a British Peace Council under the chairmanship of J.G. Crowther, a non-communist, leading member of the Association of Scientific Workers and the Guardian's scientific correspondent. In succeeding years, it was to be continuously attacked as a 'communist front organisation'. The Labour MP, Konni Zilliacus, was expelled from the party for being involved in the Council's work.

The World Peace Council's Stockholm Appeal, calling for an absolute ban on nuclear weapons, gained a purported 600 million signatures worldwide, but its calls for a new era of peace and cooperation fell on deaf ears in the West whose governments saw its activities as merely Soviet propaganda. The British section of the Council also campaigned against the huge burden of the mounting armaments bill for Britain which was still struggling to emerge from war-imposed deprivation. The Council's long-time Secretary, Colin Sweet, was tireless in his work for peace over several decades.

The end of the Second World War against German fascism, contrary to what most people had hoped, in no way meant an end to hostilities and British armed intervention elsewhere in the world. In the aftermath of that war British and American troops were immediately deployed to defeat ELAS, the Greek people's liberation army, and helped install a right-wing government in Greece. ELAS had fought heroically against the Nazi occupation of Greece and had won widespread popularity among the people. This undemocratic imposition of a brutal and quasi-fascist government led progressives in Britain to establish the League for Democracy in Greece, which campaigned for a government change of policy and highlighted the human rights abuses of the new Greek regime. It was to continue its activities over many years, and many communists played active roles in it. However the League soon joined other similar organisations, and was declared yet another proscribed organisation by the Labour Party.

British troops were sent to Saigon in 1945, ostensibly to disarm Japanese forces, but their real purpose was to help suppress the burgeoning liberation movement in Vietnam, the Viet Minh. The

British even began deploying Japanese troops in Indonesia, while awaiting Dutch forces, to fight the indigenous liberation army and help re-install Dutch sovereignty. Later, in 1948, British troops were sent to to Malaya to impose a British constitution on another unwilling country. The people there had not fought the Japanese in order to have yet another imperial authority forced upon them, and were determined to push for real freedom. The proposed constitution was rejected by most of the inhabitants and a new liberation army formed to fight for true independence.[98] This resistance was at first decried as a communist conspiracy to seize power and later simply as groups of bandits and terrorists to be exterminated. The only paper to oppose the war in Malaya and expose it in all its brutality was the Daily Worker. However, when the paper published photos showing smiling British soldiers holding up the decapitated heads of resistance fighters it was accused of fakery and of treason. Of course, the Party itself also campaigned vigorously against all these 'imperialist' interventions. Such colonial policies on the part of the government were also the main reason why demobilisation after the end of the war was delayed and it was causing significant unrest among the war-weary troops.

The Cold War

Shortly after the 1950 election it was announced that the USA were developing a hydrogen bomb. In response, a huge movement against nuclear weapons emerged. The end of the last war was still too recent for many people to willingly accept a new arms race and the potential use of such devastating weaponry on a global scale. The movement was initiated at a World Peace Congress in Stockholm in that same year. In Britain the Peace Council started a signature campaign to have nuclear weapons banned. Britain's Labour leaders were alarmed by this movement, accusing it of being communist-inspired, and added the Council to its ever-growing list of banned organisations. This led to further expulsions from Labour Party ranks of those who insisted on continuing to work with or supporting the Peace Council.

The British Peace Council announced that it planned holding a second World Peace Congress in Sheffield in November 1950. Before making the announcement, the organisers had written to the government for reassurance that nothing would be put in the way of hosting such a conference. The Prime Minister's secretary replied that 'in a free country there is no power to prohibit the proposed congress...'

so preparations went ahead. The growth in support for the Congress impelled Morgan Phillips, General Secretary of the Labour Party, to send out a circular warning all Labour Party organisations not to participate. Silence in the press about the Congress was suddenly broken when Attlee announced that it had been 'rigged', making it suddenly headline news. Attlee was then invited to address the congress, but declined.

Home Secretary Ede admitted that 561 applications for visas had been received from would-be delegates from abroad, but 215 had been refused and, at the last minute, the government cancelled its permission of landing rights for 18 charter flights from Prague, bringing other delegates. Among those denied visas was the Soviet composer, Dmitri Shostakovich, and even Picasso was only granted a visa at the last minute. One of the British delegates, Elinor Burns, commented: 'Where is the iron curtain?' Even though Sheffield City Hall was packed with 3,000 attendees, because of the many denials of visas, the Congress decided, after a day of deliberations, to transfer to Warsaw, where its work would be resumed. At its close, the Congress called for the unconditional prohibition of all atomic weapons and also demanded the banning of chemical weapons and a reduction of armed forces everywhere.

When the Korean War broke out in 1950, the Party and the Daily Worker sided with the North Koreans and the paper was immediately threatened with possible legal action. Alan Winnington, a reporter on the paper, was despatched as its war correspondent to the North and wrote his reports from there. This was considered treasonable activity by the government of the day and, as a result, his passport was withdrawn and he was forced to live in exile for 20 years, before the passport was eventually returned. He was the only Western correspondent in the North, and exposed the US use of saturation bombing and napalm.

With the eventual involvement of Chinese forces in Korea and the threat of defeat for US and allied forces, Truman actually threatened to use atomic weapons, but fortunately that threat was never carried out. After terrible loss of life on both sides a truce was declared in 1953, leaving a situation not dissimilar to that prevailing pre-war.

With the end of the Second World War, many people imagined the world had seen the last of war, but that hope had been dashed. While subsequent wars have not been fought in Europe (with the exception of Yugoslavia), there has been continuous surrogate war elsewhere in the world. It is not the place here to go into detail about these wars, but it is perhaps relevant to mention the war in Vietnam, Laos and Cambodia (1959-75) and the protracted 'civil' wars in Latin America which galvanised protest movements and campaigns throughout the world as well as in Britain. Communists were prominent in the anti-Vietnam War movements and this involvement has already been dealt with. They were also actively involved in the setting up and organising of a number of Latin American solidarity campaigns, particularly those in support of the progressive forces in Chile, Nicaragua and El Salvador as well as in the ongoing campaign to end the US blockade of Cuba.

The Party's reluctant espousal of the Campaign for Nuclear Disarmament (CND)

When CND first came into being in 1957, the Party was initially reluctant to embrace the organisation, even though several communists and sympathisers were involved in its formal establishment at a big public meeting in 1958. The actor Miles Malleson, a Party sympathiser and E.P. Thompson, who had left the Party only two years earlier, were among a whole number of distinguished individuals from the arts and sciences who were sponsors of the organisation, others were Peggy Ashcroft, E.M. Forster, Dora Russell, Fenner Brockway, Henry Moore, Doris Lessing and John Arlott.

The Party softened its attitude during the sixties and became much more supportive. It had been initially reluctant to throw its weight behind CND because it saw the organisation as the result of a purely middle class initiative and its call for all countries to commit to unilateral disarmament was seen as unrealistic; the Party supported a policy of multilateral disarmament. Its change of heart came about partly because a number of leading communists had decided to support CND, including many in the YCL who took part in the annual Aldermaston marches.

Several individual communists were elected to prominent positions in CND from the seventies onwards. Dr. John Cox was its Chair from 1971–1977, Garry Leffley was its General Secretary from 1990-94 and Kate Hudson, who is no longer a member of the Party, from 2003-2010. Another communist, professor Vic Allen, who was on its Governing Council, was accused of passing infor-mation about CND to the GDR, after papers were discovered, in 1990, in the GDR's State

Security headquarters indicating that a member of CND's Governing Council had been communicating with them. This discovery was made public in a BBC TV programme in 1999, reviving debate about Soviet links to CND. Allen had stood against Joan Ruddock for the leadership of CND in 1985, but was defeated.

Hetty Bower, an inveterate campaigner for peace and socialism, also deserves mention here. She was still marching against the invasion of Iraq in 2003 when she was 98 years old. When CND was founded in 1957 it was inevitable that Hetty would join. And she was still supporting it more than 50 years later, although in the meantime she had joined the Labour Party after the CPGB dissolved itself in 1991. Although she said that she didn't 'regret joining the party, but I do regret that I didn't leave earlier – perhaps in 1956. But I would still describe myself as a communist.'

I met her only a year before she died, but she was still getting around by herself and was as clear-minded as ever. She had come to see some new photos, communist photographer Vaughan Melzer had taken of her. She died aged 108, in 2013.

Unsurprisingly many women joined the Communist Party in the first place through their interest in peace and their opposition to war. The Party had always been in the forefront of campaigns for peace and had built international links to promote this. The other political parties rarely took initiatives in this area, and predictably accused the Party of being agents of the Soviet Union or playing into its hands. Even CND, though few communists were involved in it during the early years, suffered the same accusations.

With the Helsinki Accords, signed in 1975, ushering in a short period of 'peaceful coexistence' and a lowering of belligerent temperatures on both sides of the Cold War divide, CND lost much of its impetus. This changed once more with the election of Ronald Reagan in 1981, who, together with Margaret Thatcher, embarked on a new anti-communist crusade, the development of new weaponry and a militarisation of space.

In 1981 the moribund peace movement received a fillip when a small group of women from Wales marched from Cardiff to the US cruise missile base at Greenham Common in protest at the government's permission for cruise missiles to be stationed there and to raise public awareness. On arrival, frustrated by the lack of media attention, the women pledged to camp there until the weapons were removed.

This initially small protest soon gathered enormous support from women around the country and later that year 30,000 descended on the base to hold hands and make their opposition manifest. In 1983, around 70,000 protesters formed a human chain around the base. Despite continual harassment, arrests and evictions the camps remained there until 2000 when a memorial was installed.

The Greenham Common women became a beacon internationally for their demand for peace and the abolition of such weaponry, and again highlighted the key role women can and do play in this struggle. Although communists did not play leading roles in the initial camp, many gave vital and continued support throughout its existence. There was, though, one communist among that original group of 36 women who marched from Cardiff, and that was Margery Lewis.[99] A veteran campaigner, Margery had been on the first Aldermaston march in 1958 and her last action for peace was joining the 2003 demonstration in London against the proposed invasion of Iraq.

Other communist women like the teacher and peace activist Eileen Daffern,[100] based in Brighton, Betty Tebbs from Lancashire and Kate Hudson, later to become the general secretary of CND, were just three of the best known of those who took part in the Greenham Common camp. Another one was Newbury teacher, Philippa Lloyd.

A small anecdote that is is perhaps worth relating here, concerns Philippa's family, and underlines the wide range of people who joined the Communist Party, but also how politics can divide families irrevocably.

In 1929 Barbara Coleclough, who joined the Communist Party during the Second World War, married William Tyrrell, who went on to become Air Vice-Marshal Sir William Tyrrell, and to enjoy a successful career in the British Army and Royal Air Force. He was also made honorary surgeon to the King in 1939. They had two sons, Marcus and Timothy, and a daughter, Philippa, who, in political terms, followed in her mother's footsteps and also became an activist in CND. The marriage, unsurprisingly, perhaps, ended in separation in 1952.

Philippa related: 'We were a very divided family. My mother refused to go and see my father knighted, but much to our amusement she used Lady Tyrrell when she thought it useful – but often didn't mention it in different circumstances. My father came from the North of Ireland – a keen Presbyterian and Orangeman. At least by the time he'd been in England for many years he refused an offer of becoming an MP for Ulster on the grounds of disliking the extreme religious divisions, but he was always a loyal Tory. When his son began his national service, he said to his senior officer, "Watch him. His mother's a communist"!

He also once wrote to The Times saying [in reference to the progressive teaching at Dartington Hall, near Totnes where the family lived], "There are too many communists in South Devon schools". I wrote to him that if he ever did anything like that again, I would write and say he was married to a communist.' He was probably partly responsible for the sacking of a well-liked communist teacher at the school, the father of Philippa's friend, Nicola Seyd.

Barbara Coleclough was secretary of the local British Soviet Friendship Society, which flourished when Britain was an ally of the USSR. Philippa has remained a member of CND and took an active part in the protests at Greenham Common camp during the seventies. She opened up her house to Greenham women, camped herself on several frosty nights, tailed the cruise missile carriers in her car and helped tear down a section of the fence while US soldiers hit out at the women's hands with sticks. She was also secretary of Newbury NUT for 10 years.

It is perhaps unfair to single out only two women as examples of communist peace campaigners, but Eileen Daffern and Betty Tebbs – although exceptional women in many ways – were typical of many other communist activists. This summary of their lives will have to stand in for the many it is impossible to enumerate here.

A central tenet of communists and of the Party itself has always been a strong anti-war stance. While few members were pacifists, all believed that war was an abomination and that all measures should be taken in an attempt to prevent the use of violence as a means of solving international problems. These women, from very different backgrounds, epitomised that stance.

Eileen Daffern devoted most of her life to campaigning for peace, being an activist in her local CND group, joining the women at Greenham Common regularly, as well as travelling on delegations to various countries, both East and West, in an attempt to broaden the struggle for peace and international understanding. She helped establish strong links with the French peace movement and also wrote a number of books in French for the Bibliothèque de Travail series.

I met her shortly after she'd published her autobiography, and she invited me to visit her in Brighton, where she lived. Although it was only a few years before her death, she was still an alert, elegant and attractive woman with a flirtatious twinkle in her eye. She welcomed me warmly, and with characteristic modesty she spoke little of her own life, but showed curiosity in my life and ideas.

After her death in 2012, a commemorative event in Brighton in her honour brought together around 1000 people. The former Jesuit priest and CND general secretary, Bruce Kent, gave the eulogy. He said:

'Single-minded is too weak a word for Eileen. I was endlessly impressed by her keen intelligence, determination, world vision and capacity for efficient hard work. Many times we set off together to attend various international peace gatherings. Daffern bag-carrier was usually my allotted role. One theme was constant in Eileen's many letters: everyone can make a difference. We all have potential. Don't waste time. And she never did.'

Jenny Jones, former leader of the Green Party in the London Assembly and now a working peer in the House of Lords, was a former pupil of Eileen's and said of her:

'From the moment Eileen Daffern, our new teacher, walked into the classroom at Westlain grammar school in Brighton, in 1966, her elegant flowing silk clothes, and her insistence that French was fun, marked her out as different... She was a success in teaching; in one year, all of her 35 O-level students passed their exams.' She went on to describe Eileen as, 'a natural coalitionist, always orientating herself towards a middle ground consistent with her principles. When I was elected to the London Assembly in 2000, she insisted that the Greens should try to work with Ken Livingstone to expand the social and environmental agenda.' [101]

She was the aunt of Jeremy Paxman's partner, and he wrote a portrait of her for the Guardian in 2007:

'Now, in her 94th year, she's still at it. Every week or so there's a meeting of one or other peace group in her house in Brighton. When she's not organising petitions, the former teacher is writing letters to the newspapers. Her vigour has, perhaps, a message for everyone about growing older.' [102]

She was born in 1914 three years before the Russian revolution into a staid lower middle class family in Yorkshire. She attended Skipton

Girls' Grammar School in Yorkshire, and joined the Communist party in 1941 after being introduced to the Left Book Club. 'Marx and Lenin gave me a sense of how life works. I loved the dialectic: it was like a Bach fugue. And it gave the individual a belief that they could change the world. Above all, it was optimistic,' she said.[103]

The bombing of Hiroshima and Nagasaki in 1945 and the new threat of a third world war with nuclear weapons, convinced her that working for peace was the most important form of activism. Einstein thought that the bomb changed everything except our way of thinking, and Eileen became convinced that what was needed was a moral revolution to match the technological breakthrough. There followed years of campaigning for CND, alongside people like EP Thompson and Paul Oestreicher.

In an obituary in the Morning Star (23 January 2012) Kate Hudson wrote:

'In her long and eventful life, Eileen Daffern inspired many, myself included, not only with her dedication to the cause of peace and her communist vision of a better society but also with her dynamism, generosity of spirit and grace. But for Daffern, the real eye-opener on society which led her to down the road to political engagement was her foreign travel in the late 1930s. Working in a variety of jobs in Australia, New Zealand and South Africa, she was exposed to the working conditions of women and the inequality against which she railed so strongly.

By the time she returned to Britain in 1939, three weeks before the outbreak of the Second World War, she had become increasingly politically aware and socially conscious. The war triggered Eileen's full political development and her decision to join the Communist Party in 1941. Working as a personnel manager in wartime industry, she was particularly concerned that women should make further steps towards full emancipation and that working conditions in industry should be improved. But Daffern also threw herself into one of the greatest communist struggles of the wartime period – the campaign to open the second front so that Germany would be more rapidly weakened by having to fight on two fronts rather than throwing all its military might against the Soviet Union in the east. But the single wartime event which so profoundly shaped the rest of Eileen's life was the dropping of the atom bombs by the US on Hiroshima and Nagasaki in August 1945, at a time when Japan was already about to surrender.

After a period abroad, she and her family returned to Britain in 1960 and settling in Brighton, where Eileen joined both the local CND group and the Brighton branch of the Communist Party. Eileen's work for peace had continued throughout these years as chairwoman of South East Region CND, but in the 1980s, with attempts to introduce cruise missiles into Britain, Eileen's activity increased exponentially. She was secretary of the Sussex Alliance for Nuclear Disarmament, as well as a member of CND's national council and active on its international committee.

Among many other campaigning activities, she focused particularly on developing campaigning links with the French peace movement, for which she was made an honorary citizen of Dieppe in 1998. Eileen worked hard to foster links between the peoples of the East and West, particularly in a series of exchanges with the Peace Committees of Eastern Europe, including visits to Poland, East Germany and Hungary. She was inspired by the UN Charter, and worked hard for reform of the United Nations and for the implementation of the Final Act of the Helsinki Conference on Security and Cooperation in Europe.' [104]

Betty Tebbs, like Eileen Daffern, was active in the struggle for peace all her life. She joined the women's peace camp at Greenham Common and in 2007, as an 89 year-old, lay down in the road to help blockade the nuclear submarine base in Faslane Scotland. However, her biography is in sharp contrast to that of Eileen's.

Born in 1918, Betty joined her first trade union at 14 and spent her entire life campaigning for the rights of working women, global peace, social justice and nuclear disarmament.

She started her first job in a paper mill in Radcliffe at the age of 14. Realising that the boys working the same machine as her were being paid three shillings a week more, she complained to a colleague and then joined the union. Soon after beginning work in the big East Lancs Paper Mill in Bury, she started organising. 'I was there 17 years and at one time we had a time and motion study. They were trying to make us work harder for less, and I brought the women out on strike. There were nearly 300 of us women, but the men who worked on the process side wouldn't join us, so we were on the picket line a lot,' she said. Once the strike was over, they became, she said, 'the best paid paper mill women in Britain'.

Betty's first husband, Ernie, was killed in the Second World War, by which time they had a young daughter. Bringing up a young child alone and having to work to survive was an exhausting process, so Betty's mother sent her to stay with an aunt in Devon to recuperate. There she met a young soldier on the beach called Len. 'But he started talking to me politically,' she relates, 'and how if we had socialism we could have peace, and if we didn't have socialism we wouldn't have peace, and if we didn't have peace we couldn't have socialism! Not your conventional 'chat-up line' but it clearly worked with Betty; they were married after he returned from the war.

She and Len started out as Labour Party members, but after it accepted Marshall Aid from the USA after the Second World War they left and joined the Communist Party. Both were active, organising in their workplaces and, in Betty's case, working hard on the peace agenda and women's rights within the trade union movement. Betty also recalls 'cycling round North Manchester at night after work painting "Ban the Bomb" on railway bridges.'

Betty asked the union which factories in Warrington needed organising and was directed to a paper bag plant where, she says, conditions were 'appalling.' The mainly women workers ate at their machines, which was illegal, and the toilets were 'dreadful.' Pay was low, there was no protection from chemical glues and management retained the union cards of workers who were members. But Betty stayed there for three years to help organise, becoming Mother of the union Chapel.

In the late 1960s, she became a television news item after a 'scandalous' speech she made, declaring, that as a married woman, she was sick of being a kept woman – her argument being that pay inequalities meant that however hard they worked, women would always be dependent on their husband's income for their standard of living.

The prevalent anti-communist attitudes of her union's leadership meant that her attempts to win election to its executive were continuously blocked, so she left her job and found work driving bread trucks for the Co-op.

In the mid 1970s, at the age of 57, Betty spotted an advert in the Morning Star for a trade union organisers' course at Middlesex

Polytechnic. Encouraged by Len, she applied. Despite her terror at the interview, she was accepted straight away, recalling that 'I think I went through some red lights! So I went there for 12 months, and it were smashing.' Being in London at this time, Betty also joined the pickets at the Grunwick dispute. On finishing her course, almost at legal retirement age, she stopped paid work, but remained an active organiser. Bringing together a coalition of middle-class feminists and working class women in Warrington, she helped found the town's first battered women's refuge, despite being told by the head of the Council's Housing Committee that 'We don't have battered women in Warrington.' 'I mean we even got Warrington Rugby Club to do a sponsorship,' she said, with a laugh, 'and I bet half of them beat their bloody wives up'.

In the wake of the USA's use of British bases to bomb Libya after a bomb brought down a Pan Am jet over Lockerbie, killing 243 passengers and 16 crew, Betty also led a delegation of 150 British peace activists to Libya.

Despite her age, she continued to be active, particularly on nuclear disarmament issues. In October 2007, at the age of 89, she was arrested for blocking an access road at the Faslane nuclear submarine base in Scotland by locking herself to fellow protestors using thumb cuffs.

Despite a world which is far from perfect, Betty Tebbs still has a positive outlook on the decades of work she's put into the causes she's believed in: 'It's not all grind – what you get back from it are life-long friendships and understanding, and I feel privileged – that I met Len. He once said to me, "I'd not have married you if I didn't think that you'd be good behind the barricades"! I think I've had a good life – and it keeps you going! I've often said I don't know what I'd do if peace broke out! But it'd be lovely, wouldn't it?'

Jean Thornton, a communist and peace activist from Bradford, recalls a young David Hockney using his burgeoning artistic talent to paint a number of peace banners for the Bradford CND group in which local communists, including his father, played and active part.[105]

It is often argued by cynics and the right wing that the peace movement was a waste of time because it never achieved any of its goals: CND didn't manage to achieve nuclear disarmament; cruise missiles were not removed as a result of the Greenham Common camp; the Iraq war wasn't stopped by the more than a million who marched through London in 2003. While that is undoubtedly true, it ignores the effect of the continual pressure exerted on governments, institutions and the general public throughout this period. One could also argue that if the movement was so ineffective, then why did successive governments use their security services to spy on and infiltrate peace movement organisations (see chapter: The 'Enemy Within')? Certainly the reluctance of the public and of parliament to endorse military action in Syria in 2013 was in no small way due to the work of the Stop the War Coalition and the enormous anti-Iraq war movement.

The presence of communists in the various peace campaigns and solidarity movements has been used continuously to denigrate and smear the movements themselves as 'playing into Soviet and communist hands'. However, it is undoubtedly true that without the hard slog of communists within such movements and organisations, it is unlikely that they would have been quite as effective as they were in mobilising support and wielding political clout. The organising experience and ability of the Communist Party, together with its network of activists at home and with its fraternal parties abroad, gave it an edge over most other political groups.

The Women's Movement

'I myself have never been able to find out precisely what feminism is: I only know that people call me a feminist whenever I express sentiments that differentiate me from a doormat or a prostitute.' [106]

REBECCA WEST

'It was not until I became involved in radical political movements that I ever felt I lived fully in the present or was fully myself. All those years before I'd felt that my identity was suppressed, that I was confined to some self-created psychic prison.' [107]

ELIZABETH WILSON

Women, of course, have been playing prominent roles throughout history, but until the feminist movement of the sixties 're-discovered' them, many had been entirely ignored or overlooked by mainstream historians. Certainly today we are much more aware of the particularly significant contributions women have made to progressive causes and on the left.

Every school child learns about the suffragette movement, but it is invariably associated with middle class London ladies, like the Pankhurst family or Emily Davison who threw herself under the King's horse at Epsom. But the many working class women who threw themselves just as forcefully into the movement itself have been largely eclipsed. One of those was Mary Bamber, a prominent campaigner in the Suffrage movement on Merseyside. In 1919, she won the Orange stronghold Everton ward in the Liverpool council elections, standing for the Labour Party. Her win was remarkable for many reasons – she was the first woman to win an election in either local or national government, as no woman had been elected to Parliament in the 1918 general election, and she was also a communist who supported the Russian revolution. She remained a tireless campaigner against injustice and fought to improve women's lives particularly through the organisation of women into trade unions, promoting birth control and supporting the unemployed movement. Sylvia Pankhurst described her as 'the finest, fighting platform speaker in the country'.

Among the first leading women in the Party was Dora Montefiore, a radical campaigner who became an early propagandist for a women-centred socialism. She was a leading suffragette, born in Britain, but spent many years in Australia. She was in close contact with people like Clara Zetkin, the German communist leader, and the Soviet feminist and revolutionary Alexandra Kollontai. She came from a noted middle class family – her father had worked with Prince Albert on the planning of the Great Exhibition.

In October 1913, she was involved in a plan to take children from Dublin where an employers' lockout, organised with the aim of destroying Jim Larkin's Irish Transport and General Workers Union, had caused enormous deprivation and starvation for numerous families. Dora helped or-ganise efforts to bring some of the starving children to Britain so that they would not continue to suffer while the lockout continued. The Archbishop of Dublin wrote a public letter condemning her plan. Some of those involved in the operation were arrested and charged with kidnapping. These events, and Dora's association with the efforts to help the locked-out workers' children, were commemorated in James Plunkett's vivid portrayal of working class life in Dublin of that period in his classic novel Strumpet City.

During the First World War she joined the British Socialist Party, and in 1920 was elected to the provisional council of its successor, the Communist Party of Great Britain. When her son died in 1921, following his service in the War, the Australian government would not allow her to visit Australia until she assured them not to engage in communist propaganda. She was allowed to visit, and also used the time to make connections with the Australian communist movement, and represented the Communist Party of Australia in Moscow in 1924.

Another foundation member was Rose Smith, from a very different background. She left school with little education and became an activist in the textile mills of Lancashire during the thirties. She was at the centre of many industrial struggles there and would spend a lifetime fighting for justice and equality. She fell out with the Party over the divisions caused by the Sino-Soviet split in the sixties, and went to live in China where she worked for the Chinese communists, dying in Beijing, where she is buried.

The Scottish-born Helen Crawfurd Anderson was another of those powerful women who came out of the Suffragette movement to the Party. She was born into a religious household, becoming a Sunday school teacher, but soon threw herself into the Suffragette movement, going on hunger strikes and being arrested. She was elected on to the Party's Executive Committee in the year of its foundation in 1921 and met Lenin. She was made editor of the Women's Page of the Communist and helped set up the Sunday Worker. She was adamantly opposed to the First World War, being a devout pacifist, and campaigned on behalf of republican Spain. She became secretary of Glasgow Women's Housing Association and was active in the many rent battles of the time. She was also one of those who helped establish the League Against Imperialism, and became the first woman to be elected onto Dunoon Council. Although she wrote an autobiography, it remains unpublished.

Elizabeth Arkwright, born in 1894, was also a founder member of the Party. Her father was the distinguished bacteriologist Sir Joseph Arkwright. She had been educated at Roedean and Lady Margaret Hall, Oxford University, but had been inspired by the Russian Revolution. She married another founding member, Tom Wintringham, who was to become the commander of the British Battalion in the Spanish Civil War. She qualified as a medical doctor, but was unable to practice as she had, by then, had her first child.

Unsurprisingly, given the traditional male dominance in all areas of society, women had also been largely ignored by the mainstream trade union movement, until the Communist Party took up the issue. It made a significant contribution towards the organising of working women, which was at the time a very difficult and often thankless task. Two of the Party's founding members were the suffragettes, Sylvia

Pankhurst and 'Red' Ellen Wilkinson, who later went on to become a leading Labour MP.

In the run-up to the Second World War, there had been a big influx of young women into the engineering industry, but their low pay served to undermine that of the skilled men, and the vast majority of these women were not in trade unions. The skilled men's unions viewed women merely as cheap labour and this attitude only compounded the problem. The biggest engineering union, the AEU, was still refusing to admit women to membership at this time.

The Communist Party always stood for equal pay between men and women and for the organisation of women into the same unions, as the best way to prevent the undermining of pay and conditions, in addition to the core aim of gender equality. It has encountered entrenched opposition to this policy not only on the part of union leaderships, but also from many ordinary male members.

An early example of the Party's endeavour in this area could be seen at the Lucas factories in Birmingham in 1931 when the workforce of around 15,000 – overwhelmingly women – came out on strike. The Party initiated resistance to the Bedaux system (a time and motion system imported from the United States that was intended to intensify productivity) and the company's own 'points system' which discriminated against women and the unskilled. Jessie Eden, a local communist, who had become a shop steward at the plant, became one of the leaders of the Lucas strike.

After its 13th congress in 1935 the Party grew steadily, from a membership of around 6,500 in that year to 17,750 in 1939 before the outbreak of war. After its 1936 congress it had also agreed to call its 'cells' or 'groups' branches and to lay emphasis on building up its residential as well as its factory branches. This policy made it easier to recruit and hold more women members. In the past the Party had been very male orientated with women constituting a minority. Although Jessie Eden, mentioned above, a prominent trade union activist in Birmingham, was elected to the Central Committee in 1935 and Nellie Usher, a well-known figure in the upholsterers' union, served on the Central Committee from 1929-32, women were still very much in the background.

In theory the Party had always stood for the full emancipation of women and equality between the sexes, but in practice the story was not exactly laudable. The underlying argument was that it would be impossible to achieve true equality under capitalism and only when socialism had been established would women enjoy full equality, therefore the priority was to struggle for the overthrow of capitalism. A similar attitude pertained on the issue of race. Although such attitudes were not necessarily held by all or even a majority of members, there was often an underlying assumption that putting too much effort into fighting for women's rights or the rights of black and minority people would only divert comrades from the main struggle. Nevertheless, women in the Party, even in those early years, were not ghettoised into separate women's sections as they were in many other organisations. They did find themselves invariably given responsibility for organising fund-raising bazaars, socials and children's events, but that was more a reflection of the wider social norms than a conscious policy.

During the thirties, Party women were encouraged to become active in their local Co-operative Women's Guilds – the closest equivalent to a trade union for married women who, in their majority, did not work outside the home. A number of Party women were subsequently elected to prominent positions in the co-operative movement, like Esther Henrotte in the Royal Arsenal co-op, who was also elected onto the Party's Central Committee in 1935. In Scotland and the north of England, particularly, the co-operative movement played a significant role in the community.

Another area where women were encouraged to, and did, play prominent roles, was in residents' and tenants' associations and the struggle for fair rents, security of tenure and against slum landlordism. Although in this area there were also a number of male Party members who became tenants' leaders.

Michael Shapiro, a London University lecturer in town and country planning became the first secretary of the Stepney Tenants' Defence League (under the name of Michael Best) and was responsible for establishing a Federation of Tenants and Residents Associations. By 1938 he had also produced a Tenants' Guide published by the Labour Research Department, to explain the Rent Act to people. By this time 45 local associations had joined Shapiro's Federation. Particularly in the East End of London, where renting was the norm and slum landlordism flourished, the area became a focus of large movements and regular rent strikes. Here a Tenants' Defence League was also set up (and had grown to around 11,000 members by 1940) with three full-time officials, all communists – Maurice 'Tubby' Rosen, Ella Donovan and Harry Conn. In all the East End struggles, as well as in rent strikes and tenants' protests elsewhere in the country, it was the women who 'manned' the picket lines and who often dominated the organising committees.

Housing protests, though, were not limited to the rented sector only. On one private housing estate in East Wickham, Kent, a Party member, Elsy Borders, organised a residents' association. She and her husband found, after moving in to their new home, that it was not fit for habitation and they felt swindled by the mortgage company and so decided to withhold their payments. The mortgage company, the Equitable Building Society, in response, claimed possession of the house once she and her husband were three months in arrears. Elsy counter-claimed for the return of the money she had paid on the grounds that the mortgage company had given her the loan on insufficient security. The case came to court and she conducted her own defence. The case received considerable publicity in the press and led, in February 1939, to a mortgage strike by some 3,000 owner-occupiers in outer London. Elsy went on to become a leader of the national Federation of Tenants' and Residents' Associations.

In Birmingham, too, the Municipal Tenants' Association had as its General Secretary Jessie Eden, who had served on the Party's Central Committee. When Birmingham Council raised rents considerably in 1939, a ballot was organised by the Association and it resulted in an overwhelming vote for strike action. Every morning when the council rent collectors appeared on the estates they were met by angry crowds of women who would escort them house to house, and on 7 June, 10,000 women marched on City Hall. A week later 15 bailiffs, escorted by police, made their first attempt to enter the properties of 175 tenants under a distraint order, but the crowds prevented them from entering the houses. The struggle continued over a number of weeks, and in the end the Council was forced to capitulate and the rent increases were withdrawn.

Women and the Second World War

During the war women began to play an increasingly important role in the workforce, replacing the thousands of male workers who had been drafted into the army. They were now working in jobs previously reserved for men and were also being elected on to local union branch committees. However, they were still earning much lower pay than men even though doing the same work. This was also true in the professions, in teaching and the civil service, which were, in addition, subject to the 'marriage bar' preventing women who married from continuing to work in their chosen careers.

Early, in 1942, conscription for women was also introduced and many were called up into the Women's Auxiliary Services. Many of these women faced considerable prejudice from men who feared for their own jobs. Communists argued that the answer was not to keep women out of the workforce, but to help them organise, to become active in their unions and for women to be paid 'the rate for the job'. This task was not easy, as the unions themselves were bastions of male power. The Daily Worker was constantly attacking male dominance and in October 1942, it had a leader with the headline 'Make Way for Women' in which it attacked male prejudice not only in the workplace but also in the unions and, citing the Russian example, asked, 'Are British women less capable than Russian women?'

At a Shop Stewards National Council conference in 1941, Flo Mitten, a woman communist and engineering worker, addressed the conference and told delegates that she represented a factory employing 3,000 women. She explained how management was using the women as cheap labour and criticised the unions for ignoring women and being blind to their potential for the trade union movement. A whole number of women party members became leading shop stewards during the war period and they helped lead the mounting campaign for women's equal pay. Women were also featuring increasingly as speakers at open-air meetings.

The Party was also seeking ways of broadening the movement for women's rights and in the summer of 1941, Ted Bramley, the London District Secretary, together with Tamara Rust, a member of the District Committee, raised the issue of setting up a so-called 'Women's Parliament'. The idea was passed on to the People's Convention (still labelled a 'proscribed organisation' by the Labour leaders). As a result, the first London Women's Parliament convened in July 1941 at the Conway Hall. Over 300 delegates were present, and 'Bills' on women's work and welfare and wages were discussed by all the 'MPs' present.

The parliament was opened by well-known actress, Beatrix Lehmann and the 'Speaker' was the communist and teacher, Nan McMillan (see chapter: Influence Among Professional Workers). The Women's Parliament went from strength to strength, and its honorary secretary was the Labour councillor, Diana Pym, who later joined the Communist Party. The idea soon spread to other parts of the country and the movement caused great concern to the TUC which smelled another 'communist conspiracy' and saw it as just one more attempt to undermine the 'official movement'. A circular was issued advising unions to have nothing to do with 'women's parliaments'. Despite this disparagement, the movement did help significantly to push women's equality forward to such an extent that a Conservative MP, Thelma Cazalet-Keir, won an amendment to the Education Bill which was under debate in the House of Commons and which if passed, would have ensured equal pay in the teaching profession. Very soon after this, in 1944, a Royal Commission on Equal Pay was set up by the government.

At its 16th congress in 1943, the Communist Party elected five women on to its new Executive Committee and immediately this new Committee decided to establish a Women's Advisory Committee to give leadership on women's questions. Tamara Rust, a leading female member of the Party, raised the important question of what would happen to those women now working once the war was over. She said that 45 per cent of the women working in the engineering industry wished to remain. She also argued that the skills these women had acquired should be utilised in a new post-war society and not wasted; until there was real equality between men and women in society, she said, people's progress as a whole would be held back. As a result, the Party, in 1944, began publishing a regular monthly women's magazine, Woman Today – no other political party had an equivalent journal.

Although Party women were active in a whole number of areas, including the trade unions, they were certainly central to the peace movement and played leading roles in the various peace organisations (see chapter: The Peace Movement). On 1 December 1945 a Congress of Women was held in Paris. Delegates came from 41 countries representing millions of women who were determined to fight for peace, for women's political, social and economic rights and for conditions for the happy development of all children and future generations. Britain was represented at this congress by women who had been working in the International Women's Day Committee (IWDC) set up in 1942 during the war, and out of this congress was born the Women's International Democratic Federation (WIDF), founded in Paris in 1945.

Many progressive women in Britain, were demanding their own national organisation, independent of a single political party, that would voice their needs, demands and opinions. So on 8 March 1952, such women from all parts of the country gathered in St Pancras Town Hall,

London with the aim of setting up an appropriate organisation. They came by long distance coach, bus and train, carrying handmade banners and overnight bags, responding to the call of the IWDC, which had been campaigning intensively on behalf of women. To the delight of the assembled delegates, the Chair, Labour MP Monica Felton, announced that the target of 1,000 delegates had been exceeded – 1,398 women were there from Scotland, the Welsh mining valleys, from the textile and steel towns of Lancashire and Yorkshire and the big shipbuilding centres. They represented street groups, trade unions, women's guilds, peace organisations, political parties, International Women's Day Committees, parent-teacher associations, old age pensioners associations and others. An overflow meeting had to be organised in nearby Westminster Hall with the proceedings of the conference relayed by Tannoy from the town hall. The popularity of this event clearly demonstrated the need for a new, independent women's organisation.

The National Assembly of Women[108] was founded at that 1952 gathering. It was intended to be a broad, inclusive organisation, including communists, Labour Party members, those from faith groups and anyone else with progressive ideas and who supported its aims.

Those declared aims are inclusive and broad: 'to work for full social, economic, legal, political and cultural independence, equality for women irrespective of age, race, religion, philosophical belief, sexual orientation or nationality, aims which can only be realised fully in a world at peace. In the struggle against racism, fascism and imperialism we will work with all women and other progressive organisations that share these aims.'

It had members throughout the country and affiliations from women's groups, trades union councils, local authority equal opportunities teams, national trade unions, regions and branches as well as national like-minded organisations. However, many of the women behind the setting up of the organisation were communists or sympathisers, so inevitably it came to be labelled as a 'communist organisation' and was treated as such by many.

Evaluating the influence or impact of organisations like the NAW is certainly not easy to do, but it was, before the feminist movement took centre stage in the late sixties and seventies, one of the leading progressive women's organisations in the country, and its work for peace, in cementing better international relations and campaigning for women's rights has been exemplary. It was the only over-arching, progressive women's organisation on a national level, that reached out to women of all persuasions who wished to join in the struggle for peace, international understanding and women's rights.

After the war Communist Party women were also centrally involved with waging a concerted campaign for childcare provision in the form of nurseries, as well as women's right to have an abortion, certainly not a popular campaign in those pre-feminist days.

There were also communist women active in the professions. One example of such women is the renowned academic Erna Bennett, who devoted her life to science, where she made important contributions to plant genetics, for which she won worldwide recognition. She worked for a number of scientific bodies, rising to a senior position with the UN Food and Agriculture Organisation in Rome. Erna lived for many years in Italy and Australia, and worked for peace, justice and equality around the world. She remained a life-long communist.

Her work influenced the 1972 UN Stockholm conference on the environment and led to its call for a global programme on the conservation of plant genetic resources. But she was a controversial figure, too, because she actively opposed the organisation becoming too close to the large agro-chemical corporations. When, in 1982, corporate interests appeared to dominate the organisation's policy, she resigned, but continued to be active on public issues, lecturing, writing and advising.

Erna was born in Derry, but grew up in Belfast. During the Second World War, she served in the Middle East and Greece, in the intelligence service and in other roles. Her experience there led to her conviction that communism was the system for the future, so she joined the Party, remaining a member for the rest of her life.

The impact of the feminist movement

An indication of how far the women's movement has come is the now widespread celebration of International Women's Day. Only a few decades ago International Women's Day on 8 March was unknown in Britain outside communist and progressive circles. When a motion was moved at the Labour Party Conference in 1952 to recognise the day, it was roundly rejected.

Although women in the Party, particularly through its associated organisation, the National Assembly of Women, had always celebrated the day by organising cultural events, the date and the event were almost completely ignored by the mainstream media. Today even the BBC takes the celebration as a given and dedicates programmes to it, and events are organised up and down the country.

International Women's Day was first conceived by the leading German communist and fiery campaigner for women's rights Clara Zetkin. At an International conference on women's rights, held in Copenhagen in 1910, she launched the idea of having a celebration on one day of the year to highlight the struggle for women's emancipation. Since then, the 8 March has been a firm date in the calendar and is still widely celebrated as International Women's Day.

As an aside, in the 1980s, I found myself filming a documentary in a small, isolated indigenous settlement in the rainforest of Paraguay – one of Latin America's most backward countries – and was amazed to be invited, on 8 March, to a meeting in a forest clearing to celebrate International Women's Day, where local women who had probably never travelled much beyond their own villages, gave speeches honouring women worldwide.

The birth of the Women's Liberation Movement (WLM) at a founding conference in 1970 brought another new challenge to the Communist Party. While the Party had always promoted women's rights, there was often a perception, certainly among some male members, that true equality between the sexes could only be achieved under socialism. The WLM challenged that position forcefully, demanding immediate change and more vigorous campaigning for women's equality. The Party's long-standing National Women's Advisory Committee did, though, provide a useful forum for a discussion of feminism during the seventies, and the influx into the Party at that time of a number of young women with new and radical ideas certainly helped push the feminist agenda. Many had been inspired by Friedrich Engels' writing on women's subjugation in his book The Origin of the Family, Private Property and the State, and were increasingly impatient to give the struggle a renewed impetus. However, right from the birth of the Party, many communist women had been dissatisfied with the idea that their emancipation could only come about once socialism had been achieved. The feminist movement gave a new impetus to this dissatisfaction and ambition.

During the period of the rising feminist movement, many Party women found themselves chafing at the bit and were increasingly frustrated with the Party framework for discussion, seeing it as too narrow. Some of the key journalists and activists were also no longer prepared to confine their energies to official publications, and decided to set up their own magazine, Red Rag, without official approval. The journal first appeared in 1972, but the Party leadership was not comfortable with this initiative and tried, unsuccessfully, to bring those women members back under the Party wing. Feminists, like the journalist Beatrix Campbell, were to play significant roles in the Party's developing policy on women as well as in the wider feminist movement during that period, although Campbell left the Party during the eighties to join the Green Party.

The novelist, Elizabeth Wilson was in the Communist Party for several years during this turbulent period, and wrote for Red Rag. She has been an influential feminist and gay rights activist over many years. Now also a member of the Green Party, she remains a committed socialist and feminist. In the seventies she was involved in Gay Liberation and the Women's Movement, which defined that period for her. Her writing career began then, with activism and contributions to political 'underground' magazines such as Frendz, Come Together and Red Rag. Alongside fellow communists Bea Campbell and Jean McCrindle, she was also on the advisory panel of the pioneering feminist publisher Virago. Wilson went on to undertake academic research, particularly looking at feminist politics. In the 1980s she became a lesbian co-parent and later a parent governor at Camden School for Girls. She is currently Visiting Professor at the London College of Fashion, University of the Arts, London.

Mikki Doyle, an American communist, whose husband had been expelled from the USA in the fifties under the McCarthyite witch hunt, settled in Britain in the 1950s and soon became the Daily Worker's new Women's Editor. In this role, she took up women's issues with a feisty determination, and became a prominent activist in the women's movement during the seventies. Her viewpoint, though, was very much a class-based one, seeing women's oppression and liberation as primarily a class issue.

Laurie Penny, one of today's leading feminist and socialist journalists, while never joining the Communist Party, worked for a short time as a journalist for the Morning Star, where she cut her teeth as a young journalist.

Zelda Curtis, also a former Morning Star journalist and activist, became a founder of the Association of Greater London Older Women (AGLOW) which is still going. Like many communists or former communists, she didn't let retirement get in the way of continuing to take an active part in her community and helping to fight for justice. She had been a member of the Party for most of her life, but in old age, she struck a bitter note by declaring her anger at what she felt was betrayal by the leaders of the Party.

'I was conned and I'm angry with myself for having allowed it, and even angrier with myself for suspending my disbelief and convincing myself they were acting from the best of motives,' she says, 'Who are they? They are those in leading positions who knew but didn't tell me, who were dishonest. They used me. And what hurts me most is that those who I admired and put my trust in, didn't trust me – didn't give me the chance to make up my own mind how to act. But,' she goes on, 'one thing I am not ashamed of – I still believe in socialism. I still believe in collective action and eschew "bourgeois individualism". I want a fair and just society based on equality of opportunity. My fight is still against discrimination, racism, anti-semitism, and against censorship. I still want a world where the arts are encouraged, and where each is given the opportunity to develop their talents to the full. The only problem is that I no longer know how to get it!' [109]

Zelda Curtis's views are representative of a number of those who, in the wake of Khrushchev's revelations about Stalin, the suppression of political rights in Eastern Europe and the general disillusion that set in around the demise of the Soviet Union and the CPGB in 1991, felt let down.

Communist women in the big mining areas of the country had played important roles over decades, even if too often in the background. Annie Powell, a teacher, was a long-serving councillor in the South Wales Rhondda Valley or 'Little Moscow' as it was often called, and in 1979 was elected as the first communist mayor since Joe Vaughan in Bethnal Green in 1923.

During the last big miners' strike of 1984-85, Women Against Pit Closures (WAPC) took on a leading and key role for the first time in mining history. Traditionally miners' wives had played a background role, but these women decided it was time to take an initiative on their own. A number of them were also communists or sympathisers. Among the organisers was Anne Scargill, Betty Cook and communist Betty Heathfield from Derbyshire, then wife of the NUM's general secretary Peter Heathfield.

Women Against Pit Closures had probably one of the most profound impacts on British working class women and their roles in society than any other movement beforehand. The feminist movement of the seventies had been largely a movement of middle class women and academics and, although it did undoubtedly have repercussions beyond that demographic, its impact was limited among working class women and those from the developing world.

Communist and also a founder member of WAPC, Jean Miller, was a 42-year-old single mother of three when the strike began. Her dad had been a pit deputy and on the first night of the strike she and friends discussed what they could do to help. She said that 'miners' wives learned to do all sorts of things – standing on a platform speaking, writing, marching, organising.' For many working class women, particularly those willing to accept a traditional domestic role, feminism seemed elitist; it had hardly begun to address class issues. Most working class women were fully occupied with juggling low-paid work and bringing up a family, and had no time to reflect on feminist theory – feminism was for college and career girls. WAPC proved, though, that women's action could redefine their place in family and society, not by rejecting or refusing the role of housewife but by inspiring respect for it.

WAPC was a practical response to the problem of providing for a family through a period of great adversity. Miller was motivated also by the terrible poverty that many families suffered as a result of the strike. 'I remembered the previous strike 10 years before,' she said, 'when a woman couldn't send her kids to school because they didn't have any shoes. I was determined that if women could get together and work in support of the strike we could avoid many of these things.' Many women felt their partners had more respect for them as a result of their activities during the strike, but there were also many marriages that fell apart.

Women Against Pit Closures represented a completely new initiative on the part of women to engage in an industrial dispute. The movement brought feminist ideas into practice in an industrial dispute and empowered women to take a public role in a community that was unsurprisingly, given the nature of the industry, very male-dominated. The birth of the movement had also been influenced by the examples of contemporary women's peace movements and, particularly, the iconic women's camp at Greenham Common.

The group went on to capture headlines and change forever the image of 'miners' wives' as passive supporters. Women throughout the mining communities all over the country set up their own spontaneous WAPC groups. The overwhelming majority of the women were connected in some way to mining families, through husbands or relatives.

The group and its support work grew out of the women's experience in communal feeding of families in early 1984, but developed into a more explicitly political role. An early event was a rally at the end of May 1984, held in Barnsley, which was attended by 5,000 women from coalfields across the country. This was followed by a conference in June and a large protest march in London in August 1984. 23,000 women attended that event. It's widely accepted that the strike wouldn't have continued for as long as it did without the support of the women. Local groups organised soup kitchens, collected money and put together food parcels for mining families, travelled around the country and further afield, addressing gatherings to promote and explain the miners' cause. Many women who belonged to the movement found their lives changed dramatically in so many ways, but chiefly by the sense of empowerment it gave them.

SWOMP (Socialist Women on Male Platforms) is a more recent feminist initiative in which communist or former members of the Party were centrally involved – women like Elizabeth Wilson, Anita Wright, Mary Davis, Jo Stanley, Terry Marsland, Anita Halpin and Ann Field. It is now 19 years-old and still going strong.

Jo Stanley, one of the initiators, describes it thus: 'It's fun. It's radical. It reaches the dusty sexist corners that no other campaigning group does. And its members even sport the coolest ear-rings while battling.' How did all this begin in 1990? The Thatcher government was decimating workers' rights; the women's liberation movement had been permeating ways of thinking for over twenty years; and it was fifteen years since the 1975 Equal Pay and Sex Discrimination Acts. Most unions had Equalities Officers rather than the old-style Women's Officers, and were running women's conferences and producing educational material for women... But was women's inequality being addressed deeply enough? What real power did women have in progressive organisations, to make bigger political changes?' These were issues SWOMP was determined to address.

Mary Davis, chair of the 2010 Women's TUC, and one of the initiators of SWOMP, says: 'It just grew like Topsy. We just knew it was the right thing to do. I don't remember any formal discussions, it was just hilarious.'

'Members organised formal assaults at TUC congresses, as well as social events, always with style, Jo Stanley says, 'The point was fun, serious fun. "We decided that women didn't need yet another set of meetings to go to. So we adopted different method, characterised perhaps as 'ridicule with partying,'" says Megan Dobney (Secretary of South East Region TUC). 'It wasn't like men's meetings, with a constitution and minutes and all that' agrees Mary Davis. Anyone can be a SWOMP member. And instantly they are part of SWOMP's committee-that-never-meets. And there's no membership fee, no rule book. At different times different sisters do tasks – such as fielding the mail, booking venues, banking – as members of SWOMP's unelected and gloriously unaccountable High Command.' [110]

From obscurity to strike leader – a portrait

Sally Groves is in many ways a typical example of many women who joined the Party during the sixties from inauspicious beginnings. She relates how it happened and how she unwittingly became a strike leader.

'I was first introduced to socialist ideas by a Marxist Sociology lecturer, Richard Kirkwood, on my social work training course at NW London Poly (now Metropolitan University) in 1968. I began to see, with social work experience, how many people are poor or disadvantaged through no fault of their own whilst others, as a result of their class and wealth, can lead such privileged lives. I was then introduced to the Communist Party by a member. Later I began to do a degree course having felt I had missed out on that, but going through a separation from my then husband I moved into a bedsit and needed an income, so just went to the Job Centre and got the first job that paid reasonably well. It was a toss up between Walls ice cream factory in Acton or Trico Folberth in Brentford. Only a few weeks into the job, I found myself embroiled in a battle for equal pay.'

The big Trico car-parts factory in West London belonged to a big US multi-national. Despite the recently introduced Equal Pay Act women on the factory floor were still earning considerably less than their male counterparts despite undertaking similar jobs. When the men were given a pay rise and the women weren't, the women's anger erupted and they decided to strike. They had never been on strike before and many were not even in a union, but that didn't alter their determination.

Sally had only started working there a few weeks before the issue blew up. She was also totally inexperienced in industrial work and was certainly not a hardened political activist, although she had been a member of the Young Communist League and the Party for several years. She was quite a shy, almost timid person, certainly not one's cliché idea of a firebrand or trade union militant. However, as a communist, she knew that she could hardly stand on the sidelines and would probably be expected to provide some sort of leadership and guidance to the around 300 women, none of whom had any experience of taking industrial action.

The owners and most of the men thought the women were just plain silly and would be back at work the next day, but these women were made of sterner stuff. They maintained their strike and daily picketing for 21 weeks throughout the very hot summer of 1976. Many of the women were single with no one else to help earn the bread and butter, others had husbands who were unsympathetic or even hostile to the idea of their wives not being home to cook the supper or in the morning to get the children ready for school and do the washing and cleaning – that was still the reality for many working class women even in the seventies.

Sally was on the picket line almost every day during the strike. If not on the picket line she was touring the country with other striking colleagues drumming up support and financial help as well as liaising with the regional officers of her union, the AEU, which gave the strike its full support.

In an attempt to break the strike, the company began ferrying in spare parts in convoys of lorries during the night, so the women were forced to mount their pickets at night-time too. On one occasion Sally and a male colleague – some of the men working at the factory did support the women's strike – attempted to follow several of the lorries back to their depots to find out where they were coming from. One of the drivers realised he was being followed and slowed down on the motorway, forcing Sally's car to overtake him. He then proceeded to follow their car so closely and with his headlights full on, that they felt they would be rammed. They swerved off into a lay-by, but the lorry still came after them. They were so scared that they ran off into the countryside and Sally entered a small wood and flung herself on the ground in the leaf litter, playing possum until the lorry driver gave up his search for her and drove off. On another occasion when they were waiting in the local DHSS office trying to obtain benefit for some of

BRITAIN'S COMMUNISTS: THE UNTOLD STORY

the striking women who had no other form of income during the strike, she was manhandled by the police and carried bodily down a flight of stairs and unceremoniously dumped in the roadside gutter. Despite all this, she refused to be intimidated and continued her strike and union activities. The strike itself was a success and the women were eventually awarded the same basic pay as the men.

Later, during the national campaign against Thatcher's notorious 'Poll Tax' she became one of the local activists. Sally went on to qualify as a social worker and remained a communist.

It is impossible to sketch a portrait of the 'typical' female Party member – there is no such thing. But Sally Groves's experience above highlights a pattern and attitude that were common to many women members. Although she was a convinced feminist, she found herself at the time having to work with male union officials and gaining their full support for the women strikers, something she managed to do by avoiding an unnecessarily confrontational male versus female politicking.

Despite all the caveats, what is certainly true, is that the Communist Party, much more than any other political party, offered women an opportunity to become actively involved in politics and trade union work and gave them confidence to speak publicly and take on responsible positions in a wide variety of organisations. It demonstrated in practice that women don't have to play subservient roles to men, and that they are not condemned to the roles only of wife, mother and housekeeper.

Communists and the Labour Party - a Fraught Relationship

'The message of our programme is one of hope and confidence. The working people, acting together, can take political power into their own hands, end exploitation of man by man, and use Britain's resources to meet the increasing needs of the people. They can build a Socialist Britain which will be truly great, independent and free – a bastion of peace – a country in which all work together for a fuller, happier life, and society is organised on the principle that "the free development of each is the condition for the free development of all".'

THE BRITISH ROAD TO SOCIALISM -
THE COMMUNIST PARTY'S 1958 MANIFESTO

The creation of the Communist Party

The utopian ideal of a socialist society, in which there is justice, equality and social harmony, has been a dream of humankind for centuries, even if the term itself was not used until the nineteenth century. Early radicals, from the Middle Ages onwards, like John Ball, John Bunyan and Wat Tyler preached such ideas.

The idea of socialism as a clear concept arose in the 19th century with the French utopian socialists. Communism and the use of the term emerged in the mid-nineteenth century in connection with the ideas of Marx and Engels, when the terms socialism, social-democracy and communism were almost interchangeable. In the 20th century communism has become inalienably linked with Marxist philosophy, but also, largely negatively, with the Bolshevik revolution in Russia and the Eastern European communist countries that emerged in the wake of the Second World War.

The Communist Party of Great Britain (CPGB) was founded in 1920, immediately after the end of the First World War and three years after the Bolshevik Revolution in Russia. The Communist Information Bureau (Cominform), based in Moscow, had called for all countries to set up their own communist parties. In Britain, the Party was formed by a merger of a number of smaller Marxist parties, including the British Socialist Party, The Communist Unity Group and the South Wales Socialist Society, various socialist clubs as well as some shop stewards' groups and workers' committees. Members of the Hands off Russia campaign also joined. Several branches and many individual members of the Independent Labour Party also affiliated.

In 1921 it was refounded after the majorities of Sylvia Pankhurst's group, the Communist Party (British Section of the Third International), and the Scottish Communist Labour Party agreed to unity. The Party membership grew during a period of increasing political radicalism immediately following the First World War. The Red Clydeside movement in Scotland also gave the Party a membership a boost and a higher profile. There the Party was active in organising working people in the shipyards and surrounding industries, helping tenants fight exploiting landlords, and leading rent strikes, during the early part of the twentieth century and into the thirties.

Those foundation members were men and women who had been profoundly affected by their experiences of the slaughter in the First World War. They were determined that there would be no more such horrifying episodes in which millions of ordinary people could be sent to their deaths in a struggle for power and greed waged on behalf of a small elite. Fired by the recent example of the establishment of a 'workers' state in Russia, they were determined to change their own society in a similar way, and were convinced they could do it within a short space of time. Today, in retrospect, we may laugh at such naivety and over-confidence, but we shouldn't forget that the ruling elite were also very frightened of a Bolshevik-style revolution taking place in Britain at this time, and that's why it took such early draconian measures to suppress the emergent party.

Among the Party's early leaders were John Ross Campbell, who had been invalided out of the First World War after being decorated for 'conspicuous valour'. He was a gifted propagandist for the Clyde Workers' Committee, that organised the shipyard workers in Glasgow. He later became the editor of the Daily Worker. Harry Pollitt had been active as a young man in the Boilermakers' Society in Lancashire, before he was elected as the party's General Secretary in 1929. Several others were also Scots, including Arthur McManus a shop steward from the Clyde and Bob Stewart, a former farm labourer and hand-loom weaver, was another fiery, working class founding member. One of the few women in the leadership was Rose Cohen, born into a London East End Jewish working class family, and as a young woman, became a militant Suffragette. She later married a Russian Bolshevik and went with him to live in the Soviet Union where she died – a victim of Stalin's purges.

One other of the leading figures in those early days was the indomitable Wal Hannington, born in London, he left school at 14 to become an apprentice toolmaker, but early on demonstrated his incredible organising flair. He was largely responsible for organising the National Unemployed Workers Movement (NUWM) which became one of the most powerful working class organisations outside the official trade union movement. Two founding members from very different backgrounds were Andrew Rothstein and Rajani Palme Dutt, both of whom had enjoyed university educations. Palme Dutt, was born of an Indian father and Swedish mother. A Cambridge-educated intellectual, he was the Party's leading ideologue for many years. Although looked up to and respected by generations of Party members for his sharp mind, immense knowledge and internationalist principles, his views were invariably hardline and sectarian. Rothstein was the son of Russian-Jewish emigres. His father had been a friend of Lenin's and the latter visited the family on a number of occasions while he was in London. Rothstein studied history at Oxford and also became one of the Party's leading theoreticians, and was as hard-line and sectarian as Palme Dutt.

I got to know both men in their latter years and interviewed them on several occasions for television documentaries. I didn't warm to either, finding them both as dry as old parchment and with an off-putting, humourless earnestness. I was, though, impressed by their encyclopaedic knowledge of history and politics and strong sense of loyalty to their party. Rothstein, despite being in his eighties, when I first visited him, was able to pick relevant books off the shelves of his enormous library and find the exact quote he was looking for to underline a point he was making with no problem at all. Both men, unsurprisingly perhaps, remained rather aloof from the day-to-day struggles on the ground.

The Party was formed in the wake of the most horrendous war to engulf Europe for a century – 'The War to End all Wars'. The Russian Revolution had erupted onto the world stage only three years before, and there was a widespread feeling among all classes that the world had been radically changed and there could be no going back. The upper classes feared a Soviet-style revolution in Britain; the working classes pressed for radical change. The small group of individuals who formed this new, revolutionary party were convinced that a socialist transformation in Britain could only be a matter of a few years. They were prepared to dedicate their lives to the cause of communism.

After 1923, only three years after its establishment, the Party was already making rapid strides in its chosen fields of activity, particularly in the Miners' Federation and in the engineering industry. Its success alarmed the powers that be and already in 1925, twelve members of the Party's leadership were arrested and convicted of seditious conspiracy. Five were given 12 month sentences and the other five, six months. At the trial the judge said that the defendants 'were clearly members of an illegal party, carrying on illegal work in England and it must be stopped'.

Despite all the difficulties of continued government and establishment hostility and harassment, the Party could, by the outbreak of the Second World War in 1939, already chalk up considerable achievements. In the twenties, its members had played a significant role in the 'Hands off Russia' movement, when western nations invaded the young Soviet Union in an attempt to 'kill socialism in its cradle'. It had organised large movements against unemployment and for better welfare payments – something no other party had done. It had promoted tenants' and community organisations to counter the arbitrary power of landlords, as well as led resistance by owner occupiers to unscrupulous mortgage companies. It had mobilised workers across a whole range of industries for better wages, working conditions and for democratic control of their workplaces. In almost every area of public life it had been able to put forward an agenda very different from all the mainstream political parties and which offered a different concept for the running of society. Despite its very small size, it had given the establishment severe headaches, because it feared the Party's impact. At the same time it had been able to inspire many working class people, as well as a number of professionals, intellectuals, students and artists with its vision of socialism. It had been at the forefront of campaigns for colonial freedom, in the struggle against fascism, and been largely responsible for the wider dissemination of Marxist ideas in the country.

Communists and the Labour Party

The Labour Party was established in 1900 by the trade unions to ensure working people's representation in the Houses of Parliament. It was, in the beginning, a loose federation of socialist and social-democratic organisations. The Communist Party, set up twenty years later, saw itself as an integral part of the labour movement, but with a Marxist agenda, and sought affiliation to the Labour Party. Both parties have vied with each other over which is the true representative of the working class.

Since it was founded, the Labour Party has always been a party having strong left and right wings and, while its left-wing has often been close to the Communist Party or been willing to co-operate with it on a whole number of issues, the right wing has been vehemently opposed to any form of collaboration. The Communist Party's short-term acceptance of the Comintern's policy of 'class against class' during the late twenties and early thirties, which characterised Social Democratic parties, like the Labour party, as mortal enemies, certainly didn't help endear the two organisations to each other. So relationships between the two parties have always been volatile, but invariably hostile. However, despite everything, the Communist Party has had an ongoing impact on Labour Party policy in many ways and on a number of levels – even though this is something successive Labour leaderships have denied.

Initially, the CPGB attempted to work within the Labour Party, which, as a federation of left-wing organisations, only began allowing individual membership from 1918 onwards. However, despite the support of notable figures, such as the Independent Labour Party leader James Maxton, the Labour Party decided to reject affiliation of the Communist Party. Even while pursuing affiliation and seeking to influence Labour Party members, however, the CPGB promoted candidates of its own in parliamentary elections. As an integral part of the wider labour movement, the Party has always insisted that its goal was to affiliate to the Labour Party.

Following the refusal of its application to affiliate, the CPGB encouraged its members to join the Labour Party individually and to seek Labour Party endorsement or help for any 'communist' candidatures. At the time there was no rule forbidding individual communists from joining the party.

In the 1922 general election Shapurji Saklatvala, an Indian-born barrister, stood as a communist member of the Left Wing Group of the Independent Labour Party (ILP) for the parliamentary seat in Battersea North and won, but on this occasion he had Labour Party endorsement. Also elected, and running as a communist, but without official Labour Party support, was J. Walton Newbold, who was victorious in Motherwell, Scotland. At the following election, called surprisingly early by Stanley Baldwin in 1923, Saklatvala was this time standing against an official Labour Party candidate and lost his seat. This situation changed in 1924 when the Labour Party introduced a new rule banning communists from membership, and trade unions were also told not to nominate communists as delegates. A number of local Labour Party branches did refuse to expel the communists in their ranks and were consequently disaffiliated. This happened to 27 such local branches over the next three years.

The Labour Party's scepticism and suspicion of the Communist Party, certainly during the early years, is understandable. The leaders saw it as a party that espoused violent revolution, with a first allegiance to the Soviet Union, and that its strong internationalist stance made its loyalty to Britain questionable. There was, of course, also the fact that the Party represented a potential threat to Labour's hegemony over its working class base and it feared being overtaken on the Left. However these factors do not fully explain its almost continuous animosity to the Communist party, particularly when the latter adopted a more amenable and less absolutist position during the war years and beyond.

The Labour Party has always posited its own democratic credentials in contrast to what it saw as the Communist Party's 'conspiratorial' methods. However, as Raphael Samuel pointed out, while decrying the Communist Party's 'Stalinist' structures and its lack of democracy, it was itself hardly a model. It has always been hierarchical, leadership orientated and its purges certainly had a strong tinge of Stalinism about them. It also had little compunction manipulating the political decision-making process or of using machinations to win votes at its conferences.

The monumental 1926 General Strike marked a fault line in British political life. It shook the establishment to its roots, fearing that a united working class, once it recognised its own strength, could challenge the former's own power. Once the General Strike had been defeated, both the Labour Party and the TUC opened up a new drive to outlaw the communists and isolate them from the rest of the labour movement. The last thing they wanted was the threat of another general strike and they felt that the Communist Party would be instrumental in fomenting one.

At that time there were still around 1,500 communists active inside the Labour Party itself, joining other left-wingers to fight within it for socialist policies. In the wake of the General Strike, however, concerted measures were undertaken by the Labour Party leadership to expel any remaining communists from the party. The TUC, also, attempted to ensure that communists were no longer elected to trade union office. At the same time, the Labour Party and TUC also both set about smashing two popular working class movements: the Minority Movement and the National Unemployed Workers' Committee Movement (NUWM), both effective national organisations set up and led largely by communists. They did this by accusing the communists of fomenting armed insurrection, and stressing that the latter believed in a 'dictatorship of the proletariat' instead of democratic rule, and thirdly that the Communist Party was not a free agent, but took its orders from Moscow. To the Labour Party and TUC leaders who wanted a docile rank and file which would simply follow their leadership, communists were a terrible irritant, and were accused of being merely disrupters. In this climate, it didn't take long for the state itself to begin using its power in a more overt way in order to crush the young communist movement, and in 1925 the police raided Communist Party headquarters in King Street, Soho – a precedent then, but action that was to be repeated at regular intervals over the following years.

The SundayWorker, first published in 1925, on the initiative of Ralph Bond was the first genuine communist paper in the UK and by the beginning of 1926 it already had a stable circulation of around 85,000 and acted as mouthpiece for the Left Wing Movement.[111] At the Left Wing Movement's first annual conference in 1927, 120 organisations were represented, including 54 Labour Party and some Independent Socialist Party branches.

By this time the Labour Party and trade union leaderships had taken their anti-communist campaign into overdrive. Not only members of the Communist Party were to be expelled and isolated but anyone who even wanted to work with them, characterised by Herbert Morrison as 'elements it is not desirable to mix with'. By 1929 the Labour Party had 'loyalty' clauses inserted into its rules to exclude not only communists but those in organisations 'ancillary or subsidiary'.

Communists were particularly strong in the mining communities, but in 1927 when communists were elected by ballot to various important positions in the Scottish miners' union, the leadership refused to recognise them. In November of that same year a miners' march from South Wales to London demanding that the government address their grievances, organised by communist Wal Hannington and backed by A.J. Cooke, Secretary of the Miners' Federation of Great Britain and a member of the TUC General Council, the TUC called on Trades Councils along the route to withhold support. The trade union leadership told the world outside that the march was simply a com-munist plot to recruit members to the Party.

By 1929 the Communist Party was haemorrhaging support over the Comintern-imposed policy of 'class against class' which characterised Social Democracy as an arm of the ruling class, to be countered unremittingly. Although on the ground and among the membership this new line was adhered to more on paper than in practice, it still inflicted much damage and led to a further polarisation within the labour movement. The policy also buttressed those communists who already tended towards sectarianism and intolerance, rather than those who were more amenable to cooperation. As a result of this shortsighted policy, the overwhelming majority of organised workers swung behind the social democratic Labour Party rather than the Communist Party.

In the General Election of November 1935, the Communist Willie Gallacher was elected as MP for West Fife. He was the first communist MP elected on the Communist Party ticket. He was a founder member of the Communist Party and had been a leader of the shop stewards movement on the 'Red Clyde' in Scotland.

Gallacher had a reputation in that mining and ship-building constituency as an honest and indefatigable fighter for working people's rights. He was a man brought up in an austere culture. His father's alcoholism and early death made him a vehement teetotaller. He was so upright, that it is said that he made a member of the Party return a packet of cigarettes to a family who had given it as a token of thanks for helping them with their housing problems. For Gallacher that was corruption and not to be tolerated! His solitary presence in the House of Commons was a means of putting across communist ideas and policies in a national forum, and Gallacher functioned as a quasi one-man opposition to the consensus politics of the two main parties.

In that 1935 election the Communist Party did relatively well in one other constituency where it stood a candidate. Harry Pollitt, its general secretary, stood in the Welsh East Rhondda, where he polled 13,665 votes (Labour won with over 22,000). Following that election the Party applied again, as it had in the early 1920s, for affiliation to the Labour Party. The request was again, predictably, rejected, although the Party's request for affiliation did have significant support on the Left within the Labour Party. It's application was supported by over 1,400 organisations, including 831 trade union branches and 407 local Labour Party branches. It also had the support from notable individuals, like Sir Stafford Cripps, Aneurin Bevan and the respected Labour movement intellectual, G.D.H. Cole.

Despite the always mutual suspicions by both parties of each other, one figure who was able to overcome these to a certain extend was Harry Pollitt. Kevin Morgan in his biography of Harry Pollitt says, 'If Pollitt owed what authority he had to the Communist Party, it is equally true that the CP owed much of its credibility to its charismatic leader and to the trust and esteem in which he was held by many on the left.' He was one of the most independent minds in international communism – a thorn in the Comintern's side, as he once privately boasted.

During the war the coalition government actually held secret meetings with Harry Pollitt and other leaders of the Communist Party which neither side was keen to admit, in an attempt by the government to get the Party on board in assisting in increasing production and maintaining industrial peace during the war years. After the war, Pollitt developed a close relationship with future Labour leader Michael Foot

At the Labour Party's 1943 conference, the resolution on Communist Party affiliation was again defeated but it received 26 per cent support – the closest result ever on this issue. Throughout the Labour Party's campaign against the Communist Party and its refusal to accede to some form of united action in the face of the fascist threat, it continued to characterise the strength of the Communist Party as 'negligible'. TUC leader, Sir Walter Citrine, reiterated this view, and called the Party a 'fragment' with a pitifully small membership. In the forties, George Orwell also dismissed the CPGB as 'a tiny, barely legal organisation whose main activity was libelling the Labour Party.'[112] Such attitudes, of course, beg the question: if it was so minuscule and its strength negligible, why then all the fuss and preoccupation about its influence? The Labour Party and TUC leaderships' intransigent resistance to any form of cooperation with communists was, though, continuously subverted throughout the country at grassroots level where joint working was on the increase.

At the end of the war in 1945 the Communist Party threw all its weight behind the election of a Labour government in the hope that it would, once in power, introduce real change. A real change seemed to be what many working people in the country also wanted to see. And, although, the Labour Party did, of course, bring in some fundamental changes and sorely needed reform during its first term in office, it soon ran out of steam and began to adopt a much more cautious stance and also aligned itself totally with the US on foreign policy.

In the 1945 election, the Communist Party won two seats, this time under its own party flag – Willie Gallacher in West Fife (Scotland) and Phil Piratin in Mile End (London). The Labour leadership's fear of communism also had repercussions on those who were merely sympathetic. Several Labour MPs, including the barristers, D.N. Pritt and John Platts-Mills were both deselected, despite being sitting MPs, because of their perceived 'closeness to the Communist Party'.

Despite fighting elections on a regular basis in selected constituencies the Communist Party never made much headway electorally, garnering votes only in the hundreds or low thousands in its strongholds. On the local level the situation was not very different. In its heyday the party held a number of council seats, again particularly in its strongholds of working class Glasgow, South Wales and London's East End, but nationally the party's electoral impact was minimal. This, no doubt, was largely due to the already established position of the Labour Party as the party of the working class, but also connected with Britain's first-past-the-post system. But the bottom line was that the Party was unable to convince a sufficient number of voters that it was offering what they wanted.

Particularly at the height of the Cold War, in the late forties and into the fifties and sixties, the Party's strong identification with the Soviet Union, on the one hand, allied with a barrage of anti-Soviet and anti-communist sentiment from the media on the other, had their impact on its electoral prospects.

It is ironic that while many were willing to vote for known communists in trade union elections, they were much less willing to do so in local or general elections. This was no doubt because, even if working people didn't trust communists to represent them politically, many recognised that communists would, by and large, represent them selflessly and effectively in the workplace.

The party had reached the height of its success and political effectiveness in the later thirties, with the rising struggle against fascism. As a result of this prominence in the anti-fascist struggles, both in Europe as well as Britain, communist parties were able to retain significant support in the immediate post-war years of the early forties. The successful war alliance with the Soviet Union and the widespread admiration for the role played by the Soviets in the defeat of Hitler also helped boost the communists' image,. but this goodwill was rapidly dissipated by the Cold War.

The formation in 1947 of the Cominform (The Communist Information Bureau) represented the first official forum of the world's communist parties since the collapse of the Comintern. The British Party's signing up to this organisation, whose headquarters were based in the Soviet Union, gave the right-wing Labour leaders all the excuse they needed to once again decry the Party as an 'agent of Moscow'.

With the embers of the recent 'hot war' still smouldering, the Cold War now plunged the world into a new ice age. All the warm, cuddly feelings of the alliance against Nazi Germany, of sending British tanks to 'Uncle Joe' and British-Soviet friendship as an accepted fact of life, were swept away in a new anti-communist hysteria. The Labour Party was not slow in joining the witch hunt. It even expelled Aneurin Bevan (the future deputy leader of the party and founder of the NHS) for a short period because of his association with communists. The barrister and MP John Platts-Mills was also expelled from the party for supporting Pietro Nenni's attempt to form a coalition with the communists in Italy; this attempt was thwarted by a group of right-wing members of the Italian Socialist Party who joined with the Christian Democrats instead and formed a government. Behind the scenes of this manoeuvre was the USA, pulling the strings. Within a year, a new Western military alliance, NATO, had been set up, aimed at containing Soviet power and influence.

In 1948 Prime Minister Attlee announced that the government had decided 'to ensure that no one who is known to be a member of the Communist Party, or to be associated with it in such a way as to raise legitimate doubts about his or her reliability, is to be employed in connection with work, the nature of which is vital to the state.' This heralded a new stage in the attack on the Left in Britain and echoed what was happening in the United States. As the Daily Worker remarked the following day, 'The Labour Government is now doing what no Tory Government has ever attempted, namely to begin a witch-hunt in the civil service'.

Labour had also failed to repeal the wartime Order 1305 banning strikes, which meant that the roughly 10,000 strikes that took place between 1945 and 1951 were all illegal and many took place in an atmosphere of 'red-baiting'.

The Communist Party at its 20th congress in 1948, declared that it had not fully appreciated the scale of this drift to the right by the Labour government and called for the dismissal of its right-wing leaders and the formation of a 'Labour Government of the Left'. But its call fell on deaf ears.

W.J. Brown, a former general secretary of the civil service who had become a Labour MP was spurred on by Attlee's statement to announce in the House of Commons that he personally knew of at least two communists working in the civil service and asked how many more there were. One of those Brown referred to was E.J. Hicks who was secretary of the staff side of the Whitley Council negotiating body at the Air Ministry. He had never hidden his communist views. The other communist mentioned was Ann George, secretary to George Tomlinson, at the time Minister of Education. Both were subsequently removed from their posts.

Following Attlee's statement, 43 Labour MPs put down a motion regretting his decision, pointing out that the Official Secrets Act and other measures had always been deemed sufficient to prevent any subversive activities. Despite this, the purge continued and a whole number of communists and sympathisers lost their jobs or were demoted.

Civil servants were not the only ones in the sights of the government's anti-communist witch-hunt. The leading scientist, J.B.S Haldane,[113] who worked on two government scientific committees, was removed from any government work. Communists working in any professional capacity were now put under especial scrutiny. Some councils attempted to bring in 'political tests' for teachers, and in

Middlesex the appointment of Max Morris as a headteacher was vetoed on the grounds that he was a communist. He was later elected president of the NUT, the teachers' union.

The Cold War was very quickly taking a firm hold in the national psyche, and as a result, in the national elections of 1950, the Communist Party suffered its worst electoral setback, losing not only its two parliamentary seats, but haemorrhaging large numbers of votes. Five left wing MPs, who had been expelled from the Labour Party and who then stood as independents, also failed to get elected. Clearly the constant anti-communist crusade conducted by the TUC, the Labour and Conservative Parties together with the media, was having its effect. Membership of the Party also fell in 1950 to below 40,000 and was destined never to reach that peak again.

The fifties undoubtedly represented a climax in terms of witch-hunts against communists. In the United States the House Un-American Activities Committee (HUAC) was conducting a virulent campaign to eradicate all communist and progressive influence in the country, and the notorious McCarthy hearings were a culmination of that infamous period, which ruined so many careers and destroyed so many lives. Although the witch-hunts in Britain were not as draconian, there was certainly a shadowing of US action. Witch-hunts were, though, carried out more vigorously in parts of the British Empire, particularly in Australia, under its right-wing prime minister, Robert Menzies.[114]

In Britain during this time, the government became increasingly obsessed with the 'red menace' and, in order to clamp down on workers taking strike action, they revived wartime regulations enabling them to prosecute strikers, which they proceeded to do. However, these draconian measures only served to foment increased industrial unrest, achieving the opposite of what was intended. Even the TUC was then obliged to appeal to the government to restore the right to strike.

In 1951 the government also tried unsuccessfully to prevent young people travelling to the World Youth Festival, held in East Berlin that year, by imposing its own 'iron curtain'.

The British Communist Party's work with young people was co-ordinated through its Youth Advisory Committee and the Young Communist League. The Youth Festival was widely advertised among students and youth organisations and many young people were keen to go and experience travelling abroad – at the time a far from common experience. Some 1,700 applied to go; most were young workers, but there were also 210 students and 400 young people from the colonies.

Already at the start of their journey, many were refused entry by the French on the basis of lists supplied by the British authorities. Other delegates tried to fly to Prague and then travel by rail to Berlin, but were refused permission to overfly West Germany. Those attempting to make their way via Vienna were confronted by armed US and Austrian troops and were threatened and bullied, before being refused access to onward transport. Those who did manage to board trains were forcibly removed from the carriages.

Despite all that chicanery, most did eventually manage to get through by using inventive means and individual initiative, and were able to enjoy several days of festivity in Berlin. All Herbert Morrison's efforts to prevent their participation had failed miserably. This government-inspired action only served to demonstrate once more the shallowness of the West's much-vaunted adherence to democratic principles at this time. Later the British Council for Civil Liberties held an enquiry into the event and published the results in a pamphlet Journey to Berlin, which revealed just how the government had conspired to stop young people going to the Festival.

Despite the fundamental differences between the Communist and Labour Parties, the two have, over the course of their existence, been obliged by history to maintain a close, if fractious, relationship, despite the continued attempts by successive Labour Party leaderships to distance the party from the Communist Party. There has always been a steady trickle of members leaving one party for the other. David (now Lord) Triessman was General Secretary of the Labour Party from 2001-03, after being a member of the Communist Party for six or seven years, since joining as a student, and Jim Mortimer, the General Secretary from 1982-85, while never a member of the Party, was very close. He was a Marxist and a close friend of communist trade unionist Ken Gill, as well as writing regularly for the Morning Star.

The Labour Party, like all social-democratic parties, together with the Trades Union Congress believes in reforming or changing the social and economic system by small, cumulative steps, through the parliamentary process, although in its early days the Labour Party also included those who did believe in revolutionary change and/or considered themselves to be Marxists. Communists, who believed in root-and-branch revolutionary change, represented a fundamental challenge to the reformist ideology of the Labour Party leadership, and were ostracised because of this.

The slow decline – the Stalin revelations
and the Hungarian uprising

In 1951 the Party published its new programme for a socialist Britain, The British Road to Socialism, setting out its vision for the country. What was particularly interesting about this version was that it rejected a Bolshevik-style revolution as the only path to power and stressed that each country should adopt its own path to socialism, depending on the specific conditions of each. In Britain, it stated, a parliamentary road was possible, given the country's strong democratic traditions. It also stressed the need for a lasting peace, the restoration of Britain's independence (free from US domination) and for a socialist society.

Despite all efforts by the ruling establishment to eradicate the Communist Party and its influence in the country during the fifties, the Party survived, as did its influence, even if severely curtailed. Although still small in size – only around 35,000 members by 1952 – it was still seen as the greatest challenge to the powers that be and its ideas were feared. Its reputation, however, in the eyes of many, had been tarnished by its continued association with the Soviet Union and thus with Stalinist oppression in Eastern Europe, a fact which undoubtedly led to its steady loss of members and inability to attract new ones.

In 1956, a double bolt of lightening struck the Party. At the Soviet Communist Party Congress of that year, First Secretary of the Communist Party of the Soviet Union, Nikita Khrushchev made revelations that sent shockwaves around the world. His descriptions of Stalin's regime of terror were for anti-communists merely a confirmation of what they'd always said and believed; for communists in the West it came as a profound blow. Their image of a flawless, charismatic leader who had dragged a backward, feudal Russian empire into the modern industrial world and had led the victorious Red Army in its defeat of the Nazi menace had been shattered. To be informed by the secretary of the Soviet Communist Party that Stalin had been a monster, was difficult to digest; their vision of a utopian Soviet Union had been revealed as an illusion. This shock and disillusion was compounded in that same year when Soviet troops rolled into Hungary to suppress a popular uprising against its communist government. In the wake of Krushchev's revelations and the Hungarian uprising the Party lost a quarter of its membership – 9,000 members had left by 1958. Its youth wing lost around half its membership and its paper, the Daily Worker, lost around a third of its journalists, including the talented Llew Gardner, who subsequently became political correspondent for Thames TV. Party workers also found public campaigning increasingly difficult, facing a much increased animosity and even threats as a result of the Party's stance on Hungary.

My mother, a deeply committed member, left the Party at the time over its response to Hungary. She was as much disturbed by the Daily Worker's one-sided coverage of the uprising and the Party's inadequate response as she was by the uprising itself. It is however, a symptom of how independent the British Party felt itself to be, that it was still able to retain a solid core of its membership despite these setbacks and was able to continue campaigning for a socialist Britain. Although allegiance to the Soviet Union was always important for communists, many felt an even stronger identity with Britain and its working class traditions, which were, arguably, paramount.

A whole swathe of prominent intellectuals resigned at the time, as well as a number of leading trade unionists like John Horner. General Secretary of the Fire Brigades Union and Alex Moffatt, a Scottish miners' leader. Among the intellectuals who left were the historians Edward Thompson, John Saville and Raphael Samuel, who went on to establish a new 'dissident' Marxist force, the New Left. Although Thompson did say, later, after leaving the Communist Party, he missed the enjoyment of discussions on world issues and the comradeship. The Party, from now on, was to become a much leaner organisation, less effective, and certainly not even a potential electoral threat to the Labour Party, however it was still able to retain a strong base within the trade union movement.

Largely as a result of the damage inflicted on the Communist Party by the above events, state harassment and persecution of communists receded, certainly into the sixties, even if communists were still, at regular intervals, vilified as 'enemies of the state' and, in times of industrial disputes, still accused of conspiring to foment unrest. There was also, after the thaw in the Soviet Union in the wake of Khrushchev's revelations, a general feeling that international tensions were relaxing. The Soviet space and other scientific successes had awoken many to the fact that 'communism' could perhaps still provide an example, at least in some spheres. Only the Cuban missile crisis in 1962 threatened, for one short but awful moment, to devastate the world with a full-scale nuclear war. This was, however, followed by a new era of détente and peaceful coexistence under Brezhnev with the signing of the Helsinki Accords in 1975.

Rediscovering humanism – an attempt to recover a heritage

Marxism – the philosophical basis of the Communist Party – had deep roots in the European humanist tradition. A number of academics have maintained that there is a profound division and difference between Marx's philosophic humanism and Marxism instrumentalised as a communist ideology.

During the sixties and seventies the British Communist Party's chief aims had been to develop and broaden left unity in all areas in order to sharpen the opposition to monopoly capitalism. There was, too, particularly among the Party's intellectuals, a new emphasis on the socialist humanist aspect of Marxism and a move away from Leninist ideas and practice. One could discern this development in the writings and work of those like the English literary critic professor Arnold Kettle, the philosophy academic Maurice Cornforth, educationalist Brian Simon, and the Party's leading theoretician James Klugman. As a confirmation of that humanism, the Party also readily began to accept forms of pluralism in its attitude to the arts and culture.

In 1966 its condemnation of the persecution of the writers Daniel and Sinyavsky by the Soviet Union also represented a new milestone and a rare public demonstration of the Party's autonomy from Moscow. This independence was demonstrated even more forcibly when the Party criticised the Soviet intervention in Czechoslovakia in 1968.

In the late sixties the Party's theoretical journal, Marxism Today, began opening up its pages to a wide-ranging discussion of the relationship between culture and politics, to demonstrate that the Party's policies were not shaped by dogma. As well as an extended discussion on Marxism and Humanism in Marxism Today, Klugman issued a pamphlet, The Future of Man, whose avowed purpose was 'an attempt to recapture the humanist tradition in Marxism'. He was also behind the initiative of the Communist-Christian dialogue, in collaboration with the progressive theologian, Canon Paul Oestreicher. Christian-Communist dialogue was not entirely new, though. During the thirties and forties Rev. Hewlett Johnson, the 'red' Dean of Canterbury, was as good as being a Party member and there were several other 'fellow-travelling' clerics who viewed communism as a means of fulfilling Christian principles on earth.

Conrad Noel, the 'red vicar of Thaxted' was also one of them. He had been a member of the British Socialist Party and was involved in the ferment over the creation of the CPGB in 1920-21. While it is uncertain if he was actually a card-carrying member of the Communist Party, he was certainly as good as, working closely with local communists.

He had joined the Independent Labour Party and in 1911 became a founding member of the British Socialist Party. He was active in promoting Christian socialism, other progressive causes and local culture all his life. He was also an early member of the executive of the British Section of the League against Imperialism and subsequently became its Chair.

He provoked a national furore after he hung the red flag and the flag of Sinn Féin alongside the flag of St.George in his Church. He remained vicar in Thaxted until his death in 1942. As another example of the Party's opening-up to the Christian left, in the 1970s, a former Catholic nun, Irene Brennan, was elected to the Party's Executive Committee.

The basis of a Communist-Christian dialogue was that the cold war had prevented a working together of the two groups in areas of common humanitarian concern. The opening of this dialogue led to number of meetings and discussions taking place between representatives from the two groups. In October 1966, 700 people attended a student Communist-Christian dialogue conference, and in 1967 a meeting at the Marx Memorial Library was packed for a debate on Marxism and religion; in Coventry the following month an event, 'How to Change the World?' was also packed out.

My wife and I were two of those invited by James Klugman to join a ten-sider weekend discussion group, sponsored by Marxism Today and the Quaker Peace and International Relations Committee on the subject of 'Man, Society and Moral Responsibility'. My mother, a teacher and leading communist activist in Coventry, was also involved in the Coventry Committee for Peace and Reconciliation, set up by Canon Oestreicher and, in her role as secretary of the Coventry Peace Committee, made strong efforts to include the churches and individual Christians in the Committee's work.

This Communist-Christian dialogue was, though, not confined to intellectuals, but extended to the workplace, as well as branch and district levels of the Party. The Communist Party was making real efforts to emerge from its ghetto and to shed its widely perceived image as the 'hard line atheistic agent of Moscow'.

Coventry was the world's first 'twin city' when it formed a twinning relationship with the Russian city of Stalingrad (now Volgograd) during the Second World War. That relationship developed through ordinary people in Coventry who wanted to show their support for what the Soviet Red Army had done during the Battle of Stalingrad. The city subsequently twinned with several other East European cities like Dresden and Lidice at the height of the Cold War, when such fraternisation was severely deprecated by the Establishment.

These efforts of reconciliation and establishment of relations across the East-West divide were unique at the time and came about largely due to the city having a very progressive and left-wing post-war Labour council, but it was an initiative that also owed something to the input of leading communists in the city who had developed amicable working relationships with a number of left-wing Labour councillors, like Alderman George Hodgkinson.[115] When the city's Lord Mayor, Alderman William Callow, visited Berlin in the sixties he insisted, after being encouraged to do so by local communists, on also visiting East Berlin to meet his counterpart there, despite attempts by Willy Brandt (then mayor of West Berlin) to dissuade him.

Confronting monopoly capitalism and educating working people as to its significance continued to be a Party priority and was central to the 1968 revised edition of its programme, The British Road to Socialism. It attacked the increasing dominance of monopoly capital over the lives of people worldwide and it castigated Labour governments for attempting to 'manage' capitalism rather than taking measures to restrict monopoly power. This theoretical position on monopoly capitalism distinguished it radically from the Labour Party at this time and lent it a certain ideological superiority. Its new programme did also find some resonance among left-wing Labour Party members.

During the sixties, despite the Party's clear determination to distance itself from the Soviet Union and its relative success in achieving left unity in the trade union movement, membership still continued to decline. Among other things, this was also connected undoubtedly with the rise of a number of Trotskyist organisations which were particularly adept at attracting students and young people into their ranks, even if these new members were often very transient.

According to Geoff Andrews,[116] the new interest in the socialist humanism aspect of Marxism in the Party helped the transition to developing new forms of creative Marxism, symbolised by the role played by Marxism Today during the 1970s.

The journal helped the Party maintain a strong intellectual presence in Britain at a time when faith in the socialist world in Eastern Europe was crumbling. 'On the other hand,' Andrews writes, 'militant labourism was crucial in increasing and sustaining the Party's influence in the labour movement under the new leadership of Ramelson'.[117] Despite these achievements, the Party's fortunes were still declining. In the electoral arena, where it stood candidates, its votes were minuscule, membership was contracting and, despite the change of name of its flagship newspaper from Daily Worker to the classless title, Morning Star, in 1966, the paper's readership was also waning.

Despite the Party's inability to expand its membership base, its influence in the labour movement still remained significant. At the Labour Party conference in 1973, a draft policy document entitled Labour's Programme for Britain, contained a number of significant proposals very similar to those advocated by the Communist Party, such as the call for large-scale nationalisation, redistributive taxation and major public investment programmes.

The term Alternative Economic Strategy (AES) was used to describe these common policy proposals, which had been largely devised, and were strongly supported, by the Party. The AES was eventually adopted as official policy by the TUC at its Congress in 1977. However, the temporary 'love-in' between the left-wing of the Labour Party and the Communist Party had come to an abrupt end well before that date with the introduction in 1973 by Wilson's Labour government of the Social Contract, which was supported by both Jack Jones and Hugh Scanlon – leaders of the two largest unions.

The Social Contract, ostensibly an agreement between unions, government and employers, was to include pay restraint. The Party saw it as a means of hobbling the unions and keeping wages down. It was convinced that the employers' side of the bargain would be unenforceable.

This deep schism on the left coincided with a decline in the Party's organisational militancy and in the key role played by the Liaison Committee for the Defence of Trade Unions (LCDTU), the rank and file organisation set up, and supported, by the Party.

An Indian summer – Marxism Today and the Gramsci factor

In the mid-seventies, the Party was actively seeking new ways to gain traction in the political arena, and it brought into the leadership a number of younger thinkers who'd cut their teeth in the student movement during the late sixties. These newcomers have been characterised as the 'Gramscians'. They managed to take control of the Party's theoretical journal, Marxism Today which became their flagship, promoting radical change within the Party and also making the magazine a catalyst for new thinking on the Left in general, including within the Labour Party..

While some commentators have suggested that Marxism Today became a sounding board for Tony Blair's New Labour project, this is undoubtedly much exaggerated, even though it did attract a number of contributors and supporters from within the Labour Party. Ex-communists like Charlie Leadbetter and Charles Whelan, who were also associated with the magazine, later became advisors to Tony Blair and Gordon Brown.

Geoff Andrews's central thesis in his history of the Party (from 1964 until 1991) and the demise of the CPGB , argues that there was a battle developing between the Gramscian wing of the Party, centred very much among the younger, newer members, and the 'old guard' traditional wing. The 'Gramscians' looked to the Italian Communist Party rather than the Soviet Union for inspiration. They wanted to see a Party leaving behind the baggage of old allegiances to the Soviet Union and Eastern Europe, as well as an over-concentration on the trade union movement, and to embrace the new 'social forces' more pro-actively. Among the leaders of the Gramscians were Martin Jacques (who took over as editor of Marxism Today in 1977 after the death of James Klugman), Dave Cook (the Party's former student organiser), Beatrix Campbell and Judith Hunt (both members of the Party's Women's Advisory Committee), and Pete Carter (a former building worker and YCL activist).

Raphael Samuel's interpretation of the divisions that emerged in the Communist Party at this time is more perceptive and subtle than that of Andrews. Samuel sees the so-called Gramscian/Fundamentalist split as a false polarisation. He argues, rightly I feel, that in both camps members viewpoints, loyalties and ideological positions were more differentiated than such a divisive split would indicate.

It would probably not be helpful to go into the complexity and detail of this struggle, as it is no longer of much relevance or of likely interest to readers. I would only comment that I think Andrews's thesis that the last decade of the Party was characterised by a Gramscian versus traditionalist battle is too neat a theory to be wholly accurate. As always, reality is more complex and elusive than we would like it to be, and never fits easily into the filing cabinets we assign to it, even if such filing can often aid our understanding.

While his thesis does contain a large dose of truth, it misses key elements. A number of those Andrews calls 'Gramscians' were, I feel, less immersed in or motivated by Gramsci's ideas, than in a desire to latch onto or plug into the new social forces which appeared trendier and more exciting than the 'sluggish and conservative' trade union movement. They wanted the Party to appeal to younger people and to do that it, too, had to be transformed into something more exciting and colourful. The so-called 'traditionalists' were certainly not a homogenous grouping either, containing those who strongly believed in a trade union and working class focus, those who still clung to the Soviet Union as the Party's touchstone, and others who just felt uncomfortable with the direction in which the 'young trendies' were taking the Party. These changes also coincided with those taking place in wider society: the big industrial communities were breaking down, accompanied by a decline in the country's skilled working class; there was also an increased feeling of egalitarianism and a crumbling of cultural class barriers. This all fed into a new and heated debate about class.

Marxism Today under Martin Jacques became the flagship for the 'Gramscian' movement within the party. It also ushered in a new emphasis on culture, and the Party organised a series of quite successful cultural-political events, such as the 'Moving Left Show' in 1975, which included a mix of politics and culture, as well as the 'Festival of Marxism' in Manchester that same year.

The biggest and last large-scale politico-cultural event organised by the Party since the war was the 'People's Jubilee' held in London's Alexandra Palace in 1977 as an alternative event to the Queen's Jubilee. Around 11,000 people attended the weekend-long event. There were numerous stalls, both national and international, poetry readings, music, film shows, speeches and exhibitions. It was, in a sense, an attempt to reproduce, here in the UK, a festival similar to the popular 'Fête de l'Humanité' and 'Festa dell'Unità' organised annually by the French and Italian Party newspapers. Nigel Tanburn, the People's Jubilee organiser, said its main appeal was directed away from orthodox politics by making the cultural aspects as important as the political rally. It encapsulated the Gramscian idea that culture was, or could be, also an alternative means of political expression.[119]

It was, though, not only concepts of class that were changing. The women's movement was becoming increasingly vocal and sophisticated, music was now playing a much more central role in young people's lives, and there was also the burgeoning Gay Liberation Rights movement.

The Party's endorsement of gay liberation in 1975 was not an uncontentious position, being quite advanced at the time, even for the Party, and it was certainly far from representing a mainstream view. And the Party won a glowing endorsement for its policy from the Gay Times which called it 'the fullest and most far reaching such policy ever adopted by a non-gay organisation'. The Party gave immediate expression to its new policy by setting up its own gay liberation advisory committee. And it is perhaps also worth noting that the young gay rights activist Peter Tatchell had been a member of that British Youth delegation to the 10th World Youth Festival in East Berlin in 1973.

Marxism Today, during the seventies, began to play an increasingly polemical role not only in terms of the Communist Party's internal battles, but also in the wider political sphere, gaining a readership far beyond its previous, rather narrow Party one. The editor published controversial articles such as Eric Hobsbawm's 'Forward March of Labour Halted?' and in 1978 professor Stuart Hall's 'Moving Right Show' in which he analysed the phenomenon of 'Thatcherism' and defined it as a hegemonic project. Jacques also opened up the journal's columns to non-party writers such as the playwright David Edgar, and even included a contribution from a young Tony Blair. Two others who regularly wrote for it were Geoff Mulgan (later to become Director of Policy under Tony Blair) and Charlie Leadbetter.

Hobsbawm's article argued, amongst other things, that the dynamics that had originally driven the labour movement, such as the developments of class consciousness, class solidarity and political and electoral successes of the working class had come to an end 30 years earlier, during the late forties and fifties. The labour movement had undergone such profound crises that had fundamentally changed its make-up and consequently its role in society. He also pointed out that the changing structure of capitalism in Britain had brought with it a long-term decline in manual occupations. All this meant that the 'working class' as defined and conceived by Marx and Engels and as it had been perceived by the Party throughout its existence was no longer the same one. Consequently a rethinking on class and its role in history needed to be undertaken. He also argued that trade union 'economism' (i.e. a sole focus on wages) had led to a decline in class consciousness. His analysis gave impetus to the simmering debate within the Party.

Despite this initiation of animated debate in the Party and the new impetus provided by an increasingly high profile of Marxism Today, the Party membership fell dramatically between 1975 and '79 to 20,599. In the YCL, its youth wing, the decline was more dramatic. This decline, as Andrews says, 'was severest at precisely the time the Gramscian-Eurocommunist influence was at its peak'.[120] While the Party declined, its 'theoretical and discussion, journal,' Marxism Today was enjoying an unprecedented popularity in Left-Labour circles and won respect among political intellectuals outside the Party.

The Party had already lost some members when a hard-line, pro-Soviet faction under the leadership of Sid French, its former Surrey Regional Secretary, split off to form the New Communist Party (NCP) in 1977.

After its peak influence in the seventies, the Party's membership among students also declined, and its successors, Democratic Left (which was dissolved in England and Wales in 1998 and reformed as the New Times Network) and the Communist Party of Britain (CPB), both have virtually no presence in student bodies today. The significant contribution made by the Communist Party to student affairs was its key role in establishing the Broad Left and the latter's eventual dominance of student affairs, together with a radical politicisation of the student body during the seventies. Since then students have, apart from a few small Trotskyist groups, largely reverted to their earlier apolitical positions, and the National Union of Students today plays a very diminished role on the political front (see chapter: The Young Communist League and the Student Movement).

The decline in the Party's fortunes at this time rather undermines the argument by the Gramscian-Eurocommunists that the reason the Party had been in decline was because of its adherence to old shibboleths and outdated concepts. This conclusion, however, is not to suggest that adherence to the latter would have produced any significantly different outcome. In my opinion the Party's decline had more to do with the rapid and profound changes taking place in society at large than with internal or ideological problems: the disappearance of traditional working class communities and the industries in which they were rooted, as well as a growing political apathy that accompanied rising living standards and material preoccupations. These changes did not impact solely on the Communist Party, but similarly on memberships of all political parties, particularly the Labour Party. The Labour left was also in crisis and was unable to retard the rise of Tony Blair and New Labour. As a result of the Labour Party's crisis of identity, the Tory Party, too, was beginning to make inroads in traditionally Labour-voting heartlands. The election of consecutive Thatcher governments, with their declared aim of smashing the trade union movement and killing off socialism for good, was a challenge that neither the Communist Party, nor the Labour left or the trade unions were able to confront effectively.

The Community Charge or 'Poll Tax' introduced by Margaret Thatcher in 1990 was the one big miscalculation she made and was one of the chief factors that brought about her premature downfall. It was undoubtedly the most unpopular bill to have been introduced that century and led to massive and widespread protests throughout the country. The Communist Party did not play a leadership role nationally in this movement although the Morning Star waged a concerted campaign in its pages, and many communists were active in local Anti-Poll Tax groups. It was the Trotskyist left which was, again, more pro-active here, and reflected the debility of the communist movement in the wake of its internal battles.

The last rites

At a special Party congress in 1990 the Party under its new leader, Nina Temple, agreed to disband and form with a loose association of networks and groups under the umbrella designation of Democratic Left. At this time only around 6,300 members remained in the old CPGB. Democratic Left controversially took over the assets of the CPGB and used these to finance the new organisation. Before the final dissolution of the Party, it had become increasingly clear that the divisions within it had become insurmountable and that the 'Gramscian-Eurocommunist' faction was determined to dissolve the organisation. This it did, and also closed down Marxism Today, that, despite its relative success, had become a big financial drain on resources. Although it held most of the resources of the old Party, Democratic Left – a Left think tank and campaign group – was unable to stamp its own specific political imprint, although it continued to support various broad left campaigns and debates. Of the original British Euro-Communist project there is little remaining.

Those expelled from the CPGB during its last internal ideological struggle, together with their supporters, first formed a Communist Campaign Group which in 1988 called a conference to 're-establish' the Party, taking the name Communist Party of Britain (CPB) in an attempt to rebuild on the ruins.

Despite the divisions and splits in the communist movement and in the wake of the CPGB's dissolution, communists still continue to play a role in left-wing movements, and the Morning Star daily newspaper, allied to the CPB, but since opened up to the wider left, is still published daily.

The Stop the War Coalition was probably the biggest mass movement since the Poll Tax, and arose in opposition to Tony Blair's support for the war in Iraq and other military adventures in the Middle East. Its Co-Chairs were, until 2011, communist Andrew Murray and Lindsay German (formerly SWP) – a rare example of amicable working together on the far left. Andrew Murray is also an adviser to Len McClusky, General Secretary of the Unite union.

There are a number of cases in which individual communists are still playing an active role in the peace movement and the trade unions, although there is not a single union leader today who would claim to be a communist and very few regional or local officers either. However, ironically, the Morning Star is, today, more reliant on trade union financial support than at any time, but this is due, no doubt, to the fact that it is the only daily newspaper that covers trade union affairs in depth and offers space for the trade unions to put across their own viewpoints.

The Communist Party, throughout its history, struggled against all attempts by the establishment to marginalise it from the mainstream political scene and to ostracise it. But these attempts were only partially successful. During its lifetime it has maintained a continuous political and theoretical input to the elaboration of Labour Party policies, trade union movement strategies and in wider political discussions on the left. In the end, though, the demise of the communist-led East European bloc, together with the profound social restructuring that has taken place within the UK, contributed considerably to the Party's almost inevitable implosion.

The 'Enemy Within' –
Spooks and Dirty Tricks

'After such knowledge, what forgiveness? Think now
History has many cunning passages, contrived corridors
And issues, deceives with whispering ambitions,
Guides us by vanities.'

T.S. ELIOT

This chapter is an odd one in the sense that it's more about the activities and impact of the secret services on the Party. However a selection of the revelations below – and these must be only crumbs from the table – serve to demonstrate the way the very existence of a communist party (although, undoubtedly, it could have been any other organisation that seriously challenged the established order) evoked a response from the state's organs of control and oppression that changed the way they operate and the role they now play in buttressing and defending the state.

No government has ever seriously questioned or challenged the legitimacy of the mass surveillance, infiltration, use of 'IMs' [121] and the prejudiced anti-Left political perspective of the security apparatus that acts in the name of a democratic state. Ostensibly the secret services are there to uphold the freedom of individuals to be able to think and act as they see fit, as long as it is within recognised legal bounds, but in reality such state security organisations are there primarily to uphold the status quo of power and privilege and to monitor as well as – if needs be – to suppress dissent.

In the more recent period in which the Communist Party is no longer seen as a significant threat, the security services have transferred their attentions to other radical organisations.[122] And mass surveillance has now taken on global dimensions with the covert work of NSA in cooperation with GCHQ. All this only emphasises Marx's and Engels' characterisation of the state as, in essence, a repressive apparatus, enforcing the ruling establishment's hegemony.

From the moment it was founded in 1920, the Communist Party was subject to continuous state surveillance, harassment and investigation. Despite its minuscule size – even at the zenith of its influence it never achieved the mass membership of the French or Italian parties, for instance – it and its ideas were feared by the ruling establishment because they fundamentally challenged their privilege and the capitalist system they represented. Even with all the links the Communist Party had to the Soviet Union, these were continuously and closely monitored by the security services and never really posed a threat to Britain's security.

Despite this continual spying on its activities and its members, the very few successful prosecutions – all during the early years – were on spurious grounds, and were, in essence, attempts to intimidate its activists and prevent the Party functioning. Those individuals who chose to spy for the Soviet Union, while at some time associated with the Communist Party, were not members. The Party made it very clear that being a member precluded undertaking any spying activities on behalf of a foreign government.

Communists and the armed forces

On 14 October 1925, around 30 Special branch officers raided both the Party's national and London district offices, the Young Communist League, the National Minorities Movement offices and rooms used by the staff of Workers' Weekly. Eight leading communists were arrested (almost the entire Political Bureau) and all documents confiscated. The eight were put on trial for publishing seditious libels, conspiracy to commit breaches of the Incitement to Mutiny Act (1797) and conspiracy to seduce persons in His Majesty's forces.[123] This prosecution was in connection with the struggle for colonial freedom, fully supported by the Party, and with its attempt to build up influence in the armed forces.

Another early incident involving alleged communists and the armed forces that sent shock-waves through government was the Invergordon Mutiny of 1931. On 15 September, news hit the streets of a mutiny in the Atlantic Fleet in Cromarty Firth. Although the authorities were convinced that communists were behind it, the sailors who took action had not in fact been 'seduced' by revolutionary leaflets, but were reacting to the news that their pay was being cut by 25 percent. The sailors held angry meetings and one of those who addressed a meeting was Len Wincott who only later joined the Communist Party, but at the time he knew nothing about politics and had had no contact with the Party. 'We must strike like the miners', he said. And that is what happened. For two days 12,000 sailors stayed onboard their warships, refusing to return to their duties. Wincott drafted the sailors' manifesto.

The Daily Worker was as surprised by the mutiny as anyone, but it reproduced a copy of the manifesto in the paper and called on the armed forces to make common cause and to support the demands of the sailors. The Daily Worker premises were immediately raided by Special Branch officers who, although they had no search warrant, ransacked the building and removed piles of papers.[124] Thereafter for several weeks the paper came out with blank spaces where text had been censored. The owner of the paper 's printing press was jailed for nine months; on a previous occasion he'd got away with a fine only. Two members of the paper's staff were given two years' hard labour and three years' penal servitude respectively. The so-called ringleaders of the Invergordon Mutiny were dismissed from the service. Two of them, Len Wincott and Fred Copeman, subsequently joined the Communist Party.

A wilderness of mirrors

Undoubtedly, the most serious and foul of the dirty tricks carried out to blacken the reputation of the Communist Party was the so-called 'Zinoviev letter' case. A document, purporting to come from Grigori Zinoviev, the president of the Communist International, in 1924, urging the British Communist Party to stir up the masses in preparation for civil war, was widely publicised in the press. The letter was shown as a bona fide piece of intelligence to the first Labour Prime Minister, Ramsay MacDonald. It was agreed that the letter would be kept secret, but it was intentionally leaked to the press by the security services, when the Daily Mail published it only days before the general election in 1924. It was partially down to this (and that was probably one of the intentions) that the Labour Party lost that election. The Communist Party consistently denounced the letter as a forgery, but this was long denied by the establishment.

The British Foreign Office, belatedly, initiated a study of its own into the Zinoviev letter. For three years Millicent Bagot of MI5 delved into the archives and conducted interviews with surviving witnesses. She produced a long account of the affair, but the paper remained unpublished because it contained sensitive operational and personnel information.

Then early in 1998, reports of a forthcoming book allegedly containing revelations about the origins of the so-called 'Zinoviev letter,' based on information from Soviet archives led to renewed press speculation and parliamentary questions. In response Foreign Secretary, Robin Cook, commissioned historians of the Foreign and Commonwealth Office to prepare a historical memorandum on it. A paper was finally published in 1999 and concluded that 'it is impossible to say who wrote the Zinoviev letter' though the writer expressed that her best guess was that it was commissioned by White Russian intelligence circles from forgers in Berlin or the Baltic states.

Such dirty tricks were only the icing on the cake. Spying on the legally-established British Communist Party was endemic throughout the 20th century. In his book A Matter of Trust, the novelist Nigel West says that 'F branch (of MI5) has long established moles in most leftist organisations'. Of course this has recently been confirmed by press revelations and admission of guilt by the police. But it was widely known that MI5 had always deployed an extensive network of agents inside the labour movement.

In the thirties, MI5 managed to infiltrate an agent, Olga Gray, into Communist Party headquarters in King Street, central London. She was in place for six years, from 1931-37, but, 'She was surprised to find herself growing to like the Bolsheviks of whom she had heard such hair-raising things.' Although Gray wanted to give up her job, she was persuaded by MI5 to stay on. [125]

Another MI5 agent, Betty Gordon, spent 10 years in the Communist Party, becoming personally close to its then general secretary, Harry Pollitt. Tom Driberg, later a Labour MP, had been an MI5 informant (not a key agent) inside the Party, but was expelled after the Party was alerted by a sympathetic agent. MI5 also put an agent into CND's headquarters: one Harry Newton, who had been recruited by the

r.

security forces when a member of the Party in 1950. During the 1970s he had become Treasurer of the Institute of Workers' Control.

In the Guardian of 27 November 1985, the teacher Trevor Blackwell wrote about his close friend, Harry Newton, who was exposed as an informer. He had been named by Cathy Massiter in a banned TV documentary as the MI5 agent who had infiltrated the Campaign for Nuclear Disarmament and spied on Bruce Kent. Blackwell writes,

'Whether Harry deceived me or not I do not know. What I do know is that the ones who have truly betrayed us are those in government who have so subverted the gentle and decent qualities of English life that no one can know for certain that their best friend may not be spying on them.'

The communist graphic artist, Ken Sprague, related to me a conversation he had with a former police inspector in the 1960s. Sprague had become involved with Bertrand Russell's Committee of 100 and was under police surveillance for several months, as a police inspector later told him. This policeman, over months of monitoring Sprague's activities, had become convinced that what he was up to represented no danger to the state and he told his superiors this and also that he didn't wish to spy on people like Sprague anymore. He was summarily sacked and even lost his pension.[126]

By the time that it publicly declared that 'communist subversion' was no longer a key target for its activities, MI5 had accumulated a quarter of a million files on the Communist Party of Great Britain. This is an extraordinary degree of intelligence given the size of Party membership at any one time, even if agglomerated over the entire period from 1920. The agency claimed that it knew of 'thirteen trade union General Secretaries and at least one in eight of all full-time officials' who had been communists. MI5 carried out permanent surveillance of the Party and even installed a hidden microphone embedded in the wall of the Party's headquarters in King Street, London.[127]

Releases from the security forces into the public record of the national archives in May 2003, included files on a large number of British communists and sympathisers from all periods – during the wartime and post-war periods until 1953 (the cut-off date for the release of Security Service files at the time of writing). What the files indicate is that prominent national and regional figures in the

Communist Party were subject to permanent surveillance. The main reason the documents have been released at all is because they seem to reveal nothing much of interest.

For example, the files on Robert Robson cover the period from 1922 to 1953. He had been London District Organiser from 1927 to 1933, and was the head of the Organisation Department in 1935, and as such played a leading part in recruiting volunteers for the Spanish Civil War. Though his role in the Party seemed mostly to do with organisation, it was suspected that he was also involved with undercover work, but no evidence has been cited. Files for 1922-35 include circulars issued, Passport Office restrictions listing Robson and others, preventing their travel within the Empire, and intercepted phone conversations. There are Special Branch reports on Robson's personal life too. He had marital difficulties, suffered serious illness and his wife had turned to religion. So, scenting vulnerability, the Security Service considered turning him, but then shied away from a serious attempt to recruit him.

Bob Stewart (always Robert in the files), a Scotsman, was a founder member of the Communist Party and long-time British representative on the Comintern executive. Files released for 1926 to 1941 report extensively on his daily life. A bundle covering 1927-31 includes correspondence relating to Stewart's visit to Norwegian trade unionists and Chinese communists. Another file contains a summary of investigations on Stewart between 1922 and 1929. It includes correspondence with Zinoviev (Head of the Communist International in Moscow) relating to propaganda work in the UK and the Empire. There is a copy of a telegram sent from Stewart to the Kuomintang nationalist government in China, condemning the massacre at Wahn Sien and pledging British workers' support for revolution in China. Particular interest was paid to an informant in Ireland on visits made by Stewart to Dublin in 1929 and 1930, to pledge support for the Irish communists, including details of contacts with Irish Republicans in August 1929.

John Ross Campbell was also a foundation member of the Party, arrested in the 1926 police raid on its headquarters. He served on the executive committee of the Party and became editor of the Daily Worker in 1949. Reports of Campbell's activities from 1920-53 include speeches, pamphlets, articles, his election addresses, intercepted telegrams, telephone and written communications, along with general surveillance material, even on his wife, Sarah. One report includes internal speculation that, when Campbell was appointed editor of the Daily Worker, John Gollan was made assistant editor to make sure that he always followed the party line.

Clearly much of the espionage conducted against the Communist Party was pointless and trivial. Papers released in 2005 indicate that a wide range of people were closely watched by MI5. The anti-Apartheid activist, Rev. Michael Scott came to MI5's notice in the early 1930s when, according to the files, his 'contacts with the party were certainly close' (see chapter: Internationalism – a cornerstone of communist policy). MI5 kept tags on him, liaising with the South African security service up to 20 years later, even though by then he had little contact with the Party.

Recently released MI5 files at the National Archives (February 2014) reveal that the security services were keeping a whole number of progressive artists under close surveillance, including Benjamin Britten, his partner, Peter Pears, the writer J.B. Priestley and the actor Michael Redgrave. They also kept tabs on the newly formed National Council for Civil Liberties, founded in 1934, of which Priestley was a founder member. Pears was vice-president of the Musicians Organisation for Peace and Justice and a member of the League for Democracy in Greece, both described by MI5 as 'communist front organisations'. Another mentions 'an entertainment' compèred by Priestley in aid of CND and with performers, Sir Michael Redgrave, Peggy Ashcroft, Britten and Pears. Redgrave, one of the files said, first came to MI5's attention after he'd signed the manifesto of the 'communist-backed' People's Vigilance Committee'. It reveals once more the paranoia of the political elite and their security services in their continued search for communists under every bed. It also betrays a characteristic of most if not all secret services: their deep distrust of artists and intellectuals.

Murray Grieve, better known as the Scots poet, Hugh MacDiarmid, was first noted in MI5 files in 1931. His name had been mentioned by a group of communist journalists, meeting in a social setting at a Fleet Street pub. Soon after, an MI5 informant reported a speech by MacDiarmid in which he said Scotland 'did not end at the Cheviots but that Lancashire was its rightful boundary'. Quite how the reportage of juicy items such as this helped maintain the British Empire remains a conundrum.

Perhaps at first sight the case of Betty Reid (a leading figure in the Communist Party's Organisation Department) might suggest more purpose but not when one considers what the results of twenty years of surveillance revealed.

She first came to the attention of the Security Service in 1936 when she took up employment at the Left Book Club department of publishers Victor Gollancz. Perhaps suspicions were aroused when she toured the Soviet Union as a member of a group whose numbers were reduced to just three by Moscow's refusal to sanction visas. Either way, a close watch was established on her, and all the files contain detailed accounts of Reid's movements and meetings, reports of speeches, and copies of intercepted correspondence and telephone conversations.

The six files on Reid during the period 1936-1956 that were released in 2005 are truly inocuous, boring even. They detail her every move and conversation, even the food she ate at her favourite lunchtime café. But there appears to be little if anything of a security intelligence nature.

KV 2/2042 (1936-1950) covers the period when Reid was secretary of the Holborn Branch of the Communist Party and also Secretary of the London Council for Anti-Fascist Aid (from May 1941 the National Council for Democratic Aid), the body which supported refugees from fascist Europe in Britain. Possibly this connection with incoming foreigners made her a target.

From 1946, Reid was in charge of Party membership issues in the Party's Organisation Department in King Street. This responsibility included the vetting of membership applications, to check for infiltration from fascist or Trotskyist groups, or the security forces. Presumably, Reid's role made her a target of some interest for MI5 for the two decades that they constantly intercepted her telephone conversations.

The files contain intercepted phone calls and reports of conversations on the difficulties Reid was facing in her work over childcare. Much later in life, she came to realise that the person she thought was ideal to look after her two boys whilst she worked, and who she found by advertising in Soviet Weekly, and with whom she forged a close friendship, was in fact an MI5 plant. This belated realisation of hers received widespread publicity, especially since Reid then sought out the woman and re-established relations with her, and both began exchanging cards until Reid's death. Although even now that Reid and the spy are both dead, the released files do not confirm any illegal activities, even though the woman plant did admit her role to Reid. 'Security sources' told the Guardian that at least one withheld document was to protect the names of MI5 informants.[128]

Reid's meetings in 1955 with her contact in the Soviet embassy in

THE 'ENEMY WITHIN' – SPOOKS AND DIRTY TRICKS

London, Second Secretary Nikolai Timofeev, whom she describes as her 'cream cakes pal' are detailed. The only item of note is, it seems, that Timofeev was astounded that the men who printed the Daily Worker were not Party members.

MI5 files from 1949 on the perceived 'penetration' of the education system by the Communist Party were released in 2005.[129] One contains a note written in August of that year by MI5 on communist attitudes towards education and the recruitment of teachers as what it saw as being part and parcel of 'a struggle against the mastery of capitalism'. The report, which presumably found its way to Labour government ministers noted the way in which the Soviet Union had supposedly sought to penetrate the teaching profession across the globe and particularly in Britain.

The agency claimed to have infiltrated the CPGB and obtained extensive internal information despite the fact that the Party attached considerable significance to 'the safeguarding of membership particulars'. It was said that the Communist Party of Great Britain attached 'considerable importance' to recruiting teachers and that this was reflected in the Party having some 775 teachers amongst its 38,766 membership. The Foreign Office commented on the MI5 memorandum:

'that education is considered not only an important field for exploitation but also as analogous to an industry, is not perhaps without significance.'

It is probably not unconnected that, in 1948, the Labour government introduced security vetting, aimed at excluding communists from positions where they could supposedly damage national security. This led to 167 civil servants losing their jobs. Such vetting continued over the next few decades, even within the BBC which appointed a Special Assistant to the Director of Personnel to vet names of successful job applicants, especially graduate trainees, film editors, journalists, arts producers and drama directors. Only in 1985 did the BBC acknowledge for the first time that it vetted staff via MI5.

In the late 1940s, Sir Walter Citrine, former General Secretary of the TUC, and latterly the head of the newly nationalised British Electricity Authority demanded a purge of communists in London Power Stations. The investigation was carried out by Roger Hollis, the then head of `C' division.

The BBC, far from carrying out its supposed mission to be fearlessly independent, was up to its eyes in collaboration with the Secret Intelligence Services. It was established practice for the Chief Assistant to the Director General to liaise with MI5 on behalf of his boss, he would receive quarterly security briefings to keep the BBC informed on requirements of the security forces.

Shortly before he became BBC Director General in the 1950s, Sir Hugh Carleton Greene, unhesitatingly spoke of its propaganda role (a phrase he had no problem in employing) to the NATO College in Paris. It is little wonder that, in the cold war period, the view of the world crafted by the secret services, became the standard for public opinion.

Data collection by organisations such as the Economic League, set up by business interests to monitor trade union activists and communists, as well as the Building Employers Federation, were important from the period from the 1920s through to the 1970s. Special Branch itself also collaborated with local employers and their national self-help agencies. MI5's 'C' division handled security clearance for defence contracts and worked closely with private sector intelligence groups, such as the Economic League. Duncan Campbell, in his book On the Record,[130] suggests that the Economic League had office space in MI5 headquarters and was financially supported by it too. One of the first examples of the closeness between employers' associations and the security forces was revealed as early as 1937. The Daily Worker obtained correspondence between John Baker White and Robert Rawdon Hoare revealing that the Economic League had illegal contacts with the police.

The US State Department, via the London embassy, also supplied a vast amount of intelligence. Despite the opening of archives in the USA, little of this role has yet been revealed, no doubt because of sensitivities on the issue of interference in the affairs of sovereign states. But over a thousand pages of reports made by the US embassy in New Zealand to the State Department on the tiny local labour movement there have been declassified and show surveillance down to the level of trades councils and union branches. It is more than likely that a similar degree of interest, at least, was shown in the far more significant British labour movement.

Home Office papers released in 1995 first revealed for certain that agents were placed right at the heart of the CPGB's leadership. In September 1940, Sir John Anderson, in referring to these agents, was only in favour of prosecuting the Party leadership because of its attacks on pre-war appeasers of Hitler and its hostility to the 'phoney' character

THE 'ENEMY WITHIN' – SPOOKS AND DIRTY TRICKS

of the war at that stage, 'if that can be done without uncovering channels of information which it is essential to keep'. In other words maintaining the inside agents was more important.[131] Only a couple of low grade agents have so far been revealed. In 1950, M15 burgled the office where the CPGB's membership list was held and photographed some 55,000 records, before leaving a bug or radio-microphone there, which was only discovered in 1975.

The secret services were also not averse to using quasi independent and public organisations to assist them in collecting data on Leftists. In the 1950s, former Attorney General, Lord Shawcross, together with Common Cause, set up the Industrial Research and Information Services (IRIS), which may not have been as successful as hoped in targeting left candidates in union elections and attempting to smear them, right up to the 1980s, although it undoubtedly had a modicum of success. Particular targets were the trade unions DATA, the ETU, the NUM and the AEU, all of which had a strong communist presence. Communists knew of these activities as they experienced them at the sharp end and often suspected foul play but could not prove it.[132] IRIS's work became especially important in the area of union elections during the 1970s, particularly in the AEU and most especially in the West Midlands, where the left was ascendant. IRIS even set up what it called cells, in a deliberate parody of communist methods of work, in unions to combat the left. In this work, the planting of anti-communist scare stories in the media also played a significant role in swinging election results.

A number of trade union leaders were clearly willing to collaborate with the secret services in order to undermine communist influence in the unions. Several of these have since been 'outed' as moles: Joe Gormley, president of the NUM, the left-wing general secretaries Laurence Daly, (NUM) and Ray Buckton (ASLEF). A former chairman and former rank and file leader of the Transport and General Workers Union, Brian Nicholson, was widely respected as a 'solid left-winger', but he was later revealed by the release of papers under the 30-year rule to have been at the very least an informant (he says he spoke to anyone who asked him questions) of the security forces.

The Tory government in the early 1960s spent a fortune in public money funding anti-communist activities out of the Secret Fund, which underwrote the security services, although few at the time realised it. (Cabinet papers, released under the thirty-year rule, back these points up.) If it had been known publicly that Ford and Shell funded it in tandem with the government, undoubtedly questions would have been asked.

The eighth batch of secret files released in 2001 (a thousand files still remain closed and who knows how many were 'lost'?) 'fully vindicates those radicals who claim that the 20th century British state erected a substantial system of surveillance mainly aimed at the left'.[133] A vast number of individuals had secret files held on them detailing all manner of things. Many prominent intellectuals, often harmless individuals who simply liked to be honest in their thinking and spoke their mind, who were never in any way associated with the so-called subversive activities of social dissidents, like communists, often had bulky files of subjective comment covering their entire lives.

The tapping, bugging and mail interference by the security services was so widespread and routine that communists bore the mild inconveniences that arose, usually due to ineptitude, with good humour and disdain. A former postman in Whitechapel in 1946, where the Party had an MP – Phil Piratin for Mile End – and quite a few councillors, noticed that none of these people got their mail 'without it went upstairs to be examined'. The 'Indoor Investigation man was never off the sorting office floor… making sure that the usual addresses were taken off the frames for their journey to some secret hide-out upstairs'.[134] Communist trade unionists like Ken Gill and Mick McGahey had their phones routinely tapped and the latter had his London hotel room bugged.

Such intervention was routine until, certainly, the most recent years. Annie Machon, a former, and now disillusioned, agent of the security forces, has revealed that her duties enabled her to know that all post to the Communist Party's headquarters was routinely copied. Even when a schoolboy wrote, asking for information on a topic for a school project, he was assigned a personal file and labelled a sympathiser.[135]

Harold Wilson's outburst against 'a tightly knit group of politically motivated men', during the 1966 seamen's strike (see chapter: Trade unions – the main focus) was fed by M15's daily report on its activities to the Prime Minister. But the Special Branch of the police service focused more on provocation and dirty tricks, than on spying on the work of the Party.

In 1968, Special Branch even set up the Special Demonstration Squad, known internally as 'the hairies' for their adoption of fashionable long hair and beards. It recently came out that a number of these 'hairies' borrowed a technique from Frederick Forsyth's novel

Day of the Jackal and searched gravestones for the names of young children who would have been of a similar age to themselves for an alias. Spies were given new names, addresses, apartments, driving licences and national insurance numbers, based on these dead children.

While in March 1985 former MI5 officer Cathy Massiter revealed on Channel 4's 20/20 Vision programme, MI5's Official Secrets, that in the 1970s, the security forces engaged in systematic spying on CND, the National Council for Civil Liberties and other progressive organisations. MI5 had kept Harriet Harman, Patricia Hewitt and Bruce Kent – all to become mainstream Labour MPs or candidates – under constant surveillance. Massiter expressed disquiet about MI5's over zealous definition of the term 'subversive', as applied to the National Council for Civil Liberties and CND. She revealed that MI5's definition of subversion was being distorted and widened and that its own rules were being violated.

MI5 carried out regular surveillance of CND members it considered to be subversive. From the late 1960s until the mid-1970s, it designated CND as subversive by virtue of its being 'communist controlled'. Communists have, of course, played an active role in the organisation, and John Cox, its chairman from 1971 to 1977, was a member of the CPGB. However, from the late 1970s, MI5 downgraded CND to 'communist-penetrated'. It now says it has no current investigations in this area.

In 1985, Cathy Massiter, who had been responsible for the surveillance of CND from 1981 to 1983, resigned and made disclosures about MI5's spying on CND. She said that her work was determined more by the political importance of CND than by any security threat posed by subversive elements within it. In 1983, she analysed telephone intercepts on John Cox that gave her access to conversations with Joan Ruddock and Bruce Kent. MI5 also placed a spy, Harry Newton (mentioned above), in the CND office. According to Massiter, Newton believed that CND was controlled by extreme left-wing activists and that Bruce Kent might be a crypto-communist, but Massiter found no evidence to support either assertion.

A private detective agency, Euro-Tec, was recruited by Special Branch to spy on London dockers during the 1972 dock strike, the dispute which lead to the imprisonment of the Pentonville 5 (see chapter: Trade unions – the main focus). One Euro-Tec agent has revealed that in the early seventies thousands of shop stewards and union officials, their families and friends were regularly monitored.

Joe Gormley, President of the NUM, kept MI5 briefed on strike plans in 1972 and 1974. Many union leaders would be 'helped' along when they had serious internal trouble. Within a few weeks of the 1972 miners' strike MI5 shifted the emphasis of its work to domestic subversion from the left. MI5's F branch was massively and rapidly expanded. Even Labour leader Harold Wilson himself was under surveillance in the run up to the 1974 election; MI5 had a file on Wilson with the code-name 'Henry Worthington'. As revealed in Peter Wright's Spycatcher a group of security officers even believed Wilson to be a Soviet spy.[136]

The BBC documentary series of three programmes, True Spies in 2002 lifted the lid on some of the activities of the security forces in the British labour movement.[137] This revealed how, at the height of the left-wing militancy during the late 1960s and 1970s, Metropolitan Police Special Branch officers were infiltrated, into left-wing organisations as undercover operatives.

Special Branch's interest in actor Ricky Tomlinson, during his time as a trade unionist was also touched on in one of the programmes. He had been arrested and imprisoned for his activities during a big building workers' strike (see Chapter: Trade Unions – the Main Focus). But infiltration went much deeper than this. Activists would be nurtured by operatives and the offices of progressive organisations were bugged and burgled. Post was opened and keys copied in small plasticine blocks and passed to Special Branch and MI5.

As the left began to secure greater authority within the Labour Party, all of the techniques carried out on communists over the previous quarter of a century became even more applicable to the non-communist left. Ron Hayward, then General Secretary of the Labour Party, was told in 1974 by a private security company that the Labour Party's headquarters were bugged. He did not believe in the tip off but should have done.[138]

In 1979, the convenor and leading communist, Derek Robinson was sacked from British Leyland's Longbridge car plant, partly on the evidence of the leaking to the company's managing director Michael Edwardes (according to him in his memoirs) of the written minutes of a Party meeting concerned with opposing the plan of running down British Leyland. The reality of the plot is open to speculation but MI5 is supposed to have had an agent in place, code-number 910, very close to Robinson. It has been claimed that 910 was a Communist Party member, working at Longbridge and was also 'a highly placed union official' a member of the AUEW. He knew the main union leaders and was 'an easy man to look after; he would enjoy a couple of pints in an ordinary pub somewhere where he may not be recognised, and then always wanted to eat fish and chips in your car before he got home, and that's the way you ran him', his handler reported. The information he supplied concerned the unions' intentions, especially on strikes. All his reports were instantly sent on to MI5, which held him in the highest regard as a 'very, very highly valued' agent.

Notoriously, during the 1984-5 miners' strike, when Stella Rimington was Assistant Director of MI5's F Branch (she was later to become Director General of MI5), the spooks had a field day. Interventions to undermine the strike through the establishment of a 'National Working Miners' Committee' was only the tip of the iceberg. The story splash on 28 October 1984 in the Sunday Times about NUM Chief Executive Roger Windsor's fund-raising meeting with Libyan leader Colonel Gaddafi led to subsequent allegations that Windsor was an MI5 'mole' within the NUM, although denied by both Windsor and the NUM.

Documents released in 2005, revealed the extent of Special Branch surveillance of the Anti-Apartheid Movement (AAM) in Britain during the early 1980s. The Branch, which acted as the monitoring body for MI5, penetrated the organisation from top to bottom. Officers would report on such trivial details as a supermarket worker handing out leaflets to work colleagues. The numbers attending meetings and the subjects discussed were reported; even the left-wing bias of posters stored in a member's garden shed was noted! The files, released to the BBC under the Freedom of Information Act, indicate that the finest detail of the events of the AAM executive committee or annual conference were regularly reported to the Special Branch. Profiles of each and every member of the 30 member executive were developed and it was noted that 13 of these were members of either the South African or British Communist Party.

Although Britain never underwent the full corrosive and socially destructive process that McCarthyism wrought on the USA, there was nevertheless regular harassment of left-wing activists, many of whom were communists; letters were regularly opened, phones were tapped, premises raided and the iniquitous and secret, system of blacklisting was used widely. In the former colonies, however, persecution of communists and those who associated or sympathised with them and their ideas could be as severe as in the USA. In the colonies and

Commonwealth anti-communism was much more strident and McCarthyite methods were implemented, as in Australia under its ardent right-wing Prime Minister Robert Menzies. Many communists there, including ther renowned anthropologist and friend of Peter Worsley (see below), Fred Rose, was forced to leave the country and seek employment elsewhere.

My own mother and father experienced blacklisting during the 1940s – my mother was summarily sacked from her nursing job at a big London hospital, after photos of Russian Bolsheviks were found in her room; my father lost his job as a machinist in a small machine tool factory in Shropshire and found himself blacklisted throughout the region's engineering industry. He was obliged to work as an insurance salesman from then on. But they are just two of many such incidents. Blacklisting, like racial or gender discrimination is always extremely difficult to prove, but everyone on the Left knew it was taking place. It was implemented particularly strictly in so-called key industries or security-sensitive areas, but went on everywhere that trade union organisation was strong and effective. The BBC as well as the Civil Service vetted all prospective applicants with MI5's active cooperation. Communists were on no account to be employed. A friend of mine who worked freelance for the BBC during the seventies was asked directly by his line manager about his political affiliations and was told clearly that if he were a 'card-carrying member' of the Communist Party, he would find no more employment with the organisation.

While Britain's state secret services did not often carry out their own blacklisting work, they readily passed on information concerning leftists and trade union militants to the relevant bodies which would then ensure that such individuals were blacklisted. For years some of the biggest names in British business subscribed to a secret blacklist containing thousands of names with the power to deny work and destroy livelihoods. From the Millennium Dome to the iconic Olympic Park, some construction firms paid for information on workers they feared could delay work and cost them money.

Academics were also blacklisted

The renowned sociologist and anthropologist Peter Worsley details his own blacklisting in his autobiography.[139] As a young, but already renowned anthropologist, he was asked to come for interview at the British government's then Colonial Office to be considered for a research job at the Rhodes-Livingstone Institute (RLI). He wasn't offered the job and was told subsequently by Max Gluckman, who had been the director of RLI and was on the interviewing board, that he would have been given the job but MI5 had blocked his appointment. At the same time Max told him that several important figures in the academic world of anthropology had confided that they would ensure that 'as a Marxist' he was never given a post in anthropology. That came to pass and was largely the reason for Worsley's career change to sociology.

According to the Guardian's obituary of Worsley (29 March 2013) he was 'a social scientist of remarkable range and influence' who 'did much to define and popularise the idea, first expressed by the French demographer Alfred Sauvy, that developing countries constituted a "third world".'

The article went on to describe how the security services stymied his career: 'The course of Worsley's career was shaped by the intervention of MI5, on account of his communist associations. They snooped on his Swahili teaching in East Africa and spiked his plan to do fieldwork in central Africa despite the support he received from Max Gluckman, professor of social anthropology at Manchester University, where Worsley had a post-graduate studentship.' He became the first professor of sociology at Manchester University and his best-selling book Introducing Sociology became a basic text for all aspiring sociologists, selling over half a million copies worldwide.

In his autobiography he also writes about his experiences as a university staff member during the student rebellions of the sixties, demonstrating how communists in their actions often belie the extremist label they were usually given. Worsley writes almost, it seems, as an apology for his non-militant behaviour: 'Whatever my ideological politics, brought up in a political culture that eschewed violence and preached the rational resolution of differences, I found these radical methods difficult to accept, although I never condemned them.' [He is here referring here to student occupations and raids on university offices]

As John Sutherland said in his review of James Smith's book, British Writers and MI5 Surveillance, 1930-60, in the New Statesman,[140] 'one of the most mythologised aspects of the British secret state was its attempt to keep tabs on literary intellectuals. The idea that poets, novelists or playwrights could have been crucial to the progress of the communist "menace" was, he wrote, "an enduringly attractive one", and it flattered the writers, and caused the spooks to go into paroxysms of paranoia.' The three sections of James Smith's book deal with the Auden circle; the folksinger and songwriter Ewan MacColl and theatre director Joan Littlewood, together with George Orwell and Arthur Koestler.

'There is, ironically, an uncanny parallel between Orwell's nightmare vision of an all-seeing dictatorship and his own status for more than a decade as a target for the close scrutiny of the British security services and then his own role as an informant.

MI5 bugged conversations between Joan Littlewood and friends connected with Theatre Workshop, but Smith says: 'whatever its covert origin, none of this evidence gathered by MI5 indicated illegal activity or even anything particularly sinister'. MI5's spying is often a comedy of errors. The security services – MI5 often, and Special Branch unfailingly – were useless at spying on intellectuals or for that matter on anyone else. They were invariably incapable of understanding the relevance or significance of what was being said.'

Of course, spooks and plods aren't literary critics. Sutherland quotes Hugh Trevor-Roper, remarking that, 'the intelligence establishment ranged between "pretty stupid" and "very stupid", and never "had much use for ideas". Orwell said: 'the policeman who arrests the "red" does not understand the theories the "red" is preaching. This is more than a sneer: to be 'an intellectual' was itself grounds for mistrust. It's often apparent from the files that the things these writers actually wrote went unread by those investigating them.

'Arthur Koestler's story is the darkest and most interesting,' Sutherland writes, 'One intelligence officer described him as "one third genius, one third blackguard, and one third lunatic", which seems about right. In his communist years, Koestler really was close to the German communist propaganda chief, Willi Münzenberg, and his escape was accomplished through blackmail, bluster and outright lying. 'Koestler,' Smith says, 'launched an energetic campaign to ingratiate himself with whatever office or agency of the British secret state he could establish contact with.'

It is amazing how much time was wasted on red herrings. A great deal of energy was spent fretting over the influence Ewan MacColl and his then wife Joan Littlewood had in the BBC – Children's Hour, specifically. In the files, a 1944 minute on surveillance of the Independent Labour Party, dismissed nine years previously as no threat, observed:

'In the course of officially ignoring the ILP we have accumulated a file of 22 volumes about it.
The occasional voice of good sense is the blessed exception. One MI5 officer called Ogilvie calmed the waters after Special Branch reported on Orwell's "advanced Communist views" and "alarming tendency to dress in a Bohemian fashion both at his office and in his leisure hours". Ogilvie, who had actually read Orwell, indicated dryly that their man wasn't really on board with the Moscow line.'

As Smith levelly acknowledges, 'the most impactful relationship between the secret state and writers during these years was not in any subversive effect the latter had on the former: rather, it was the way in which the former provided career boosts to the latter. Leftish writers – whether careerists such as Spender and Koestler or simply apostate one-time sympathisers such as Orwell – made good propagandists. The upshot of the cultural cold war, more or less, was that the British government caused the printing of very many copies of Animal Farm.'
Sutherland concludes by saying that:

'What this whole history of surveillance of the Communist Party demonstrates is the paucity and banality of the results, at tremendous costs to the country. This small party never really represented a threat or significant challenge to the establishment, although there was, of course, always the potential of a real challenge.' [141]

This short description of the ongoing relationship between the Communist Party and Britain's security services demonstrates, I feel, that the stigmatisation of both the Party, its many sympathisers, fellow travellers and individual members was a central preoccupation of the Establishment. It also reveals, based on those files and papers that have been released into the public domain, that the Party and its followers were hardly the deadly and dangerous elements they were made out to be. This work by the security services did, though, serve to cement the idea of communists being an 'alien' or subversive force in society and it also ruined or stymied the careers of many individuals.

GRAHAM STEVENSON

A Summing Up

'*Every true man is in some sort, until his youth dies and his eyes harden, the potential builder of a New Jerusalem. At some time or other, every one of us has dreamed of laying his brick in such a work. And even if this thing that is being builded here with tears and blood is not the golden city that we ourselves have dreamed, it is still a thing to the sympathetic understanding of which each one of us is bound by whatever he owes to his own youth.*' [142]

ARTHUR RANSOME

'*My commitment to the cause was for life, and it was an exhilarating moment to be alive and young. We simply knew, all of us, that the revolution was at hand.*'

JAMES KLUGMAN

Communists and the Communist Party in Britain have been largely dismissed and ignored by historians on the rationale that the party was always small and never won significant electoral support in the country. That is true, but one also has to assess its significance using a different measuring stick to the one used for mainstream parties. Its long-serving General Secretary, Harry Pollitt, described it as 'a small party of the elect... not a party of passive members, but activists.' Rather than aiming for a mass party, he said, we want people we can rely on in a crisis.[143] Hardly anyone joined the Party unless they were willing to devote considerable time and energy to it.

Most members of the Communist Party were far removed from the image their media-portrayal would suggest. Certainly in the early years they were encouraged to see themselves as a 'new kind of individual', upright, responsible and unwaveringly committed to the cause of socialism. Certainly in its early days, members were expected to be clean-living, family-orientated and conservatively dressed; beards and Bohemian lifestyles were very much frowned upon. In its instructions to members partaking in a march in London's St. Pancras in 1926, The Party emphasised, for instance, that members should 'Remember you are organised workers, not a mob.'

What also often distinguishes them from many of their fellows is that they invariably express their beliefs in a coherent politicised framework which provides them with a structural body of theory with which to place their ideas and arguments. This can sometimes by perceived as an arrogant 'know-it-all' mindset, but is more often simply a reflection of a holistic Marxist understanding of society.

A history of the Communist Party can be written in various ways and, as is well demonstrated in the publications of research projects making full use of oral evidence, such evidence is often very different from the documentary. Interviews with those who took part in organisations and events often provides a picture at variance with 'official' historical narratives, based largely on documentary evidence.

In the foregoing pages I have attempted to demonstrate that the overwhelming majority of communists in Britain were, and are, not a group of militant fanatics or subversive agents out to impose a totalitarian regime on the country. On the contrary, I hope readers will have grasped that the Communist Party, even though never a large organisation, and the many who have passed through its ranks, have made a significant and often valuable contribution to Britain's cultural, political and social life. It can be seen clearly from those areas covered in this book, together with the few short biographies of selected individuals, that communists came from all walks of life, from the working class, middle class and even a few from the aristocracy, they were young and old, men and women.

Of course, it could be argued that all the communist individuals mentioned here would have made similar contributions to society whether they had been in the Communist Party or not. After all, there are thousands of selfless, courageous and socially committed activists also from all walks of life, who belong to a multitude of other organisations or none. How are communists in any way different? I would suggest, that communists, even if they were attracted to the Party in the first place because of their, perhaps, strongly developed social conscience or sense of solidarity with the less fortunate, would have been significantly changed by their experience. The experience of belonging to a close-knit and 'comradely' group – indeed an international fraternity – of like-minded individuals, together with an introduction to the theory of Marxism, will have left an indelible impression on most of them and significantly influenced the way they thought, behaved and worked. That is something few other organisations or groups could boast of.

Overall I believe it is also justified to argue that communists have, on the whole, made a positive contribution to life in Britain. Far from being the 'outsiders' they have been characterised, manipulatively attempting to insert themselves into democratic organisations by subterfuge and guile, they have been in the forefront of attempts to encourage ordinary people to become politically aware and take political action. They have been consistently committed to encouraging participation in the political and social processes of the country, particularly at a grassroots level.

People who become communists have a variety of motivations, some persuaded of the validity of the communist project by their readings of Marxist classics, but the overwhelming majority have been motivated by a deep-seated feeling of solidarity and an abhorrence of poverty and injustice; they saw the Communist Party as the organisation best suited to fight for and achieve the social and political goals they embraced. Most were motivated by an ideal.

Despite not being a major political force, the Party was always an active pressure group. Even if it failed electorally, its members were rarely isolated or marginalised, even at the height of the Cold War; on the contrary, they invariably won respect and managed to effect many changes in the political and social arena, however small.

Interestingly, a not insignificant number of members came from a Christian background, particularly ex-Catholics. And, certainly, the Christian principal of treating one's fellow human beings as one would wish to be treated, the concept of mutuality, of helping the poor and deprived and helping to build a more egalitarian world, could all be easily reconciled with communist ideology. The writer Graham Greene in many of his novels deals with the recurring dilemma facing those who, in our imperfect world, experience a crisis of faith and who may then toy with the attraction of communism as an ideology that 'gets things done' and can achieve real change.

Most of those who spent a considerable time as ordinary members of the Party or even their whole lives, invariably pursued careers in which they could make a social contribution or, outside work, used their free time to promote social justice and equality of opportunity. Many, even after leaving it, and maybe rejecting some or all of its policies, invariably remained committed to some form of radical social change or socialist vision. Some, particularly once the extent of Stalin's purges became better known, set up their own Trotskyist organisations, the first of which was formed in London's Balham in 1932.

There were only very few former members who became virulent anti-communists and, it has to be said, often made careers out of it. This apostate status was often an ideal entry card and acceptance into establishment circles and useful in terms of career enhancement. Certainly ex-communists like Arthur Koestler and the electricians' union officials, Frank Chapple and Les Cannon – given a life peerage and a knighthood respectively – fall into this latter category.

What characterised most communists is that they entered politics not for any career opportunities the Party might offer, nor with the ambition of holding high office or being in power. The Communist Party was certainly not the vehicle for pursuing such goals in life; it was a battered bicycle compared with the Bentleys and Rolls Royces of the mainstream parties.

Raphael Samuel in his book, The Lost Word of British Communism, underlines the fact that the Communist Party was seldom, if ever, confrontational or rabble-rousing; it was invariably circumspect, cautious in its tactics and activities. Its main appeal was not to wild revolutionaries but more to serious minded workers and 'respectable' individuals; communists were, in the main, 'clean living', organised and disciplined. The Party's first general secretary, Harry Pollitt, symbolised those characteristics. He always wore a suit and waistcoat, and told other comrades that they should never turn up to address meetings without a clean shirt.

The reasons why individuals joined the Communist Party over the years can probably be reduced to a few substantive ones. Those who then left after shorter or longer memberships will probably have had a wider range of reasons for doing so. Undoubtedly, many will have resigned because, over time, they developed ideological differences with the Party and found that they disagreed with significant aspects of its policy. Many will also have been disillusioned by what had been happening in the Soviet Union, particularly during the Stalin period. But, particularly at the height of the Cold War, some will have wished to distance themselves from the Party for legitimate career reasons.

As I have also attempted to demonstrate, the pressures on Party members were enormous as was the amount of hatred and ostracism they faced. Many of those who remained members despite this often forewent careers, advancement, promotion and recognition – it was a considerable sacrifice not only for the individuals concerned but also for their immediate families. Membership certainly brought no privileges, and those prepared to take on full-time jobs on behalf of the Party were expected to work around the clock and on a virtual subsistence salary. The famed 'Moscow Gold', whatever the actual financial support from Moscow was, certainly didn't find its way into the pockets of Party functionaries or members.

Francis Beckett, writing about the Communist Party Chairperson at its last conference, underlines this point: 'had she [Marian Darke] chosen the Labour Party instead of the Communist Party, she would in 1991 have probably been a member of Neil Kinnock's shadow cabinet, instead of presiding over the last Congress of a fast diminishing Communist Party.' [144]

Of course, because the Communist Party never held political power in Britain, we can have no idea how its individual members would have behaved if it had. Maybe little better or worse than those in any of the other political parties – power and power structures tend to impose their own templates on individual thinking and behaviour, and few seem to be able to withstand the 'cloning' that invariably takes place and the concomitant subordination of one's own moral and ethical principles to party loyalty. We can only judge them on what they actually did as part of a small, radical and oppositional party.

While many were often blind at the time to the deficiencies of the Soviet Union and many of the crimes committed by Stalin in the name of communism, they rarely became ovine imitators of Soviet methods. They were as much formed and moulded by Britain's democratic and political pluralist traditions than anything else and, certainly in the trade unions and working class movement, they became very much an accepted, integrated and respected part.

While neither communists nor the Communist Party have played central or decisive roles in Britain, they have, since their existence, been an integral and ever present factor in the life of the country. Despite continuous attempts to demonise and to marginalise them by labelling them as agents of a foreign power, as an alien growth on the body politic, they have persisted in their attempts to build the basis for a genuine socialist society.

What is also hardly disputed is that Marxism, as a philosophy, has had a seminal influence in the area of ideas, e.g. in literary criticism, philosophy, sociology and economics, even though this impetus has not come exclusively from communists. To be a Marxist requires viewing the world dialectically and holistically, and to understand the historical process as a consequence of conflicting, antagonistic forces. It usually, also, implies a radically critical attitude to capitalism as an exploitive, profit-making system, and proposing some form of socialism as the solution to its seemingly intractable problems.

There is little doubt, viewed historically, that communism and the highpoints of its popularity and attraction are now in the past, even though one of its successor parties, the Communist Party of Britain (CPB), still exists, as does Democratic Left and those self-defined communist individuals, even if only in their hundreds now, and there is still a significant number outside these organisations who would characterise themselves as Marxist thinkers.

The communist movement in Britain and worldwide has to be looked at from within the historical context. The appeal of communism for many grew out of the inability of the capitalist system to create a world free of wars, of injustice, poverty and deprivation. The horrors and mass slaughter of the First World War and the worldwide slump that followed in the twenties encouraged many to look at alternative ideas for running society, and communism appeared to be one of the most attractive. The successful Bolshevik Revolution seemed to show the way forward to a state controlled and run by working people for their own benefit and which promised an end to the boom and bust of capitalism.

The settling of East European Jews in western countries during the late 19th and early 20th centuries after fleeing the pogroms there was also highly significant in boosting the fortunes of communist and socialist organisations. These were once again reinforced by the next wave of Jews fleeing German fascism, and many of these too threw in their lot with the communists, who they saw as the most effective force, able and committed to fighting fascism. A description of western communism, particularly in Britain and the USA, is impossible without giving due credit to the thousands of those from a Jewish background who not only made up a significant proportion of its membership but also took on leading roles.

Another factor which helped give communism a boost during the first half of the twentieth century was the more 'black-and-white' social and class situation during that period; issues appeared to be more clear-cut and polarised. Many progressives were fired also by a feeling of urgency, of revolution or radical social change being 'around the corner'. Even the wars that were fought at that time, like the Spanish Civil War or the battle against Nazism, could easily be categorised as battles between 'good and evil' and it was easier to choose sides.

Social issues, too, seemed to be much more clearly defined during the earlier part of the twentieth century, whereas today there is a multitude of organisations involved in social or environmental campaigns, each separately doing their own thing; there is no central organising body or recognised political party to give focus or leadership. Allied to that, there is also a widely held mistrust of political parties and even the whole idea of 'leadership'.

Today the waters are more muddied and wars are invariably complicated by religious, ethnic, racial and ideological undertones. The 'great causes' such as the battles against mass hunger and poverty, illiteracy and environmental degradation are often perceived as 'too big' to be tackled effectively. People are increasingly focussing their idealism on single issues rather in 'saving the world'.

The 20th century could, with a certain justification, be defined as the communist era, in which the communist movement flourished worldwide, but it is perhaps an era now gone for ever. It was characterised by tightly-knit groups of like-minded people, whether political parties, religions or social groups, in which members felt a strong sense of cohesion, common purpose, comradeship and solidarity; they believed that they were actually changing the world. It is difficult to describe that tribal sense of belonging – comparable perhaps to that allegiance of football fans to a particular team – of one's own life being given with purpose and goals; also the deep satisfaction by being involved and of being educated by the movement itself. There was also, perhaps, much self-delusion, but on the whole it was for those who belonged to the movement over longer periods, a positive and life-enhancing experience.

John Gorman's autobiography, Knocking Down Ginger, provides a fascinating and vivid description of his upbringing in London's East

End, his joining the Communist Party as a young man, to his resignation from the Party in 1956 after Khrushchev's revelations about Stalin and the Soviet intervention in Hungary. It is one of the best descriptions of what life in the Party for ordinary members was really like.

He explains the attraction, but also the shame he felt once Stalin's tyranny had been revealed:

'In the Party, I had found the comradeship that is built when a group of people are banded together against a common enemy, the romance of struggle against great odds. They were good days…My shame was for the extent to which I'd been gullible in my adulation of Stalin and my unquestioning support for Soviet Communism, when so many were its innocent victims.'

He goes on to explain the sleepless nights he experienced and heart-searching he undertook before he was able to break loose from a Party that had very much defined his life over many years. However, despite feeling no longer able to call himself a communist and belong to the Communist Party, he remained committed to radical social change:

'Our society is torn by violence, greed, racial intolerance and the pursuit of private wealth, with minimal concern for community or the very earth on which we live. There has to be a better way, and that way surely lies in a society based upon cooperation, not competition. Within me, the gleam of socialism remains undimmed.'

His experience is typical for a large number of communists, certainly of those who joined in the thirties or forties. That feeling and that vision, Gorman describes so well, remained for those who stayed in the Party as well as for many of those who left. He also makes clear that in the Party discipline was accepted by most members as a prerequisite for an effective organisation; it was not imposed by coercion, and if it had, the Party would have ceased to exist very quickly.

Looking back over the history of communism, it is certainly difficult to explain the continuous, vitriolic and vehement hatred that has been aimed at communists by the mainstream media and established political and business elites, since the concept was first elaborated by Marx and Engels. Certainly in those countries where communists have never held power and done nothing deserving of such a reaction, it can only be explained in terms of the power of communist ideas. The hatred has certainly been more malicious and vindictive than anything directed at fascism and fascists or other right-wing extremists. Just look at how the western allies and the German ruling class treated the Nazis after the war – with kid gloves; whereas those who supported and worked for the former GDR, who were in no way responsible for millions of dead, for fomenting a world war or of genocide, have been hounded and denied basic justice, or the way not only communists, but anyone at all socialist or progressive, was treated by the US authorities during the McCarthy era.

What is certain, is that the capitalist system against which communists have consistently fought and against which they have polemicised is unable to offer solutions to the great existential problems of our time, and it is still subject to deep economic crises, as predicted by Marx and Engels. Capitalism is also the same unequal and unjust system it always was, but in an era of monopoly and finance capitalism that injustice and lack of fairness are even crasser, despite the fact that we are living in a materially much richer world and one with the technological means of providing everyone with a decent life.

The demise of communism and of communist parties has also been paralleled by a wide-spread depoliticisation of people throughout the world, but perhaps particularly in the developed West. This period is characterised by an increasing apathy, cynicism and decoupling of most people from the political process, as well as a loss of hope, of faith in a future of progress. People no longer feel that politics and engagement with politics are able to bring about meaningful change. Such widespread attitudes endanger the development of new political ideas, the health of societies and indeed democracy itself.

It is significant that despite the demise, in 1989, of the communist-run countries in Eastern Europe and the implosion of communist parties throughout the world, communist ideas refuse to go away. And despite the fact that the Communist Party and communists hardly play significant roles today, they continue to be used as bogeymen by the ruling elites to attack progressive movements or even the expression of liberal views. The Daily Mail's intemperate attack on Ed Miliband's father as a 'Marxist who hated Britain' in an attempt to slur the son, was one of the most recent. Conservative Prime Minister David Cameron then took up the cudgel by accusing Ed Miliband of 'wanting to live in a Marxist universe', for threatening to regulate energy prices for consumers. The Chancellor, George Osborne said Miliband's suggestion was 'out of Das Kapital' to which Miliband responded by asking if regulation was a good idea or a communist plot, allowing Cameron to retort: 'I'll leave the Communist plots to him!' [145]

In the USA, President Barack Obama is characterised by some of his opponents as a 'crypto-communist', among other epithets. This is symptomatic of the way the right-ring ruling elites still use the communist bogeyman to counter opposition or demands for a more just society.

There is also a continuous stream of films, books and radio programmes that deal with the experience of life 'under communism', virtually all of which provide a predictable and extremely one-sided picture, with the aim of reminding the public, should anyone still think that communism has any validity for our society today, that it is an evil, oppressive ideology.

I mention these examples here simply to demonstrate that communism appears to be living on beyond its widely declared interrment. The fact that ideas of communism and Marxism are still deemed powerful and dangerous enough to warrant continued demonisation or demontage is perhaps argument enough to suggest that they may still have relevance for our society today.

Tony Benn has stated that 'all political careers end in failure.' And certainly communism as an alternative system to capitalism has demonstrably failed to gain traction, but, as I hope I've been able to demonstrate, that doesn't mean that those individuals and their ideas achieved nothing and are therefore irrelevant. Perhaps we should recall Mao's memorable adage when asked to evaluate the lasting influence of the French revolution: 'It is too early to pass judgement'!

Finally, I'd like to conclude with a quotation from Malcolm MacEwen's autobiography, The Greening of a Red, because I feel it expresses succinctly what I hope I have also been able to demonstrate and underline in the pages of this book.

'I would not have written my story if my purpose had merely been to add to the number of confessions by former communists. The world has been drenched with stories, true and false, honest and mischievous, about the crimes, mistakes and inefficiency of communism, but there is a dearth of information about the real life of the Communist Party, and about the contribution that communists have made to the progress and liberation of humanity

– not least by paying the highest price for resisting Franco in Spain, defeating Hitler, frustrating American imperialism in Asia and opposing military dictatorships – and, I might add, contributing in all likelihood the largest number of Stalin's purges.'

BIBLIOGRAPHY

Alexander, Bill, *British Volunteers for Liberty*, Lawrence & Wishart, 1983 and, together with Williams, Colin and Gorman, John, *Memorials of the Spanish Civil War*, International Brigade Association, 1996.

Andrews Geoff, Fishman Nina and Morgan Kevin (eds), *Opening The Books essays on the social and cultural history of the British Communist Party*, Pluto Press 1995.

Andrews Geoff, *Endgames and New Times – the final years of British Communism 1964-1991*, Lawrence and Wishart, 2004.

Bosch, F. Xavier, Archie Cochrane: *Back to the Front, Barcelona XI* Cochrane Colloquium 2003.

Bounds, Philip, *British Communism and the Politics of Literature 1928-1939*, Merlin Press, 2012.

Branson, Noreen, *History of the Communist Party of Great Britain, Volumes III and IV*, Lawrence & Wishart, 1985 & 1997.

Brogan, Hugh, *The Life of Arthur Ransome*, Hamish Hamilton, 1985.

Beckett, Francis *Stalin's British Victims*, Sutton Publishing, 2004 and *Enemy Within – The Rise and Fall of British Communism*, John Murray, 1995.

Birch, Chris, *My Life*, St. Christopher Press, London, 2110.

Blackman Peter, *Footprints*, Smokestack Books 2013.

Callaghan, John, *Cold War, Crisis and Conflict: the CPGB 1951-68*, Lawrence & Wishart, 2003

Chambers, Colin, *The Story of Unity Theatre*, Lawrence & Wishart, 1989.

Clarke, Kate, *Chile in My Heart*, Bannister Publications, 2013.

Cohen, P, *Children of the Revolution*, London, Lawrence & Wishart, 1998.

Cope, Dave, Central Books – a Brief History 1939-1999, Central Books, 1999.

Cope, Dave (compiled by), *CPGB Bibliography online*:
http://www.amielandmelburn.org.uk/cpgb_biblio/searchfrset.htm.

Courtois, Stéphane (ed), *The Black Book of Communism: Crimes, Terror, Repression* (Original title Le Livre noir du communisme) Harvard university Press, 1999.

Croft, Andy, *Red Letter Days*, Lawrence & Wishart, 1990
Comrade Heart: A Life of Randall Swingler, Manchester University Press, 2003
After The Party: Reflections on life since the CPGB; Lawrence & Wishart; 2012

Croft, Andy and Mitchell, Andrew, (eds) *Red Sky at Night: socialist poetry*, Five Leaves press, 2003.

Daffern, Eileen, *Essays on a Life – politics, peace and the personal;* B&M Publishing, 2007

Dash, J. *Good Morning Brothers*, Lawrence & Wishart, 1969.

Davis, Mary, *Class and Gender in British Labour History*, Merlin Press, 2011

de la Mora, Constancia, *In Place of Splendour: the Autobiography of a Spanish Woman*, Harcourt, Brace and Company, 1939

Docherty, Mary, *A Miner's Lass*, Preston, 1992

Feaver, William, *James Boswell Unofficial War Artist*; Muswell Press 2007.

Feeley, Pat, *The Gralton Affair*, 1986.

Finch, John, Cox, Michael and Giles, Marjorie (eds), *Granada Television--The First Generation*, Manchester University Press; 2003.

Fishman, Nina, *The British Communist Party and the Trade Unions, (1933–45)*, Scolar Press, 1995.

Arthur Horner: *A Political Biography*. Volume 1 (1894-1944), Volume 2 (1944-1968), Lawrence and Wishart, London 2010.

Foster, G & C. Woolfson, *The Politics of the UCS Work-in*, London, Lawrence & Wishart, 1986.

Frow, Ruth, Edmund Frow (Eddie) *1906-1997 – the making of an activist*, Working Class Movement Library 1999.

Gabbidon, C.M., *Party Life (between the wars)* D.Phil thesis, Sussex university 1991.

Gorman, John, *Knocking Down Ginger*, Caliban Books, 1995.

Gralton, Margaret, *My Cousin Jimmy*, 1991.

Green, John *Ken Sprague – People's Artist*; Hawthorn Press and Artery Publications, 2002.
Red Reporter, Artery Publications, 2011.

Green, John & Boncza, Michal – *Hung, Drawn and Quartered*, Artery Publications, 2009.

Groves, Reg, *Conrad Noel and the Thaxted Movement: an adventure in Christian socialism*, A. M. Kelley, 1968.

Guckian, Des, *Deported – Jimmy Gralton a Undesirable Alien*, 1986.

Halpin, Kevin, *Memoirs of a Militant*, Manifesto Press, 2012.

Herbert, Michael and Taplin, Eric (eds), *Born with a Book in His Hand – a Tribute to Edmund Frow*, North West Labour History Group, 1998.

Hill, May (ed), *George Sinfield – his pen a sword*, Esme Sinfield, 1975.

Hodgkinson, George, *Sent to Coventry*, Maxwell, 1970.

Hogarth, Paul and Richard Ingrams, *Drawings on Life: the Autobiography of Paul Hogarth* 1997.

Hogenkamp, Bert, *Deadly Parallels: film and the left in Britain 1929-39*, Lawrence and Wishart, 1986
Film, Television and the Left in Britain: 1950-1970, 2002.

Howe Mark (ed) *Is That Damned Paper Still Coming Out? – the very best of the Daily Worker/Morning Star*, Peoples Press Printing Society, 2001.

Hyde, D., *I Believed*, London, William Heinemann Ltd. 1950.

Jacks, Digby, *Student Politics and Higher Education*, Lawrence & Wishart, 1975.

Jones, Jack, *Union Man: An Autobiography*, London, Collins, 1986.

Kasrils, R, *Armed and Dangerous: My Undercover Struggle Against Apartheid*, Heinemann African Writers Series, 1993.

Kay, Jackie, *Red Dust Road*, Pan MacMillan, 2011.

Keable, Ken, *London Recruits – the Secret War Against Apartheid*, Merlin Press, 2012.

Kehoe, Louise, *In This Dark House, A Memoir*, Schocken Books, Random House, 1995.

Kessel, Lippmann, *Surgeon at Arms*, Pen & Sword, 1958, reprinted 2011

Klugmann, J., *History of the Communist Party of Great Britain Vol. II 1925-26*, London, Lawrence & Wishart, 1969.

Koch, Stephen, *Double Lives: Stalin, Will Munzenberg and the Seduction of Intellectuals*, Harper Collins, 1995.

McEwan, Malcolm, *The Greening of a Red*, Pluto Press, 1991.

MacIntyre, Stuart, *Little Moscows: Communism and Working Class Militancy in Inter-War Britain*, Croom Helms, 1980.

McCrindle, Jean and Rowbotham, Sheila, *Dutiful Daughters: Women Talk About Their Lives*, Pelican books, 1979

Marsh, Kevin and Griffiths Robert, *Granite and honey – the story of Phil Piratin*, Communist MP, Manifesto Press, 2012.

Morgan, K. *Labour Legends and Russian Gold: Bolshevism and the British Left: Part one.* Lawrence & Wishart, 2006.
Ramsay MacDonald, Haus Publishing, 2006.
The Webbs and Soviet Communism: Bolshevism and the British Left: Part Two, Lawrence & Wishart, 2006.
Harry Pollitt. Lives of the Left, Manchester University Press, 1993.
Against fascism and war: ruptures and continuities in British communist politics 1935-1941, Manchester University Press, 1989.

Morgan, K., A Flinn, G Cohen. *Communists and British Society 1920-1991*, Rivers Oram Press, 2007.

David Howell, Dianne Kirby, Kevin Morgan. *John Saville: Commitment and History*, London: Lawrence & Wishart, 2010.

Morgan, K. *Bolshevism, Stalinism and the Comintern 1919-43: Perspectives on Stalinization*. Edited by N. LaPorte and M. Worley, Palgrave, 2008.

Morgan, K., Andrew Flinn, Gidon Cohen, *Agents of the Revolution. New biographical approaches to the history of international communism in the age of Lenin and Stalin.*

Morgan, Kevin, Cohen, Gidon, Flinn, Andrew, *Communists and British Society 1920-1991*, Rivers Oram Press, 2007.

Morgan, K. *Opening the Books: essays in the social and cultural history of the British Communist Party*. Edited by with G. Andrews and N. Fishman. , Pluto Press, 1995.

Morgan, Marguerite, *Part of the Main*, People's Publications, 1990.

Morgan, Dave, *A Short History of Dave Morgan*, self-published, 1992.

Morris, Aubrey, *Unfinished Journey*, The Polemecist and Artery Publications 2006.

Morris, Linda and Radford, Robert, *AIA– the Story of the Artists International Association 1933-1953*, The Museum of Modern Art, Oxford 1983.

Newton, Kenneth, *The Sociology of British Communism*, Allen Lane, The Penguin Press, 1969.

Nicholson, Jock, *A Turbulent Life*, Praxis Press Glasgow 2009.

Olden, Mark, *Murder in Notting Hill*, Zero Books, 1996.

Paynter, Will, *My Generation*, George Allen & Unwin, 1972.

Pearce, Ivor, *Laurie Smith & Alice Bolton.*

Peck, John, *Persistence: The Story of a British Communist*, 2001.

Pentelow, Mike, *Norfolk Red: The Life of Wolf Page, Countryside Communist*, Lawrence & Wishart, 2009.

Piratin, P., *Our Flag Stays Red*, Thames, London, 1948.

Platts-Mills, John, *Muck, Silk and Socialism*, Paper Publishin, 2002.

Podmore, Will, *Reg Birch: engineer, trade unionist, communist*, Bellman Books, 2004.

Pollitt, Harry, *Serving My Time* (autobiography), 1940.

Pollitt, Marjorie, *A Rebel Life*, Red Pen Publications 2007.

Rafeek, Neil C., *Communist Women in Scotland: Red Clydeside from the Russian Revolution to the End of the Soviet Union*, IB Taurus, 2014

Riordan, Jim, *Comrade Jim: The Spy Who Played for Spartak*, Harper Collins, 2009.

Taylor Graham and Dromey Jack, *Grunwick: The Workers' Story*, Lawrence and Wishart., 1978.

Seifert, Roger and Sibley, Tom, *Revolutionary Communist at Work – a political biography of Bert Remelson*; Lawrence and Wishart; 2012.

Simon, Brian, *A Life In Education*, Lawrence and Wishart, 1998.

Smith, James, *British Writers and MI5 Surveillance 1930-1960*, Cambridge University Press, 2013.

Starrett, Bob, *As I See It*, Feir Play, Glasgow, 2013.

Stewart., B, *Breaking the Fetters: the Memoirs of Bob Stewart*, Lawrence & Wishart, 1967.

Stonor Saunders, Frances, *Who Paid the Piper?: The CIA and the Cultural Cold War*, 2000.

Trory, E., *Between the Wars: Memoirs of a Communist Organiser*, Crabtree Press, 1974.

Wainwright, John L. The *Last to Fall (the life and letters of Ivor Hickman – an International Brigader in Spain)*, Hatchet Green Publishing, 2012.

Warren, Nick, *Thirty Years in a Turtleneck Sweater*, Ebury Press 2005.

Watters, Frank, *Being Frank*, Frank Watters, 1992.

Winter, Richard, *Power, Freedom Compassion*, Willow Tree Press, 2011.

Worley Matthew, *Class Against Class: The Communist Party in Britain Between the Wars*, I.B. Tauris, 2002.

Worsley, Peter, *An Academic Skating on Thin Ice*, Berghahn Books, 2008.

Westacott, Frederick, Clark, Joseph William Russell and Clark, Joe, *Shaking the Chains: A Personal and Political History*, 2002.

Williamson, John, *Jailed by McCarthy*, William Maclellan 1955.

Wynn. Bob, *Skilled at all Trades: History of the Farmworkers' Union, 1947-1984*, Frontline 1993

Youngday, Biddy, *Flags in Berlin – an account of life in Berlin 1928-1945*, Mary Brimacombe and Clare Lowy, 2012.

For those who wish to read more biographies of communists,
the best source is Graham Stevenson's online Communist Biographies:
http://www.grahamstevenson.me.uk

FOOTNOTES

1. http://www.grahamstevenson.me.uk

2. Samuel Raphael, Theatres of Memory, Verso, 1994 p. viii

3. London Review of Books 25.10.12

4. Courtois, Stéphane (ed), The Black Book of Communism: Crimes, Terror, Repression (Original title Le Livre noir du communisme) Harvard university Press, 1999

5. Orwell, George, The Road to Wigan Pier, New York: Harcourt Brace & Company, 1961

6. Hinton, James, Coventry Communism: a study of factory politics in the Second World War, History Workshop Journal No. 10, 1990 p.92

7. Hinton, James 'The Communist Party, Production and Britain's Post-war Settlement' Opening the Books p.160

8. Morgan, Kevin, Against Fascism and War, Manchester University Press, 1989

9. Richard Crossman (ed) The God that Failed : Six Studies in Communism (1950) p8.

10. George Orwell, 'England Your England' (1940), collected in The Collected Essays, Journalism and Letters of George Orwell vol 2 (1970) p95.

11. George Orwell, Inside the Whale, Gollancz 1940, collected in The Collected Essays, Journalism and Letters of George Orwell vol 1 (1970) p562

12. Andrew Boyle, The Climate of Treason (1979)

13. Stephen Koch, Double Lives: Stalin, Willi Munzenberg and the Seduction of the Intellectuals (1995) p184

14. This essay is confined to observations about Communist writers ; for other aspects of the Party's cultural life see: Andy Croft, (ed) A Weapon in the Struggle : the Cultural History of the Communist Party in Britain (1998)

15. Andrei Alexandrovich Zhdanov was appointed by Stalin to oversee cultural affairs and who brought in a very narrow and prescriptive view of culture.

16. http://www.theguardian.com/world/2014/apr/29/bill-ash

17. Cope, Dave, Central Books – a Brief History 1939-1999, Central Books, 1999

18. Lessing, Dorothy, Under My Skin Volume One of My Autobiography, to 1949, Harper Collins, 1994

19. Chambers , Colin, The Story of Unity Theatre, Lawrence and Wishart, 1989, p.281

20. ibid

21. Dickson, Andrew, The tin hut revolutionary, Guardian G2 12 June 2014

22. Beckett, Francis, Enemy Within, p.68

23. Morgan, Kevin, Opening the Books, Pluto 1995

24. Guardian Review 31.08.2013

25. Tudor-Hart is the author of many books and scientific articles. His most recent book, The Political Economy of Health Care: A Clinical Perspective explores how the NHS might be reconstituted as a humane service for all (rather than a profitable one for the few) and a civilising influence on society as a whole. The book provides 'a big picture' for students, academics, health professionals and NHS users that Tudor Hart hopes will inspire them to challenge received wisdoms about how the NHS should develop in the 21st century.

26. http://www.independent.co.uk/news/ obituaries/madeleine-sharp- obituary-doctor-and-peace-campaig ner- who-worked-tirelessly-for- humanitarian-causes-in-vietnam-lao s-and-cambodia-9257520.html

27. http://www.telegraph.co.uk/news/obit uaries/10158057/James-Gibb.html

28. AIA - The Story of the Artists international Association by Lynda Morris and Robert Radford 1983

29. Brian Simon Times Higher Education 15 Jan 1996

30. The Guardian, Brian Simon obituary 22 January 2002

31. Norman MacKenzie, Guardian Obituaries, Wednesday 3 July 2013

32. Lenin in conversation with Lunacharsky in February 1922 said: 'you must remember, of all the arts, the most important for us is the cinema.'

33. Bert Hogenkamp, Deadly Parallels: film and the left in Britain 1929-39; Lawrence and Wishart, 1986.

34. Working Class Movement Library (Ewan MacColl - Journeyman: xv- xvi)

35. Bert Hogenkamp, Film, Television and the Left in Britain, p. 1

36. The Guardian obituary by Ian Christie, 4 December 2001

37. Finch, John, Cox, Michael and Giles, Marjorie (eds), Granada Television—The First Generation, Manchester University Press; 2003

38. Peter Frost, She invented the drama documentary, Morning Star 25.01.2014

39. Blacklist -The Inside Story of Political Vetting by Mark Hollingsworth and Richard Norton- Taylor, The Hogarth Press, 1988

40. Report in Daily Worker 24 October 1933

41. Branson Noreen, History of the Communist Party of Great Britain 1941-1951, p.177

42. ibid

43. Dash, J. Good Morning Brothers, Lawrence & Wishart, 1969

44. Gorman, John, Knocking Down Ginger, Caliban Books 1995

45. Seifert, R and Sibley T, Revolutionary Communist at Work, Lawrence & Wishart p. 118

46. ibid p.114

47. Francis Beckett, Enemy Within p.232

48. Platts-Mills, John, Muck, Silk and Socialism: Recollections of a Left-wing Queen's Counsel

49. Watters, Frank, Being Frank, 1992 and The Guardian obituary by Graham Stevenson, Monday 12 August 2002

50. Kevin Morgan, obituary of Edward Frow in the Independent, 23 May 1997

51. Raymond Postgate was educated at Oxford, where he gained a first class honours degree in 1917. In 1918 he married Daisy Lansbury, daughter of the renowned Labour Party leader, George Lansbury and, as a result, was barred from the family home by his Tory father. From 1918 Postgate worked as a journalist on the Daily Herald, then edited by his fa- ther-in-law, Lansbury. He was a founding member of the British Communist Party in 1920, when he left the Herald to join the staff of the Party's first weekly, The Communist. Postgate soon became its editor and was briefly a major pro- pagandist for the Party before leaving it in 1922, disagreeing with the Communist International insisting that British communists follow Moscow line. However he remained a man of the left all his life and also a key player in left-wing journalism. He returned to the Herald, before joining Lansbury on Lansbury's Labour Weekly in 1925–1927. He went on to publish a number of biographies novels and a study on Soviet Russia for the Fabian Society. Always a keen gourmet and wine enthusiast, he is perhaps best remembered today as the founder of the Good Food Guide. He is the father of children's author Oliver Postgate.

52. Wilfred Willett's life was made into a moving drama by the BBC in 1981 called 'Wilfred and Eileen' about a Great War soldier who recovers from terrible injuries to marry his sweetheart. It was directed by David Green. He was horrifi- cally injured during the First World War, and it was assumed he'd die, but he survived thanks largely to his courageous wife who rescued him from almost certain death in the hospital. He became a founder member of the Communist Party and a renowned naturalist. He also led a campaign of justice for farm workers.

53. Haldane is generally credited with a pioneering role in the development of neo-Darwinian thinking. His uncle was Richard, later Lord, Haldane, Secretary of State for War in the run-up to the First World War; his father was also a scientist, philosopher and a staunch Liberal.

54. Claud Cockburn, perhaps the paper's most renowned member of staff, resigned as The Times' Washington corre- spondent to join the Daily Worker in 1935.

55. Is That Damned Paper Still Coming Out? Mark Howe (ed)

56. The Economic League was an organisation dedicated to opposing what they saw as subversion and action against 'free enterprise'. The organisation maintained a list of alleged leftwing troublemakers, which corporate members of the League used to vet job applicants, often denying jobs on that basis. In

the late 1980s press investigations revealed the poor quality of the League's data, and following a 1990 parliamentary inquiry and further press reporting, the League closed down in 1993. However, key League personnel continued similar vetting activities through other organisations. The organisation was founded in December 1919 to January 1920 by a group of industrialists and William Hall MP. Hall had been Director of the Naval Intelligence Division of the Admiralty from 1914 to 1919. The organisation's chief function was to promote the point of view of industrialists and businessmen, and to keep track of communists and other leftwing organisations and individuals.

57. Gracie Fields was probably the best loved British performer of the era – star of music hall and cinema

58. The Story of the Daily Worker by William Rust, People's Press Printing Society, 2010 (new edition)

59. http://www.theguardian.com/media/2005/mar/03/guardianobituaries.pressandpublishing

60. Callaghan, John, Opening the Books – Essays on the Social and Cultural History of the British Communist Party, Pluto Press, 1995

61. Named after the great US singer, actor and communist, Paul Robeson

62. Reginald Bridgeman was born in London; he was the oldest son of a Brigadier, who was the son of the 3rd Earl of Bradford. He had a distinguished career in the Civil Service, rising to become chargé d'affaires in Vienna, and, in 1920, was appointed counsellor of embassy in Tehran. After a visit to India he left the service, horrified by what he saw of British imperialism there and began a close association with the Communist Party.

While Bridgeman was never actually a card-carrying member of the Communist Party, he was certainly a 'fellow traveller', and was especially close to Harry Pollitt, the Party's general secretary. In practice, and to all intents and purposes, even while a member of the Labour Party, Bridgeman acted like a Communist.

He himself once stated: 'Communist influence is gaining ground throughout the world. Social Democracy represented by the ILP, LP, TUC, in close cooperation with Federation of British Industries, is a waning force, while the masses everywhere are revolting against capitalism.'

From 1925, Bridgeman worked as secretary in the Chinese Information Bureau. He was head of the British delegation sent by the House of Commons to the League against Imperialism (LAI) in Brussels. He contested Uxbridge for Labour in the 1929 election, but was expelled from the party only a short time after, because of his membership in the LAI, an organisation proscribed by the Labour Party. After the League's dissolution, he was readmitted to Labour in 1938 and was adopted as Labour's prospective candidate for Hendon.

Bridgeman was expelled again in 1941 and after the Second World War he joined the Britain-China Friendship Association and was a member of the British-Soviet Friendship Society (both proscribed organisations as far as the Labour Party was concerned). He also sat on the National Council for Civil Liberties. In 1962, he was

nominated vice-chairman of the
Co-ordinating Committee for
Nuclear Disarmament. Bridgeman
died in 1968.

63. The League Against Imperialism by
Jean Jones, Socialist History Society
pamphlet, 1996

64. George Padmore was born
Malcolm Nurse in Trinidad in
1903, was a leading Pan Africanist,
journalist, and author who left
Trinidad in 1924 to study in the US
and from there moved to the Soviet
Union, Germany and France,
before settling in London and,
toward the end of his life in Ghana.
In 1924, he travelled to the USA to
take up medical studies.

During his college years he
became involved with the Workers
(Communist) Party and when
engaged in party business adopted
the name George Padmore. He
officially joined the Communist
Party in 1927 and was active in its
involved in recruiting black
Americans.

He was an energetic worker and
prolific writer, was noted by the US
Party's trade union leader William Z
Foster as a rising star and was taken
to Moscow to deliver a report on
the formation of the Trade Union
Unity League to the Communist
International in 1929. Padmore was
asked to stay on in Moscow to head
the Negro Bureau of the Red
International of Labour Unions
(Profintern). He was even elected to
the Moscow City Soviet.

As head of the Profintern's Negro
Bureau, Padmore helped to produce
leaflets and pamphlets and
contributed articles to Moscow's
English-language newspaper, the
Moscow Daily News. He was also
used periodically as a courier of
funds from Moscow to various
foreign Communist Parties.

In July 1930, Padmore was
instrumental in organizing an
International Congress of Negro
Workers in London which had to be
transferred to Hamburg at the last
minute because the Labour
government banned it. He became
editor of the monthly publication
The Negro Worker on behalf of the
International TradeFof Negro
Workers (ITUCNW).

In 1931, Padmore moved to
Hamburg and accelerated his
writing output, continuing to
produce the ITUCNW magazine
and writing more than 20
pamphlets in a single year. His
German sojourn came to an abrupt
end by the middle of 1933, however,
when the offices of the Negro
Worker were ransacked by right-
wing gangs following the Nazi
seizure of power. Padmore was
deported to England by the
German government in 1933.

One consequence of the time
Padmore spent in the Soviet Union
was an end of his time as a resident
of the United States. As a non-
citizen and a communist, Padmore
was effectively barred from re-entry
to America once he had departed.

65. Callaghan, John, Opening the
Books – essays on the social and
cultural history of the British
Communist Party, Pluto 1995, p.16

66. ibid

67. Rafeek, Neil, Communist Women in
Scotland. p.47

68. Alexander, Bill, British Volunteers
for Liberty, 1983 and Memorials of
the Spanish Civil War, 1996.

69. Bill Alexander, obituary in the
Guardian 14 July 2000

70. The Committee of 100 was set up
in 1960 by the philosopher
Bertrand Russell and other leading

figures to undertake direct action in order to pressure government to undertake nuclear disarmament.

71. See above – short biography of Reginald Bridgeman

72. ibid p143

73. Olden, Mark, Murder in Notting Hill , Zero Books, 1996.

74. ibid

75. Peter Blackman poems, Smokestack Books, 2013

76. See short biography in Camden New Journal The Review section 9 October 2008

77. Keable, Ken (ed) London Recruits: The Secret War Against Apartheid, Merlin Press, 2012

78. See Graham Stevenson Communist Biographies. Nan Berger had joined the Communist Party in 1939. In 1940, she began working at the Bank of England and promptly set up a staff committee for temporary clerks, but found her-self summarily dismissed. Her subsequent career as a civil servant in the statistical office of the Ministry of Fuel and Power, eased by the changed circumstances of the later wartime period, was considerably more successful.

Though a low graded worker in the Ministry, she developed a statistically valid and rational plan for assuring the distribution of fuel in a fair way. When aged only 33, she was awarded an OBE in the New Year Honours' list of 1948, quite an achievement, given the emerging Cold War. Afterwards she became a freelance journalist.

79. Kasrils, R, Armed and Dangerous-my undercover struggle against apartheid, Heinemann 1993.

80. This notorious and divisive policy led to a labelling of Social

Democrats and those to the right of the Communist Party as part and parcel of the 'class enemy' – the ruling class. Everyone not considered to be within the 'revolutionary vanguard' of the working class became an actual or potential enemy of that class and thus an ally of the ruling class; on the political front, social democrats were denounced as 'social fascists' and mainstream artists and intellectuals denounced as lackeys of the bourgeoisie. This 'Class against class' policy was officially overturned in 1935 at the Comintern's seventh congress. This notorious and divisive policy led to a labelling of Social Democrats and those to the right of the Communist Party as part and parcel of the 'class enemy' – the ruling class.

81. Middleclass Recruits to Communism in the 1930s, lecture and seminar by Professor Nicholas Deakin March 2013

82. Aubrey Morris left school at 14 in 1933 without any formal qualifications and took up taxi driving. He and his young family were keen to see something of the world, but in those pre-war days foreign travel was only for the very rich. Despite having very little money, he decided to take the risk of motoring through France and Italy on a shoestring, by taking the family in his black London cab. No one had ever taken a black cab abroad at the time and his friends thought he was mad. However his enjoyable and successful experience prompted him to begin offering tours to his fellow cab drivers. They were so popular that he then set up his own small travel company.

Then after the war, with many former RAF pilots now unemployed and old troop-carrying planes available at relatively cheap prices, the possibility of air travel and foreign holidays for ordinary working people became feasible for the first time. Aubrey took advantage of this situation and launched the first air travel package business, first taking football fans to European away matches and then branching out into the holiday business, thus becoming, in the 1950s, one of the pioneers of package holiday travel as we have come to know it.

His company, Riviera Holidays was so successful that it was eventually bought out by Thomsons Travel, making Aubrey a millionaire. Although he had left the Communist Party in 1956 and was now very rich, he remained a sympathiser and supporter of many progressive causes and proudly called himself a socialist until his death. He was a founder and supporter of the radical monthly Red Pepper. In his autobiography, Unfinished Journey, he relates the whole magical story in detail.

83. Costello, John and Tsarev, Oleg, Deadly Illusions, Crown, 1993

84. Branson, Noreen, History of the Communist Party of Great Britain 1927-1941 (1985) p.284

85. ibid p. 297

86. ibid p.304

87. ibid . p 309

88. ibid p.316

89. Branson, Noreen, History of the Communist Party in Great Britain from 1941- 1951, p.4

90. ibid p9

91. ibid p5

92. ibid

93. Andrews, G. Endgames and New Times – the final years of British Communism 1964-1991 p.34

94. Beckett, Francis, Digby Jacks obituary, The Guardian, Tuesday 29 November 2011

95. Jacks, Digby, Student Politics and Higher Education, Lawrence Wishart, 1975

96. Rafeek, Neil, Communist Women in Scotland: Red Clydeside from the Russian Revolution to the End of the Soviet Union, IB Taurus, 2014. p.27

97. The Socialist Sunday School 'ten commandments' which were printed in some of the editions of the hymn book.
1. Love your schoolfellows, who will be your fellow workmen in life.
2. Love learning, which is the food of the mind; be as grateful to your teacher as to your parents.
3. Make every day holy by good and useful deeds and kindly actions.
4. Honour good men, be courteous to all men, bow down to none.
5. Do not hate or speak evil of anyone. Do not be revengeful but stand up for your right and resist oppression.
6. Do not be cowardly. Be a friend to the weak and love justice.
7. Remember that all good things of the earth are produced by labour. Whoever enjoys them without working for them is stealing the bread of the workers.
8. Observe and think in order to discover the truth. Do not believe what is contrary to reason and never deceive yourself or others.
9. Do not think that he who loves his own country must hate and despise other nations, or wish for war, which is a remnant of barbarism.
10. Look forward to the day when all men and women will be free

citizens of one fatherland and live together as brothers and sisters in peace and righteousness.

98. See Alan Sillitoe's novel Key to the Door for a vivid description of a national service soldier's take on this episode

99. See Guardian obituary Other Lives 7 September 2013. While she was still in her teens, her father sent her, unaccompanied, on an educational trip to Germany. It was an uncomfortable experience witnessing the early days of Hitler's regime, and she cut the visit short.
Her father also encouraged her to learn about motor mechanics – she was still driving at the age of 90. In the mid-1930s, Margery moved to Oxford and joined the Communist party. Margery and her husband joined in the demonstration against Oswald Mosley and his followers at the Battle of Cable Street in 1936. During the Second World War, she joined the FANYs (the First Aid Nursing Yeomanry) as an ambulance driver in Oxford and Salisbury. She became a counsellor for Compassionate Friends – the support group for bereaved parents, after losing her own son, aged 32. Margery had boundless energy and curiosity. She loved music, especially jazz, and literature.

100. Daffern, Eileen, Essays on a Life: Politics, Peace and the Personal, 2007

101. Jenny Jones, The Guardian, Sunday 5 February 2012

102. ibid

103. Jeremy Paxman, The Guardian, Thursday 5 April 2007

104. Hudson, Kate, obituary for Eileen Daffern, Morning Star , 23 January 2012

105. http://www.theguardian.com/uk-news/2014/apr/09/jean-thornton-obituary

106. Rebecca West, Young Rebecca: Writings, 1911-1917, Indiana University Press,1989

107. Elizabeth Wilson Mirror Writing, an autobiography, Virago, 1982

108. A more detailed history of the NAW can be found at http://www.sisters.org.uk.

109. http://zeldacurtis-alife.blogspot.co.uk

110. Jo Stanley, article on SWOMP in Herstoria, 2012

111. See chapter on communists in the film industry.

112. Smith, James, British Writers and MI5 Surveillance, 1930-1960

113. J.B.S. Haldane was an eminent biochemist and geneticist. He left Party in 1956 in the wake of the Hungarian uprising.

114. Worsley, Peter, An Academic Skating on Thin Ice

115. Hodgkinson, George, Sent to Coventry, Maxwell, 1970

116. Andrews, G. Endgames and New Times – the final years of British Communism 1964-1991

117. ibid

118. ibid

119. ibid p.151

120. ibid

121. 'IM' was the term used by the GDR's state security apparatus for its unofficial collaborators or 'Mitarbeiter'.

122. Lubbers, Eveline, Secret Manoeuvres in the Dark: Corporate and Police Spying on Activists, Pluto, 2012. Lewis, Paul,

Undercover: The True Story of Britain's Secret Police by Paul Lewis, Rob Evans, 2013

123. Klugmann, James, History of the Communist Party of Great Britain Vol. 2 The General Strike 1925-1926, Lawrence Wishart, 1969

124. Branson vol.I, p 69

125. Francis Beckett, Enemy Within, p.79

126. Green, John, Ken Sprague People's Artist, Hawthorn Press

127. Hennessey, Peter , The Secret State, Penguin 2003

128. Norton-Taylor, Richard, the Guardian September 5th 2005

129. Foreign Office paper FO 371/77385 1949 National Archives

130. Campbell, Duncan and Connor, Steve. On the Record: Surveillance, Computers, and Privacy: the Inside Story

131. The Guardian, 8 February 1995

132. Morning Star 3 January1995

133. Robert Taylor, New Statesman 19 November 2001

134. Bill Connor of Heywood, Lancashire, the Guardian 1 February 1997

135. Annie Machon, Spies, Lies and Whistleblowers, The Book Guild (2005)

136. Wright, Peter, Spycatcher, Bantam Doubleday Dell Publishing Group, 1988

137. The True Spies series was first shown on BBC Two beginning Sunday 27 October 2002

138. Robin Ramsay, 'The Clandestine Caucus' (self-published pamphlet 1996) The Guardian, 27 September 2005

139. An Academic Skating on Thin Ice; Berghahn Books, 2008

140. Review of British Writers and MI5 Surveillance, 1930-60, James Smith, Cambridge University Press, 2013, by John Sutherland in New Statesman, 8-14 March 2013

141. ibid

142. Brogan, Hugh, The Life of Arthur Ransome, Hamish Hamilton, 1984. Arthur Ransome, the author of the beloved children's book, Swallows and Amazons, was at this time the correspondent for the Daily News in Russia during the Bolshevik Revolution. He made this comment in a 1918 letter to his mother, in reference to the revolution.

143. Harry Pollitt in the Daily Worker 16 January 1935

144. Francis Beckett, Beckett, Francis, Enemy Within,

145. Simon Hoggart's Sketch 'It's all a communist plot, The Guardian 10 October 2013.

INDEX

Ackland, Valentine 39
Adamov, Arthur 56
Airlie, Jimmy 136, 142
Akhmatova, Anna 45
Aldridge, James 44
Alergant, Joyce 213
Alexander, Bill 166, 170, 199, 208, 321
Ali, Tariq 221
Allende, Salvador 39
Allen, Bob 179
Allen, Vic 234
Allison, George 162
Almond, Brian 42
Amaral, Lucien 108
Ambler, Eric 46
Amiel, Barry 74
Amis, Kingsley 39
Amis, Martin 14
Anderson, Lindsay 102, 105, 113
Anderson, Sir John 298
Anderson, Tom 225
Andrews, Geoff 9, 279, 282, 283, 284, 286, 321, 324, 333, 334
Anstey, Edgar 94
Aragon, Louis 40, 45
Archer, Jeffrey 46
Arden, John 60
Arkwright, Elizabeth 247
Arkwright, Joseph (Sir) 247
Arlot, John 234
Arundel, Honor (Morfydd) 52, 53, 54, 105

Arup, Ove 72
Ash, Bill 48
Ashcroft, Peggy 295
Ashleigh, Charles 42
Asquith, Herbert Henry 75
Askey, Arthur 55
Atkinson, Conrad 220
Atilla the Stockbroker 50
Attlee, Clement 24, 52, 126, 150, 274, 233, 274
Ayrton, Michael 24
Austen, Jane 42
Auden, W.H. 56, 291
Audley, Maxine 55
Peter Avis 141

Baines, Harry 84
Bagot, Millicent 292
Baker White, John 298
Baldwin, Stanley 268
Ball, Fred 42
Ball, John 263
Bamber, Mary 246
Baron, Alexander 42
Barke, James 39
Barker, George 44
Barker, Clive 60
Barker, Dennis 106
Barr, Andy 185
Barr, Sammy 136
Barriedale, Keith (professor) 151
Bart, Lionel 14, 55, 58

Barzey, Jimmy 174
Barzman, Ben and Norma 116
Bass, Alfie 14, 55, 105, 190
Bates, Alan 113
Bates, Ralph 39, 42, 169
Bates, Winifried 169
Beauchamp, Kay 146, 148, 175
Beckett, Francis 9, 63, 135, 223, 313
Beckett, John (MP) 164
Beeching, Jack 39
Behan, Brendan 39, 183
Belafonte, Harry 27
Bellamy, Edward 50
Benge, Alfreda 222
Benn, Caroline 88
Benn, Tony 49, 175, 318
Bennett, Erna 252
Berger, John 24, 78, 82, 84
Berger, Nan 176
Berger, Harry 198
Bergman, Ingrid 44
Bergman, Ingmar 102
Bernal, J.D. 24, 43, 64, 65, 205
Bernal, Martin 66
Bernstein, Sidney (Lord) 58, 101, 106, 107
Bernstein, Alec 108
Berry, John (Jack) 44
Best, Michael 247
Bevan, Aneurin 52, 70, 72, 213, 230, 272, 273
Bevin, Ernest 172, 206
Billany, Dan 42
Binder, Pearl 80
Binnington, David 87
Birch, Chris 321
Birch, Reg 49, 133, 141, 325
Black, Misha 80
Blackman, Peter 49, 165, 174, 321
Blackwell, Sam 212
Blackwell, Trevor 293
Blair, Tony 14, 283, 285, 286, 288
Blair, Lionel 188
Blair-Reisz, Betsy 115, 116
Blackett, Lord 24
Blunt, Anthony 38
Blumenfeld, Simon 42
Bond, Edward 60
Bond, James 21
Bond, Ralph 94, 95, 98, 99, 105, 141, 270

Bonnar, Robert 42
Bose, Subhas Chandra 160, 166
Boston, Sarah 16
Bogarde, Dirk 43, 113
Boswell, James 53, 80, 81, 322
Boughton, Rutland 75
Boult, Sir Adrian 24
Bowles, Sally 43
Behan, Brendan 183
Bolt, Robert 39
Borders, Elsy 250
Bowen, Elizabeth 39
Bowden, John 74
Bower, Hetty 233
Bowman, Aubrey 75
Bowman, Dave 141
Bradsworth, Colin (Dr.) 169
Bragg, Melvyn 47
Bradley, Ben 162, 163, 171
Brain, Gus 141
Bramley, Ted 123, 189, 212, 213, 251
Brandt, Willi 281
Branson, Clive 171, 208
Branson, Noreen 9, 202, 319
Bratherton, J. (Alderman) 96
Brecht, Bertolt 45, 55, 57, 58, 60, 113, 187
Brennan, Irene 280
Brennan Ward, Frank 146
Brett, Ken 141
Brezhnev, Leonid 278
Bridgeman, Reginald 161, 163, 164, 165, 172
Bridges, George 179
Briffault, Robert 39
Brinson, Peter 102
Britten, Benjamin 14, 24, 43, 56, 175, 295
Britton, Lionel 58
Briggs, Asa 24
Brockway, Fenner 164, 175, 230, 234
Brook, Peter 57
Brooks, Ern 83
Browne, Felicia 169
Brown, Isabel 123
Brown, W.J. (MP) 174
Brown, Gordon (Prime Minister) 283
Buckle, Desmond J. 161, 172
Buckton, Ray 142, 299
Buñuel, Luis 104

Bunyan, John 263
Burgess, Anthony 49
Burgess, Guy 38, 88
Burra, Edward 83
Burns, Elinor 233
Burns, Emile 161
Burt, Cyril 91
Burton, Humphrey 108
Bush, Alan 14, 46, 56, 75, 102, 202

Calder-Marshall, Arthur 24, 39
Callaghan, John 9, 165, 321
Callow, William 281
Cameron, Ken 140
Cameron, David (Prime Minister) 177, 318
Campbell, Duncan 298
Campbell, Ian 76, 77
Campbell, John Ross 125, 146, 265, 294, 295
Campbell, Beatrix 256, 283
Cannon, Les 312
Carr, Rose 128
Carritt, Michael 171
Carritt, Bill 213
Carleton Greene, Hugh 298
Carter, Pete 283
Carter, Trevor 172
Carpenter, Maurice 39
Carver, Bill 210
Casson, Sir Hugh 24
Casson, Lewis 56
Cassou, Jean 40
Castle, Barbara (MP) 133, 175
Caudwell, Christopher 41, 46
Cavalcanti, Alberto 94, 105, 108
Cazalet-Keir, Thelma (MP) 252
Chambers, Colin 57, 60, 61, 321
Chamberlain, Neville (prime minister) 60, 99, 150, 194, 195, 196, 198, 201
Chandler, George 42
Chaplin, Charlie 27
Chapman, Harry 212
Chapple, Frank 312
Childe, Gordon 66
Christie, Ian 112
Christie, Julie 113
Churchill, Winston 46, 170, 196, 202, 203, 204, 207, 229
Citrine, Walter 127, 128, 272, 297

Clark, Kenneth (MP) 104
Clarke, Kate 321
Clegg, Arthur 172
Cliff, Tony 219
Coates, Ken 133
Cochrane, Kelso 173
Cockburn, Claud 147, 148
Cohen, Max 42
Cohen, Nat 170
Cohen, Rose 265
Coldstream, William 80
Coleclough, Barbara 236, 237
Coleman, Fitzroy 173
Conn, Harry 249
Connolly, James 183
Connolly, Nora 115
Cornforth, Maurice 52, 279
Cook, A.J. 271
Cook, Dave 43, 220, 283
Cook, Betty 257
Cook, Robin (MP) 292
Cooley, Mike 134
Cooper, Charles 101, 102, 110
Cope, Dave 10, 322
Copeman, Fred 291
Corbett, Anne 88
Corbyn, Jeremy 155
Cordwell, Reg 97
Cornford, John 38, 39, 216
Costello, Mick 10, 133, 217
Cotter, Judith 221
Cole, G.D.H. 271
Cole, Sidney 94, 103, 104, 113, 194
Coleclough, Barbara 236, 236, 237
Coleman, Fitzroy 174
Cornforth, Maurice 53, 279
Coulthard, Dorothy 130
Courtois, Stéphane 14, 322
Cox, John 234, 301, 322, 328, 339,
Craig, David 39
Crane, George 206
Crawfurd, Helen 164, 247
Cripps, Stafford 52, 58, 150, 272
Croft, Andy 3, 4, 5, 9, 47, 49, 51, 75, 49, 322, 327
Crowe, Bob 142
Crowther, J.G. 231
Crosland, Anthony 51
Crossley, James 158
Cromwell, Oliver 65, 200, 208

Cunard, Nancy 38, 39, 43
Currie, Edwina 46
Curtis, Zelda 256, 257

Dadoo, Yusuf 180
Daffern, Eileen 234, 236, 240, 236, 237, 239, 238, 322
D'Arcy, Margaretta 60
Dash, Jack 129, 176, 322
Darke, Marian 142, 313
Darling, Julia 39
Day-Lewis, Cecil 39, 46
Davison, Madge 184, 185
Davis, Mary 66, 67, 257, 258, 320
Davison, Emily 245
De la Haye, Ina 58
Deakin, Nicholas 9, 13, 14
Deakin, Arthur 129
De Sica, Vittorio 116
De Francia, Peter 82
Defoe, Daniel 42
Devlin, Bernadette 184
Dickens, Charles 42, 46, 59
Dickinson, Thorold 105
Dignam, Mark 55, 106
Dillon, Eillis 63
Dimitrov, Georgi 41
Disraeli, Benjamin 46
Dixon, Bob 49
Dmytryk, Edward 112
Dobb, Maurice 64
Dobney, Megan 260
Doherty, Len 42
Doy, Gen 222
Doyle, Mikki 254
Donovan, Ella 249
Dovzhenko, Alexander 97
Driberg. Tom (MP) 292
Dunn, Jack 133
Durkin, Tom 213
Durkin Pat 212

Ede, Jams, Chuter 233
Eden (McCulloch), Jessie 16, 248, 250
Edgar, David 285
Edwardes, Michael (Sir) 302
Einstein, Albert 27, 239
Eisenstein, Sergei 95, 97, 99, 101, 102
Elias, Sid 122
Ellenberg, David 75

Elliott, David 79
Eliot, T.S. 289
Elton, Arthur 94
Elvin, George 94
Éluard, Paul 40
Engels, Friedrich 18, 27, 50, 65, 255, 264, 286, 290, 317
Epstein, Jacob 78
Etheridge, Dick 133
Eyles, Arthur 166
Evans, Bill 74

Fairhall, John 223
Fanon, Franz 159
Farsky, Tony 91
Faulkner, Hugh 67
Feaver, William 83, 322
Fell, Alison 43
Felton, Monica (MP) 253
Field, Ann 42, 59
Fields, Gracie 150, 330
Fielding, Henry 22, 33
Fisher, Hannah 114
Fitton, James 80
Fleming, Ian 74
Foot, Michael 15, 155, 272
Foot, Paul 219
Ford, Anna 217
Forman, Stanley 100, 102, 110
Foster, John 10, 322, 340
Forster, E.M. 39, 202, 234
Forsyth, Frederick 301
Fox, Ralph 39, 46
Francis, Harry 141
Franco, Franciso (General) 36, 168, 169, 319
Freeson, Reg (MP) 190
French, Sid 286
Frisch, Max 55
Frost, David 60
Frost, Peter 10, 107, 328
Frow, Eddie 43, 140, 142, 143, 322, 323, 325, 329
Frow, Ruth 322
Fucik, Julius 41

Gaddafi, Colonel 301
Gallacher, Willie 41, 100, 192, 207, 208, 214, 266, 269
Gambon, Michael 55

Garaudy, Roger 45
Gardner, Llew 275
Gaster, Jack 74, 211
Gavin, Barrie 108, 109
Gehlen, Reinhard 32
George, Ann 272
German, Lindsay 286
Ghandi, Mahatma 68
Gibb, James (Jimmy) 55, 75
Giles, G.C.T. 86, 320
Gilbert, Tony 173
Gill, Eric 80, 81
Gill, Tess 74
Gill, Ken 142, 276, 298, 300
Ginsberg, Jean 71
Gluckman, Max 305
Goddard, Robert 36
Goldberg, 'Fannie' 210
Goldfinger, Ernő 73, 74
Gollan, John 169, 218, 295
Gollancz, Victor 51, 296, 327
Goldman, Willy 42
Goodwin, Dennis 212
Gorley, Robert 57
Gordon, Alex 139
Gordon, Betty 290
Gorman, John 10, 50, 58, 59, 132, 199, 315, 316, 322
Gormley, Joe 299, 302
Gould, Julius 222
Gowing, Lawrence 55
Gralton, Jimmy 182, 183, 323
Gralton, Packie 183
Gramsci, Antonio 41
Grassic Gibbon, Lewis 39
Gray, Mary 224
Gray, Olga 299, 292
Greaves, Desmond 172
Green, Nan 169
Greene, Graham 38, 39, 57, 311
Greenwood, Walter 43, 142
Grierson, John 56, 94, 99
Grieve, Murray (Hugh McDiarmid) 295
Groves, Sally 10, 260, 262
Guedes, Eduardo 112
Guy, George 141

Haldane, J.B.S. 64, 147, 149, 150, 198, 274
Haldane, Richard (Viscount) 74

Hall, Stuart 285
Halpin, Kevin 133, 323
Halpin, Anita 141, 259
Hannington, Wal 41, 118, 119, 120, 121, 206, 271
Hamilton, Patrick 38, 39, 44
Harman, Harriet 301
Harper, Frederick 42
Hart, Finlay 206
Hart, Richard 176
Hastings, Jack (Earl of Huntingdon) 81, 82
Haylett, John 10
Hayward, Ron 302
Haxell, Frank 141
Healey, Dennis 14, 188
Heath, Edward (PM) 134, 135, 157
Heathfield, Betty 257
Heathfield, Peter 257
Heinemann, Margot 39
Hellman, Lillian 115
Henderson, Hamish 39, 44
Henderson, Stan 213
Hendy, John 74, 75
Hepworth, Barbara (Dame) 24, 78, 81
Herman, Josef 82
Heslop, Harry 42
Hewitt, Patricia 301
Hicks, E.J. 274
Hikmet, Nazim 40
Hill, Christopher 25, 37
Hitchcock, Alfred 60
Hitler, Adolf 105, 118, 121, 122, 126, 127, 171, 205
Hill, Christopher 46, 64, 65
Hilton, Rodney 64
Hinton, James 22, 24
Hoare, Robert Rawdon 298
Ho-Chi-Minh 69
Hobday, Charles 39
Hobsbawm, Eric 29, 65, 285
Hodgson, Jack 180
Hodgkinson, George 279, 321
Hogarth, Paul 81, 323
Hope, Vida 56, 103
Horniman, Guy 162
Hoskins, Bob 55
Honecker, Eric 100
Holland, James 80
Holloway, Stanley 113

Holmes, Walter 146, 148
Holt, William 42
Horner, Arthur 120, 121, 124, 127, 141, 206, 322
Horner, John 278
Hosey, Sean 179, 180
Hoover, J. Edgar 115
Hopkins, Harold 17, 155
Hopkins, Kelvin 155
Howells, Kim (MP) 221
Howerd, Frankie 60
Hudson, Kate 234, 236, 239
Hughes, Ken 55
Huston, John 77
Hunt, Judith 283
Hunt, Tristram 65
Hunt, Alan 220
Hunter, Ian 112
Huntley, Jessica and Eric 174
Hurd, Douglas 47
Hurt, John 110
Hutchinson, Lester 162
Hutt, Allen 53
Huxley, Aldous 38
Huxley, Sir Julian 24, 95
Hyde, Douglas 62

Isherwood, Christopher 43
Isserlis, John 52

Jacks, Digby 223, 323, 221
Jackson, Tommy 41, 45, 46
Jacques, Hattie 56
Jacques, Martin 220, 283, 284, 285
Jagan, Cheddi 174, 176
Jagger, Mick 42
James, C.L.R. 162
Jeffrey, Lionel 174
Jenkins, Clive 223
Jennings, Humphrey 94
John, Augustus 78, 81, 151
John, Gus 174
Johnson, Hewlett (Dean of Canterbury) 152, 279
Johnson, Wallace 159
Joliot-Curie, Frédéric and Iréne 27, 231
Jordan, Colin 173, 190
Jordan, Pallo 180
Jones, Claudia 40, 173, 174
Jones, G. J. 203

Jones, Lewis 42, 121
Jones, Bill 127
Jones, Jack 131, 282, 323
Jones, Jenny 238, 334
Joseph, Helen 176

Kalla, Georgia 109
Kane, Jock 127
Kane, Mick 122, 123
Karlin, Marc 110
Kapp, Yvonne 39
Kasrils, Ronnie 178, 179, 180, 181, 323
Kay, Jackie 16, 39, 323
Kay, John 16
Katz Otto 37
Kehoe, Louise 73, 323
Keable, Ken 9, 177, 179, 323
Kelly, Gene 114
Kempson, Rachel 56
Kenyatta, Jomo 164
Kennard, Peter 222
Kent, Bruce 238, 293, 301
Kerrigan, Peter 128
Kerrigan, Rose 225
Kessell, Lippman 67
Kettle, Arnold 46, 279
Keynes, J.M. 95, 150
Kinnock, Neil 218, 313
Kinsey, Tom 82
Kirby, Edward 210
Klingender, Francis 80, 84
Klugman, James 9, 208, 279, 280, 283, 309, 323, 335
Knight, Laura 81
Koestler, Arthur 14, 17, 62, 306, 307, 312
Koch, Stephen 37, 38, 323
Kollontai, Alexandra 246
Kossoff, David 55
Kristol, Irving 62
Krushchev, Nikita 278

LaCour-Scott, Joan 113
Laine, Cleo 174
La Rose, John 174
Larkin, Jim 180, 246
Lansbury, George 155, 164
Lansbury, Violet 154
Lambert, Dave 42
Lamche, Gustav and Ann 110

Landis, Harry 55, 142
Lardner, Ring 112, 113
Lassally, Walter 55, 101
Laybourn, Keith 38
Lawrence, D.H. 44
Lawrence, Martin 41
Lazarus, Abe 121
Lean, David 112
Le Corbusier 71
Le Carré, John 38
Leadbetter, Charles 283, 285
Leger, Fernand 78
Lehmann, Rosamund 38
Lehmann, Beatrix 56, 152, 251
Lees, Robert 112
Leeson, Robert (Bob) 48
Leffley, Garry 232
Legg, Stuart 94
Lenin, Vladimir 73, 93, 142, 143, 145, 239, 247, 265
Lessing, Doris 38, 39, 53, 234
Lestor, Joan (MP) 190
Levy, Hyman 64, 65
Lewenstein, Oscar 58, 107
Lewis, Lou 133
Lewis, John 205
Lewis, Margery 236
Levitas, Max 187, 208
Lindey, Christine 9
Lindsay, Jack 39, 43
Lipton, Julius 42
Litherland, Jackie 39
Littlewood, Joan 55, 59, 60, 183, 306
Livingstone, Ken 148, 226
Llewellyn, Emrys 122
Lloyd, A.L. 46, 76, 77
Lloyd, John 211
Lloyd, Philippa 10, 224
Loach, Ken 105, 182
London, Jack 50
Loren, Sophia 114
Losey, Joseph 111, 114
Loveless, George 153
Low, David 202
Lukács, György 45
Lubetkin, Berthold 71, 72, 73, 74
Ludmer, Maurice 190
Lunacharsky, Anatoly 36
Lund, Beryl 57
Lurcat, Jean 78

Lutyens, Elizabeth 43

Mbeki, Thabo 178
Macaulay, Rose 202
McArthur, Douglas (General) 32
McArthur,, Archie 223
McCarthy, Joseph (Senator) 275, 311, 317
MacClean, Donald 191
McClellan, Lawrence 114
MacColl, Ewan 46, 53, 77, 97, 306
McCrindle, Alex 52, 53, 105
McCrindle, Jean 256, 324
McClusky, Len 288
MacDiarmid, Hugh 44, 49, 295
MacDonald, Ramsay (PM) 291, 324
MacEwan, Malcolm 319, 323
McGahey, Mick 133, 300
McGrath, John 60
McGraver (Canon) 183
McKay, Claude 175
Mackenzie, Norman 90
MacLean, John 225
McLeod, Lewis 101
Mcmanus, Arthur 265
MacMillan, Harold (PM) 86
McMillan, Margaret 224
McMillan, Nan 89, 90, 251
McMichael, Joan 67, 68, 213
MacNeice, Louis 38
MacKenzie, Norman 90
McShane, Harry 119
Major, John (PM) 104
Malleson, Miles 58, 234
Mandela, Nelson 85, 177, 178, 179
Mandelson, Peter 14
Manifold, John 52
Manley, Norman 173
Mann, Charlie 98
Mann, Tom 119
Mannin, Ethel 36
Manning, Olivia 39, 43
Mantel, Hilary 14
Marley (Lord) 185
Marsland, Terry 259
Martyn, Carolyn 225
Marrowitz, Charles 60
Marx, Karl 18, 19, 25, 28, 50, 239, 264, 278, 290, 317
Mason, John 197

Mason, Margery 61
Masters, Sam 168
Massiter, Cathy 293, 301
Matthews, Geoffrey 39
Maugham, Somerset 44, 48
Maxton, James (MP) 162, 267
Meacher, Michael 155
Medley, Robert 78
Mellows, Liam 182
Melzer, Vaughan 233
Menon, Krishna 160, 166
Menuhin, Yehudi 24
Menzies, Robert (PM) 275, 304
Mickiewicz, Adam 36
Mikado, Ian 230
Miles, Bernard 106
Miller, Arthur 27, 57
Miller, Jean 258
Miller, Karl 14
Miliband, Ed (MP) 318
Milligan, Spike 11, 155
Mitchell, Warren 55
Mitten, Flo 251
Moffat, Abe 124, 127, 206
Moffatt, Alex 278
Montagu, Ivor 94, 99, 100, 103, 106
Montefiore, Dora 246
Montand, Yves 114
Moore, Frances 39
Moore, Henry 78, 81. 234
Moore, Roger 106
Moore, Sammy 133
Monckton, Sir Walter (QC) 213
Morgan, Dave 324
Morgan, Geri 79, 82
Morgan, Marguerite 90
Morgan, Kevin 9, 29, 60, 65, 143, 271, 321, 327, 328
Morley, Iris 39
Morris, Aubrey 189, 324, 332
Morris, Lynda 222, 328
Morris, Max 87, 142, 275
Morris, William 18, 81
Morrison, Herbert 100, 151, 172, 195, 197, 201, 205, 270, 276
Mortimer, Jim 276
Morton, Leslie 46, 64, 65, 76
Morton, Cyril 133
Mosley, Oswald 129, 1497, 173, 188, 189, 190

Moumbaris, Alex and Marie Jose 179
Mountbatten (Lord) 207
Münzenberg, Willi 37, 38, 3064, 323
Mulford, Wendy 39
Mulgan, Geoff 285
Murdoch, Iris 39
Murphy, Dylan 38
Murray, Andrew 288
Mussolini, Benito 148, 167

Nash, Paul 78
Nehru, Jawaharlal 160, 163, 165, 166
Nenni, Pietro 273
Neruda, Pablo 40
Newbold, J. Walton 268
Newton, Harry 292, 293, 301
Newton, Kenneth 324
Niemeyer, Oscar 15
Niemöller, Pastor 24, 56
Nicholas, T.E. 195
Nicholson, Ben 47, 81
Nicholson, Brian 299
Nicholson, Fergus 220
Nixon, Barbara 58
Nkrumah, Kwame 161
Noel, Conrad (Rev.) 279, 323

Obama, Barack (US President) 318
O'Casey, Sean 43, 60, 151, 183
Oestreicher, Paul (Rev.) 239, 279, 280
Olden, Mark 173, 325
Olive, Paul 141
Ongley, John 52
Orwell, George 14, 17, 37, 38, 62, 168, 200, 272, 306, 307, 327
Osborne, John 107
Osborne, George 318
Owen, Bill 55, 103
Owen, Jack 150

Padmore, George 164
Paice. Eric 141
Page Arnot, Robin 150
Pankhurst, Sylvia 14, 66, 174, 245, 246, 248, 264
Pappianou, E. 172
Papworth, Bert 206
Parker, Charles 46, 76, 77
Pargeter, Edith 39
Paterson, Frank 147

Palme Dutt, Rajani 41, 66, 164, 171, 265
Pasternak, Boris 40
Paul, Leslie 227
Paxman, Jeremy 238
Peck, John 43, 325
Peck, Leonard 57
Pelling, Henry 38
Pentelow, Mike 141, 325
Peppin, Geraldine and Mary 75
Percival-Davies, John 120
Perks, Jeff 108, 109
Phelan, Jim 42
Philby, Kim 38, 191
Philipps, Wogan (2nd Baron Milford) 15
Phillips, Peter 53
Phillips, Morgan 128, 233
Phillips, Trevor 221
Picasso, Pablo 15, 27, 45, 78, 79, 116, 215, 233
Pinder, Winston 174
Piper, John 81
Piratin, Phil 100, 189, 198, 207, 210, 269, 300, 324, 325
Platts-Mills, John 74, 75, 267, 271, 323
Pollitt, Harry 125, 168, 205, 210, 265, 271, 292, 309, 312, 324, 335
Postgate, Raymond 145
Ponsonby, Lord 151
Ponti, Carlo 114
Poulsen, Charles 42
Powell, Annie 257
Powell Anthony 35
Powell, Enoch 46, 175
Powell, Margaret 169
Powell, Len 195
Power, Mike 135
Prebble, John 39
Press, Ron 180
Priestley, JB 42, 151, 153, 202, 295
Priestly, Frank 147
Prince Albert 246
Pritt.D.N (QC) 74, 75, 207, 209, 269
Pudovkin, Vsevolod 95, 96, 97
Pym, Diana 251

Rafeek, Neil 225, 324, 331, 333
Ramelson, Bert 10, 130, 131, 132, 133, 135, 168, 282
Rampling, Tom 210

Ransome, Arthur 39, 309, 321
Rattenbury, Arnold 39
Rawsthorne, Alan 43
Ray, Satyajit 102
Reagan, Ronald (President USA) 112, 177, 235
Reckitt, Eva 100
Redgrave, Vanessa 60, 219
Redgrave, Michael (Sir) 56, 295
Redmond, Phil 48
Read, Herbert 81
Reed, John 27
Reid, Betty 295, 296
Reid, Jimmy 136
Reisz, Karel 105, 113, 114
Renior, Jean 102
Rewcastle, Martin 83
Richardson, Tony 106, 112
Richardson, Maurice 39
Ricardo, David 64
Rickword, Edgell 39, 46, 64
Ritchie-Calder, Lord 24
Rivera, Diego 27, 82
Roberts, Tom 121
Robeson, Paul 27, 43, 56, 161
Robinson, Dereck 302, 303
Robson, Robert 292
Rochfort, Desmond 85, 220
Rogerson, Maud 170
Ronksley, Bill 142
Roosevelt, Franklin D. 170
Room, Aaron 97
Rose, Fred 304
Rose, Millicent 80
Rosen, Harold 90, 189
Rosen, Michael 90, 109, 189
Rosen, Maurice 'Tubby' 208, 210, 213, 249
Ross, Jean 43
Rotha, Paul 94
Rothman, Benny 16
Rothermere, Lord 149, 188
Rothstein, Andrew 265
Rowe, Cliff 78, 79, 83
Roughton, Roger 39
Rudé, George 65, 170
Ruddock, Joan 235, 301
Russell, Bertrand 95, 171, 293
Russell, Dora 229, 234
Rust, William 'Bill' 146

Rust, Tamara 249, 251
Rutherford, Margaret 112
Ryan, John 166

Saklatvala, Shapurji Dorabji(MP) 160, 161, 268
Salt, Waldo 112
Samuel, Raphael 65, 268, 278, 283
Sapper, Alan 94, 142
Sapper, Laurie 142
Sartre, Jean-Paul 55, 60
Sauvy, Alfred 305
Sayle, Alexei 15, 222
Saville, John 278, 324
Saxton, Reginald (Dr.) 169
Scanlon, Hugh 131, 282
Scargill, Anne 257
Scargill, Arthur 136, 139
Scott, Adrian 112, 113
Scott, Joe 128
Scott, Michael (Rev.) 171, 295
Scott, Noll 156
Searle, Chris 39, 49
Seaton, Arthur 43
Sedley, Bill 213
Sedley, Stephen 74
Seifert, Sigmund 74
Seifert, Michael 74
Seifert, Roger 10, 134, 325
Sellars, Peter 15
Serota, Nicholas 83
Seyd, Nicola 10, 111 237
Shelvankar, D 169, 172
Shapiro, Michael 210, 249
Sharp, Madeleine 67, 70
Shaw, George Bernard 27, 50, 95, 151, 153, 184
Shawcross, (Lord) 299
Shepherd, Dick 230
Shostakovich, Dmitri 233
Sibley, Tom 9, 10, 134, 325
Signoret, Simone 114
Sinclair, Betty 184, 185
Simmons, Tony 100
Simon, Brian 86, 88, 89, 279
Simon, Ernest 87
Sillitoe, Alan 43
Sitwell, Edith 44
Shelley, Percy Bysshe 41
Slater, Montagu 39, 43, 46, 56

Slater, Mary 169
Slipman, Sue 219
Smith, Reggie 43, 46
Smith, Rose 247
Smith, Herbert 42
Smith, James 305, 307, 325
Smith, Laurie 326
Snow, CP 24, 38, 43
Sommerfield, John 39
Spencer, Stanley 78, 82
Spencer, George (MP) 124
Spender, Stephen 38, 39, 62, 307
Sprague, Ken 4, 83, 84, 108, 109, 141, 293, 322
Spratt, Phillip 162
Spriggs, Jack 137
Sraffa, Piero 64
Stafford Cripps, Richard (MP) 58, 150, 272
Stalin, Josef 14, 17, 29, 34, 37, 82, 217, 268, 280, 312, 313, 316, 319, 321, 324
Stanley, Jo 10, 259
Steer, Bernie 135, 176
Stevenson, Graham 3, 4, 5, 9, 10, 142, 307, 325, 327, 329, 332
Stewart, Bob 294, 265, 325
Stewart, Edwina 182, 184, 185
Stewart, Jimmy 185
Stonor-Saunders, Frances 62, 325
Strachey, John 51
Straight, Michael 38
Strand, Paul 54
Sutherland, John 305, 306, 307
Sykes-Davies, Hugh 39
Swift, Mr. Justice 164
Swingler, Randall 14, 39, 43, 44, 46, 52, 53, 56, 64, 322
Swinton (Lord) 202

Tagore, Rabindranath 27
Tait , Jim 142
Tanburn, Nigel 286
Tatchell, Peter 285
Tayler, Julian 74
Taylor, Graham 325
Taylor, Cleston 176
Tawney, R.H. 88
Tebbs, Betty 149, 150, 153, 154
Tebbs, Len 236, 237, 240, 242
Terry, Mike 178

Thatcher, Margaret (Prime Minister) 60, 75, 124, 138, 140, 156, 177, 223, 235, 259, 286
Thomas, Dylan 39
Thomas, J.H. (MP) 146
Thomas, Jim 121
Thomas, Edward 166
Thomson, George 46, 65, 66
Thompson, Willie 38
Thompson, E.P. 46, 65, 234, 239, 278
Thorez, Maurice 51
Thorndike, Sybil 56, 95, 106
Tocher, John 133
Toller, Ernst 56
Tomlinson, George (MP) 274
Tomlinson, Ricky 137, 138, 302
Toynbee, Arnold 216
Toynbee, Philip 39, 216
Trease, Geoffrey 39
Townsend-Warner, Sylvia 38, 46
Townshend, Pete 218
Tressell, Robert 42
Trevor Roper, Hugh 306
Triessman, David (Lord) 276
Trotsky, Leon 41
True, Arthur 131
Truman, Harry S. (President USA) 26, 32, 229, 233
Tudor-Hart, Edith 81
Tudor-Hart, Julian 67, 68
Tudor-Hart, Alex 68
Turner, Vic 135, 176
Tyler, Wat 18, 263
Tyrrell, William (Sir) 236
Tyrrell (Lady) 236
Twain, Mark 145

Upward, Edward 38, 39
Ustinov, Peter 57

Vaptsarov, Nikola 41
van Gyseghem, André 58, 106
von Braun, Werner 32
Vorhaus, Bernard 111, 112
Vorhaus, Hetty 112
Vitezslav, Netzval 41

Wake, George 133
Ward, Bert 42, 214
Ward, Frank Brennan 146

Warren, Des 137, 138, 325
Watkins, Peter 107
Watkinson, Ray 81
Wallis, Dave 42
Watt, Harry 94
Walters, Ian 50
Watt, Graham 68
Watters, Frank 136, 325
Waugh, Evelyn 38
Wayne, John 112
Webb, Lily 121
Webb, Sidney and Beatrice 27, 206
Weinberg, 'Queenie' 208
Weinstein, Hannah 104, 112, 113
Wesker, Arnold 59, 77, 190
Wesker, Leah 59
Wolf, 'Barney' Barnet 59
Wells, H.G. 99, 149, 221
West, Alick 46, 64
West, Rebecca 243
Whelan, Charles 283
Widdecombe, Anne 46
Wight, Clifford 82
Windsor, Roger 301
Williams, Eric 172
Williams, Nigel 48
Williams, Raymond 39, 46
Williams, Vaughan 43, 77, 202
Williamson, Johnny 324
Willis, Ted (Baron) 42, 55, 103
Willis, Fred 143
Willett, Wilfred 145
Wilkinson, Ellen (MP) 14, 162, 187, 248
Wilson, Elizabeth 243, 257
Wilson, Harold (PM) 130, 175, 230, 282, 300, 302
Wilson, Mary 47
Wincott, Len 289
Winnington, Alan 206, 231
Wintringham, Tom 42, 144, 166, 200, 247
Winstanley, Gerrard 18
Whitfield, David 139
Whitman, Walt 41
Woddis, Jack 98
Woddis, Roger 42, 177
Wood, Charles 106
Woolf, Virgina 42, 81
Woolfson, Charles 320

Worsley, Peter 114, 304, 305, 326
Worthington, Henry 302
Wright, Anita 259
Wright , Nick 10, 141, 221
Wright, Peter 302
Wyatt, Robert 222

Yospa, Manny 101
Young, Stan and Muriel 82, 84

Zetkin, Clara 244, 253
Zhdanov, Andrei 41, 45
Zilliacus, Konni (MP) 229
Zinoviev, Grigory 202, 291, 292, 294
Zoschenko, Mikhail 45
Zuckermann, Sir Solly 24